The New Naturalist Library

A SURVEY OF BRITISH NATURAL HISTORY

MOTHS

The aim of this series is to interest the general reader
in the wildlife of Britain by recapturing the enquiring
spirit of the old naturalists. The editors believe that
the natural pride of the British public in the native
flora and fauna, to which must be added concern for
their conservation, is best fostered by maintaining a
high standard of accuracy combined with clarity of
exposition in presenting the results of modern
scientific research.

The New Naturalist

MOTHS

Michael E. N. Majerus

With 16 colour plates and over 180 black
and white photographs and line drawings

HarperCollins*Publishers*

HarperCollins*Publishers*
77–85 Fulham Palace Road
Hammersmith
London W6 8JB

The HarperCollins website address is:
www.**fire**and**water**.com

Collins is a registered trademark of HarperCollins*Publishers* Ltd.

First published 2002

ISBN 0 00 220141 0 (Hardback)
ISBN 0 00 220142 9 (Paperback)

Printed and bound in Great Britain by the Bath Press
Colour reproduction by Saxon Photolitho, Norwich

Contents

Editors' Preface

In nearly half a century since the publication of E. B. Ford's New Naturalist *Moths*, there have been exciting advances in our understanding of the biology of moths. In particular, moths can now tell us more than ever before about the ways in which natural populations evolve, even over short periods within an ecologist's lifetime. Michael Majerus brings us these developments in this new book. As a boy he eagerly devoured Ford's earlier volume, which greatly influenced his subsequent career, and he sees this present book as a direct outcome of that early stimulus. Like his eminent predecessor, he combines an infectious enthusiasm for the natural history of the group with a disciplined scientific approach and a particular fascination for ecological genetics, a field in which moths provide excellent tools for digging into evolutionary questions. This book sets the rich complexity of moth biology in an evolutionary context and shows how the study of this group illuminates more general principles; in sharing his enthusiastic affection for moths the author brings us an alluring introduction to topics such as insect biology, mimicry, predation, dispersal and ecological genetics. By drawing attention to the many unsolved questions to which naturalists might contribute, even without expensive equipment, he tempts us to become active participants in the study of moths as they evolve before our eyes, adapting to the rapid environmental changes that result from human activities.

Author's Foreword and Acknowledgements

There are many things that this book is not. It is not a book about moth collecting. It is not a book about how to identify moths. It is not a book about how to study moths. But it is a book about moths: about their lives, their behaviour, their struggles to survive and reproduce within a hostile environment, their multitude of enemies, their extraordinary capabilities in avoiding them, and their future in the face of human-driven change. It is also a book about their beauty.

I was incredibly flattered when I was asked to write this book. I have been a fan of the New Naturalist series since I was ten and a fan of E.B. Ford for just as long, for it was on my tenth birthday that I was given a present of Ford's *Butterflies*. To emulate Ford in writing two books for the New Naturalist series I felt was a great honour. However, I only accepted this undertaking after considerable thought and with some trepidation.

I think it necessary to make it clear that this book is neither a revision nor simply an updating of Ford's wonderful New Naturalist *Moths*. Indeed, although professionally my field of expertise is that of ecological genetics, a field of science that Ford founded, I have tried to avoid the basic genetical ground covered in Ford's *Moths*. This is largely because the fundamentals of genetics described so clearly by Ford nearly half a century ago have changed little, and I would still recommend anyone with an interest in the way that characteristics of moths are inherited to read Ford's two books, *Butterflies* and *Moths*.

This book is concerned more with the place of moths in the biological world. It is thus a book on the natural history of moths, dealing with their behaviour, ecology and evolution. The first chapter introduces the subject of moths, discusses human perceptions of them and describes how they are related to what most people would recognise as the other group of the order Lepidoptera, the butterflies. Chapter 2 describes the basic life cycle of moths, treating each of the four major stages separately while showing how they fit together in the overall cycle from generation to generation. In Chapter 3, the basic processes of evolution that have moulded and continue to mould moths are discussed.

Chapters 4–8 consider how moths live their lives, in a context of their interactions with one another and the rest of their environment. The backdrop of these chapters is a very simple equation that is relevant to all populations of all organisms. It is simply that changes in population size depend on the birth rate, the death rate and any migration into or out of the population. Chapter 4 deals with reproduction and all that that entails, from sex determination through the various and complex aspects of courtship and mating to the point when females finally lay their eggs. Chapter 5 follows the life cycle through the main feeding stage, the larval stage, to the pupa and finally the adult. Here host plant preferences and habitat specialisations are considered. The adult theme is continued in Chapter 6 with a consideration of moths' flying abilities, their dispersal, migration and distributions. Death rate is considered in Chapter 7, in which the various biotic enemies of moths, including man, and other causes of moth death, are described. Chapter 8 tells the other side of the story in a discussion of the many and various survival traits that moths have evolved to foil those that would make a meal of them.

Chapter 9 is the only chapter that appears to deal with one single phenomenon. It is the phenomenon of melanism. Here the case of the rise and fall of melanic Peppered moths is considered in the wider context of melanism, in relation both to industrialisation and otherwise. The importance of cases of melanism in moths as examples of the action of natural selection is stressed.

The final chapter considers the interrelationship between moths and man. Positive and negative interactions are considered from both the human and the moth point of view.

The book is furnished with a glossary to help with scientific words where I have felt that their use was either necessary or desirable. I have used references sparingly to avoid disrupting the flow of the text. All scientific references mentioned are included in the bibliography at the end of the book.

Throughout the book I have used the English names of moths (where I know them), giving the scientific name on first usage in each chapter. The names used follow Skinner (1984), Emmet (1991a) and Bradley (2000).

I have had a passion for moths from a very young age. I still have. I am also a trained scientist. My training has added tremendously to my appreciation for and fascination in the moths that I encounter. I hope that in this book I have introduced some readers to scientific ideas and principles that will enhance the way they look at these beautiful insects, while leaving untarnished the magic and mystery of moths.

Acknowledgements

Many people have assisted in bringing this book to publication. These may be reasonably divided into four groups. First, I am grateful to a number of people who have helped me with the illustrations. Many of the photographs are my own. However, nearly all of those that are not were taken by John Bebbington. These include Plates 2b, 2d, 3d, 4c, 4f, 5b, 6d, 6e, 6f, 7c, 8c, 8d, 9a, 9b, 9e, 9f, 10e, 10f, 11c, 11d, 11e, 12a, 12b, 12c, 13f, 16c, 16d and 16e. John also contributed a number of the black and white photographic figures. He is acknowledged where appropriate in the legends for these. I am extremely grateful to John for allowing me to use his pictures and for the many hours of interesting discussions on moths that we have had over the years. Dr Clair Brunton and Mr Jim Stalker were heavily involved in the research that led to Plates 14d and 14e. I am grateful to Anne Bebbington for her skill in producing a number of the line drawings for me. Tamsin Majerus produced several of the computer-generated line figures, and also helped with many other details of the production. Finally, I am grateful to Professor Charlie Ellington and to the journal *Nature* for allowing me to use Plate 5a.

The second group I wish to thank are all those at HarperCollins who have helped in the publication of this book. In particular I would like to thank Isobel Smales for persuading me that writing this book, when there was already a *Moths* in the New Naturalist series, really was a good idea. I also thank Katie Piper, Claire Marsden, Liz Bourne and other members of the production team for their advice, tolerance and patience with me while this book has been in the pipeline. Special thanks are due to Dr Sarah Corbet who read the whole manuscript and made innumerable cogent and helpful suggestions.

Mothing in the Canadian Rockies: from left, Nic Majerus, John Acorn, Kara Majerus, the author and Kai Majerus.

The third group are all the graduate and postgraduate students past and present who have helped me in my research on moths and in particular my investigations of melanism and resting-site preferences. They are too many to mention each by name, but special thanks should go to Dr Rory Howlett, Dr Carys Jones, Dr Clair Brunton and Mr Jim Stalker. In this context I also wish to thank Dr Yoshiaki Obara and Dr John Acorn for many interesting conversations and correspondences about Lepidoptera and for guiding me admirably around the insects of their respective countries.

The final group who deserve my gratitude are all the members of my family and one or two friends, again past and present, who have put up with my moth-related eccentricities over the last 40 years or so. Among them, my mother, Muriel Majerus, who used regularly to ferry me down to the New Forest from north-west London in the 1960s, staying in a bed and breakfast while I watched over a moth trap all night. My father Fernand Majerus regularly brought moths back from his travels to the Far East and Australasia, when I was a child. Iain Ross ran up and down alpine meadows for me in the 1970s. My wife, Tamsin, has had to put up with moths in the bedroom, the bathroom, the bidet and the fridge. My children, Kara, Nic and Kai, are developing into extremely proficient field assistants, although they have not yet reached their teens.

One incident from my childhood comes to mind. It became something of a tradition that I would rear Indian Moon moths, *Actias luna,* so that some adults would emerge around Christmas. These were used as live Christmas decorations from Christmas Eve until the day after Boxing Day. The moths remained motionless as long as the lounge light was left on overnight. All was well until the year Granny stayed over Christmas night and, being financially astute, switched the lounge lights off. I was woken at three in the morning to a house in chaos and was requested to retrieve my moths from various parts of the building.

So, to all those who have had to put up with me, I extend my heartfelt thanks, and I dedicate this book to them.

M.E.N.M.
Cambridge
April 2001

1

Of Moths

Of Moths and Butterflies

The question that I have been asked most often in over 40 years of collecting, studying and talking about moths and butterflies is: 'What is the difference between a butterfly and a moth?' There is no easy answer, but the question itself has always been something of a puzzle to me, for it implies that moths and butterflies are similar enough that people have difficulty in telling one from the other. Yet the public perception of the two is strikingly different. In short, butterflies are nice, and moths are nasty.

Many times I have wondered why public views of moths and butterflies should be so disparate: I have even met a number of people who have phobias about moths, yet actively like butterflies. The answer, I think, lies in the cumulative effect of several things.

First, butterflies are brightly coloured and fly by day, flaunting themselves in the sunshine, while moths are often creatures of the night and many have dull and dowdy colours. As Penny Haddrill, one of my postgraduate students, put it, 'the trouble with moths is that they are brown and hairy and they flap'. One of my close friends in the Department of Genetics in Cambridge, Dr John Barrett, calls them LBJs (little brown jobs). Yet, in Britain, there are more species of day-flying moth than there are species of butterfly. Many of these day-flying moths are brightly coloured and as such are often misidentified as butterflies.

Second, moths invade our homes at night, flying in through our windows, attracted by our lights, which they fly around rapidly. And of course they eat our clothes. Many people believe that this is a general characteristic of moths and that it is the adult moths that eat fabrics. This belief goes back to the Old Testament of the Bible, where the book of Isaiah (Chapter 51, verse 8) warns:

> 'For the moth shall eat them up like a garment, and the worm shall eat them like wool: but my righteousness shall be for ever, and my salvation from generation to generation.'

Moths also appear in a poor light in the New Testament where, in St. Matthew's Gospel, Jesus is recounted to say during the Sermon on the Mount:

> 'Lay not up for yourselves treasures on earth where moth and rust doth corrupt, and thieves break through and steal: but lay up for yourselves treasures in heaven, where neither moth nor rust doth corrupt, and where thieves do not break through nor steal: for where your treasure is, there will your heart be also.'

In fact the number of species of 'clothes moth' in Britain can be counted on one's fingers, out of a total of over 2,000 moth species. They are all small moths from a single family, the Tineidae. Most are now uncommon, having declined dramatically as man-made fibres have come to dominate our apparel. The adult moths of these species do not eat clothing, but the caterpillars do.

Third, and perhaps more legitimately, moths have the reputation of doing considerable damage to many crops and some garden plants. The army worms of Africa, the cutworms of many British allotments, vegetable gardens and herbaceous borders, and the winter moths and Codling moth, *Cydia pomonella*, that attack our fruit trees, are some of the more renowned and obvious pests. There can be no doubt that the larvae of moths are responsible for a considerable amount of damage. However, humans have harnessed the feeding capacity of some moths for our own benefit. For example, the pyralid moth, *Cactoblastis cactorum*, was successfully introduced into Queensland, Australia, to control the Prickly Pear Cactus, which had become a serious pest in the early part of the twentieth century, having originally been introduced as an enclosure plant for sheep.

It is somewhat ironic that although we tend to think of butterflies as beautiful delicate insects, and moths as dowdy and drab, it is a group of the latter, the silk moths, that provide the raw material for some of our own most beautiful creations. The commercial Silk Worm, *Bombyx mori*, long extinct in the wild, is farmed in vast numbers to produce the silk for many of our finest fashion garments. It is the larvae of this rather unattractive moth, with its dull and reduced wings, that manufacture silk from modified salivary glands, particularly when they weave the cocoons in which they pupate.

The difference between moths and butterflies

There are a number of stock answers to the question 'what distinguishes a moth from a butterfly?'. Moths fly by night while butterflies fly by day. Moths are usually brown or grey or black, while butterflies are brightly coloured and

Fig. 1.1a (left) A Privet Hawk moth, *Sphinx ligustri*, resting with the wings in a roof-like posture.

Fig. 1.1b (below) A Moorland Clouded Yellow butterfly, *Colias palaeno*, with the wings held straight up from the body.

Fig. 1.2a (left) The thick abdomen of the Kentish Glory, *Endromis versicolora.*

Fig. 1.2b (above) Butterflies (for example, the Swallowtail, *Papilio machaon*) have relatively thin bodies.

patterned. Moths hold their wings down across their bodies in a roof-like pose when at rest (Fig. 1.1a), while butterflies hold theirs perpendicular (Fig. 1.1b). Moths have thick bodies (Fig. 1.2a), while butterflies are slender-bodied (Fig. 1.2b). Finally, the antennae of moths taper to a point (Fig. 1.3a), while those of butterflies end in a club (Fig. 1.3b). However, there are problems with all these answers. Many moths are characteristically day-flying and many of these are beautifully coloured and very strikingly patterned. In Britain, one has only to think of some of the burnet moths (Plate 13f) or tiger moths (Plate 1c) to

Fig. 1.3a (left) Moth antennae typically taper to a point.

Fig. 1.3b (below) Typical butterfly clubbed antennae.

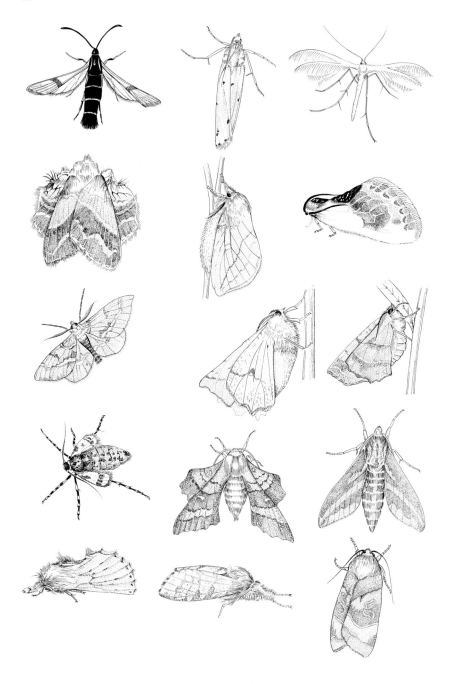

Fig. 1.4 The resting postures of some moths. (Drawings by Anne Bebbington.)

see that this is so. In the tropics, many spectacularly coloured and patterned moths are found. Some are day-flying, such as the Zodiac moth, *Alcidis zodiaca* (Plate 1a), of tropical Australia, while others, such as the moon moths (Plate 1b), are active at night. Although most moths hold their wings together along their bodies when at rest, a significant minority hold them perpendicular, the Early Thorn, *Selenia dentaria*, being an obvious example (Plate 7b). Indeed, the British moths display a diverse array of resting postures (Fig. 1.4). Furthermore, many butterflies hold their wings flat early in the morning while warming up in the sunshine. Moths of many families do have thick bodies compared with most butterflies (for example, Plate 1d). However, those of many other families, including two of the largest families, the Geometridae and the Pyralidae, have very slender bodies and are at least as delicate as most butterflies (for example, Plate 1f). The tapered antennae of moths and the clubbed antennae of butterflies are perhaps the most reliable distinguishing characteristic, although two families, the skipper butterflies (Hesperiidae) and the burnet moths (Zygaenidae), still give scope for confusion, for both have antennae with a club which tapers to a point at the end (Fig. 1.5).

So, there appears then to be no strictly correct answer to the question of what distinguishes moths from butterflies. In fact, the butterflies appear to be what is called a monophyletic group within one of the major divisions of the order Lepidoptera, the Ditrysia. Their monophyly means that they have all evolved from one ancestor that split off from the moths. The Ditrysia are defined on the basis of the female genitalia. In this huge group which includes

a

b

Fig. 1.5 The distinction between tapering moth and clubbed butterfly antennae is confused by two groups of Lepidoptera.
a) The antenna of a skipper butterfly, with the clubbed end tapering to a point.
b) The antenna of a burnet moth, which has a club-like swelling before tapering to a point.

about 95% of all the Lepidoptera, two apertures exist on separate abdominal segments, one for mating and the other for egg-laying. In primitive moths, either a single aperture serves both functions or, if two apertures are present, they are on the same segment. The monophyletic butterfly group is called the Rhopalocera (Duméril 1823) on the basis of their clubbed antennae. Until recently, this group included two superfamilies, the 'true butterflies' or Papilionoidea and the skippers or Hesperioidea. However, Scoble (1986) has given a well-reasoned argument for including a third superfamily within this group. This superfamily is the Hedyloidea, which is represented by a single genus, *Macrosoma*, of 35 known species confined to tropical America. Inclusion of this superfamily within the Rhopalocera seems to be taxonomically justified as evidence suggests that they are a sister group to the Papilionoidea, having diverged from this group after the Rhopalocera split off from other ditrysians. However, their inclusion also increases difficulty over what is a butterfly and what is a moth, for the *Macrosoma* are nocturnal, do not have clubbed antennae and generally sport dull colours of browns, greys or whites.

Fig. 1.6 A classification of the main lineages of the Lepidoptera. The Ditrysia contain the following superfamilies of moths in Britain: Tineoidea, Yponomeutoidea, Gelechioidea, Cossoidea, Tortricoidea, Sesioidea, Zygaenoidea, Scheckensteinioidea, Epermenioidea, Alucitoidea, Pyraloidea, Pterophoroidea, Drepanoidea, Geometroidea, Bombycoidea, Noctuoidea. The butterflies Papilionoidea and Hesperioidea are usually placed within the Ditrysia, after the Pyraloidea and Pterophoroidea, but before the Geometroidea, Drepanoidea, Bombycoidea and Noctuoidea. (After Scoble 1992.)

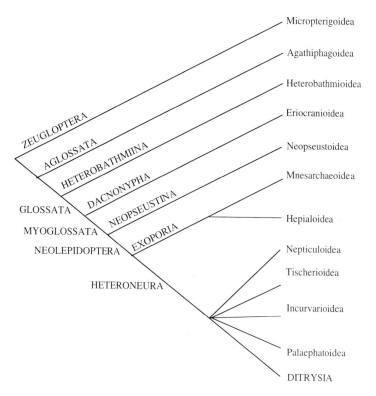

Leaving aside the Hedyloidea, the butterflies are all closely related. However, the same cannot be said of moths, or the Heterocera as Duméril (1823) termed them. Many evolutionary splits have given rise to the different main moth lineages. These are shown in Figure 1.6. Within the Ditrysia, some appear to have diverged before the Rhopalocera split off, others afterwards.

In summary, there is no single difference that separates all butterflies from all moths. Indeed, perhaps the safest definition of moths that I know is that attributed to Dr David Sharp: 'The only definition that can be given of Heterocera is the practical one that all Lepidoptera that are not butterflies are Heterocera' (Holland 1968).

Moth myths

The difference in perception of 'nice' butterflies and 'nasty' moths is reflected in the differences in the way the two groups have been used in literature. As already intimated by the two biblical quotations earlier, over the centuries, moths have had a bad press. Butterflies are usually thought of and written of in terms of their beauty and delicacy. Moths, however, tend to be connected with decay and death. I remember when writing my doctoral thesis, which concerned the evolutionary genetics of the Angleshades moth, *Phlogophora meticulosa*, seeking an appropriate quotation that would reflect my enchantment with these elusive inhabitants of both night and day. My searches led to frustration as I came upon passage after passage reflecting moths in a poor light. Finally, I did find one, but only one, quotation that I thought would suit. It is the final sentence of Emily Brontë's *Wuthering Heights*:

'I lingered round them, under that benign sky: watched the moths fluttering among the heath and harebells; listened to the soft wind breathing through the grass, and wondered how anyone could ever imagine unquiet slumbers for the sleepers in that quiet earth'.

Still to this day this passage instantly transports me back to days spent on windswept upland heaths in northern England, Scotland or Lapland, watching Black Mountain moths, *Psodos coracina*, (Plate 14a), or the small yellow and white underwings, *Anarta* species (Fig. 1.7), flying over heather and grass in

Fig. 1.7 The Broad-bordered White Underwing, *Anarta melanopa*.

the sunshine. But this is the exception. To most people, moths have a darker side.

Perhaps the species of moth most associated with legend is the Death's-head Hawk moth, *Acherontia atropos*. The skull marking on its thorax (Fig. 1.8), the way it holds its dark brown wings back along its body, slightly parted to reveal the yellow, blue and black markings along the abdomen, all contribute to the impression of a skeletal Death in his dark cowl (Fig. 1.9). This impression has given the moth its name and has drawn this species into disrepute, aligning it with the forces of darkness. In Hungary, for example, the entry of a Death's-head into a dwelling place is considered a harbinger of an imminent death in the family. In France, it was thought that a single scale from a wing of a Death's-head in one's eye would cause blindness. Consequently, a Death's-head fluttering around a candle, shedding scales with every beat of its wings, was not welcomed. More recently, the Death's-head was used to great effect in the Oscar-winning film *The Silence of the Lambs*. From a lepidopterist's point of view the film was a disaster, for the pupae that were drawn from the mouth of one of the victims of the serial killer had jug-handled, tongue-like proboscises and were obviously not those of a Death's-head. Furthermore, in one scene the proboscis is shown unrolled by a needle to a length of perhaps five centimetres (Fig. 1.10). The proboscis of a Death's-head is a relatively short, stubby organ and does not exceed two centimetres.

The association of moths with death is also found in English literature. J. Wyatt, writing in 1973, recalls, 'In Lancashire big moths are known as "night buggerts". I remember being told as a boy that if one came into the house

Fig. 1.8 The skull mark on the thorax of a Death's-head Hawk moth, *Acherontia atropos.*

Fig. 1.9 The Death's-head Hawk moth at rest, with its 'skull', and with its wings slightly apart showing the 'ribs'.

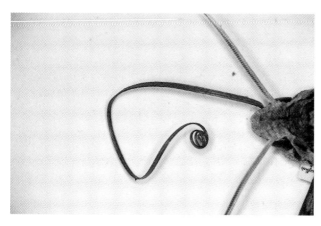

Fig. 1.10 The proboscises of many Hawk moths, such as this Convolvulus Hawk moth, *Agrius convolvuli*, are long and thin, and of the type shown in the film *The Silence of the Lambs*, but the proboscis shown in the film could not have been that of a Death's-head Hawk moth, which is short and stubby.

there would be a death in the family.'

From the *Newcastle Weekly Chronicle* of 11 February 1899 comes, 'Clothes moths are "ghosts", and every time one is killed there is a danger of injuring a relative'. Earlier, in his *Evolution of an English Town*, M.S. Calvert (1828) writes,

> 'It be an ill sign to the dying if a dark winged moth make at the bed light and fall at it, but it be a good sign should a light winged one come thrice and go its way unharmed. Even if it do fall at it, it doth say nothing worse than the ailing one will soon die but that the death shall be the freeing of a happy soul.'

Pale or white-winged moths have frequently been said to be the souls or ghosts of the dead. Thus, 'a large moth seen in the room of a dying person is sometimes believed to be the soul quitting the body. It must not be killed' (Opie & Tatem 1989). M. Trevelyan (1909), in *Folk-Lore of Wales*, records that, 'Aged people used to say that white moths were the souls of the dead, who in this form were allowed to take farewell of the earth'. In the same book, speaking of witches, he notes, 'When they die their souls pass out of their bodies in the shape of a "great big moth".'

From Cornwall comes a charming little poem, titled *The White Moth*:

> 'The light above the poet's head
> Streamed on the pane and on the cloth,
> And twice and thrice there buffeted
> On the black pane a white-winged moth:
> 'Twas Annie's soul that beat outside
> And "Open! open! open!" cried.'

On a brighter note, another common connection is between moths and the arrival of post. Thus, from various volumes of *Notes and Queries* (1849–date) comes: 'If a moth persists in flying round about you it is said to be a sign that you are about to receive a letter. According to the size of the moth will the letter be' (1869); or, 'If a moth flies round the lamp once, it is a sign of a postcard, twice a letter, three times a parcel' (1922); or still, 'If a moth flies around the light at night a letter will come in the morning' (1954).

Moth facts

Worldwide there are nearly 200,000 species of moth. They form the major part
of the Lepidoptera, which thus comprises the Earth's second largest order of
organisms, after the beetles (Coleoptera), making up about 10% of all known
species. Moths occur throughout the terrestrial world, from inside the Arctic
Circle to the tropics. Diversity increases with decreasing latitude and decreasing altitude. Most moths feed on flower nectar as adults and the foliage or
other parts of living plants as larvae. However, many other foods are taken by
particular species. A few species are predators or parasites. All moths have
scales and most have wings, although a few have lost their wings secondarily.
For example, a number of species of the family Geometridae, such as the
Winter moth, *Operophtera brumata,* have wingless females but are descended
from species in which both sexes are fully winged.

Moths vary in size from the pigmy moths (Nepticulidae), *Stigmella acetosa* having a wingspan of only two to three millimetres, to the Owlet moth, *Thysania
agrippina,* from Brazil, which has a wingspan of 300 millimetres. The moths
with the largest wing area are the Atlas moths, *Attacus atlas* and *Coscinocera her-
cules* from tropical Southeast Asia and northern Australasia. The heaviest
moths are females of some species of Cossidae. Some of the females of members of the genus *Xyleutes* from Australia can lay up to 18,000 eggs during their
lives and may have abdomens 70 millimetres long with a girth of over 20 millimetres.

Moth names

All described species of moth have a scientific name. Many, but by no means
all, have an English name as well. Conventions developed since the binomial
system of taxonomy was introduced by Carl Linnaeus in the second half of the
eighteenth century, govern scientific nomenclature. These conventions, over-
seen by the International Commission for Zoological Nomenclature (ICZN),
are based largely on the law of priority: that the first used name for a species
takes precedence over later names. Because of the importance of priority, the
full scientific name of a species of moth, or any other organism for that matter, should have four parts. These are the generic name (the name of the
genus to which the species is assigned), the name of the species, the name of
the person who first bestowed the specific name on the species and the date
on which this name was first published. Thus the full scientific name for the
Death's-head Hawk moth is *Acherontia atropos* (Linnaeus) 1758. The brackets
around the describer's, or authority's, name indicate that the species was originally assigned to a different genus, in this case, the genus *Sphinx.* The reason
for the strict rules over scientific nomenclature is to attempt to ensure that
there is one, and only one, unambiguous name for each species, that can be
used anywhere in the world, and to ensure that no two different species share
the same name.

Colonel A. Maitland Emmet, in his wonderful treatise on the origins and
meanings of the scientific names of British Lepidoptera (Emmet, 1991b), pays
tribute to Linnaeus, noting that in 1758 he laid the foundations to the scientific names of the Lepidoptera. In so doing, he used a wide variety of bases for
the names (see Box 1.1a), to the extent that few new types of name have subsequently been devised.

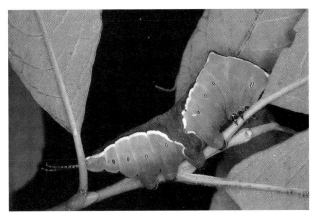

Fig. 1.11 The burgundy-coloured saddleback and the horns of the Puss moth larva give it its Latin name, *Cerura vinula*, meaning horned and of wine.

I would heartily recommend Colonel Emmet's book to any naturalist who has wondered over the scientific names of any species of organism. An understanding of the origins of and rationales behind these names not only provides an intrinsic interest to anyone with an enquiring mind, as most naturalists have, but also acts as a considerable *aide-mémoire*. Thus, knowing that the two parts of the scientific name for the Puss moth, *Cerura vinula*, mean, respectively, horned (from the abdominal appendages of the larvae) and of wine (from the colour of the saddle-shaped mark on the larva's back), immediately brings an image of the striking larva of this moth to mind (Fig. 1.11, Plate 9e and 9f).

Unlike scientific names, the common English names of species do not have to follow any strong rules of priority. So, for example, the Peppered moth, *Biston betularia*, was formerly called the Salt and Pepper, yet the more recent name is now used, rather than the original.

The English names have a similar range of rationales behind them to the scientific names given in Box 1.1a. Examples are given in Box 1.1b, where for each name type, I have given an example of a common name with the reason for the name if it is not obvious.

It is a shame that there is no book as scholarly as Colonel Emmet's on the origins of the English names of British moths. That said, it perhaps helps maintain the pleasure of personal realisation, recognition and understanding, when one first recognises why some moths have the common names that they have. Many are obvious. Thus one only has to see a Burnished Brass, *Phalaena chrysitis*, (Plate 1e) or a Dot moth, *Melanchra persicariae* (Fig. 1.16), a White Satin, *Leucoma salicis* (Fig. 1.17), a Figure of Eighty, *Tethea ocularis* (Plate 3a), a Silver Y, *Autographa gamma* (Fig. 1.12), or a Twin-spot Quaker, *Orthosia munda* (Fig. 1.18), to understand the name. However, many are less obvious and have to be sought. The origin of the name of the Blackneck, *Lygephila pastinum*, is not difficult to find if the thoracic region of the moth is examined (Fig. 1.19). The Spectacle, *Abrostola triplasia*, also becomes obvious if viewed head-on (Fig. 1.20), so that the ringed anterior markings on the thorax can be seen. Harder, and requiring some imagination, is the Mother Shipton, *Callistege mi*, (Fig. 1.21), which has markings on the forewings that could be seen as the hooked nose, eye and pointed chin of an old woman. These markings are said to resemble the face of a Yorkshire witch named Mother Shipton.

Box 1.1a Types of name used by Carl Linnaeus in naming 542 species of Lepidoptera in *Systema Naturae*, Edition 10, 1758. (Adapted from Emmet 1991.)

1. Named after a character in classical literature (for example, *Venessa atalanta*, the Red Admiral butterfly: named after Atalanta, the famous beauty and athlete who raced her suitors and killed them if they lost).

2. Named after the larval foodplant (for example, *Aglais urticae*, the Small Tortoiseshell butterfly: from Stinging Nettle, *Urtica dioica*).

3. Adopting a name previously used for the insect in the literature (for example, *Cerura vinula*, the Puss moth: Linnaeus used the name previously used by Mouffet) (see text p. 21).

4. Named after a character in the wing pattern (for example, *Autographa gamma*, the Silver Y) (Fig. 1.12).

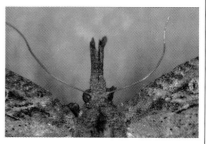

Fig. 1.13 The elongate labial palps of the Snout, *Hypena proboscidalis*, resemble a nose or proboscis.

thing (for example, *Lymantria monacha*, the Black Arches, resembling a nun's habit) (Fig 1.14).

Fig. 1.14 The Black Arches, *Lymantria monacha*.

9. From fancy (for example, *Catocala nupta*, the Red Underwing, from *nupta* meaning a bride) (see text, p. 25).

10. Named after the habitat (for example, *Crambus pratella*, from *pratum*, a meadow).

11. Named because of difficulty in classification (for example, *Triphosa dubiata*, the Tissue, meaning doubtful as to whether this was a distinct species from *Rheumaptera cervinalis*, the Scarce Tissue).

12. Named after the season when the adult appears (for example, *Operophtera brumata*, the Winter moth, occurring on the shortest day).

13. Named after an individual entomologist or friend (for example, *Dichrorampha petiverella*, after James Petiver: 1660–1718).

Fig. 1.12 The Silver Y, *Autographa gamma*, with the Y or gamma mark on the forewing shown enlarged (inset).

5. Named by comparison with a previously named species (for example, *Celestrina argiolus*, the Holly Blue butterfly, which was smaller than the previous species described by Linnaeus, *Polyommatus icarus*, the Common Blue butterfly).

6. Named after a structural character (for example, *Hypena proboscidalis*, the Snout: the elongate labial palps resemble a proboscis) (Fig. 1.13).

7. Named after some characteristic behaviour (for example, *Phyllodesma ilicifolia*, the Small Lappet, looking like a bunch of dead leaves when at rest).

8. Named by analogy with the appearance or behaviour of some person, creature or

Box 1.1a (cont.)

14. Named after a place name, such as the type locality (for example, *Mormo maura*, the Old Lady, from Maurus, an inhabitant of Mauritania, from where the type specimen was taken).

15. Named as a result of its position in a series of species (for example, *Emmelina monodactyla*, the first in a series of six species of a family described by Linnaeus with the wings divided into finger-like feathery lobes).

16. Named for its aesthetic appearance (for example, *Utethesia pulchella*, the Crimson Speckled, from *pulcher*, beautiful).

Box 1.1b. Examples of Lepidoptera whose common English names appear to be derived for similar reasons to their scientific names. (The order of reasons is the same as in Box 1.1a, except for 3 which has been amended.)

1. Adonis Blue butterfly, *Lysandra bellargus*, after the beautiful youth loved by Aphrodite.

2. Juniper Carpet, *Thera juniperata*, from the common name of its foodplant, juniper.

3. (Derived from a previous Latin name.) The Vestal, *Rhodometra sacraria*. The scientific name of this species, given by Linnaeus, is *sacraria*, meaning a female keeper of a temple, a priestess, a vestal virgin. The vernacular name was probably taken from the Latin name.

4. Gold Spot, *Plusia festucae*, from the iridescent markings on the forewings.

5. Small Angleshades, *Euplexia lucipara*: similar to, but smaller than, the Angleshades, *Phlogophora meticulosa*.

6. Dotted Fan-foot, *Macrochilo cribrumalis*, named after the structure of the expansible hairy scent-pencils on the forelegs of the males (Fig. 1.15).

7. Drinker moth, *Philudoria potatoria*, from the often-observed habit of larvae drinking dewdrops.

Fig. 1.15 The name of the Dotted Fan-foot, *Macrochilo cribrumalis*, derives from the structure of the feathery scent brushes on the front legs.

8. Lobster moth, *Stauropus fagi*, from the resting posture of the larva (Plate 8f).

9. The Vestal, *Rhodometra sacraria*, because the simple yet beautiful pattern suggests chastity.

10. Fen Wainscot, *Arenstola phragmitidis*, from the fen lands that this species inhabits.

11. The Uncertain, *Hoplodrina ambigua*, because of the difficulty in distinguishing this species from others of the genus, such as the Rustic, *Hoplodrina blanda* and the Powdered Rustic, *Hoplodrina superstes*.

12. July Highflyer, *Hydriomena furcata*, because it flies in this month.

13. Blair's Shoulder-knot, *Lithophane leautieri hesperica*, named after its discoverer in Britain, K.G. Blair.

14. The Burren Green, *Calamia tridens occidentalis* (Plate 16d), named after its colour and the Burren, County Clare, Ireland, where it was first found in 1949 and where it is well established and locally common.

15. Least Yellow Underwing, *Noctua interjecta*, because it is the least of three, the others being the Large Yellow Underwing, *Noctua pronuba*, and the Lesser Yellow Underwing, *Noctua comes*.

16. Beautiful Yellow Underwing, *Anarta myrtilli*, named by comparison with the other yellow underwings. The forewings of this small, day-flying underwing are patterned in purple and white and are superb when fresh, particularly when seen in contrast to the yellow and black hindwings.

Fig. 1.16 The reason for the naming of the Dot moth, *Melanchra persicariae*, is obvious.

Fig. 1.17 The wings of the White Satin, *Leucoma salicis*, have an obvious shimmering quality.

Fig. 1.18 The Twin-spot Quaker, *Orthosia munda*.

Fig. 1.19 The Blackneck, *Lygephila pastinum*. The dark marking at the back of the head and front of the thorax gives this species its English name.

Fig. 1.20 (above) To understand the name of the Spectacle, *Abrostola triplasia,* the adult moth should be seen from the front.

Fig. 1.21 (right) The markings on the forewing of the Mother Shipton, *Callistege mi.* With a little imagination, the markings can be seen to resemble the face of an old woman, such as the renowned witch, Mother Shipton.

Many English names cannot be understood simply by looking at an adult moth, for some relate to the larval foodplant, an aspect of behaviour, or the habitat or geographic distribution of the species. Yet a certain feeling of achievement may be gained by understanding the names, and most make some sort of sense and help one to remember some critical feature of the species.

Of course, the namers of moths were also people of imagination with their own fancies. The rationales behind some moth names are now hidden and, since the deaths of their authorities, they will remain so, although they may be speculated upon. Thus, for example, Emmet (1991b) draws attention to Linnaeus' habit of naming species with brightly coloured underwings after the fairer sex, with brides and fiancées particularly featured (Table 1.1). He wonders whether eighteenth-century brides in Sweden were in the habit of wearing gaudy underwear to stimulate the groom, or whether maybe Linnaeus thought that they ought to do so.

The lack of international conventions relating to vernacular names of moths can lead to confusion in two ways. First, it means that the same species of moth may be called by different names in different countries, even if the same language is used. For example, *Celerio lineata* is the Silver-striped Hawk moth in Britain, but the Striped Morning Sphinx in America; the Dark Sword Grass, *Agrotis ipsilon,* becomes the Ypsilon Dart, while our Garden Tiger moth, *Arctia caja,* is the Great Tiger moth on the other side of the Atlantic. The problem is of course compounded in other languages. Second, the same name may be applied to two different species. Thus, for example, the Grey Dagger in Britain is *Apatele psi,* while in America it is *Apatele grisea.*

An inordinate fondness for moths

I have often wondered why moths have held such fascination for me throughout my life. To be honest, I have no answer. Possibly it was merely an extension

Table 1.1 The names of species that have brightly coloured hindwings or 'underwings' have a common theme, being named after women, and in particular, brides or fiancées. (Compiled from information in Emmet 1991.)

Roeslerstammia pronubella	From *pronuba*, a bridesmaid. The pale yellow underwings of this small moth give it some similarity to the Large Yellow Underwing, *Noctua pronuba*.
Cacoecimorpha pronubaba	As for the previous species.
Archiearis parthenias, Orange Underwing	*Parthenias*, the son of a concubine, or from *parthenos*, a maiden.
Arctia caja, Garden Tiger moth	Caia or Caja, a Roman lady's name.
Arctia villica, Cream-spot Tiger moth	*Villica*, a female housekeeper in charge of a villa.
Callimorpha dominula, Scarlet Tiger moth	Diminutive of *domina*, the mistress of the household.
Syntomis ancilla	*Ancilla*, a maidservant.
Noctua pronuba, Large Yellow Underwing	*Pronuba*, a bridesmaid.
Noctua comes, Lesser Yellow Underwing	*Comes*, a comrade, companion. It is probable that Hubner, the authority of this species, was using *comes* as a common-law wife.
Catocala nupta, Red Underwing	*Nupta*, a bride.
Catocala electa, Rosy Underwing	*Electa*, a fiancée.
Catocala elocata, Esper's name for the Rosy Underwing	*Elocatus*, hired out: a prostitute.
Catocala promissa, Light Crimson Underwing	*Promissus*, promised, pledged in marriage.
Catocala sponsa, Dark Crimson Underwing	*Sponsa*, a fiancée or bride.
Catocala nymphagoga, Esper's name for the Dark Crimson Underwing	*Nymphagogos*, the person who leads the bride from her home to the bridegroom's house.

of a fascination with insects generally. I apparently caught my first butterfly when four and may have simply assumed that moths and butterflies were virtually the same. I certainly never really distinguished between the two in my mind. By the age of six, I was aware that there was no sensible distinction between the two groups, for day-flying Six-spot Burnets, *Zygaena filipendulae* (Plate 13f), with their semi-clubbed antennae, were a common sight on the thistle heads on Ruislip–Northwood Common, near my home. I also began to appreciate at around this time, or a little later, that there were far more moths than butterflies. The abundance of moths was brought home to me the morning after one warm summer night in the early 1960s. I had left the bathroom light on, with the window open, to attract moths. The bathroom was crowded when my father went to shave in the morning, hawk moths 'rubbing shoulders' with thorns, hook-tips, underwings, prominents, ermines and tiger moths. I remember that my father was not best pleased, while, once his anger had abated a bit, I was delighted and amazed at the diversity of the occupants of the bathroom.

I suppose that it was at about this time that I began to wonder about where all the moths went. It was obvious that there were more individual moths than butterflies, yet butterflies were far more apparent, at least in the summer months. The answer was before my eyes in the intricate colour patterns and behaviours of the moths. Many species were both camouflaged and secretive. I began to understand that moths were there, in the garden, or surrounding woodlands, but that they were masters of disguise. At age ten I obtained my first mercury vapour moth trap. Having read Ford's wonderful book *Moths* (Ford 1955) in that year, I questioned why each new species encountered looked the way it did. How did the colour patterns and the way a moth held itself when at rest contribute to its defence? The Peppered moth story had a considerable influence on me and I remember the excitement of finding both melanic and non-melanic forms of this moth in the trap that June of 1964. However, I soon realised that a moth trap is an unnatural setting for a moth. If one is to really understand why moths, or any other creatures, are the way they are, they should be seen in their natural habitats, behaving normally, with as little interference from the observer as possible. And with a group that is largely active at night, that has meant many late nights lurking about in dark woodlands or on deserted moorlands, often to the intrigue and puzzlement of officers of the local constabulary.

For many species, the best way to get to know them is to breed them through a generation or more. One gets to know the life history, the anatomy and the different behavioural strategies employed at different stages of development. Fortunately, most moths mate readily in captivity and are easy to rear. I am sure that caring for families of caterpillars as a child helped me develop at least two personal traits that I think are commendable now: attention to detail and patience. The importance of keeping detailed notes on each family reared, the methods used, the successes and the failures, was drawn from Ford's two New Naturalist volumes (Ford 1945, 1955). The patience came from the moths themselves. Privet Hawk moths, *Sphinx ligustri*, Emperor moths, *Saturnia pavonia*, Puss moths and Buff-tips, *Phalera bucephala*, that readily laid eggs in captivity, were of fairly immediate interest as the eggs hatched and the young larvae had then to be fed, cleaned and cared for. But once they had disappeared below the surface of the soil provided for them, or spun their silken cocoons, the wait of nine or ten months until they emerged as adults seemed an interminably long time for me then.

I am grateful for one other lesson that I learned at that time and again I have to point to the writings of Professor Ford. It was within the pages of his books that I discovered that the study of moths and butterflies, if applied carefully, had a scientific relevance and value that extended far beyond the bounds of the Lepidoptera. Studies on moths had impinged on many aspects of general biology, in particular genetics and evolution, and on medicine. Furthermore, British scientists working on British species of moth, many of which were the very species that I commonly found in my moth trap or in the local woods, had conducted much of the work.

British moth collecting

The Industrial Revolution began in Britain during the first half of the eighteenth century. The profits made by some people, through industrial endeavour and from interests in the Empire, led to great wealth, which in turn allowed them, or their descendants, leisure time for hobbies. The British have the strongest tradition of collecting insects of any nationality in the world. The earliest known collection still surviving in its original form is that of James Petiver, now housed in The Natural History Museum in London, dating from the late seventeenth and early eighteenth centuries, just prior to the birth of the industrial age. Collections were brought back from far-flung regions of the Empire throughout the nineteenth century and many dating from this period are still preserved in museums and private collections scattered around Britain. The Lepidoptera were very well represented in these collections, for many were relatively easy to distinguish and they had and have the advantage that they are easy to transport and preserve. Adult specimens, if kept in the right conditions, retain their colours with little deterioration over time.

The scientific literature on moths dates to 1634 and the publication by Sir Theodore de Mayerne (physician to Charles I) of *Theatrum Insectorum*. This book bears the name of Thomas Moffet as author, but was probably a compilation of his writings and those of Gesner, Penny and Wooton and possibly others. This book is the earliest known book on insects to be published in Britain and was translated into English in 1658 by Edward Topsel. Moths are included as nocturnal forms of butterflies.

Theatrum Insectorum was followed by Christopher Merrett's *Pinax rerum Naturalium Britannicarum, continens Vegetabilia, Animalia et Fossilia, in hac Insula reperta Inchoatus* in 1666, the year of the great fire of London. In the eighteenth century, John Ray's *Historia Insectorum* was published in 1710, followed by Petiver's *Papilionum Britanniae* in 1717 and Eleazar Albin's *Natural History of English Insects* in 1720. The wonderful works of Benjamin Wilkes entitled *One Hundred and Twenty Copper-plates of English Moths and Butterflies* were published between 1747 and 1760 and give details of the early stages of the species depicted. In 1766, Moses Harris produced one of the most famous books on the Lepidoptera. This is *The Aurelian or Natural History of English Insects; Namely, Moths and Butterflies. Together with the Plants on which they Feed,* which includes superb and accurate plates of some 38 British butterflies and 85 species of moth. Although the book is exceedingly rare, Hamlyn published an excellent facsimile, with an introduction by Robert Mays, in 1986.

The first British book to adopt Carl Linnaeus' system of nomenclature was John Berkenhout's *Outlines of Natural History of Great Britain and Ireland*, published in 1769. However, Moses Harris also used Linnean names, together with English names, in his second book, *The Aurelian's Pocket Companion*, in 1775.

The turn of the nineteenth century saw a quickening of the pace, in terms of both the books on Lepidoptera and the founding of entomological societies. The first entomological society in the world was The Aurelian Society, which was already in existence in 1743. This society, a second of the same name founded in 1762 and The Society of Entomologists of London were all relatively short-lived, none surviving to the nineteenth century. However, in 1801, a third Aurelian Society was founded. This became the Entomological Society of London in 1806 and the Entomological Society of Great Britain in 1824, before joining with the Fellows of the Linnean Society to form the Zoological Club of the Linnean Society, which exists to this day as the Zoological Society of London.

Other societies were formed. Pre-eminent among them must be the Entomological Society of London, founded in 1833. This has become one of the most influential entomological societies in the world and, following royal consent on its centenary, is now the Royal Entomological Society. Others include the South London Entomological and Natural History Society (now the British Entomological and Natural History Society) and the Amateur Entomologists' Society, founded in August 1935.

With the growth of entomological societies went the publication of a number of entomological journals. Thus, in 1832, the *Entomological Magazine* was first published. This was followed by a variety of journals from the Entomological Society of London, which to this day publishes a series of high quality journals on all aspects of entomological research. The *Entomologists' Annual* followed in 1855, with the *Entomologist's Weekly Intelligencer* starting the following year. The *Entomologist's Monthly Magazine* and the *Entomologist's Record and Journal of Variation*, founded in 1864 and 1890 respectively, still appear to this day. They are augmented by the *Entomologists' Gazette*, the *British Journal of Entomology and Natural History* and the *Bulletin of the Amateur Entomologists' Society*. Entomologists in Britain are thus well served with journals in which to publish the fruits of their interest.

The Victorian era was a great period for entomology, and the names of many lepidopterists of that age are remembered and revered by those who study moths today. Professor J.O. Westwood, H.T. Stainton, Edward Newman, the Reverend W.F. Kirby and J.W. Tutt, to name just a handful, all came from this period.

Moths and the study of evolution

Many of the lepidopterists of the late Victorian era embraced the new ideas in biology that gained prominence at that time. The ideas that arose from the reading of Charles Darwin and Alfred Russel Wallace's essay *On the Tendency of Species to Form Varieties; and On the Perpetuation of Varieties and Species by Natural Means of Selection* to the Linnean Society of London on 1 July 1858, form the bedrock of modern biology. Darwin's theory of evolution gave lepidopterists a new focus, for few groups of organisms were, or are, more suitable for the study of evolution through natural selection and sexual selection than the Lepidoptera. It is perhaps an irony that the most famous example of evolution in action, that involving the occurrence and spread of a dark or melanic form of the Peppered moth in industrial parts of Britain, was proceeding at the time of the publication of Darwin's two great works, *On the Origin of Species* (1859) and *The Descent of Man* (1871). Yet it was not until after Darwin's death that Tutt first proposed a valid mechanism suggesting that industrial melanism provided evidence to support Darwin's theory (see Chapter 9).

The rediscovery of Mendel's laws of genetics at the turn of the twentieth century gave birth to the field of evolutionary genetics. Darwin's evolutionary theories were placed on a theoretical framework of the laws of inheritance by R.A. Fisher, Sewall Wright, J.B.S. Haldane, Theodosius Dobzhansky and others. The outcome was the so-called neo-Darwinian synthesis, drawn together in the 1930s and 1940s. Much of this work was theoretical, but it gave birth to a new empirical field of study, ecological genetics. The aim of this was to collect data from field observations and experimentation that would allow alternative evolutionary hypotheses to be evaluated. It is perhaps not surprising that the father of this field of study, E.B. Ford, was a lepidopterist of some repute. Ford's experience of Lepidoptera, gained in the company of his father, H.D. Ford, gave him the insight to realise that moths and butterflies were possessed of an exceptional array of characteristics that made them suitable for the study of evolution in extant populations. In the late 1920s much was already known of the life histories of many species of moth and butterfly. These species were relatively easy to maintain and breed in captivity. They produced large numbers of progeny, making them convenient for the study of Mendelian genetics and the segregation ratios expected of Mendel's laws. Above all, Ford recognised that the form and structure of the wings of Lepidoptera were an unsurpassed vehicle upon which the outcome of evolution could be seen. The word Lepidoptera is derived from Greek, meaning scaled wings. The pigmented scales that clothe the wings and bodies of moths and butterflies are multiple minute units which, by a combination of chemical pigments and the physical characteristics of light reflection and diffraction, may give rise to an infinite variety of colour patterns. Upon this infinite variety, evolution, through natural selection and other processes, may indeed be seen writ large on the wings of moths and butterflies.

With few exceptions (notably fruit flies of the genus *Drosophila* and snails of the genus *Cepaea*), the classical studies of ecological genetics involved the Lepidoptera. These included exhaustive work on the phenomenon of industrial and other types of melanism in moths, which has provided irrefutable evidence of the role of natural selection in biological evolution (Chapter 9). Work on the Scarlet Tiger moth, *Callimorpha dominula*, provided pivotal evidence with which to judge the roles of selection and sampling error in evolution (Chapter 3). Studies of mimicry and other defensive strategies of the Lepidoptera have shown that complex sets of traits, which are only successful in concert, may evolve gradually through selection (Chapter 8).

These studies formed the core of evidence supporting evolutionary theory until advances in molecular genetics brought other types of variation, particularly at the protein and DNA levels, within the capabilities of researchers.

A call to arms to all 'moth-ers'

The rise of molecular genetics has resulted in the deflection of research funding from long-term studies of evolution in natural populations of moths of the type instigated by Ford, Bernard Kettlewell, Sir Cyril Clarke, Philip Sheppard and many others. Some work is still carried out by a few professionals. For example, the frequencies of the forms of the Peppered moth are still monitored regularly in a variety of locations by Paul Brakefield, Laurence Cook, Bruce Grant, David Lees and myself. However, now, perhaps more than at any time in the last century, amateur moth and butterfly collectors may play an important role in science.

Human activity is changing Britain now as fast as at any time in history. Our impact on the ozone layer, the 'greenhouse gases' that we belch into the atmosphere, our use of insecticides, herbicides, fungicides and agricultural antibi-

otics, our planting of huge swathes of monoculture crops, the increasing use
of genetically modified crops, and our introduction of an army of alien species
of plant and animal, all have enormous effects on the ecological communities
within our islands. The impacts of environmental change are being professionally monitored to some extent, but resources are thin and only a limited
number of organisms or ecosystems can be kept under scrutiny given these
scarce resources. The naturalists of Britain can be grouped according to their specialisations.
Most numerous are the ornithologists, followed by the lepidopterists, with
other specialisations lagging some way behind numerically, although not in
enthusiasm or dedication. Because of their popularity and the considerable
wealth of knowledge that we already have of them, I would argue that the
Lepidoptera are the most suitable group for the study of the impact that
human-induced environmental change is having on the terrestrial fauna of
these islands. Birds are comparatively large organisms with relatively long generation times and are less likely to be quickly affected by small changes in the
environment, particularly at the microhabitat level. Within the Lepidoptera
the British butterflies, although certainly more popular, offer much less scope
for study than the moths, largely as a result of the paucity of species of the former compared to the latter.

This then is a call to arms to moth-watchers and collectors throughout
Britain. Get out your nets, your cameras, your trowels, your moth traps, your
'sugar' recipe, your sweep nets, your beating trays and most importantly your
notebooks and pens, and start recording. Too often in the past, we have only
noticed deleterious changes to our fauna and flora after the event and when it
is too late to reverse the trend.

2

Life History and Anatomy

Moth life cycles

Most insects fall neatly into two groups with respect to the life cycle. Both groups have an egg and an adult stage. It is what fills the life history space between these two that divides the two groups. In one group this space is filled with nymphs that are similar in structure to the adults that they develop into, except that they are wingless. The wings of this group develop in little wing buds arising from the second and third thoracic segments and lying along the top of the abdomen. Because the wings develop externally to the main body, this group, which includes grasshoppers, cockroaches, true bugs, mantids and dragonflies, is referred to as the Exopterygota (meaning outside wings). Exopterygote insects pass through a number of instars as they feed and develop, shedding their external skin as they grow.

The second group has two main stages between the egg and adult. These are the larval and pupal stages. The larvae, which are called caterpillars or maggots in some orders of insects, feed and grow like nymphs of exopterygotes, shedding their skins as they get larger. However, these larvae show no external sign of wings, the wing buds developing internally. This group, which includes the four largest orders – beetles (Coleoptera), bees, wasps, sawflies and ants (Hymenoptera), true flies (Diptera) and moths and butterflies (Lepidoptera) – is thus called the Endopterygota (internal wings). The pupa, also referred to as a chrysalis in some groups, is a non-feeding stage. In some orders, including the Lepidoptera, the developing wings can be seen on the outside of the pupa, lying ventro-laterally, either side of the legs, antennae and proboscis (Fig. 2.1).

The transitions between the life history stages of insects are called metamorphoses. The two major groups of insects, the exopterygotes and the endopterygotes, are sometimes said to show hemimetabolous and holometabolous metamorphosis respectively, in reference to the extent of the changes that occur during metamorphosis.

In this chapter, I will describe the different life history stages of moths, consider the form and function of each stage and briefly examine how the transitions between the various stages are achieved.

Egg

The resourcing and laying of eggs

All moths start life in the outside world as eggs. Females contribute to the well-being of their offspring in a number of ways. First they may have a strong influence on the genetic make-up of their young by choosing male partners that carry good genes to fertilise their eggs (Chapter 4). Second, they provision the eggs that they lay with a store of nutrients for the development of the embryos inside. Females of some species also protect their eggs by putting a cocktail of

Fig. 2.1 Ventral view of pupae of the Spurge Hawk moth, *Hyles euphorbiae.*

defensive chemicals within the yolk, or, as in the tussock moths (Lymantriidae), covering them in a layer of fine irritant, or urticating, hairs (Plate 2b). The way that eggs are laid may also have a defensive element. For example, laying eggs in batches several layers high may help protect those in the lower layers from egg parasitoids such as 'fairy flies', which are tiny Hymenoptera of the family Mymaridae, and those of the related family Trichogrammatidae. However, perhaps a more crucial aspect of egg-laying behaviour is the choice of oviposition site. Most females choose a site to lay their eggs carefully, picking a place on, or close to, food. For most species, this means choosing to lay eggs on or in plants (Fig. 2.2, Plate 2a), or more rarely lichens or fungi, of one or a limited number of species. This, however, is not

Fig. 2.2 Eggs of the Winter moth, *Operophtera brumata.*

Fig. 2.3 Females of some moths, such as these White Satins, *Leucoma salicis*, will lay their eggs almost anywhere. Two egg batches can be seen on the mosquito netting across the window.

always the case, and some species will deposit eggs some distance from food (Fig. 2.3).

The eggs of moths vary considerably in size and shape. Many are hemispherical, but others are ovoid, rectanguloid (Fig. 2.4), cuboid, severely flattened or extremely elongate. Undoubtedly particular shapes are adaptations to particular situations. For example, the eggs of most species that oviposit within plant tissue are somewhat elongate, making egg-laying easier. This elongation is extreme in eggs of the yucca moths (*Tegeticula* spp.), which are up to 20 times as long as they are wide. The variation in the size of moth eggs shows some correlation with the size of the moth that lays them, but this is not strong and some small species lay larger eggs than species many times their size.

Fig. 2.4 The rectanguloid eggs of the Feathered Thorn, *Colotois pennaria.*

Egg colour also varies greatly between species and again the reasons are mainly defensive. Many are green or brown and are laid as appropriate on leaves or twigs so that they are camouflaged. Those of many pyralid and tortrix moths are scale-like and virtually transparent so that they are well camouflaged irrespective of the substrate on which they are laid. Some camouflage is more specific, in that particular elements of the environment are resembled. Thus, for example, the eggs of the Puss moth, *Cerura vinula*, are laid in twos and threes and mimic dark red leaf galls (Fig. 2.5); those of the Small Emerald, *Hemiostola chrysoprasaria*, resemble plant tendrils, and those of *Langsdorfia franckii* (Cossidae) look like plant seeds. In a few species, particularly those with larger eggs, the shape of the egg is disguised by what are called disruptive patterns, dark lines across a paler ground colour. The eggs of the Lappet moth, *Gastropacha quercifolia*, are a good example of this.

Although most moth eggs are rather inconspicuous in colour, a few are brightly coloured and stand out from the substrate upon which they are laid. These are the species whose eggs are chemically defended, for example, the yellow eggs of the Six-spot Burnet, *Zygaena filipendulae*, and others of this genus, which are laid in large batches and are provided with cyanogenic glucosides by their mother.

Egg structure

In structure an egg is initially composed of three main parts, the yolky core that contains the new embryo usually towards the base or back end of the egg, a membrane surrounding the yolk and a shell or chorion. The shell is coated on the inside with a waxy layer that helps to control water loss. It is punctured by one or more minute perforations called micropyles. It is through these that sperm enter the egg to fertilise it. In addition, these pores and others called

Fig. 2.5 Eggs of the Puss moth, *Cerura vinula*, on a sallow leaf.

aeropyles allow gas exchange through the chorion so that the developing embryo can obtain oxygen for respiration. In some species of moth the micropyles are situated at the top of the egg, as they are in butterfly eggs. These eggs are said to be upright. However, in the majority of moths, micropyles are sited at one end, the eggs then being described as of the 'flat' type, irrespective of their exact shape.

The eggs of most moths are laid very soon after fertilisation. In many species this may be some time after mating, for female Lepiodoptera have the capacity to store sperm in a specialised organ called a spermatheca. They only release sperm for fertilisation when eggs are ready to be laid. Once eggs are fertilised and laid, the development of the embryo may begin immediately or there may be a substantial dormant period, as is the case for many species that pass the winter as eggs. The rate of development in eggs appears to be controlled primarily by juvenile hormone (Nijhout & Riddiford 1974, 1979). Once the embryo does start to develop, cells divide rapidly in the yolky fluid and an elongate tube-like structure forms, which curves around into the shape of a ring within the shell. Legs develop facing towards the shell at first, but after a time the embryo starts to wriggle so that the legs are turned inwards. By the time the embryo is ready to hatch, it fills virtually the whole of the space within the eggshell.

The embryo, which may now be thought of as a larva, or caterpillar, has no egg tooth for breaking out of the chorion, unlike many other insects. Instead it simply eats a hole in the chorion through which to hatch (Fig. 2.6).

Larva or caterpillar

Larval structure

The young larva, when it has released itself from its eggshell, has two main functions: to obtain enough to eat and to avoid being eaten. In the context of the whole life cycle, the larval stage is the main feeding stage. Indeed, in some Lepidoptera it is the only feeding stage, for the adult mouthparts of some moths are functionless. This main feeding function is evident as soon as the larva hatches, because the first meal for most larvae is a portion, if not the

Fig. 2.6 A clutch of Emperor moth eggs, *Saturnia pavonia*, that have hatched.

whole, of their eggshell. This meal, as well as being an easily available source of food for the neonate larva, may provide the larva with vital minerals and, in some cases, symbiotic bacteria that help in the digestion of plant material. Certainly, this meal appears to be essential to the larvae of many species, for if denied it, they die.

The defensive strategies that are used by caterpillars to avoid being eaten, either by predators or parasites, are largely similar to those used by adult moths. I will thus discuss these in Chapter 8, which is devoted specifically to the subject of defence. Here, I will consider the basic anatomy of moth larvae and their adaptations for feeding and dispersal.

In shape, most larvae are cylindrical with a heavily sclerotised head capsule, adorned with hard mouthparts adapted for chewing, simple eyes and very short antennae. The mouthparts are typical of many insects, comprising sclerotised mandibles usually with molar and incisor regions, maxillae, labrum and labial palps. Two labial palps fused together form a central structure below the mandibles called a spinneret. This is of great importance as it is from this organ that the larva extrudes silk at various times in its development. The glands that produce the silk, of which there are two, are very elongated modified salivary glands. In species of moth that use a lot of silk during their larval stage, these glands can occupy a significant proportion of the body.

The simple eyes of moth larvae should correctly be called stemmata, rather than ocelli. Usually there are 12, arranged in two groups of six each side of the front of the head, close to the mouthparts. Dethier (1963) has argued that the structure and positioning of these simple eyes will provide well-focused but rather poorly resolved images. Each stemma gives a separate image, so that what the larva sees is likely to be a coarse mosaic of its surroundings.

The two short antennae are located either side of the head between the stemmata and the mandibles. They usually have three or four segments, although some leaf-miners have fewer. Segment 2, in particular, bears a number of sensory structures including a single bristle. The antennae are well armed with sensory receptors and play a role in food detection and selection.

The first three body segments behind the head correspond to the thoracic segments of the adult moth. The first of these bears a breathing pore or spiracle that is lacking from the others. Each segment bears a typical pair of jointed insect legs made up of coxa, trochanter, femur, tibia, tarsus and tarsal claw. These are the true legs of the larvae. There is surprisingly little variation in the structure of legs in different families, although they are reduced in some leaf-mining species, and elongated in some notodontids, such as the Lobster moth, *Stauropus fagi* (Plate 8f).

The abdomen has ten segments (referred to as A1–A10). These house the gut. In addition, some of the segments bear what are called prolegs or false legs. These are not true legs, so the generalisation that insects have six legs is not compromised here. These prolegs are, in essence, fleshy outgrowths of the body wall. Most commonly, prolegs are carried on segments A3–A6 and A10 (Fig. 2.7); those on A10 are slightly different in structure from the rest and are called claspers. The distribution of prolegs varies considerably. Members of the Geometridae typically have no prolegs on segments A3–A5, so they are reduced to just two pairs (Fig. 2.8). These larvae walk by forming a loop, looping the body upwards between the true legs and the prolegs, and are thus commonly called loopers (in America they are termed inchworms) (Fig. 2.9).

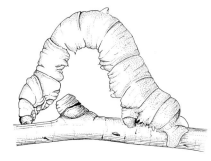

Fig. 2.7 (top) A larva of the Oleander Hawk moth, *Daphnis nerii*, showing the positioning of the prolegs.

Fig. 2.8 (above) In the geometrid 'stick' caterpillars, the prolegs are reduced to the two hindmost pairs.

Fig. 2.9 (left) Looper caterpillars walk by drawing the hind claspers up to the true legs then moving the true legs forward again. (Drawing by Anne Bebbington.)

In plusiines, such as the Silver Y, *Autographa gamma*, prolegs are only obvious on segments A5, A6 and A10. Other reductions are seen in some leaf-miners where the prolegs are either absent or reduced to small wart-like structures. In a few families of microlepidoptera, the number of pairs of prolegs is greater than five. However, these larvae are very small and, as a rule of thumb, caterpillars that are observed with more than five pairs are almost certain to be sawflies, not moths.

Prolegs work by a sort of telescopic action. They are muscular and end in a circular pad bearing numerous microscopic hooks. These hooks, or crotchets, give the caterpillar an excellent grip.

Fig. 2.10 Larva of the Poplar Hawk moth, *Laothoe populi*, showing the tail hook.

Fig. 2.11 The larva of the Puss moth, *Cerura vinula*, has two extendible, whip-like tails.

The last three abdominal segments of some moth larvae differ from the other segments in having other protuberant structures. For example, the larvae of most species of hawk moth (Sphingidae) have a hook-shaped 'tail' rising from A8 (for example, Fig. 2.10, Plates 2c, 9d). In the Puss moth and related kitten moths, the A10 claspers are modified into a pair of elongate, extendible whip-like tails (Fig. 2.11).

Larval moulting

Because the larval stage is the main feeding stage, part of its primary function is to grow larger. Although the soft bodies of lepidopteran larvae seem to be elasticated, there is a limit to how much the outer cuticle can stretch as the larva grows. In consequence, moth larvae, like those of other insects, have to shed their skin, or moult, at intervals as they develop.

The stage between two moults is referred to as an instar, so the larva that hatches from an egg enters the first instar. The number of instars through which moth larvae pass before they pupate varies from three to eight, but five is most usual.

For moth larvae, moulting is a perilous time because the larva has to attach its old skin to the substrate so that it can pull itself out. This process typically takes about two days in temperate climates and for this period the larva is more or less immobile in one position.

The process of moulting comprises three distinct stages: the separation of the outer cuticle from the underlying epidermal cells (called apolysis), secretion of a new cuticle, and the discarding of the old cuticle (called ecdysis). The first stage is initiated when the cells of the epidermis divide rapidly under the influence of juvenile hormone and become more dense. A tension is produced between the surface of these cells and the inner cuticle surface. These then separate producing a subcuticular space. Moulting fluid containing enzymes that break down the proteins and enzymes in the inner cuticular layer are then secreted into the subcuticular space. These enzymes (proteinases and chitinase) are initially in an inactive form. This is essential otherwise they would digest the newly forming cuticle being secreted by the epidermis. The newly forming cuticle consists of a procuticle layer which gradually increases in thickness and a cuticulin layer directly below the moulting fluid filled subcuticular space. Once the cuticulin has been formed, the enzymes in the moulting fluid are activated and begin to digest the inner layers of the old skin. The larva reabsorbs these so that up to 90% of the resources within the old skin are retrieved before the old skin is shed. As already suggested by the consumption of eggshells by neonate larvae, little of use in the way of nutrients is wasted by caterpillars. By the time the old skin is sloughed off, the old cuticle consists of just the two outermost, thin layers. Just prior to the final shedding of the old skin, the larva secretes a layer of wax onto the surface of the new cuticle. This layer prevents too much water being lost by evaporation through the new cuticle.

To shed its old skin a larva sucks in air through its mouth, causing the gut to expand and put pressure on the old cuticle. This then splits along precisely defined weak fault lines. Rhythmic muscular contractions control the section of the larva that swells at a particular moment, so that the split in the old skin lengthens. Once the old skin has split sufficiently, the larva pulls itself out, headfirst, leaving the old skin attached to the substrate. This remnant is called the exuvia.

Following ecdysis, the new skin of the larva is soft and unexpanded. Despite now being mobile, having moved off its temporary attachment to the substrate, the larva is still very vulnerable due to its softness. However, it now increases the protection afforded by its new skin by hardening it. To increase the potential growing space that the new skin will provide, the larva again increases its volume by drawing in air before the cuticle hardens.

Hardening of the cuticle involves a complex chemical process known as tanning. In moths this tanning involves the formation of strengthened links between protein molecules in the cuticle. The strengtheners are quinones, which are derivatives of tryosines, just as the dark melanin pigments are. As the cuticle hardens, it usually also becomes significantly darker as a result of the production of a hard protein called sclerotin, or as a result of the polymerisation of excess quinone molecules, a process that forms melanin. A suite of hormones, such as juvenile hormone, ecdysone and bursicon, controls the complex sequence of events in moulting.

Duration of the larval stage

The length of the larval stage is very variable between species. Development rate is dependent on temperature and food quality. For some British species in which the larval stage occurs in high summer, the time between egg hatch and pupation may be as short as two weeks, but this is exceptional. For species that feed on leaves and do not overwinter as larvae, four to eight weeks is more usual. Those that overwinter as larvae may be in this stage of the life cycle for up to ten months. In a few species that feed on food with a low nutritional value, the larval stage may last for years. Larvae of several of the clearwing moths (Sesiidae), which feed on the wood of trees, frequently pass two or occasionally three winters as larvae. Thus the Orange-tailed Clearwing, *Synanthedon andrenaeformis*, spends two winters in stems of Wayfaring trees or Guelder Roses, while the Hornet moth, *Sesia apiformis*, and the Lunar Hornet moth, *Sesia bembeciformis*, spend almost two, or sometimes three years in the wood of the lower trunks and upper roots of poplars, sallows or willows. The larvae of the Reed Leopard, *Phragmataecia castaneae*, also spend two winters in the stems of their foodplant, the Common Reed. Larvae of the Ghost moth, *Hepialus humuli*, which feed on the roots of grasses and a variety of herbaceous plants, take two years to reach maturity in most parts of Britain, but three years in more northerly locations. A three-year larval stage is also usual for the Leopard moth, *Zeuzera pyrina*, which feeds on the wood of the trunks and branches of a variety of deciduous trees and shrubs. The longest larval stage among British moths is that of the Goat moth, *Cossus cossus*, which feeds on the wood of various deciduous trees, including many fruit trees. It will feed for three or four years and then spin a cocoon in which it incorporates particles of wood or earth. However, it does not pupate immediately and remains as a fully developed larva for a final winter before pupating and emerging as an adult in the fourth or fifth year of its life.

Larval dispersal

Moth larvae have three main ways of getting about. One is simply walking, for which they use both their true legs and their prolegs. The other two involve the production of silk. Larvae may attach a strand of silk to a piece of vegetation and then lower themselves slowly down using the force of gravity. This may be thought of as a sort of abseiling, although in this case they are manufacturing the 'rope' as they descend. The other method, which is only adopted by very small larvae, is to generate silk in the same way, but once hanging by a thread, these larvae are carried away on the breeze, the silken attachment to the substrate breaking. These larvae continue to 'fly' on the wind until they bump into something solid.

The main reasons that larvae need to move are to find supplies of food, to escape predators once detected and to find suitable pupation sites. Walking is used for all three of these reasons. In particular, many larvae of larger species, such as the hawk moths, engage in long perambulations once they have finished feeding, climbing down to ground level and frequently walking some distance before digging into the ground to form a subterranean cell in which to pupate. Larvae that indulge in these long pre-pupation walks frequently change colour, usually becoming darker and duller.

'Silk-dropping' is used mainly by arbivorous species to escape predators. If disturbed, larvae will drop off the branch, later climbing back up their own silk thread. However, full-grown larvae of some arbivorous species that pupate in the earth will also use this method as a short cut to the ground. Silk parachuting by very young larvae is used primarily as a method of finding food. This is particularly prevalent if overwintered eggs of species that feed on deciduous trees hatch before bud-burst. This habit, which is found most commonly in the geometrid and tortricoid moths, may play a significant role in dispersal in some species, because, if conditions are right, these small larvae may be carried very considerable distances as elements of the aerial plankton.

Pupa

The final larval moult gives rise to the pupal stage. The purpose of the pupal stage seems to be to allow the insect to accomplish an almost complete internal reorganisation and overhaul.

Pupal structure

Most moth pupae are roughly bomb-shaped. They are usually cylindrical, blunt at the head end and tapering towards the tail, sometimes ending in a point (Figs. 2.1 and 2.12). The outer shell is heavily sclerotised and is usually shiny and smooth. Seen dorsally, the pupa has a head, a well-defined thoracic region and an abdomen apparently comprising eight segments, although an additional two can be seen if the pupa is viewed ventrally. On the ventral surface, a variety of structures of the adult moth can be seen, either standing proud or impressed into the pupal case. These include the labrum and labial palps, the eyes and antennae and the legs and forewings.

Pupa formation occurs when the larva moults for the last time. The pupal stage is essentially immobile, although some movement of the abdominal segments is possible in most species, and a few species, such as some notodontids, have the ability to move slowly through soil by use of their anal cremaster at the end of the abdomen.

The general immobility of moth pupae would make them vulnerable to predators and parasitoids. However, in most moth species pupation is preceded by behaviours that place the larva in a situation in which the resulting pupa will be less vulnerable to attack than if it were formed in a fully exposed position. In some species, this entails the construction of a chamber underground or in debris at ground level. In others a cocoon, formed of silk from the modified salivary glands, is constructed. Cocoons may be made almost anywhere, underground, at ground level, on the surface of rocks or bark, or under bark

Fig. 2.12 The bomb-shaped pupae of the Atlas moth, *Attacus atlas*.

Fig. 2.13 A pupa of the Common Footman, *Eilema lurideola*, on the inside of bark.

(Fig. 2.13), within wood or plant stems or among plant foliage (Plate 2e). Most species are fairly specific about where they form their cocoon and pupate.

Cocoon manufacture

The cocoon is manufactured out of silk produced by the large, modified salivary glands. Initially, a strand of silk is attached to surrounding matter at a number of points, forming a meshwork of guide ropes around the larva (Fig. 2.14). The larva then constructs the cocoon inside this meshwork from within

Fig. 2.14 The initial meshwork cocoon frame of a silk moth larva.

Fig. 2.15 The finished cocoon of a silk moth.

(Fig. 2.15). Some species incorporate plant material or soil into their cocoons. For example, the Puss moth and the kitten moths, which make their cocoons on tree trunks, chew off bits of bark and add this to their constructions, giving them greater rigidity and making them highly cryptic. The Short-cloaked moth, *Nola cucullatella*, uses fine fragments of thin bark stripped off twigs in the same way (Fig. 2.16).

The cocoons constructed by moth larvae vary tremendously in strength. Some cocoons are simply a thin meshwork of silken strands that hold leaves or other bits of material together to provide a chamber for the pupa. In other species, a much thicker, more complete silken cocoon is constructed. This is most pronouncedly seen in the silk moths (Saturniidae). In Britain we have just a single representative of this family, the Emperor moth, *Saturnia pavonia*.

Fig. 2.16 The Short-cloaked moth, *Nola cucullatella*, incorporates fine fragments of thin bark in its cocoon.

Fig. 2.17 The larva of Blair's Shoulder-knot, *Lithophane leautieri hesperica*, remains as a larva within its cocoon for several months before it pupates.

Emperor moth larvae make a cocoon shaped like a pitcher, with a valve of strong outward-facing hairs at the narrower end allowing the moth to emerge, but preventing predator or parasite entry.

Usually, once a larva has constructed its cocoon, it sheds its final larval skin, thereby pupating almost immediately. However, in Blair's Shoulder-knot, *Lithophane leautieri hesperica*, the larva remains in the cocoon for several months before it pupates (Fig. 2.17), thereafter completing its development into an adult relatively quickly.

The pupal stage may last a few days, or many months, depending on temperature and whether the species overwinters in this stage. Some arctic species that overwinter as pupae do not hatch the first year after pupation if conditions are not appropriate. These emerge the following year or even later, effectively missing unfavourable summers.

Emergence

The final stage in the metamorphic drama that is the immature life of a moth is its hatching from the pupa. Its transformation from the crumpled, damp and flaccid jumble of tissues and scales that clambers out of the pupal case (Plate 2f) or cocoon into the beautifully coloured and patterned creature that results is remarkable. I well remember the first time I saw an adult moth hatch and even now, having seen this miracle thousands of times, I still find it spellbinding.

Emergence from the pupa is similar to emergence by larvae from an old skin. The pupa splits along weak fault lines and the moth pulls itself out. If the pupa is within a cocoon, the adult moth has to exit from this as well as its old pupal case. Some species are armed with barbs or sharp projections on the anterior surface. By wriggling within the cocoon, these are able to cut through the silk to make an exit. Others soften the silk of the cocoon prior to emergence. Thus, the Puss moth secretes a solution of potassium hydroxide from its mouth, which softens up the mixture of silk and wood fragments at the exit end of the cocoon. The pupae of wood-boring clearwing moths, which are formed just below the bark inside the burrows that they made when larvae, wriggle part way out of the bark before the adult moth emerges. Emerging

Fig. 2.18 Cocoons of the Six-spot
Burnet, *Zygaena filipendulae*, with
the pupal exuviae protruding
from the cocoon.

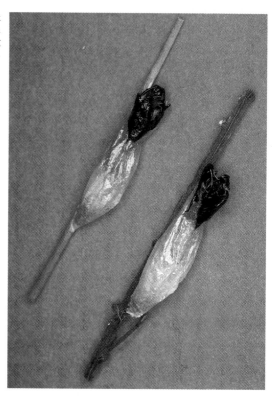

burnet moths also use the cocoon to help them get free of their pupal case,
leaving the exuvia caught on the fibres around the exit hole in the cocoon.
Cocoons of these moths are a frequent sight on grass stems in midsummer,
with the empty, black pupal cases protruding from them (Fig. 2.18).

Once free of pupal case and cocoon, the soft adult moth will find a place that
provides a firm foothold before beginning to expand its wings. Often this
involves simply turning back towards the cocoon and using it as a platform
from which to hang to allow the wings to expand. However, those species that
pupate underground, once free of their pupal chamber, still have to make a
considerable effort pushing through the soil to the surface before they can
attain their full adult form.

The expansion of the wings is achieved by pumping haemolymph into the
veins of the wings, stretching them to their full size. Once they are fully
expanded, the haemolymph is withdrawn back into the body. The wings, which
are still soft and floppy, remain hanging down from the thorax to dry and hard-
en (Fig. 2.19). Only once they are fully hardened will they be moved into the
position that the particular species adopts when at rest (Fig. 2.20).

The process of expansion and drying takes from about half an hour to two
hours, depending on the species of moth and the temperature, humidity and
airflow in which emergence takes place.

Most species emerge from their pupa at a specific time of the day. In many
night-flying species, this eclosion takes place in the late afternoon. Conversely,

Fig. 2.19 (left) A Garden Tiger moth, *Arctia caja*, with wings hanging down to dry.

Fig. 2.20 (below) The Garden Tiger moth, *Arctia caja*, in its normal resting position. (Courtesy of John Bebbington.)

the majority of day-flying species emerge in the morning. Presumably, these specialisations are adaptive, serving to reduce the time between emergence and when the moth can first take to the wing to begin essential activities, such as seeking a mate or finding food.

The adult moth

The final stage in the life cycle of a moth is the adult stage: the actual moth. The fundamental role of this stage is to reproduce, which is discussed in Chapter 4. However, adult moths have many other activities, including feeding, dispersing, resting at appropriate times and avoiding the great variety of causes of death that they may face. Morphologically, adult moths show adaptive features related to all these activities.

In basic structure the adult moth is again a segmented insect that can conveniently be divided into three parts comprising the head, thorax and abdomen. The head is both the sensory and feeding centre of the moth. The thorax supports the locomotory structures, the legs and wings. Finally, the abdomen houses the digestive tract, much of the respiratory apparatus, most of the fat stores and, most importantly, the reproductive organs. Although the three main parts obviously work in concert, it is convenient to focus on the main features of each in turn when considering the general anatomy of the adult insect.

Head

The head of a moth supports or contains the mouthparts, the suction pump that aids the uptake of fluids, the brain and two of the major sensory organs, the antennae and the eyes. The external skeleton of the head, or head capsule, is made up of cuticular plates, or sclerites, that meet along seams known as sutures. These sclerites are covered in hair-like scales. Internally, the head is supported by a series of struts that make up the tentorium, rather like the crash bars placed internally in some rally cars. These struts provide rigidity

Fig. 2.21 The pro-
boscis of a microlepi-
dopteran, curled
under the head.

and give anchorage to many of the muscles within the head.

Mouthparts

The most obvious feature of the mouthparts of most moths is the coiled, tongue-like organ known as the proboscis (Figs. 1.10 and 2.21). It is formed from the fusion of the two maxillary galeae (extensions of the maxillae). When not feeding the proboscis is held coiled up under the insect's head (Plate 3c). It is used to suck up fluid and is uncoiled for this purpose (Fig. 2.22). Almost all moths have a proboscis with the exception of some primitive groups, such as the Micropterigidae, and a few species in which the mouthparts have become severely reduced secondarily i.e. having evolved from species with normal mouthparts, so that the adults are incapable of feeding. The main mouthparts in primitive species that have no proboscis, such as *Micropterix calthella*, are the mandibles. These are used in concert with the inner surface of the labrum to grind pollen grains. In more advanced taxonomic groups of moths, functional mandibles do not occur.

The proboscis of moths of the family Eriocraniidae, the most primitive family of moths to possess this specialised structure, is relatively simple. The fusion

Fig. 2.22 A Brown-
line Bright-eye,
Mythimna conigera,
feeding on Buddleia.

between the two maxillary galeae that make up the suction tube is rather weak and is attached to external muscles only. These moths do not visit flowers, but use their proboscis to suck up plant sap or water.

In higher moths the proboscis is more complex, in respect of both the internal structure of the tube and its musculature, which involves both internal and external muscles. Here the combination of increased blood pressure in the proboscis and relaxation of some of the muscles causes the proboscis to uncoil. Recoiling of the proboscis results largely from its inherent elasticity, but is aided by muscles, at least in more advanced families.

Most moths imbibe fluid through the proboscis by a pump action. The cavity formed within the mouthparts and the pharynx, or throat, make up the pump. It is operated by three sets of muscles. One set controls the flow of fluid to and from the pump, while the other two control the contraction and dilation of the pump.

Eyes

The eyes of adult moths are compound eyes. Moths have two large round or oval compound eyes, set on the front sides of the head (Plate 3b). In general the eyes of night-active species are larger than those of diurnal species and those of male moths are larger than those of females of the same species.

Each compound eye (Plate 3d) is made up of numerous hexagonal facets, or ommatidia. The number of facets varies greatly, ranging from as few as 200 in some microlepidoptera to 27,000 in the Convolvulus Hawk moth, *Agrius convolvuli* (Yagi & Koyama, 1963). Each facet has a transparent cornea, a crystalline cone and a light sensitive layer called the retinula, which contains sensory cells giving rise to nerve fibres and surrounded by pigment cells. The cornea is convex and so acts as a lens. The crystalline cone that lies beneath the cornea is also a lens and may be very powerful. The thickness of the cornea and crystalline cone are inversely related. In diurnal species of moth, the cornea tends to be thick and the cone is short, while in nocturnal species the cornea is thin and the cone is long. Beneath the crystalline cones lie retinula sense cells that are attached to a nerve fibre running to the brain. The retinula cells each have a self-secreted rod running down their length to the nerves. In most diurnal Lepidoptera the retinula cells are approximately the same width along the whole of their length. However, in nocturnal species, the outer portion is heavily constricted and so is much thinner than the inner section. This constriction affects the type of image that is produced by the eye.

Ocelli

The compound eyes are not the only light sensitive organs on the head of an adult moth. Most moths also have a pair of ocelli, one above each eye (Plate 3d). In this the Lepidoptera differ from most other insects, including their nearest relatives, the Trichoptera (caddis flies), which have three ocelli. An ocellus is in effect a simple single-lensed eye. The image produced by the ocelli of adult moths is unfocused. Consequently, it is thought that their function may be in orientation during flight. The nerves from the ocelli are connected directly to the motor neurons to the wings. With the ocelli positioned on top of the head and with a wide field of view, changes in the position of the horizon relative to the moth would be immediately appreciated and corrections in the flight path could be made rapidly as appropriate.

Antennae

The antennae of moths are highly modified appendages from what ancestrally was the second segment within the head. They are paired and are largely sensory in function. The shape of moth antennae varies from fine filaments to thick feathery organs (for example, Plate 3f). However, the antennae of most species of moth taper to a point. The burnet moths (Zygaenidae) are sometimes regarded as being exceptional in this respect. However, while the antennae of this family have a distinct bulge towards the end, from the bulge they again narrow, ending in a blunt point (Fig. 1.5).

A moth antenna comprises a base segment, called the scape, a second segment, the pedicel, and a variable number of other segments that are similar to one another and make up the flagellum. It is the variation in the shape of the segments that make up the flagellum that is responsible for the great variety of antennal types. Each segment may be a relatively simple cylinder, just bearing hairs and sense cells, or it may have extensions, which may be single or paired. The flagellum segments within each sex of a species are relatively invariant. However, there is often a considerable degree of sexual dimorphism, male antennae usually being more complex than those of the female (Plate 3e and 3f). This is adaptive, for in many species it is the males that are attracted to females for mating, the attraction being through scent (p. 97). Antennae are able to move and do so by means of muscles from the head to the scape and from the scape to the pedicel. The flagellum does not contain muscles.

The sensory capacity of the antennae is based upon tiny sense organs, called sensilla. Sensilla vary in both their shape and their function. They can respond to either chemical or mechanical stimuli, or both. The sensitivity of a sensillum to a chemical cue appears to depend upon the number of pores it carries. Some are multiporous, some have just a single pore and some have no pores at all. Multiporous sensilla show the greatest sensitivity to chemical cues, while those that lack pores only respond to mechanical stimulation.

Thorax

The most obvious feature of the thorax of moths is that it is the site from which the organs concerned with locomotion, the legs and particularly the wings, arise. The thorax has three segments (prothorax, mesothorax and metathorax) each of which has a pair of legs. The wings, of which there are two pairs, arise from the mesothorax and metathorax. In a few species, the wings are much reduced or absent in females, or occasionally in both sexes (p. 195).

The prothorax is the smallest of the thoracic segments, largely because, in contrast to the mesothorax and metathorax, it does not have to house large flight muscles. The prothorax does, however, give rise to the first pair of legs.

Legs

The legs of moths, like those of other insects, are divided into a series of jointed parts. From the body end these are the coxa, trochanter, femur, tibia and tarsus. The main functions of the legs are walking and standing. The joints between the various sections of the leg move in different planes from each other so that in combination they provide considerable flexibility and manoeuvrability. This flexibility allows moths to stick their legs out at a wide range of angles when resting on uneven surfaces (Fig. 2.23). For holding onto sub-

Fig. 2.23 The jointed legs of moths mean that they are able to stand on uneven surfaces.

strates when at rest the tip of the tarsus is armed with clinging claws.

Walking and standing are not the only functions of the legs. In most moths the tarsi are armed with sensilla. Like the antennae, these may bear sensilla sensitive to chemical or mechanical stimuli. Certainly in some species the sensilla on the tarsi of females are important in the detection of chemicals exuded by plants, so that they act in foodplant recognition, promoting or inhibiting egg-laying as appropriate. The legs of many male moths carry scent brushes or scent pencils (for example, Fig. 1.13), which give off pheromones used in attracting a mate or in allowing a potential mate to determine whether a suitor is of the correct species or sufficient quality.

Moths frequently also use their legs to clean their antennae. In many the tibia is armed with a structure called the epiphysis, which lies proud of the inner surface of the tibia. In such species cleaning antennae involves the moth drawing the antenna between the tibia and epiphysis, thereby prising particles from the antenna.

Wings

The wings of moths vary greatly in shape and size. From the thin wings of many species of smaller microlepidoptera, fringed delicately with fine hairs, to the massive wings of some of the larger silk moths, the range in scale is enormous (p. 20). Yet, despite this variation, nearly all moth wings share two features in common. First, they are covered in pigmented scales. Second, their main function is flight.

In the most primitive groups of moths, the forewings and hindwings are of similar sizes, as are the mesothoracic and metathoracic segments. However, in the majority of families, the forewings are larger than the hindwings, and the mesothorax, having to house larger muscles to power these larger wings, is bigger than the metathorax.

The way that the wings are attached to the body is complex, but crucially allows the wings to be both moved up and down as they flap and to swivel, permitting the rapid changes in angle necessary to generate the aerodynamic forces to give lift during flight (p. 139). A series of sclerotised plates, some of them remarkably flexible, are involved in the joint. The complex arrangement of plates and flexible cuticle is also involved in the folding back of the wings along the body into the resting position employed by most moths. In some species, including most geometrids, the ability to fold their wings back has been secondarily lost.

A moth wing is effectively composed of two membranes and a series of veins. The veins are tubes that connect to the haemocoele. In adult moths that have dried their wings after emergence, the veins are virtually empty tubes because the haemolymph used in wing expansion has been withdrawn from them. However, each of the larger veins contains a nerve and a trachea, the latter providing a means of gaseous exchange. In comparison to many other insects, the arrangement of veins of moths is relatively simple, most veins running from the wing base out to the edge of the wing. Relatively few cross veins are present. The venation is important taxonomically and has been extensively used in all levels of classification within the order Lepidoptera. Description of all the names and numbers that have been assigned to the different veins is outside the scope of this book. However, I find the nomenclature used by Wootton (1979) both sensible and simpler than some others and Scoble (1992) gives a clear and concise review of wing venation in the Lepidoptera with appropriate references.

The position in which moths hold their wings when at rest is highly variable (Fig. 1.4). However, this considerable variability has been split by Tweedie & Emmet (1991) into just three main categories. First, some hold the wings back along the body in a roof-like position or in some cases curled around the body. This posture is referred to as tectiform (Figs. 2.24, 2.25 and Plate 7a). Second, many geometrids and some other species adopt a position with the wings held out flat and away from the body (planiform) (Figs. 2.26, 2.27 and Plate 10c). Third, the majority of butterflies and a few moths, such as the Early Thorn, *Selenia dentaria* (Plate 7b) hold the wings up above the body. This posture is termed veliform.

The many variations of these three main themes are intricately correlated with the resting sites chosen by moths and the colour patterns sported by their wings and bodies. These have most often evolved as a result of natural selection acting to reduce predation by predators that find their prey by sight. I shall return to the rationale behind some of the more unusual postures that are adopted by moths when I discuss moth defences in Chapter 8.

When flying, moths may beat their wings in phase or out of phase. Most often, the wings of primitive species are not tightly coupled, so they are beaten out of phase. Primitive families, such as the swifts (Hepialidae), have a finger-like projection from the back of the forewing, called a jugum. This helps in wing folding, but does not keep the forewings and hindwings linked as a single unit when in flight. Rather, as slow-motion film of male Ghost moths, *Hepialus humuli*, displaying over their lekking sites has shown (Mallett 1984), the forewing rises before and in front of the hindwing, before coming against it in the down stroke.

Primitive families of moths with a jugum can be contrasted with most more advanced families that have a wing-linking system. This involves a hook or series of bristles on the underside of the forewing (called a retinaculum) and a set of bristles, or sometimes just a single bristle at the base of the hindwing (called a frenulum). The interlocking of the frenulum with the retinaculum holds the wings together. Exceptionally, a third type of arrangement is seen in

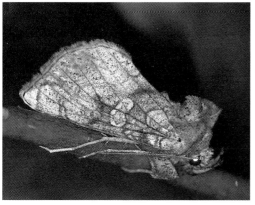

Fig. 2.24 (above left) The Golden Plusia, *Polychrysia moneta*, with wings held in the tectiform position.

Fig. 2.25 (above) The Great Prominent, *Peridea anceps*, with wings held in the tectiform position.

Fig. 2.26 (left) A Narrow-winged Pug, *Eupithecia nanata*, with wings held in the planiform position.

Fig. 2.27 (below left) The Light Emerald, *Campaea margaritata*, rests with wings out in the planiform position.

most butterflies and most moths of the superfamily Bombycoidea, although not the hawk moths (Sphingidae). Here the front margin of the hindwing is simply extended so that there is a large overlap with the hind margin of the forewing. Although the wings are not locked together, this overlap, in conjunction with the timing of wing muscle activity and the dynamics of flight, serves to keep the wings synchronised in phase during flight.

Scales

Having described the features that give the Lepidoptera the second half of their names (pteron, meaning wing), it is appropriate to deal now with the features that contribute the other part of the name: the scales (lepis). Although I am dealing with the scales directly after discussing the wings of moths, scales are not only found on the wings. In fact, the antennae, mouthparts, head, thorax, legs and abdomen may also be clothed in scales.

Moth scales vary tremendously in shape. They may be hair-like or widely expanded like a ping-pong paddle. However, essentially, they all have the same basic structure. Typically they have a stalk that fits into a socket, and a blade (Fig. 2.28). The lower surface of the blade is usually plain and unsculptured. However, the upper surface is a complex of longitudinal ridges and troughs crossed with smaller ridges and sporting a series of holes into the interior of the scale, which contains pigment granules (Fig. 2.29). Apart from the pigment granules, the interiors of the scales in more advanced Lepidoptera are hollow. This gives the scales some utility as an insulating material.

This is of course not the only function of scales. Scales play the major role in the colour patterns of moths. The colours produced may be either structural colours, as seen in the iridescent bronzy green of the Burnished Brass, *Diachrysia chrysitis* (Plate 1e), or pigmental colours, which in moths produce most of the colours visible to the human eye. In moths structural colours are produced either as a result of the scattering of light off the ridges and other components of the scales, or by interference off scales that are spaced regularly across the wings at intervals that are similar to the wavelength of light. A third type of structural colour, diffraction colour, occurs in some butterflies.

Pigment colours are found in all Lepidoptera. The pigments that have been identified are varied and diverse. They include pterins (white, yellows to reds), melanins (black, browns to reds, occasionally yellows), ommochromes (red to brown), flavonoids (various colours, for example, yellow, red, blue) and biliverdins (blue, green). The melanins, of which there are many different types, are by far the most common pigments, and comprise the major colour components of a great many of our British moths. Much rarer are the flavonoids, which occur in many moths, but are rarely common. Moths cannot synthesise flavonoids, so when these occur in moths it is assumed that they have been sequestered from foodplants. Bile pigments such as the biliverdins and related compounds are generally green or blue. They are metabolised by the moths themselves and are frequently combined with yellow carotenoids to produce green coloration. Other types of pigment undoubtedly await discovery.

Through the colours and patterns that they produce, the scales of moths play crucial roles in both intraspecific and interspecific communication (p. 103), in protection from predation (Chapter 8) and in thermoregulation (p. 242). In addition, they are used in the distribution of pheromones from scent brushes, they give some protection from damage or abrasion to both body and wings and they play a role in the aerodynamics of flight (p. 139).

Abdomen

The final section of the moth body plan is the abdomen. As the abdomen is the site of greatest gaseous exchange through the spiracles, one might regard it as the most important part of the body in terms of respiration. It also contains the majority of the gut and fat reserves, thereby also being the main food-processing part of the body. Perhaps most crucially it houses the gonads (ovaries and testes) and other parts of the reproductive system. In addition, in

Fig. 2.28 An electron micrograph of scales on a moth wing.

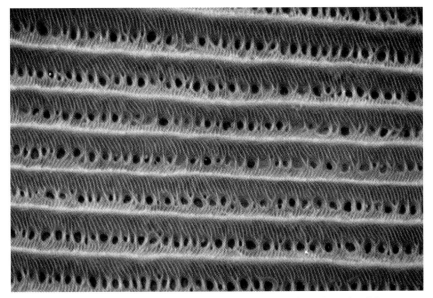

Fig. 2.29 An electron micrograph of the detail on the upper surface of a scale of the Burnished Brass, *Diachrysia chrysitis.*

some moths, such as members of the Uraniidae, Pyralidae and Geometridae, tympanal organs that, like our ears, are sensitive to sound, are situated at the base of the abdomen. Finally, a variety of glands are contained in the

abdomen. Most of these are involved in reproduction and will be discussed in
Chapter 4. However, some glands are thought to contain repellents and probably have a defensive role.

Sound production

Sound is produced by a variety of species of moth in a variety of ways. In many,
sound is generated by rubbing two parts of the body together. Thus, legs may
be rubbed against protuberances on the wing or specific wing veins, wings may
be rubbed against the thorax and the pupae of many moths can rub their
abdominal segments together. Some moths, particularly arctiids, lymantriids,
pyralids and some noctuids have a row of minute tymbal organs that can produce sound. These are situated on the metathorax in arctiids, on the abdomen
in lymantriids and some noctuids and on the tegulae of some pyralids. Sound
is produced when muscles contract and relax causing the tymbal organ to first
distort and then return to its resting position, thereby producing a pulse of
sound.

Sound may be produced in other ways. Some tiger moths may produce
sound as they expel noxious liquids or foams from the prothorax when disturbed. A few noctuids have the ability to produce sound as they vibrate their
wings, the sound being caused by the percussive action of blister-like features
on the forewings. Perhaps most famously, Death's-head Hawk moths,
Acherontia atropos, have the ability to produce sound by expelling air from the
pharynx through the proboscis. Several authorities have suggested that this
'piping' has a role in bee appeasement when moths enter bees' nests to steal
honey. The sound, which consists of a low-pitched squeak followed by a higher pitched squeak, has been said to mimic sounds made by queen bees. These
sounds have been known since the eighteenth century. However, as far as I
know, I was the first person to have these sounds broadcast on the radio, at the
request of John Holmes, a BBC producer for Radio 4's *Natural History
Programme*.

Hearing organs

Many species of moth have hearing organs. These vary in both structure and
anatomical position. The majority consist of a stretched membrane, or tympa-
num, sited over an air sac. Usually these are found on the abdomen, but some
are situated on the metathorax or at the base of the wings. Other types of hearing organ consist of modifications of the mouthparts in some hawk moths and
sound-sensitive hairs in some moth larvae.

Hearing organs in the moths probably evolved in response to predators,
principally bats, that hunt using sound. Many moths are certainly able to detect
the ultrasounds emitted by hunting bats and take evasive action (p. 212).

Moths may also respond to sound made by other moths. For example,
ultrasounds produced by the tymbal organs of males of the Lesser Wax moth,
Achroia grisella, cause females to orientate towards males, thereby having a
function in mate detection. The sounds made by another pyralid, *Syntonarcha
iriastis*, also act to attract females to calling males, but being of a much lower
frequency than those of the Lesser Wax moth, they are effective over much
greater distances.

Both male and female Polka-dot Wasp moths, *Syntomeida epilais*, call by
sound. This species is a member of the tiger moth family, a family in which

sound is commonly used in defence as a warning of unpalatability or to interfere with bats' sonar (p. 213). The calls of the sexes of the Polka-dot Wasp moth are substantially different, suggesting that they possibly have a role in gender recognition (Scoble 1992). Moreover, as it seems highly probable that the use of sound in courtship in this species has evolved secondarily, this may be an example of sexual selection through sensory exploitation. Here, mate choice based on sound may have evolved through the exploitation of traits originally evolved for some reason unconnected with mating.

Conclusion

Moths are complex insects, in respect of both their life histories and their morphological make-up. Different species show a great many variations on the various themes I have mentioned. The brief and somewhat generalised descriptions of the various stages of the life cycle of moths and the basic anatomical components of the stages related in this chapter do little more than brush the surface of a subject that has been examined in great detail. For those readers who wish to look deeper into the intricacies of the way that the different stages of a moth's life are put together, I warmly recommend Malcolm J. Scoble's 1992 book *The Lepidoptera: Form Function and Diversity*.

Despite over a century and a half of close study, there are still many gaps in our knowledge of the structures of the Lepidoptera. Sadly, the advances that need to be made are largely in areas that require facilities and equipment that are not available to most lepidopterists, such as pigment chemistry, pheromone analysis, the function of microstructures, behavioural neurology, biochemistry and molecular genetics. However, in the ensuing chapters, in dealing with the natural history of moths in their environments, I hope to point to many opportunities for lepidopterists, denied expensive high-tech equipment, to make valuable contributions to our knowledge of moths and science in general.

3

Moths and Evolution

Moths and evolutionary theories

Life is a struggle for existence. Some live and reproduce: others die without leaving issue. This is the basis of modern evolution and so lies at the centre of modern biology. Studies of the Lepidoptera, more than any other group of organisms, have helped us to formulate ideas of the processes by which the diversity of life that inhabits the Earth got to be the way it is. This group of insects has been at the heart of most of the major debates on evolution since Darwin first put forward his theory of biological evolution through the processes of natural selection and sexual selection. The polymorphisms in some swallowtail butterflies showing Batesian mimicry (p. 208) were at the centre of the debate, in the early 1900s, between those who thought selection was the most important factor in evolution and those who gave this prime role to genetic mutation. Once this problem was resolved in favour of the selectionists, the question of the relative import of selection compared to chance in the form of random genetic drift held centre stage for two decades. It was resolved by studies of a population of the Scarlet Tiger moth, *Callimorpha dominula*, in Berkshire, which provided the first data allowing the relative merits of these opposing views to be assessed. One of the first examples of evolution in action, and still one of the best today, concerns the increase in dark or melanic forms of many species of moth, most notably the Peppered moth, *Biston betularia*, in Britain (see Chapter 9).

There are several reasons why until recently the Lepidoptera took pride of place among the groups used to study evolution. They include the beauty of many members of the order. The aesthetic pleasure in watching these beautiful insects has long attracted observers, both young and old, with inquiring minds. The ease with which many different species can be collected, bred and observed has also made them useful tools in scientific research. The large number of progeny produced means that they are amenable for the study of inheritance. For example, the genetics of many different colour pattern forms of the Magpie moth, *Abraxas grossulariata* (Fig. 3.1), were analysed in the first two decades after Mendel's laws of inheritance were rediscovered in 1900. The multiple elements that comprise the colour patterns on the wings of moths, each individual scale, its colour, shape and lay, and the combination of physical and chemical colours, together meld into a feature with infinite possibilities of design and variation. As genes are responsible for much of this make-up in any individual, variations in these colours and patterns can be passed from generation to generation and can be moulded and changed by the forces of evolution. The scales on the wings of a moth or butterfly thus provide the perfect medium through which to see the products of the forces of evolution.

In this chapter, I will briefly introduce these 'forces' of evolution. However, I do not wish to write a full introductory discourse on basic genetical and

Fig. 3.1 The inheritance of colour pattern variation in the Magpie moth, *Abraxas grossulariata*, was analysed in the early 1900s.

evolutionary theory, as I have done previously (Majerus 1994, 1998). Rather, I will try to explain here some of those features of the evolutionary genetics of moths that go to show how my fascination in these wonderful insects has been enhanced by understanding how evolution has shaped their form and behaviour.

Biological evolution

There are over 180,000 described species of moth on Earth and many thousands, probably hundreds of thousands, of others that await description. They will never all be described, for two reasons. First, due to natural changes on Earth and to human activity, many will become extinct before they are found. Second, the rate at which new species are discovered and described is just too slow to keep up with the number of new species that form as a result of evolutionary processes.

So what are these evolutionary processes? In general terms there are just two, although each of the main mechanisms of evolution has many subgroups. These are selection and chance. Selection, which centres on the mechanism first proposed by Charles Darwin and Alfred Russell Wallace in their joint paper in 1858 (p. 29), involves variation among individuals, with some varieties being more likely to survive and reproduce than others. This main mechanism has to be coupled with the features of the successful individuals being passed on to progeny through genes. Selection encompasses not only natural selection in the sense of survival of the fittest, but also sexual selection through male competition or female choice, kin selection, whereby some die or forgo reproduction in order to increase the chances of survival of relatives, and even species selection, in which features not of individuals but of whole populations play a role in whether the population continues or dies out. I will return to the various types of selection presently, for they underlie much of the discussion in this book. The alternative, chance, also has a part to play in evolution and in some ways is more fundamental as it affects all genes that show variation.

Random genetic drift

Chance, by which in the evolutionary context we mean random genetic drift, is a sort of numbers game. Take, for example, two normal randomly shuffled packs of 52 cards. The red and black cards in each pack may be taken to represent two forms of a gene that code for different colours of some element of a moth's colour pattern, one producing red, the other producing black. Each pack now represents the germ cells or gametes of one of the parents. If we allow this pair of parents to produce ten offspring, we can do this by picking one card from the top of each pack ten times. Each pair of cards represents one offspring and the colours of the cards show its genetic constitution, or genotype, in respect of this colour trait. Now count up the number of red and black cards in these offspring. If you get exactly ten reds and ten blacks, there has been no genetic drift. The frequency of reds and blacks is exactly the same in the progeny as in the original parental generation: that is equal numbers of each. But sometimes you will get 11:9 or 12:8 or even a more extreme bias. This happens just by chance through sampling error and the likelihood that reds are in excess over blacks is exactly the same as the reverse.

This happens to real moths too. The eggs and sperm that go to make the next generation are in effect drawn randomly from pools of sperm and eggs at fertilisation. The frequency of red and black genes, or alleles, in the pool of gametes in the next generation will be determined by their frequency at fertilisation at the beginning of the generation. Therefore, if the initial frequency of reds and blacks was 50% of each, but the sample that were successful in fertilisation was slightly biased with 51% being red alleles, this would be the frequency of reds in the next generation and so in the sperm and eggs produced by that generation. At each generation, the frequency of reds could increase or decrease just due to chance. Over long periods of time, one or other of the alleles would reach such low frequency that it would run the risk of not being present in the sample of gametes that produced a new generation. Once that has happened, the allele will have been lost from the population. Thus, the main effect of this random genetic drift is to remove genetic variation from populations. In theory, if random genetic drift were the only evolutionary mechanism affecting genes, the different alleles of each gene would gradually be lost over long periods of time, until each gene was represented by only one allele. All members of a population would end up being genetically identical. Despite nearly four billion years of evolution, this quite obviously has not happened. The reason is that while drift acts to reduce variation, another process, genetic mutation, acts to generate new variation.

The effects of drift are most profound in small populations, whether this small size is a result of a crash due to harsh conditions, or to fragmentation of a larger population due to habitat destruction or to founder effects when just a few individuals form new colonies. This is simply because sampling effects will have a proportionately greater magnitude in small samples than in large samples. While one would not be too surprised to get seven reds and three blacks if picking ten cards from a fair pack, getting 7,000 reds and 3,000 blacks from a very large number of packs appears highly unlikely.

There are two fundamental differences between selection and random genetic drift. First, drift acts on all genes that show variation in their code composition at each generation, whereas selection only acts on a proportion of those variable genes that have an effect on the organisms that carry them. Second, while drift lacks direction, selection often has direction, one allele increasing until it replaces another.

The Hardy–Weinberg law

One of the few biological laws, the Hardy–Weinberg law, is central to our thinking about the ways in which evolutionary processes affect genes and the characteristics that they control in populations. This law was formulated independently, in 1908, by two mathematical biologists. It states that given a number of assumptions there will be a strict relationship between the frequency of alleles in a population and the genotypes that these produce, and that these frequencies will not change over time. The relationship is that if there are n alleles of a gene, then the frequency of the genotypes will be the product of the frequencies of the alleles that make up that genotype when homozygous or twice the product for heterozygotes. Thus, if a gene has only two alleles in a population, say alleles M and m, at frequencies p and q respectively (so p+q = 1 as these are the only alleles), the three possible genotypes will have frequencies as follows: $MM = p^2$, $Mm = 2pq$, $mm = q^2$. This rule can be extended to more than two alleles. Figure 3.2 illustrates the relationship between allelic and genotypic frequencies for a three allele system.

The assumptions underlying the Hardy–Weinberg law are crucial:

i) The organisms in question must be diploid (having two sets of chromosomes).

ii) The organisms must reproduce sexually (this applies to almost all Lepidoptera).

iii) The population size must be infinitely large.

iv) Mating must be random with each individual having an equal chance of mating with each other individual.

v) There must be no genetic mutation in the population.

vi) The population must be independent of other populations so that there is no migration into or out of the population.

vii) Finally, there must be no Darwinian selection.

The Hardy–Weinberg law is an odd law because quite obviously the assumptions upon which it is based can never hold true. No population is infinite; there is always mutation, and in species that have independent sexes, as in almost all moths, mating is never random because it is not possible to reproduce with a member of the same sex. The value of this law is not then in its accuracy. Rather it provides a null hypothesis predicting the baseline for when nothing of biological interest is happening. When populations are found that over time appear to break the Hardy–Weinberg law, it simply means that one or more of the law's underlying assumptions is being contravened and, consequently, something worth investigating is going on. Put another way, if the Hardy–Weinberg law is found to apply to a genetic trait in a population, then in most instances, the conclusion would be that there is no selection (but see stable genetic polymorphism, p. 64) and that drift is the only evolutionary process acting on the trait. The relative importance of drift and selection may thus be tested by seeing whether the Hardy–

Fig. 3.2 The derivation of the expected frequencies of the genotypes due to a gene with three alleles. The alleles m', m" and m* have frequencies p, q and r respectively. The assumptions of the Hardy–Weinberg law apply.

		Alleles in female gametes →	m'	$m"$	$m*$
	Allelic → frequencies ↓		p	q	r
Male gametes ↓		Genotypes and frequencies of offspring ↓ ↓ ↓			
m'	p		$m'm'$ p^2	$m"m'$ pq	$m*m'$ pr
$m"$	q		$m'm"$ pq	$m"m"$ q^2	$m*m"$ qr
$m*$	r		$m'm*$ pr	$m"m*$ qr	$m*m*$ r^2

The frequencies of the six genotypes are thus:

$m'm'$	$m'm$	$m'm*$	$m"m"$	$m*m"$	$m*m*$
p^2	2pq	2pr	q^2	2qr	r^2

Weinberg law does or does not apply over a period of time.

The assessment of the relative importance of selection and drift was at the forefront of evolutionary debates for much of the twentieth century and the Lepidoptera played a crucial part in the often heated and acrimonious controversies that were generated. Before considering the case studies that played a role in these debates, some explanation of the way selection operates is needed.

Darwinian selection

Darwin's theory of evolution by natural selection is based upon just seven points (Darwin 1859). Four of these Darwin knew, from observation, to be true. The other three were deductions that Darwin believed, on the basis of the four observations, had to happen.

1. Fact – Organisms produce far more offspring than are necessary to maintain a stable population.
2. Fact – Most populations remain relatively stable in size over time.
3. Deduction – Therefore, many of the progeny produced must die before reaching reproductive maturity.
4. Fact – Almost all the characteristics of an organism vary.
5. Deduction – Therefore, some variants will be more successful in the struggle for life or in the struggle to reproduce than will others.
6. Fact – There is a resemblance between the traits possessed by parents and those of their offspring.
7. Deduction – Therefore, the characteristics of one generation that give them success in survival and reproduction will be inherited by their progeny, which will, therefore, have these success-giving traits. Over time, advantageous traits will spread to all individuals of a population, while disadvantageous traits will be naturally selected out of the population.

From these seven points, it may be seen that Darwin's theory is both a genetical theory and a population biology theory. Crucially, the final two points recognise that individuals of a species vary and that some of the variation is passed from one generation to the next, i.e. it is inherited. This genetic variation is necessary for selection to operate and cause change over time. If all individuals were identical, they would all have the same fitness. For individuals to vary, something must generate the variation. Ultimately that something is mutation. Mutations are essentially mistakes in the copying of genetic material as one cell divides to produce two daughter cells (or four sex cells).

Mutations may be small, involving just a single change in the nucleotide base code of DNA, or large, involving rearrangements of large sections of chromosomes, or even the loss or gain of whole chromosomes or chromosome sets. Large mutations are comparatively rare and are usually deleterious so that they are usually selected out of the population soon after they arise. However, small changes in the genetic code within a gene can produce changes in the trait controlled by that gene and so affect the chances of survival of individuals expressing the new mutation. While most changes have no effect on fitness, a sizeable minority of mutations are deleterious, while a much smaller minority are beneficial. By definition, selection will not act directly on those mutations that do not affect fitness and these mutations will increase or decrease in frequency just through random genetic drift. However, both deleterious and beneficial mutations will be affected by selection. Mutations that have a negative effect on fitness will be selected out of the population. Beneficial mutations will increase in frequency.

When we consider variable genes in populations, we have to consider not only the effect of the different alleles of a gene, but also the relationship between these alleles and their expression when they occur together. This means that we have to take genetic dominance into account. In the simplest case, consider one gene with two different forms or alleles. One allele causes red pigment to be produced. The second allele causes yellow pigment to be produced. Such genes are known in a number of moths, such as the Scarlet Tiger, the Cinnabar, *Tyria jocabaeae*, and several of the burnet moths (Zygaenidae) (Plate 15f). As most moths are diploid, i.e. they carry two copies of each of their chromosomes, they will carry two copies of this gene. Individuals that carry two red alleles (i.e. they are homozygous for the red allele) will obviously be red, just as those that carry two yellow alleles will be yellow. The critical question is what happens in individuals that are heterozygous for the two alleles, which is to say that they carry one allele of each type. There are three possibilities. First, the red allele may dominate the yellow allele so that only red is produced. The red allele is then said to be dominant over the yellow allele, which is said to be recessive. The reverse may also occur, the yellow allele being dominant over the red. The third possibility is that both alleles are expressed with the result that the individual is intermediate, either orange, or being part red and part yellow. If this is the case, the alleles are said to show no dominance or incomplete dominance, depending on whether the result is precisely halfway between the two extremes or is closer to one than the other.

It is important to recognise that genetic dominance does not imply anything about predominance or commonness of an allele. For example, the alleles of many moths that give rise to industrial melanic forms are dominant to the non-melanic alleles, yet these melanic forms vary in frequency over time and space. In some populations, particularly in industrial areas, the melanic forms became the predominant form for a time, but in many species have subsequently begun to decline in frequency. In other populations, the form controlled by the dominant allele has never achieved a majority in the population (see Chapter 9).

Darwin, in preparing material for *On the Origin of Species*, was aware that his theory would be highly controversial. He saw that it had to embrace and explain all aspects of life on Earth. Thus, as we shall see in Chapter 4, he formulated his ideas on sexual selection specifically to explain the considerable differences that he observed between males and females of many types of organism. Species that had two or more distinctly different forms were also a problem to him, for he could not imagine how a population could contain more than one 'fittest' form. I shall turn now to this question of species that are polymorphic, for these were the subject material for much of the work conducted in evolutionary biology in the twentieth century.

Genetic polymorphism

Genetic polymorphism was defined by Ford (1940) as 'the occurrence together in the same locality of two or more discontinuous forms of a species in such proportions that the rarest of them cannot be maintained merely by recurrent mutation.'

This is a very precise definition. It excludes seasonal varieties (not the same time) and geographic races (not the same place). It also excludes continuous variation and variants that occur at very low frequency as a result of recurrent mutation.

Transient and stable polymorphisms

During the spread of a novel advantageous mutation, while the frequency of the forms is changing in one direction, then the polymorphism is said to be transient. An obvious case would be the melanic form of the Peppered moth, which increased in frequency in many industrial areas in the second half of the nineteenth century (p. 217). The expectation is that the allele controlling the fittest form will become fixed, reducing the alternative allele, or alleles, to the status of rare mutations. However, if during the spread of an initially beneficial allele it loses its advantage, then the frequency of the genotype may stabilise at specific levels, or may change in a regular cyclical manner. The polymorphism can then be maintained indefinitely at or around particular equilibrium frequencies. Such polymorphisms are termed stable or balanced.

The maintenance of balanced polymorphisms

Natural selection versus random genetic drift

The relative importance of the two central processes of evolution, natural selection and random genetic drift, has been hotly debated for a hundred years. This controversy may be couched as a question. Which evolutionary changes are the result of selection? The corollary is that those evolutionary events not driven by selection must have occurred through genetic drift. In the main, this controversy centred on conspicuous genetic polymorphism of the type defined by Ford. This is because such polymorphisms were amenable to study and because they were a quandary for the early Darwinian evolutionists. Selectionists found it difficult to envisage how two or more forms could be maintained in a population unless they were selectively neutral. Indeed, when Darwin (1859) defined the concept of natural selection in *On the Origin of Species,* he specifically disassociated the concept from natural polymorphisms:

> 'This preservation of favourable variations and the rejection of injurious variations I call natural selection. Variations neither useful nor injurious would not be affected by natural selection, and would be left a fluctuating element, as perhaps we see in the species we call polymorphic.'

Up until the early 1940s, most scientists who studied evolution followed this view, believing that conspicuous polymorphisms had to be selectively neutral. Variations in the frequencies of forms over time were therefore attributed to random genetic drift.

Two English scientists, Sir Ronald Fisher in Cambridge and Professor E. B. Ford in Oxford, disagreed strongly with this interpretation of polymorphism. Fisher, in 1922, had already shown mathematically that two or more alleles of a species could be maintained in a population by selection. At equilibrium, the selective forces for and against each allele are balanced precisely so that each type of allele has the same overall fitness. Fisher proposed two basic types of mechanism that would maintain polymorphism. First, heterozygotes could be fitter than homozygotes so that both the alleles carried by the heterozygote are maintained in the population. Second, the fitness of a form could be inversely correlated with its frequency, so that a form became fitter if it decreased in frequency relative to other forms.

Darwin saw evolution as a slow, gradual process. Thus, early evolutionary biologists viewed selection as a rather weak force. However, Ford took a different view. Having considered Fisher's mathematical analysis of polymorphism, Ford speculated that change might be slow not because selective forces are weak, but because they are strong and balanced. Polymorphisms maintained by balancing selection would change only very slowly as the overall relative fitnesses of the forms changed in response to alterations in the balance of selective advantages and disadvantages. Ford then came to a remarkable and surprising deduction. He saw that the most temporally stable and geographically widespread polymorphisms would be those that would be the subject of the strongest balancing selection. In such cases, the frequencies of genotypes and phenotypes would be maintained through time and space at stable equilibrium points, so that they could only deviate slightly from these frequencies before the balancing selection brought them back into equilibrium.

As evidence to support this insight, Ford used the most ubiquitous type of balanced genetic polymorphism: the occurrence of two distinct sexes. The way in which the ratio of the sexes is usually maintained in precise balance, with each sex having equal frequency, illustrates the power of balancing selection beautifully.

Selection maintains the sex ratio

In most species in which sex is determined genetically, populations contain approximately equal numbers of males and females. Why should this be so? One answer is that in most species, including moths, sex is determined by the segregation of the sex chromosomes during meiosis in the sex that has two different sex chromosomes (the heterogametic sex), and that this will generate a 1:1 ratio of gametes bearing the large or small sex chromosome from the heterogametic sex. This is true as far as it goes. However, many other mechanisms of sex determination, which can produce different sex ratios, exist, and would have become prevalent if they were beneficial.

An explanation based on the stability of the common 1:1 ratio would be more convincing. The explanation, usually attributed to Fisher, was first put forward by Darwin (1859) in the first edition of *On the Origin of the Species* (Darwin removed this explanation from subsequent editions). Assume that the sex ratio of the next generation is determined by genes acting in the parental generation. This might result from genes acting in the heterogametic sex to alter the ratio of male and female determining gametes produced, or from genes acting to alter the success of the two types of gamete during fertilisation. Consider what happens if a species' sex ratio is displaced from parity, either through chance or sex-biased mortality, or through the action of a sex ratio modifier gene. Say, there are now fewer males than females. In forming the next generation, each zygote will have one mother and one father. It follows that the average contribution made by each male is now greater than the average made by each female. In other words, males are now fitter than females and will be selected for. Furthermore, the bigger the skew in the sex ratio, the larger will be the selective benefit in producing the rarer sex. Only when the sex ratio returns to parity will the restoring force disappear. In this way, we can see that the evolutionarily stable equilibrium point is to have equal numbers of males and females, for it is only at this ratio that the reproductive value of a son is precisely equivalent to that of a daughter.

Ecological genetics

It was Fisher and Ford's adherence to the view that selection maintained polymorphism that placed them in opposition to those who considered polymorphisms to be non-adaptive, and particularly to Sewall Wright from Chicago, one of the chief advocates of random genetic drift. As this debate fired up, Fisher and Ford began to collect evidence to resolve the controversy. Indeed, in the 1930s, Ford initiated a long-term programme of research into some of the most well-known conspicuous polymorphisms. This programme involved a meld of observation and experimentation, in both the laboratory and, more critically, in the field. This approach to the practical study of the causes and consequences of genetic variation in populations became known as ecological genetics. Many of the species used as subject material in this research programme were Lepidoptera. They included examples of transient polymorphisms involving industrial melanism in several moth species (Chapter 9), and a number of balanced polymorphisms involving moths or butterflies. The first of these was the study of a balanced polymorphism involving colour pattern in the Scarlet Tiger moth.

Genetic polymorphism in the Scarlet Tiger moth

The Scarlet Tiger moth (Plate 1c) is a colonial, day-flying moth that, in Britain, inhabits marshland and hedgerow habitats. In one famous British colony, at Cothill in Berkshire, it is naturally polymorphic for its colour pattern. Three forms occur, all controlled by two alleles of a single locus with no dominance. The normal form, *dominula*, and the rarest form, *bimacula*, are homozygotes, while the heterozygote, *medionigra*, is phenotypically intermediate between these (Fig. 3.3). By examining old collections, Ford established that the maximum frequency of the so-called *medionigra* allele prior to 1929 was in the region of 0.024. In both 1936 and 1938, Ford visited the colony and found several specimens of the *medionigra* form, concluding that this form had increased in frequency.

Fig. 3.3 Forms of the Scarlet Tiger moth, *Callimorpha dominula*, from Cothill, Berkshire. Top – f. *dominula*, middle – f. *medionigra*, bottom – f. *bimacula*.

Fisher and Ford surveyed this colony from 1939 to 1946. In 1939 and 1940, they collected data simply by catching individuals and recording the phenotypes. However, from 1941 onwards they used multiple mark–release–recapture techniques, which, with mathematical analyses developed by Fisher, allowed accurate estimation of the frequency of the two alleles, the average survival rate, and the population size allowing for recruitment into the adult population at the beginning of the flight season and the natural decline in adult population towards the end of it. The estimates obtained for these parameters were the first on which the alternative explanations of a polymorphism, selection or drift, could be tested.

Fisher (1930) had already shown that it is possible to calculate the extent to which random genetic drift could alter allele frequencies between generations in a population of given size. Using this method and an assumed breeding population of 1,000 adults each year from 1939–1946, Fisher & Ford (1947) demonstrated that the changes in the frequency of the rarer allele, unhelpfully termed the *medionigra* allele in the literature, (Table 3.1) were too large to be attributable to genetic drift alone. In the conclusion to this classic paper they wrote:

> 'Thus our analysis, the first in which the relative parts played by random survival and selection in a wild population can be tested, does not support the view that chance fluctuations in gene ratios, such as may occur in very small isolated populations, can be of any significance in evolution.'

This interpretation was challenged by Professor Sewall Wright (1948). His criticisms concerned three points in particular. First, there were no population size estimates for 1939 and 1940 and the largest drop in the frequency of *medionigra* occurred between 1940 and 1941. Second, he argued that real and apparent population sizes could be very different if whole broods were wiped out by catastrophic events such as would occur if females lay most of their eggs in one place. Third, he suggested that even if the forms did differ in fitness, such differences might fluctuate randomly so that frequency changes would have no trend, but would fluctuate in response to random variations in conditions year on year.

These criticisms were answered by Ford in turn (Ford 1964). He pointed out that visits to the colony were difficult in 1940 because of the constraints of war. Yet, on the few visits made that year the moths had been flying in considerable numbers. To invalidate Fisher and Ford's conclusions the population size for 1940 would have had to be about the same as the number actually caught and this Ford asserts was certainly not the case. Second, because female Scarlet Tiger moths scatter their eggs randomly (Sheppard 1951) and do not lay them in batches as do most moths, it is highly unlikely that whole broods would be wiped out by accidents. Here Ford makes a blistering attack against Wright, accusing him of making theoretical deductions on evolution unsupported by study, or any knowledge of the ecology of the species under consideration or the situation concerned. Third, although Wright's third point was justified at the time, continued monitoring of the Cothill colony has shown that the level of 2–3% reached in the early 1940s has largely been maintained since (Table 3.1). This is not consistent with the idea of random fluctuating changes in frequency.

Table 3.1 The occurrence of the *dominula, medionigra* and *bimacula* forms of the Scarlet Tiger moth, *Callimorpha dominula*, at Cothill, Berkshire, from 1939 to 1988. Data from Fisher & Ford 1947, Ford & Sheppard 1969, Ford 1975 and Jones 1989. From 1941 to 1961 population size was estimated using mark–release–recapture, but subsequently very few recaptures were made. The estimates for 1962 to 1972 were obtained from an unweighted regression of population size on the number of moths captured in those years when seven or more were recaptured. From 1973 mark–release–recapture was again used. (After Jones 1989.)

Year	Numbers captured			Total	Estimated population size of total colony	Allele frequency (% of *medionigra*)
	dominula	*medionigra*	*bimacula*			
1939	184	37	2	223	?	
1940	92	24	1	117	?	11.1
1941	400	59	2	461	2000–2500	6.8
1942	183	22	0	205	1200–2000	5.4
1943	239	30	0	269	1000	5.6
1944	452	43	1	496	5000–6000	4.5
1945	326	44	2	372	4000	6.5
1946	905	78	3	986	6000–8000	4.3
1947	1244	94	3	1341	5000–7000	3.7
1948	898	67	1	966	2600–3800	3.6
1949	479	29	0	508	1400–2000	2.9
1950	1106	88	0	1194	3500–4700	3.7
1951	552	29	0	581	1500–3000	2.5
1952	1414	106	1	1521	5000–7000	3.6
1953	1034	54	1	1089	5000–11000	2.6
1954	1097	67	0	1164	10000–12000	2.9
1955	308	7	0	315	1500–2500	1.1
1956	1231	76	1	1308	7000–15000	3.0
1957	1469	138	5	1612	14000–18000	4.6
1958	1285	94	4	1383	12000–18000	3.7
1959	460	19	1	480	5500–8500	2.2
1960	182	7	0	189	1000–4000	1.9
1961	165	7	0	172	1200–1600	2.0
1962	22	1	0	23	216	(2.2)
1963	58	1	0	59	470	(0.8)
1964	31	0	0	31	272	–
1965	79	2	0	81	625	1.2
1966	37	0	0	37	315	–
1967	50	0	0	50	406	–
1968	128	3	0	131	978	1.1
1969	508	38	0	546	5712	3.5
1970	444	31	0	475	4493	3.4
1971	637	9	0	648	7084	0.7
1972	335	5	0	340	3471	0.8
1973	230	1	0	231	1000–2000	0.2
1974	836	11	0	847	2000–3000	0.7
1975	50	2	0	52	<1000	1.9
1976	167	3	0	170	1000–2000	0.9
1977	12	0	0	12	<500	–
1978	39	1	0	40	<1000	1.3
1988	611	11	0	622	4000–6000	0.9
Totals	**19,979**	**1,338**	**28**	**21,345**		

Subsequent work on the Scarlet Tiger moth vindicated the Fisher–Ford view, with two opposing selective factors being identified. On the one hand, experiments were designed that allowed the relative fitnesses of the different forms to be assessed. Young larvae of known genetic make-up were marked radioactively by feeding larvae on Comfrey, their preferred foodplant in Britain, containing an isotope of sulphur, S^{35} (Kettlewell 1952). These were released both in the Botanic Gardens in Oxford and in a colony at Sheepstead Hurst, near Cothill. Final instar larvae and adults from these colonies were sampled, marked individuals being detected by use of a Geiger counter. The conclusion of this work was that the *dominula* form had a strong survival advantage over the other forms.

Conversely, mating choice experiments showed that the forms mate disassortatively (Sheppard 1952); individuals prefer to choose mating partners of any genotype other than their own. Such a mate preference system produces selection that is inherently negatively frequency dependent, conferring an advantage on rarer genotypes (Table 3.2). In the Cothill colony, this selection is strong enough to maintain the *medionigra* and *bimacula* forms, despite their innate survival disadvantage.

Table 3.2 Disassortative mating in the Scarlet Tiger moth, *Callimorpha dominula*, favours the rarer forms.

Imagine that two alleles were present at equal frequencies and were in Hardy–Weinberg equilibrium. The frequencies of the three forms would then be as follows :

dominula	*medionigra*	*bimacula*
0.25	0.5	0.25

If moths prefer to mate with genotypes other than their own, the two alleles would have equal reproductive fitness, because each of the homozygote forms (*dominula* and *bimacula*) would be preferred by the same proportion of the population (75%). The heterozygote, *medionigra*, although favoured as a mating partner by only 50% of the population would have no effect as it carries both alleles.

If on the other hand, the *medionigra* allele were much rarer (say 0.04), as in the wild, the frequencies of the forms might be:

0.9594	0.0319	0.0016

With disassortative mating preferences, it is now obvious that the rare allele gains an advantage because it is rare. The *bimacula* form is a preferred mate of over 99% of the population, and the *medionigra* form is preferred by over 96% of the population. Conversely, less than 5% of the population actively prefers to mate with the *dominula* form.

Further support for the balancing selection explanation came from Sheppard's work using artificial and manipulated colonies of the Scarlet Tiger moth. In one colony he raised the frequency of the rarer allele, *medionigra*, to an abnormally high level. In the other, he introduced this allele at a very low level. His rationale was that if the polymorphism was maintained by selection, the frequencies of the *medionigra* allele in these two colonies would converge.

In 1951, at Hinksey, near Oxford, Sheppard set up an artificial colony of the Scarlet Tiger moth in a habitat that appeared suitable for the moth, but from which the moth had not previously been reported. The colony was founded by releasing 4,000 eggs from crosses between the *dominula* homozygote and the *medionigra* heterozygote. The initial frequency of the *medionigra* allele in this population was thus 0.25. In 1952, 30 larvae were collected. These produced 21 *dominula* and nine *medionigra* adults, giving a frequency for the *medionigra* allele of 0.15. By 1960, the colony was well established, with adults flying in good numbers in both 1960 and 1961. The frequency of the *medionigra* allele, based on substantial adult samples, had declined further from the initial release level to 0.0625 in 1960 and 0.0731 in 1961 (Table 3.3) (see Ford 1964 for review).

Table 3.3 The phenotypic frequencies, and the frequency of the *medionigra* allele from Shepherd's artificial colony of the Scarlet Tiger moth, *Panaxia dominula*, at Hinksey. (Adapted from Jones 1989.)

Year	dominula	medionigra	bimacula	%m allele
1951	2000 eggs	2000 eggs	–	25.00
1952	21 larvae	9 larvae		15.00
1960	269	32	3	6.25
1961	217	35	1	7.31

In 1954, Sheppard introduced the *medionigra* allele into an established natural colony of the Scarlet Tiger moth at Sheepstead Hurst, over a mile from the Cothill colony. Here the *medionigra* and *bimacula* forms do not occur, except presumably as rare mutants (of 11,102 individuals caught between 1949 and 1954, all were of the *dominula* form). To introduce the *medionigra* allele into this colony, Sheppard scattered eggs from 50 crosses between *dominula* males and *medionigra* females in suitable situations. The following year, two of a sample of 875 moths were of the *medionigra* form. Samples of adults caught at this colony on a number of occasions over the next 15 years (Table 3.4) show that the frequency of the *medionigra* allele increased to around 0.02.

Table 3.4 The phenotypic frequencies, and the frequency of the *medionigra* allele from Shepherd's artificial colony of the Scarlet Tiger moth, *Callimorpha dominula*, at Sheepstead Hurst. (Adapted from Jones 1989.)

Year	dominula	medionigra	bimacula	%m allele
1949–1953	all	–	–	0
1954	introduction of *medionigra* allele			
1955	873	2	0	0.11
1960	398	9	0	1.11
1961	405	9	0	1.09
1964	739	13	0	0.86
1969	509	25	0	2.34

In both of these colonies the frequency of the *medionigra* gene has moved towards the level at which it is maintained in the Cothill colony, the convergence in the Hinksey colony being from a frequency in excess of the Cothill equilibrium frequency and, in the Sheepstead Hurst colony, from a frequency below equilibrium.

Fisher and Ford's 1947 paper on the Scarlet Tiger moth reported only the first of a series of studies relating to the selection-drift argument. Other studies, including many on Lepidoptera, have confirmed the most important of

Fig. 3.4 Unbanded (left) and banded (right) forms of the Riband Wave, *Idaea aversata.*

their findings: that except in very small populations, selection, not random genetic drift, is responsible for the maintenance of conspicuous polymorphisms. A wide variety of different selective mechanisms have been shown to be involved in different cases and it is perhaps pertinent to review these briefly here.

Selective systems that will maintain balanced polymorphism

Many of the moths that occur in Britain are polymorphic for their colour patterns. In many species obvious melanic forms occur. In others, the ground colour is variable or a specific element of patterning is either present or absent. For example, the Riband Wave, *Idaea aversata*, is most commonly rather uniform in colour across both forewings and hindwings apart from a pair of thin cross lines. Alternatively, a dark band may traverse the wings between the cross lines (Fig. 3.4). Colour polymorphism is also common in larvae (for example, Plate 15b, 15c and 15d). Very little, or in many cases, no scientific attention has been paid to most of these polymorphisms other than describing the forms and rather intermittent recording of their frequencies. The reasons for the evolution of more than one form within a population are of great evolutionary interest because their coexistence seems contrary to the central tenet of Darwinian evolution: 'the survival of the fittest' (p. 59). Here is an area in which lepidopterists may make a significant contribution to knowledge simply by recording the frequencies of the forms of species that they encounter with a little care and publishing their findings when they have accumulated a reasonable data set (Majerus 1990). They can of course go further and breed from the different forms to work out how they are inherited. Further still, they may consider the reasons for the maintenance of forms at specific frequencies or any changes in frequency recorded. To do the latter, some knowledge of the types of mechanism that may be involved in the maintenance of genetic polymorphisms may be helpful.

Heterozygote advantage

Of the wide variety of mechanisms that will lead to the maintenance of a genetic polymorphism, the most obvious occurs when carriers of two different alleles of a gene (heterozygotes) are fitter than those that carry two copies of the same allele (homozygotes). This situation is known as heterozygous advantage. The frequency of the alleles and the different genotypes depends on the relative fitnesses of the homozygotes and the heterozygote.

Examples of demonstrated heterozygote advantage are few, partly because it is a difficult phenomenon to detect. However, some cases are known. For example, in the Mottled Beauty, *Alcis repandata*, the frequency of heterozygotes between the normal and the *conversaria* alleles is greater than expected on the basis of the Hardy–Weinberg equilibrium. Indeed, by breeding this species in harsh conditions, Ford was able to increase the advantage of the heterozygote over both homozygotes. In the larvae of the Angleshades, *Phlogophora meticulosa*, there is evidence that one of the five genes that control the colours of later instar larvae is maintained, at least in part, through heterozygote advantage.

Although relatively few polymorphisms maintained by heterozygous advantage have been identified, even since the advent of molecular techniques for distinguishing between heterozygote genotypes and dominant homozygotes, heterozygous advantage has been given considerable prominence in the literature on polymorphism. This is because heterozygote advantage is the expected outcome of Fisher's (1928) theory of the evolution of genetic dominance. Fisher's theory depends on three points. First, it was known, from observation of those genes that were first examined in detail, that major genes have multiple effects on the phenotype. Second, Fisher realised that a particular allele is only dominant to another with respect to one, or a number, of particular phenotypic effects, while for other characteristics the dominance may be incomplete or reversed. Third, observation showed that a character controlled by a particular allele exhibited slight variations in expression due to the action of modifier genes.

Fisher then reasoned that selection would tend to promote the favourable effects of an allele and suppress the deleterious effects, by acting on the modifier genes. Advantageous traits of either allele would be expressed in the heterozygote, while deleterious effects would be suppressed. The heterozygote would thus express only selectively advantageous characteristics and so would be superior to the homozygotes, which would express all the traits controlled by an allele, irrespective of whether they were good or bad.

Environmental heterogeneity

Natural environments are complex mosaics of different habitats containing many varying niches. They are thus said to be heterogeneous and this environmental heterogeneity may lead to the maintenance of polymorphism. On a large geographic scale we may think of polymorphisms in moths showing industrial melanism between industrial and non-industrial regions. Here melanics are favoured in polluted habitats and non-melanics in unpolluted ones. Migration between the two types of habitat may prevent either form becoming fixed in any particular population (see Chapter 9). However, environmental heterogeneity may promote polymorphism on a smaller scale.

With respect to a particular organism, an environment may be classed as either coarse-grained if an individual organism spends most of its life in one niche, or fine-grained if it moves from one niche to another and covers all the different niches randomly through its lifetime. The environments of most moths may be considered coarse-grained because females usually lay their eggs in carefully chosen situations, which determine to a large extent the niche in which the early stages will develop. In both fine- and coarse-grained environments polymorphism will be maintained if over all the niches the average fitness of the heterozygote is higher than that of either homozygote. Effectively this is just an extended case of heterozygote advantage. However, if there is competition in a coarse-grained environment, then rarer morphs may gain an advantage if the niches in which they do best are less crowded, leading to a negative frequency dependant aspect in the overall selection. This mechanism is only powerful enough to produce polymorphism in a limited range of cases if individuals of the various phenotypes, or morphs, are randomly distributed across the niches within an environment at the start of a new generation. But in most species this will not be the case. Most species will show some degree of morph-specific habitat selection. If different forms are suited to particular niches, the frequencies of the forms will then become determined by the relative proportions of the different niches as well as the differences in the fitnesses of the forms in each niche. Known examples in the Lepidoptera include the habitat selection shown by a variety of species of cryptic moths with melanic forms (p. 239) and the resting-site selection in the Pine Beauty, *Panolis flammea*. In the latter, three forms, controlled by a single gene, the alleles of which control the amount of grey scaling on the wings, preferentially rest on different parts of pine trees (Majerus 1982).

Apostatic selection

The term apostatic selection was first used by Bryan Clarke (1962) to describe a situation in which predators take a disproportionately high number of the commoner form of a prey species compared with the number of the rarer form taken. The rarer form thereby gains an advantage because of its rarity, and, indeed, becomes increasingly fit if its frequency declines. The fitness of a form is here obviously inversely correlated with its frequency.

Evidence that this type of selection may maintain polymorphism was first obtained by John Allen in a long series of experiments using pseudo-caterpillars of different colours offered to birds at different ratios (for example, Allen & Clarke 1968). The pseudo-caterpillars were made of a flour and lard dough coloured with food dyes. Allen was able to show that when green and brown dyed 'caterpillars' were placed out at low density in ratios of nine green: one brown or the reverse, over time the rarer form invariably suffered lower predation than expected from its degree of camouflage. Although the situation was somewhat artificial, these elegant experiments established the potential for polymorphism to be maintained if predators did indeed form searching images for common types of prey. Later, during my own studies of the causes and consequences of larval colour polymorphism in the Angleshades moth (Plate 15a and 15b), I was able to adapt Allen's basic experimental design, substituting real caterpillars for his pastry baits. The substitution made no difference to the patterns of predation shown by a variety of wild birds, and I was able to demonstrate that apostatic selection plays a crucial part in the maintenance of the complex of colour pattern larval variants in this species (p. 192). I have no doubt that apostatic selection is also important in maintaining green, brown and other larval colour forms in many other species, such as the Elephant Hawk moth, *Deilephila elpenor* (Plate 10e and 10f).

Non-random mating

Mating is rarely random. The majority of systems in which mating is non-random produce negative frequency dependent selection. We have already seen an example of this in the case of disassortative mating in the Scarlet Tiger moth (p. 70). However, other types of mating preference will also favour forms when they are rare. The reason is easy to appreciate. Assume that a constant proportion of females prefer to mate with males of a particular form. When the preferred type of males is rare males of this type gain a greater advantage than when they are common because the preferring females are shared out between fewer males of the preferred form. The rarer the preferred males become, the greater the advantage that accrues to them as a result of the choosy females.

Coevolution between species

Finally, polymorphism may be produced by a variety of coevolutionary systems. Two examples will suffice to illustrate the diversity of this process. Predators and prey and hosts and parasites are involved in evolutionary arms races, each member of an interaction vying to gain the upper hand. If one imagines a relationship between a parasitoid wasp and its moth host, it is easy to think of a variety of ways in which either participant can improve its chances of survival. The wasp can increase its ability to find hosts, improve its discrimination between low and high quality hosts, fine-tune the number of eggs it lays in a host to the quality of that particular host and improve its ability to overcome the host's immune system. The host may conceal itself, may evolve defensive strategies such as dropping off the foodplant when attacked by a wasp, or develop a variety of chemical immunity systems.

Taking immunity as an example, if we imagine that some individuals in a host population have one type of immunity, while a much smaller number have a second mechanism, it seems rational to assume that selection will favour wasps that can overcome the common type of immune response of the host. Moths with the rarer type of immunity will thus gain an advantage because it will be more profitable for wasps to be adapted to the common host type. Consequently, the rare form will be less adversely affected if attacked by parasites and will gradually increase in frequency until, due to its increased abundance, it becomes a profitable target for the wasp's counter-defence. The selective roles of the two types of host thus change and the whole system cycles, first one type of immunity and then the other being beneficial.

As a second example, we can consider Batesian mimicry, a common phenomenon among the Lepidoptera worldwide, although examples in Britain are few. Batesian mimics are fakes. They are palatable species that have warning coloration to resemble other species that are unpalatable. Batesian mimicry may lead to polymorphism again because it involves negative frequency dependent selection. As the degree of protection afforded a Batesian mimic will be dependent on predators having learnt that its model (the unpalatable species that it resembles) is inedible, the fitness of the mimic will depend on its frequency relative to that of the model. As the mimic becomes commoner relative to its model, its fitness will decline because there is an increased chance that a naïve predator will come across a palatable mimic before it has encountered a model. This negative frequency dependent selection leads to an equilibrium between the mimetic form and the non-mimetic form or between forms that mimic different models.

The evolution of Batesian mimicry is a fascinating subject in itself and I will discuss the evolution of both monomorphic and polymorphic Batesian mimicry in Chapter 8.

Transient polymorphism

In contrast to balanced polymorphism, we can consider the second type of conspicuous polymorphism defined by Ford: transient polymorphism. Transient polymorphisms are generally rare because, at any moment in time, most of the advantageous alleles within a genome will already have been selected to fixation. Only rarely will new advantageous mutations occur in stable environments. However, in changing environments the potential for mutations to be selectively beneficial increases. Thus most of the well-documented cases of transient polymorphisms have occurred in changing environments in which human activity has been the main cause of the change (for example, industrial melanism in moths, pesticide resistance, antibiotic resistance). Two fates are possible for a new advantageous mutation. First, the mutation can spread to fixation, reducing the original allele to the status of a recurrent deleterious mutation. Second, the initial advantage of the new mutation can be lost as its frequency increases, leading to a balanced polymorphism maintained through negative frequency dependent selection, a selection/migration balance, or heterozygote advantage.

Let us consider the pattern of spread of a new advantageous allele that has arisen by mutation in a previously invariable gene. We would expect such an allele to increase in frequency in the population as a result of its selective advantage. If the new allele, or at least those individuals that express it, maintains its advantage as it increases in frequency, it will eventually spread through the whole population and become fixed (i.e. reach a frequency of 100%). The rate of spread would be dependent mainly on the relative fitnesses of the three genotypes and the genetic dominance of the advantageous mutation. Dominant advantageous mutations increase in frequency rapidly when at low frequency, but only slowly once they have attained a high allelic frequency. Conversely, the rate of increase of an advantageous recessive allele is initially slow, but once it becomes common, the final spread to fixation is rapid. This slow initial increase occurs because only a small proportion of recessive alleles are present in the homozygous state when the recessive allele is at low frequency: most are present in the heterozygote state where they are not expressed and so are not exposed to selection.

It is this behaviour of genes, and particularly the fact that recessive alleles can 'hide' in heterozygotes, that explains why there is so much hidden genetic variation contained in most populations of most sexually reproducing species. This hidden variation is important in evolution, for it provides a repository of genetic variation that may come into play when conditions change.

Continuous variation

So far, I have discussed the evolution of different traits that are controlled by the alleles of one or a small number of genes. However, Darwin saw evolution as a slow process in which organisms in populations change gradually over long periods of time. Much of the variation in the traits that selection acts upon is continuous and so does not constitute polymorphism. So, for example, variation in moth wing length, antennal length, the number of facets in a compound eye, the number of scales that make up a wing-marking character, the number of days that larvae take to feed up, the duration of copulation, all show continuous variation. Such variation may be a consequence of genetic factors in the form of polygenic systems, or of a large range of environmental factors, or a combination of the two. Saying that a trait is controlled by a polygenic system simply means that it is affected by alleles of many genes, each having a small positive or negative effect. The problem with traits that show continuous variation is that it is difficult to know how much of the variation should be attributed to genetic factors and how much is just environmental flux.

Heritability

Both polygenic systems and environmental influences usually produce continuous variation in the trait that they affect. As variation produced purely in response to environmental conditions experienced by an organism during its life cannot be inherited, this cannot be passed down the evolutionary line. It is thus helpful to know what proportion of the variation in a trait that exhibits continuous variation is due to genetic rather than environmental factors. The techniques used to analyse so-called Mendelian traits cannot be used because segregation of individual genes cannot be recognised in the phenotypes. Therefore, other methods of analysis have to be used.

The proportion of the variation in a particular character that is due to genetic differences rather than environmental differences is called the heritability of the trait. More precisely, heritability is defined as the fraction of the total variation of a trait, in a given sample or population, that is due to genetic rather than environmental factors.

Different methods have been developed to measure heritability in different types of organism. In moths, the most applicable is the mass selection method, a technique that was first developed for increasing yields in domesticated animals and crop plants.

The procedure is simply to breed the next generation from those individuals that are best with respect to the trait being improved. If phenotypic variation is due in part to genetic differences among individuals, mass selection will change the genetic characteristics of the stock.

Assume that the trait under consideration is normally distributed (has a bell-shaped frequency distribution), as is often true for quantitative traits such as wing length. We need then be concerned with just two measures, shown in Figure 3.5. First, the selection differential, which is the difference between the average of the selected parents and the average of the population as a whole (or a randomly chosen sample from the population). Second, the selection response, which is the difference between the average of the progeny of the selected parents and the average of the parental generation.

If the variation is all due to environmental causes, the distribution of the selected parents' offspring will be the same as that of the parental population. On the other hand, if the phenotypic variation is all genetic, the mean of the offspring will be the same as that of the selected parents. The most common situation is that the variation is partly genetic and partly environmental. In such cases there will be a selective response, but the mean of the offspring will not be as high (or low) as that of the selected parents. Heritability will then be

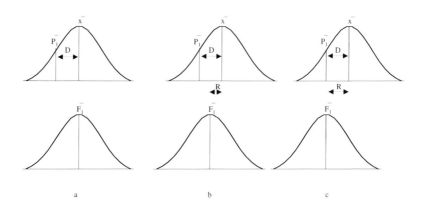

Fig. 3.5 The selection differential, D, and selection response, R, are the crucial parameters in estimating heritability using the mass selection method. X gives the mean for the population as a whole. P_1 and F_1 are the means for the trait in the parental and first filial generations respectively. (Courtesy of Tamsin Majerus.)

estimated by the ratio between the selection response and the selection differential. If we let R represent the selective response and D represent the selective differential, we simply have:

the heritability, $h^2 = R/D$.

In the Angleshades moth, heritability studies using this method on a Surrey population in 1977 gave an estimate of 0.46 for the heritability of the length of the front margin of the forewing.

It is important to recognise that the heritability of a trait is not fixed. The heritability will change if the genetic variation in a trait changes, as, for example, when alleles are gained by mutation or lost by selection or random genetic drift. Thus in quoting estimates of the heritability of a trait, it is essential to specify the source of the material and the period when the heritability was estimated.

Selection acting on polygenic systems

Stabilising selection

The variation in characteristics that vary continuously usually has a normal distribution, with most individuals being close to the average for the trait and the extremes tailing off on either side of the mean (see Fig. 3.6). It is easy to envisage selection acting on variation with this type of distribution in three ways. First, and in fact most usually, selection may favour the mean and act against the extremes. If the mean value of a trait is in fact the optimum in terms of fitness, and individuals showing either greater or lesser development of the trait are progressively less fit, selection is said to be stabilising.

Stabilising selection acts on the majority of polygenic traits in most species. Most of the size features of moths, the precise tone of colours, the number of eggs produced by females (although not the number of eggs actually laid), and many behavioural characteristics are under stabilising selection. This is what we should expect, because past selection should have acted to engineer the

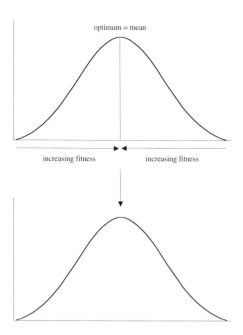

Fig. 3.6 A normal distribution is typical of continually varying traits. Under stabilising selection, individuals with values of the trait close to the mean are most fit. Individuals towards the extremes of the distribution are eliminated. (Courtesy of Tamsin Majerus.)

mean of a trait to the optimum value for that trait.

Directional selection

It is possible that changes in some aspect of the biotic or physical environment of a population change the optimum value for a trait away from the mean towards one of the extremes (Fig. 3.7). For example, a population may be in a situation exposed to high winds, favouring individuals with smaller wings than elsewhere. Individuals from the favoured end of the distribution, that is to say with smaller wings, will be at an advantage and so will make a greater contribution to the next generation, with the result that genes producing a reduction in wing area will increase in frequency. The distribution of the variation in the trait will thus change, becoming skewed to the smaller end. While this change is taking place, selection is said to be directional. Eventually, the mean value for the trait will converge on the new optimum value for the particular population. Once this happens, selection becomes stabilising again.

Probable examples of directional selection in moths include the reduction in the past of wing sizes in populations of species that fly on windswept cliff tops or alpine heaths, compared with populations in more sheltered situations. Analysis of the genetics of the reduction or loss of wings in females of some winter Lepidoptera, by hybridisation with related species that have winged females, suggests that directional selection acting on polygenic systems has been responsible for the loss of flight. More recently, many species of cryptic Lepidoptera have shown a gradual and general darkening of their ground colours in environments affected by soot pollution from industry (see p. 241).

Fig. 3.7 Under directional selection, individuals
towards one end of the
distribution are
favoured. If the trait has
high heritability, the distribution shifts in this
direction in subsequent
generations until the
mean and the optimum
coincide and the trait
comes under stabilising
selection. (Courtesy of
Tamsin Majerus.)

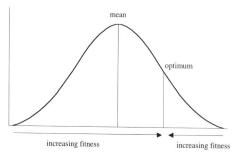

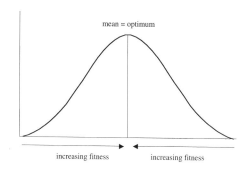

Disruptive selection

The third way in which selection may act on a polygenic system is undoubtedly the rarest. It involves the situation in which a species has two or more optimal phenotypic values for a trait, at least one higher and one lower than the
mean (Fig. 3.8). In the simplest case we may imagine that both very long wings
or no wings are selectively favoured, while individuals with medium length
wings are comparatively unfit. Here selection is said to be disruptive. The
expected outcome of disruptive selection would be the evolution of some
mechanism that reduced the production of the unfit intermediate phenotypes.
It is possible that this could be achieved by the development of assortative mating preferences, so that the two favoured types rarely mated with each other.
Such assortative mating preferences may lead to speciation if they become
complete. Alternatively, the genes that produce a favoured phenotype may
become tightly linked into a supergene, as has been proposed for the various
genes controlling elements involved in the polymorphic Batesian mimicry of
some swallowtail butterflies (p. 209). The two forms of females of the Water
Veneer, *Acentria ephemerella*, one fully winged and the other apterous, represent
one of the rare cases of this type (p. 116).

Although the expected outcomes of disruptive selection, either speciation or
the evolution and maintenance of balanced polymorphisms, occur only rarely
on an ecological timescale, disruptive selection does play an important part in
one type of variation in almost all species of moth. This is the variation
between males and females of a species. Because males and females often play
rather different roles in reproduction, largely as a result of the different contributions that eggs and sperm make to the offspring, the two sexes are

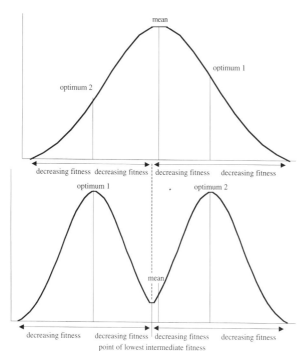

Fig. 3.8 Under disruptive selection individuals with trait values either side of the mean are favoured. Disruptive selection may lead to speciation or to the evolution of stable polymorphism. (Courtesy of Tamsin Majerus.)

exposed to different selective pressures. These different selective pressures may reinforce the fundamental difference between males and females, which by definition is the size of sex cell produced (p. 92), and may lead to differences in morphology, physiology and behaviour of the sexes. In some cases, such as the Muslin moth, *Diaphora mendica*, differences between the sexes extend to time of flight during the day or night and many other aspects of behaviour and coloration (Fig. 3.9)

Fig. 3.9 Sexual dimorphism in the Muslin moth, *Diaphora mendica* (left – male, right – female).

The role of heritable variation in evolution

An organism is the sum of all its expressed genes, which depends on the genes present, their interactions with one another and their interaction with the environment. The ultimate source of all heritable variation is mutation. However, the variation between individuals within sexual species is also the product of recombination, both through the random assortment of genes on individual chromosomal pairs and as a result of chiasmata formation and crossing over between members of a chromosome pair during meiosis, the specialised cell division that leads to the production of sperm and eggs. In effect, mutation acts to modify the basic components of the genome, while sex is a mechanism that allows genetic shuffling. It may be argued that mutation is the more fundamental source of variation. However, the question still arises, which is the more important process in terms of evolution? Upon which of these types of variation does selection act? Do adaptations evolve as a result of selection acting upon novel mutations that by chance arise concurrently with environmental change? Or conversely, does selection act primarily upon varieties that are generated each generation through the random assortment of genes and recombination during sexual reproduction?

The case of industrial melanism in the Peppered moth provides one of the best-known examples where a mutation produced a novel, advantageous phenotype (Fig. 3.10), which then increased in frequency through the action of natural selection. However, most other adaptations appear to have evolved as a result of selection acting upon variants created by the reassortment of pre-existing genes. Again, examples can be drawn from the evolution of melanism in moths. For instance, the darkest melanic varieties of the Common Marbled Carpet, *Dysstroma truncata*, are produced by a set of three complementary genes with additive effects. Evidence from the examination of old Lepidoptera collections suggests that the dark alleles of these genes all existed prior to widespread industrialisation. However, only over the last 150 years has pollution in industrial areas increased the fitness of those individuals carrying dark alleles for all three genes. It is these dark forms that now predominate in most industrial areas, with the less melanic forms being present in rural areas of southern Britain. Predominantly non-melanic populations are now confined to the Highlands and Islands of Scotland.

Fig. 3.10 The typical (left) and *carbonaria* (right) forms of the Peppered moth, *Biston betularia.*

The effect of changes in population size

To my mind, the best demonstration of the wealth of variation that exists in most natural populations of moths occurred in 1976. Before describing the observations of the summer of that year, the relationships between selection, variation and population size need to be explained. If most selection acting on a population is stabilising selection, then it is imaginable that while population size remains stable, selection will be constant. Put another way, in a population of stable size, selection each year will eliminate a constant proportion of individuals at either end of the distribution of variability (Fig. 3.11a). If the population begins to increase in size, it implies that selection has been relaxed. It therefore follows that the cutoff lines indicating which individuals survive and which die are moved away from the mean and optimum (Fig. 3.11b). More genetic variants thus survive and the extent of variation in the population increases. The reverse is also true. If a population begins to decline in size, it implies that selection has become harsher, moving the cutoff lines closer to the mean and optimum (Fig. 3.11c). Genetic variation is thus expected to decline while population size is declining. It is important to realise that it is only while population size is changing that the relaxation or increased stringency of selection will lead to a change in the amount of genetic variation. Once population size has stabilised, even if at a new level, the selection cutoff lines will return to their original positions and the level of genetic variation will stabilise again.

The summers of 1975 and 1976 were long and hot, and the winter between these summers was mild. Conditions for moths and many other insects were abnormally favourable. The result was a considerable increase in the populations of these insects. Perhaps most notable for those that remember the summer of 1976 were the 'plagues' of ladybirds that swamped many coastal resorts in July and August. However, my attention at the time was on moths. In July I

Fig. 3.11 The theoretical effect of changes in population density on genetic variation. a) Showing the situation when population size is stable. The vertical lines represent selection lines. b) While population size is increasing, selection is relaxed, i.e. the selection lines move out from the mean. More extreme forms then survive and the spread of variation increases. c) While population size is decreasing, selection is intensified, i.e. the selection lines are drawn closer to the mean. Only individuals close to the mean (and optimum) survive, and the amount of genetic variation is reduced. (Courtesy of Tamsin Majerus.)

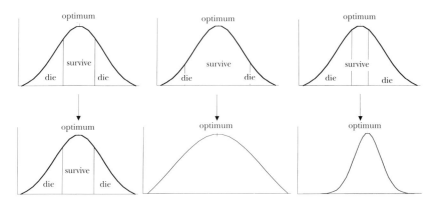

Fig. 3.12 A Robinson mercury vapour moth trap.

spent five nights running a Robinson moth trap (Fig. 3.12) in my mother's garden on the edge of the New Forest. The nights were hot and humid and perhaps the best conditions that I have experienced for light trapping in Britain. Three times each night the trap was hurriedly emptied into a lighted shed that had been stripped of furniture for the purpose. The daylight hours were spent sorting, scoring and releasing the catch in the shed. The minimum catch on any one of those five nights was 30,000 moths. The pertinence of the case is not the wealth of moths; it is the number of abnormal varieties that were obtained that week. Taking account of the numbers of individuals of different species caught compared with other years, I calculated that unusual forms were between 2.3 times and 16.5 times as common (depending on species) in that year as on average over the period between 1977 and 1989, when the house was sold and I could no longer trap there.

Types of selection

In this chapter we have already seen that selection may be of various types. In the main I have discussed natural selection: the struggle for survival. However, I have also mentioned sexual selection: the struggle to find and secure a mate, preferably of high quality, and to reproduce. This type of selection will be discussed in more detail in Chapter 4. Other types of selection, artificial selection, kin selection and species selection are also recognised.

Artificial selection

Artificial selection need detain us a moment only. It involves human attempts to exaggerate specific traits of a species by breeding from those individuals that show the required traits most strongly. Most artificial selection involves domesticated animals or crop plants. In respect of moths, I can only think of three types of situation in which it has been used to any appreciable extent. First, silk moths, particularly the Silk Worm, *Bombyx mori*, have long been subject to selection to produce silk with specific characteristics of strength, texture and colour. Second, some attempts have been made to selectively breed deleterious traits into pest species, such as the army worms. In particular, scientists are currently investigating the use of inherited bacterial pathogens of insects in integrated pest management schemes involving moths (see p. 261). Third, some moth enthusiasts use artificial selection to breed unusual forms of species. I have used this technique to look at the amount of underlying variation in the degree of black speckling in the Peppered moth. Others have used artificial selection to produce series of spectacular specimens of a wide range of species. Many of the products of such breeding programmes are now retained in museums and other collections. For example, the collections at The Natural History Museum in London house some extraordinary series of Garden Tiger moth, *Arctia caja*, with forewings either virtually all brown or all cream, and the hindwings all red or all blue.

Kin selection

In discussing selection, the tone is usually rather selfish. Organisms struggle to survive and reproduce for their own selfish interests and often at the expense of others. However, there are many cases in which organisms appear to act not selfishly, but for the good of a group of individuals, a population or the species as a whole. Here, individuals appear to act altruistically. Rather than trying to outcompete others in their population, they act cooperatively, aiding others, sometimes apparently to their own detriment. It is generally recognised that biological evolution involves the passage of heritable material – the genes – down the generations through reproduction. We must then ask, how can genes for cooperative behaviours evolve? What mechanism can lead to an individual increasing the reproductive success of another individual at the expense of its own reproductive success?

At one time there was a common view that many traits, particularly behavioural traits, had evolved simply 'for the good of the species'. However, since the 1960s, the view that selection acts through the phenotype to promote the passage of genes, has held sway. The concept of the 'selfish gene' is now well known (Dawkins 1976). This has brought the evolution of apparently altruistic behaviours into sharp focus.

Detailed investigations of apparently altruistic acts have shown that in many cases, even if a behaviour seems to benefit others, it also increases the reproductive success of the acting individual. This then is not true altruism, for the definition of altruism is behaviour that increases the lifetime reproductive success of another at a cost to one's own lifetime reproductive success. Such cases therefore need no special explanation. Such behaviours will evolve through the normal processes of natural and sexual selection. However, there are behaviours of true altruism observed in the natural world.

An easy example to understand is that involving the many social insects that forgo their own reproduction to aid that of their queen. Here, the evolutionary rationale leading to the altruistic behaviour can be appreciated if the relationship of the helpers to their queen and to their nest mates is considered. In a bumblebees' nest, for example, the workers are all daughters of the same queen. The queen and all the female bees have two sets of chromosomes. The male that the queen mated with had just one set of chromosomes (i.e. he was haploid), this set being passed to all his daughters (but not to sons produced by his mate, which result from unfertilised eggs). The daughters of a queen thus share three-quarters of their genes for they all get half their genes from their father (which are all the same), and half their genes from their mother, of which half are the same and half different. In terms of genetic relatedness, these sisters are thus more closely related to each other than they would be to their own daughters to whom they would only contribute half their genes. Thus, worker bumblebees increase the passage of copies of the genes they contain by helping the queen to produce more sisters rather than reproducing themselves.

The important point here is the degree of genetic relatedness. In almost all moths, full siblings share approximately half their genes by direct descent. Exceptions occur in the few species in which females regularly reproduce parthenogenetically, i.e. without the eggs being fertilised by a male, and in occasional instances of parthenogenetic reproduction in species, such as the Silk Worm, that normally reproduce sexually. Kin selection in most species is most evident in the behaviour of parents, particularly the female parent, towards offspring. However, kin selection may also have been important in the evolution of some fundamental life history traits, such as adult longevity (p. 205) and some common phenomena, such as chemical defence and associated bright and conspicuous colour patterns (p. 199).

Species selection

Species selection is perhaps the most difficult type of selection to explain. It involves the loss of a complete species as a result of the evolution of heritable systems, that while advantageous in the short term, ultimately lead the species into an evolutionary cul-de-sac. In short, the idea is that different species that follow different evolutionary paths will, in so doing, by chance make themselves more or less liable to extinction.

Two quite different types of example may help to explain the type of situation that could lead to species selection. In the first, we may consider two closely related moth species. Ancestrally, both fed on a wide range of plant species. However, one of the species gradually evolves a digestive system that enables that species to utilise the leaves of the commonest plant species more efficiently. Over time, it evolves to specialise on that one food, thereby out competing the other species where the favoured plant occurs. The other species retains its more catholic diet, but is excluded from use of the food of its related species because of that species' greater efficiency. In the short term, the specialist gains an advantage. However, should the preferred foodplant of the specialist be eradicated by some environmental change, such as climate warming, the specialist will be in extreme jeopardy because of its specialisation. A similar scenario might involve a species that gave up a camouflage colour pattern to gain protection by mimicking some inedible species with bright coloration. Once the palatable species has followed this evolutionary path, it is at risk if the species it mimics becomes extinct, for now it is conspicuous and no longer gains protection by resembling a species that predators will learn to leave alone (see Batesian mimicry, p. 206).

In the second case, we can consider one of the rare species of moth, such as some species of the family Psychidae, that have forgone sexual reproduction.

Secondary asexual reproduction or parthenogenesis has evolved many times in many different types of organism. The reason that it has evolved so often is that it gives females that reproduce this way an initial advantage. The main point is that in diploid species that reproduce without sex, females produce only daughters. These gain an advantage because sex is costly.

To show that sex is costly, consider a moth with a 1:1 sex ratio that provides no parental care outside the normal resourcing of the egg by the mother. Half a female's progeny are female and half are male. But then imagine a female that had a gene mutation that allowed her to modify her reproduction so that she only produced daughters, and did it from cells that were not fertilised by sperm. We will assume that such a female produces daughters that were genetically identical to herself. Effectively she has produced clones. When rare, the mutation that gave the female this capacity would double in frequency in each generation because she is producing twice as many daughters as a female without the mutation and producing both sons and daughters in equal measure. This result has been expressed by saying that there is a 'twofold cost of sex', arising from the needless production of males. The problem arises if the asexual mutation spreads through the whole population. Now, all the females will be more or less the same, having derived from the female that first reproduced without males. The population is thus genetically invariant. Again, should the environment change appreciably, this population would have a much lower likelihood of surviving the change than a sexual species that was able to throw up an array of genetic variants, at least some of which could cope with the new conditions.

Asexual reproduction is very rare in the Lepidoptera. Most species reproduce sexually, with males and females playing specific roles in the generation of offspring. The strategies that are used by different species to produce quality sex cells, to find, attract and recognise mates, to succeed in the fertilisation game and to give offspring a reasonable chance of survival are extraordinarily varied. It is this subject of sexual reproductive strategies of moths that is the main theme of the next chapter.

4

The Sex Lives of Moths

Population demography

Moths vary tremendously in their abundance. Some species are very common, others exceedingly rare. The rarity of a species is dependent upon the size of the geographic range of the species and population density across this range. In some species, the range is continuous, so the species has, in effect, a single population. The majority of species are, however, divided into a series of more or less independent populations. The size of each of these populations may increase or decrease over time.

Birth, death and migration

Four factors affect changes in population size over time: the birth rate, the death rate and levels of both immigration and emigration. Other factors obviously impinge on the population demography of a species. The amount of a variety of limited resources, such as food or space, will have a major influence. So, changes in population size are largely a function of birth, growth, dispersal and death. Having introduced moths and their anatomy in the first two chapters, and the evolutionary processes that shape moths and all other organisms in Chapter 3, I intend to structure the next five chapters around the factors that affect population size. In this chapter, I will briefly discuss the interrelationship between the main factors that affect population demography, before dealing with the first of these factors, birth, and all the various topics, largely sexual in nature, that lead to birth. The ensuing chapters will deal with resources and habitats, dispersal and distributions, death and the avoidance of death.

Perhaps the easiest way to consider theories of population size is to consider what happens when a moth establishes itself in a new location devoid of enemies or of other species that compete with it for resources. We might think of a species arriving on a volcanic island that has already been well colonised by its foodplant, but which few other animals have colonised. On this new island, due to the availability of plentiful food and the lack of competitors or enemies, we may expect that the population size would increase rapidly. This population increase would be driven largely by the number of offspring produced each generation. Plotting increase in population size during this period of the history of the colony would show an almost exponential increase. Eventually, however, as the population becomes rapidly larger, we would expect that the food available would become limiting. The increase in numbers would introduce competition between members of the colony into the equation. This would impose a constraint on the rate of population increase. At some point, the mortality due to the competition for food and space would reach a level such that, of the offspring produced by each pair in a generation, only two would survive to reproduce. The population would then have reached the carrying capacity of its new island and population size would stabilise at a level exactly equal to this carrying capacity.

Mathematically, these ideas can be written as a simple equation:

> Population size (at a given moment in time) = population size at a previous point in time + birth rate - death rate + immigration - emigration (all since that previous point in time).

Changes in population size over a given period of time are thus affected just by the four factors over that period of time.

The intrinsic rate of natural increase and the carrying capacity

In our new colony, we can describe the rate of population size change over time using an equation that incorporates both the intrinsic rate of natural increase, r, which is effectively the birth rate, and the carrying capacity, K.

Thus: $dN/dt = rN\,(1\text{-}K/N),$

Where dN/dt is the change in population size, N, over time, t. This equation is called the logistic equation. The plot of the population size growth that it describes initially increases with ever-increasing speed, but then slows as mortality due to intraspecific competition kicks in. Thus an S-shaped plot is produced. The logistic equation may also be embellished to incorporate interspecific competition for resources or other causes of mortality, such as that due to predators or parasites.

In reality, natural populations rarely behave precisely as theory predicts, for it is rare that a species colonises such an ideal environment with plentiful resources and no enemies. However, parts of the pattern produced by the main components of the logistic equation, r and K, have been observed in British moths. Perhaps the best example in recent times is that of the colonisation of Britain by Blair's Shoulder-knot (*Lithophane leautieri hesperica*) (Plate 16a). This species, first reported in Britain from the Isle of Wight in 1951 (Blair 1952), has spread rapidly northwards. Its larvae (Fig. 4.1) feed on a variety of cypress trees, including Monterey Cypress, *Cupressus macrocarpa*, Lawson's Cypress, *Chamaecyparis lawsoniana*, and the common hybrid hedging conifer *Cupressocyparis* x *leylandii*. A consistent pattern of increasing population size has

Fig. 4.1 Larvae of Blair's Shoulder-knot, *Lithophane leautieri hesperica.*

been seen in many parts of southern and central Britain. In Cambridge, for example, my first moth-trap record of this species is from 1983. The number of males caught increased in each of the next eight years, so that by 1991, it was vying with the Green-brindled Crescent, *Allophyes oxyacanthae*, the Brown-spot Pinion, *Agrochola litura*, the Beaded Chestnut, *Agrochola lychnidis*, and the November moth, *Epirrita dilutata*, as the most common late autumn capture. Since 1991, the numbers caught have stabilised and have remained fairly consistent. Of course, in this case, it is certain that the initial increase in Cambridge was in part due to moths arriving from more southerly counties. However, a large part of the increase was surely the result of a high reproductive output and the utilisation of a food resource that was little used by other herbivores. The subsequent stabilisation in the population density suggests that the carrying capacity around Cambridge has now been reached.

As population size is a consequence of birth rate, death rate and migration, I shall discuss each of these in turn, starting here with birth.

Reproduction in moths

Birth is the outcome of reproduction. In moths, reproduction is almost exclusively sexual. In the very few species that are able to reproduce asexually, for example *Dahlica triquetrella* and the Lichen Case-bearer, *Dahlica lichenella*, this ability has evolved from sexual lineages. The asexuality of these species is thus said to be secondary, and is usually referred to as parthenogenesis (see p. 87).

Sexual reproduction is a complex behaviour. In moths, which confer no parental care on their offspring once the eggs are laid, reproduction begins with the production of sex cells, or gametes, and ends with oviposition. I use oviposition as the end point of the process rather than birth because there is some ambiguity over the definition of birth. In humans, the moment of birth is easily defined and is the same from the perspective of both the mother and the baby. However, in egg layers, it is not clear whether birth occurs when the eggs are laid or when the eggs hatch. Possibly from the mother's perspective, she gives birth when she lays her eggs, while from the perspective of her progeny, they are born when they exit their eggs into the outside world.

Gamete production

If a moth is to reproduce successfully it has to produce gametes, find an appropriate mating partner, which should be of the opposite sex and of the same species, elicit a mating response from the partner, copulate and then, if female, lay eggs. The first part of this process is perhaps the most fundamental and complex.

The production of gametes, sperm in males and eggs in females, involves an unusual type of cell division called meiosis. Normally when cells divide during growth, two copies of their parental cell are produced, each with precisely the same genetic material as each other and the parental cell from which they are derived. The process usually involves the precise duplication of the nuclear chromosomes carrying genetic material in the form of genes and the division of this duplicated material into precisely equal halves. The parental cell will carry two complete sets of chromosomes, thus producing four sets when these are duplicated as a prelude to cell division and being reduced back to two sets as the two daughter cells are formed. This type of cell division is called mitosis. The condition of carrying two sets of chromosomes is known as diploidy.

In meiosis, the diploid parental cell also precisely duplicates the genetic material, but it divides twice, producing not two, but four daughter cells, each with just one set of chromosomes. The products of meiosis are thus haploid rather than diploid. Diploidy is restored when the nuclei of two haploid cells, one sperm and one egg, fuse together at fertilisation.

The process of meiosis is critical in evolution because it shuffles genetic material producing variation that selection can act upon. The ultimate source of new genetic variants is mutation. Mutations occur when mistakes happen in the copying of the basic molecule of inheritance, DNA. It is this amazing molecule that comprises the so-called blueprint of life. The basis of this blueprint is the order in which nucleotide bases, of which there are four, adenine, cytosine, guanine and thymine, occur along a strand of DNA. It is this order of bases that is precisely copied when DNA replicates. However, very occasionally the copying process goes wrong, so the order of bases is changed. If this occurs within a part of the DNA that codes for an important metabolic chemical, the precise constitution of that chemical is likely to be changed to some extent. When such a change occurs during the mitotic division of most growing cells, it may result in some abnormality in the individual in which it occurs, but it will not be passed on to the individual's progeny. It is only if such a mutation occurs in the cell lines that give rise to gametes that the new variant can be inherited and so have the chance of becoming a long-term part of evolution.

Although the ultimate source of all genetic variation is mutation, most new variants arise as a result of the bringing together of different varieties of genes from different individuals through the process of sexual reproduction (p. 87). During sexual reproduction, genes are shuffled in two ways. First and most obviously, genes from two different individuals are brought together at fertilisation. However, there is another source of reshuffling, which occurs within the parents prior to fertilisation when gametes are produced by meiosis. During the first part of the meiotic division, when the chromosomes have replicated, the two strands of each of the two chromosomes of a chromosomal pair lie together. Four strands, or chromatids, thus lie alongside each other. Before these divide they may form what are called crossover points or chiasmata. These are formed when two chromatids break at the same point and then join up again, but in so doing, join to the other chromatid. This process of recombination changes the order of alleles that lie close together on the same chromosome and so have a high likelihood of being inherited together.

In most species, recombination is an integral part of meiosis in all sexually reproducing individuals. However, in a few groups recombination is confined to one sex. Perhaps most well known in this respect are fruit flies of the genus *Drosophila*. Here, recombination is inhibited in males. The same is true of some other true flies (Diptera). Rather less well known is the fact that recombination seems to be suppressed in one sex in the Lepidoptera, but here it is the females in which it does not occur (Robinson 1971). How or why recombination is confined to males in the Lepidoptera is not currently known.

Gamete production varies to some extent between the two sexes. Although both eggs and sperm result from meiosis, whereas meiosis leads to four sperm in males, only one of the haploid products of meiosis in females will be the female gamete. The other three products give rise to the yolk of the egg. The second difference involves the number and size of gametes produced. Sperm are very small, effectively comprising just a cell nucleus containing the chromosomes, a tail for locomotion, and a few specialised organelles, called mitochondria, which act like batteries and power the locomotory movements of the tail. The female gamete is much, much larger. The nucleus again contains the chromosomes. However, this nucleus makes up only a small proportion of the total volume of the egg cell, the rest of the cell being the cytoplasm, which contains a rich cocktail of organic molecules and various organelles including numerous mitochondria. Thus, whereas males can produce vast numbers of their minute and energy-cheap sperm, females produce very many times fewer of their large, energy-rich eggs.

Intriguingly, male moths of most species make two types of sperm: eupyrene sperm, which may be considered normal in that the sperm has a nucleus, and apyrene sperm, which lack a nucleus. Apyrene sperm cannot fertilise eggs, and their function is unclear, although it has been speculated that they are involved in sperm competition. This production of two types of sperm occurs in most Lepidoptera, and appears to be specific to the moths and butterflies.

Sex determination

It is in fact the difference in the size of the gametes produced by the two sexes that is the only definer of which sex is male and which is female. Females produce large, usually sessile gametes; males produce small mobile ones.

Sex chromosomes

The definer of the sexes is not the same as the mechanism that determines sex. In the majority of sexually reproducing organisms the difference between development into a male or into a female is determined by a single, somewhat unusual pair of chromosomes, called the sex chromosomes. While most chromosomes occur in pairs that are largely the same throughout their length (autosomes), the members of a pair of sex chromosomes are very different, one being much larger than the other. The two are similar along a short portion of their length (called the pseudoautosomal region), but both the longer and the shorter sex chromosome contain some portion that is not matched by the other sex chromosome. In most animals, including humans, females have two copies of the larger of the two sex chromosomes (termed the X chromosome). Males have just one X, but they also have one of the shorter type (called the Y chromosome). Females produce gametes of only one type, carrying an X chromosome, and are thus known as the homogametic sex. Males are the heterogametic sex because they produce gametes of two different types, carrying either an X or a Y chromosome.

In most Lepidoptera the situation is rather different, for males have two sex chromosomes of the same type while females have one of each type. To distinguish this pattern from the more usual XX/XY system, the chromosome that is present in both sexes is called Z and that present in only one sex is called W. Thus, in moths, males are homogametic (ZZ) and females are heterogametic (ZW).

Species with ZZ/ZW sex determination are often mentioned in textbooks almost as an afterthought: a simple note that in some groups; birds, almost all moths and butterflies and a few reptiles, fish and groups of invertebrates, the sex chromosomes are switched around. However, although most work on sex determination has been conducted on XX/XY systems, that on ZZ/ZW systems, particularly in the moths, is interesting because of both the similarities to and the differences from sex determination in XX/XY systems such as those of man and of fruit flies. In addition, the heterogamety of females rather than males in ZZ/ZW species may have considerable effects on the way selection acts on some sexual traits.

In humans and other XX/XY vertebrates, sex is largely determined by the presence of a Y chromosome rather than the number of X chromosomes present. This is seen in people with Turner's syndrome, who have just one sex chromosome, an X (notated as XO). Such people are phenotypically female, although sterile. Conversely, in fruit flies, the Y chromosome is unimportant in sex determination, and it is the number of X chromosomes compared with the number of sets of autosomes that determines sex. A fly that has the same number of sets of X chromosomes as autosomes is a female. When the ratio is 1 X chromosome : 2 sets of autosomes, a male is produced. Abnormal fruit flies with other numbers of X chromosomes and/or autosomes also sometimes occur, and these produce flies with abnormal sexual characteristics.

In the Lepidoptera, it appears that the critical determinant of sex varies between species. In the Silk Worm, *Bombyx mori*, which has been more closely studied genetically than any other species of moth, females are ZW and males are ZZ. However, in other species of moth with ZZ males, females may be ZO, ZZW, or even ZZWW. The presence of both ZO and ZZW females suggests that the W chromosome is essential in female determination in some species (ZZW species), but not in others (ZO species). Working with Silk Worm strains with extra chromosomes and translocated fragments of the W chromosome, Tazima (1964) showed that in this species the W chromosome does carry female-determining genes, localised to one end of the W chromosome. Changing the ratio of sex chromosomes to autosome sets had no effect on sex determination.

Thus, in the Silk Worm, the W chromosome is pivotal to sex determination. However, this mechanism of sex determination is not found in all moths. Obviously, femaleness cannot be determined by genes on the W chromosome in the few species that are referred to as ZO, for females of these species have just one sex chromosome, a Z. They have lost the W chromosome some time in their past evolutionary history.

The complexities of lepidopteran sex determination may be realised from the consideration of one extraordinary little species of British moth. This is the psychid *Dahlica triquetrella*. This moth, like many of its family, has wingless females. The larvae feed on lichens, mosses, dead insects or decaying plant material from within a case constructed of silk and adorned by sand granules, frass and dead insect body parts. The larva pupates inside this case. The adult, when ready to emerge, manoeuvres itself to the posterior opening of the case, and, still inside the pupal case, wriggles halfway out before eclosing. The female then, without the attentions of a male, starts to oviposit, placing her eggs inside the larval case that she has just exited. She is able to do this because, in Britain, this species reproduces parthenogenetically. Amazingly, males of this species have never been recorded in Britain and probably do not occur here. However, males are known from other parts of Europe, and in some locations reproduction can be either sexual or parthenogenetic. It was for this reason that J. Seiler initiated a painstaking research programme on the sex determination of this moth, which spanned over 50 years.

Seiler found that three types of female appeared to exist. Some have two sets of 31 chromosomes giving a diploid number of 62 (60 autosomes plus a Z and a W). Others have two sets, but have only 61 chromosomes because they lack the W chromosome (i.e. these were ZO). The third type has four sets of chromosomes, comprising four of each of the autosomes, but just two sex chromosomes, both Zs. These are known as tetraploids. In the wild tetraploid females reproduce by thelytokous parthenogenesis, which means that they only produce female offspring and do so without fertilisation. Of the diploids, ZW females reproduce sexually in the normal way while ZO females, like the tetraploids, produce just daughters without mating. In fact, the situation is slightly more complicated than this, because ZO females can reproduce either sexually or parthenogenetically, depending on whether sperm is available for fertilisation.

Because some females are ZW and others are ZO, this is obviously one of the species in which the W chromosome plays no role in determining femaleness. Indeed close examination revealed no difference in the viability or reproductive efficiency of ZW compared with ZO females (Seiler 1959, 1960). This deduction is strengthened by a consideration of the morphology of individuals with abnormal sex chromosome complements. ZWW moths are female, while ZZW and ZZWW moths are male. The simplest explanation is that it is the number of Z chromosomes, and not the presence or absence of the W chromosome, that is crucial here in sex determination.

In captivity, sexual diploids can be crossed with parthenogenetic tetraploids. Such crosses produce offspring of two types, parthenogenetic tetraploid females, and triploid intersexes, with three sets of chromosomes. These results suggest that only some eggs are fertilised and reinforces the view that sex determination in this amazing little moth depends on the ratio of Z chromosomes to sets of autosomes. The ratios of Z chromosomes to autosomes and the sexuality of the moths are given in Figure 4.2.

Fig. 4.2 Variation in the sex chromosome complements of *Dahlica triquetrella* and the phenotypes that they produce.

Sex chromosome complement

ZO : 2A	normal female or parthenogenetic female
ZW : 2A	normal female or parthenogenetic female
ZZ : 2A	normal male
ZWW : 2A	normal female
ZZW : 2A	normal male
ZZWW : 2A	normal male
ZZ : 3A	highly variable sexual mosaics
ZZ : 4A	parthenogenetic female

Comparison of the Silk Worm and *D. triquetrella* shows clearly that the mechanism of sex determination varies between species. Unfortunately, in the vast majority of moths we do not know whether it is the W chromosome or the ratio of Z chromosomes to sets of autosomes that is important. Furthermore, the precise biochemical mechanism of sex determination in ZW systems remains to be uncovered. However, the alteration from male to female heterogamety has some interesting evolutionary consequences.

The consequences of females having different sex chromosomes

The Lepidoptera, along with the birds, are arguably the most sexually dimorphic groups of organism known. The sexual dimorphism in these groups involves features that may be involved in choosing a mate, such as bright male adornments in many birds, butterflies and day-flying moths, or scent and olfactory organs as in some butterflies and many nocturnal moths. It seems beyond the bounds of coincidence that these two groups just happen to be those with heterogametic females. Indeed there are theoretical reasons for believing that this connection between sexual dimorphism and female heterogamety is a direct consequence of females only having one Z chromosome.

According to Darwinian theory, many male adornments are a result of sexual selection by female choice. If this is true, some females must have a genetically controlled preference to mate with males having particular characteristics. The genes that control these mating preferences must, ultimately, have arisen by mutation. Most novel mutations are recessive; that is they are not expressed if there is a second, dominant allele present. If a mate preference gene first arises on an autosome of a female, it will thus not be expressed. Indeed, its initial spread could only be by random genetic drift. This would also be the case if it arose on an X chromosome of a female homogametic species. However, should such a mutation lie on a W chromosome or the non-pairing part of a Z chromosome in a female heterogametic species, such as a moth, the mutation would immediately be expressed. Its evolution would thus be much less dependent upon the vagaries of random genetic drift in its initial stages and so would be more likely.

A second intriguing observation involves the lack of chromosomal crossing over during meiosis in female Lepidoptera mentioned previously. Again we may ask is it merely coincidental that in both fruit flies and moths, chiasmata formation is suppressed in the heterogametic sex, in the former this being the male and in the latter the female? Personally, I am always somewhat suspicious of apparent biological coincidences and I suspect that there is a logical evolutionary or genetical reason for this pattern.

Sexual mosaics and hermaphrodites

Most sexually reproducing organisms have two types of sex organs. In some species the male and female sex organs are on the same individual, but in most, including the Lepidoptera, they are usually on different individuals: the males and the females. Yet very occasionally in moths, individuals with both male and female primary sex organs occur. Furthermore, individuals that are part male and part female in respect of other characteristics also occur as rarities (Fig. 4.3). Individuals of this type are most often noticed in species with a strong degree of sexual dimorphism in noticeable features such as the colour pattern. The commonly used term for an organism that is part male and part female is a hermaphrodite, after the child born to the goddess Aphrodite and the man Hermes. Their son became captivated by the nymph Salamacis and joined with her to become one, part male, part female, being. The correct name for a moth that is made up of some male and some female parts is a sexual mosaic.

The most spectacular sexual mosaics are those where the divide between the male and female parts is straight down the middle. Such examples are very

Fig. 4.3 The antennae of a sexual mosaic Emperor moth, *Saturnia pavonia.*

rare, but they are very notable when they occur. More commonly, the mix of male and female parts is not so clean, and male and female elements are dotted around the insect, as in the Emperor moth, *Saturnia pavonia*, pictured on Plate 4b.

Sexual strategies

The difference in the sizes of gametes produced by males and females and their energy requirements lead to differences in the basic strategies that males and females should have in regard to mating. Males, with their high sperm production, at rather little energetic cost, should endeavour to mate with as many different females as possible, spreading their sperm widely to gain as much paternity of the following generation as possible. Females, on the other hand, because they have invested so heavily in each of their relatively few eggs, should try to ensure that these eggs are only fertilised by sperm from males that are fit as a result of carrying good genes. Thus males should be highly promiscuous, while females should be choosy.

While these are the basic rules, other factors come into play when specific examples are considered. These factors include the longevity of both sexes, their relative emergence times, the abundance of potential mates, the ability of each sex to attract or seek out the opposite sex, the degree of mate choice, the costs of mating, the levels of mate guarding, the mechanisms used by males to ensure paternity and the competition between sperm to succeed in fertilisation. This variety of factors has led to some truly amazing sexual features among the moths.

Finding a mate

To take just one of these features, the ability to attract a mate, we may consider the Emperor moth. I remember returning to Cambridge from a field trip in April 1984. I had left a number of Emperor moth cocoons in a large Perspex cage outside the laboratory with instructions that any that emerged should be isolated until my return so that their virginity should be maintained. Arriving at the field station at around four in the afternoon, I noticed a male flying across the car park, close to the cage. Uttering some uncomplimentary things about the capabilities of one of my colleagues, I assumed that this moth had eclosed from my stock and somehow managed to escape the cage. But then another male appeared and then another. Within 15 minutes there were over 20 flying around the cage. In the cage was a single newly emerged female hanging from the roof of the cage, her abdomen distended and her scent glands exposed. Although the Emperor moth is not particularly abundant in the Cambridge area, a fresh virgin female hung out on a sunny April afternoon will invariably pull in upwards of a dozen males in the late afternoon by the power of her scent.

This attraction of males by females is the normal pattern among moths. Females release volatile chemicals, called pheromones, that act as messages to males of their own species. In the case of the Emperor moths, the male has an extraordinarily acute sense of smell as a result of his highly sensitive antennae (Fig. 4.4), which he uses to track up the scent plume towards a 'calling' female. There are reports of males being able to detect females from as much as eight kilometres away. The female herself, by utilising a very strong male attractant, frequently gathers more than one male to her, with the result that she has a group of suitors to assess and choose from.

The problems of initially finding a mate vary in different species of moth. In high density species, the problem is not great. However, in low density species, particularly if they are short lived, it is imperative to have an efficient mechanism of finding or attracting the opposite sex. Although the interests of males and females are often in conflict, as shown by the differing basic strategies resulting from differences in gamete size mentioned above, the machinery of males and females to get together works beautifully in concert, for here the interests of the sexes are the same. Given that most moths are nocturnal, mate-finding using vision is not an option for many species. Sound might be used to advertise location to members of the opposite sex, and is employed by some insects, such as grasshoppers, cicadas and some beetles. However, sound does not travel very far and because many species of moth do not live in close colonies and have the ability to disperse widely, a system of attraction over greater distances would have obvious advantages. Scent fulfils this requirement.

In most species of moth, males fly to females rather than the reverse. Examination of the antennae of many moth species shows that the antennae

Fig. 4.4 The male Emperor moth, *Saturnia pavonia*, has exceptionally sensitive antennae.

of males are frequently more feathery than those of females (Plate 3e and 3f). This greater development supports the view that males are usually attracted to the scent of females, not vice versa. Further circumstantial evidence comes from the high male to female ratio for many species in moth light trap catches, suggesting that males fly far more than do females. A third piece of suggestive evidence is that while the females of a number of British moths have no wings or have vestigial wings that are useless for flight, the males are fully winged. The reverse is not true for any moth species.

Detailed studies of the anatomy and neurology of the antennae of the Tobacco Horn-worm, *Manduca sexta*, have confirmed this view. A single antenna of a male Tobacco Horn-worm has just under 100,000 sensilla, while an antenna of a female has 100,000–150,000 sensilla (Lee & Strausfeld 1990). From this one might imagine that the females are better adapted than males to pick up scent attractants when needing a mate. However, examination of the sensilla showed that two types occurred. One type are those that are specifically sensitive to pheromones: the other type are sensitive to an array of general environmental scents. The male antennae are armed with both types, each antenna having about 43,000 pheromone-specific sensilla and 55,000 general sensilla. Conversely, the female sensilla are all of the general type.

If it is usually males that are attracted to females, then the female's role in the system is to manufacture a cocktail of pheromones to attract the males. Studies of a variety of pest species of moth have shown that alcohols, aldehydes and acetate esters are most frequently utilised, and that the cocktail produced by a species is usually very specific in respect of both the component chemicals and the concentrations of these components within the cocktail. The pheromones are released from glands on the posterior abdominal segment. These glands are extruded by females when they are 'calling' males. Anyone who runs a moth trap will know that completely still nights do not produce very good catches. Similarly, attempting to mate moths in a confined space, such as a room or laboratory, with the windows shut, is often unsuccessful. The reason for both is that the dispersal of female pheromones requires some breeze. Female moths in mating condition usually call from a relatively exposed position so that the pheromone will be dispersed by the wind. She has control over when she calls and will do so when wind conditions are favourable. A night when the wind is what we might describe as a mild breeze and is relatively constant in both strength and direction is best. If the wind is insufficient or is too strong, or the direction is constantly changing, females will not call.

A consistent breeze will disperse the pheromone from a female downwind in a plume. Males that fly through this plume are stimulated to fly upwind with slight side-to-side oscillations in direction, which probably help them to maintain their position in the plume.

The signals that males receive in the form of pheromone molecules, which dictate the pattern and intensity of upwind flight, involve the number of pheromone molecules detected. A pheromone molecule that hits a pheromone-sensitive sensillum on a male antenna will enter the sensillum through a pore. Once inside the sensillum, it will interact with the target site of a protein molecule specific to that type of pheromone, which effectively binds it. The pheromone binding protein then transports the pheromone molecule to a position where it reacts with a receptor protein, thus triggering a neuronal signal. The pheromone molecule is then degraded. Each pheromone molecule received will lead to one nerve impulse and the male moth will react to changes in the number of nerve impulses received.

Although it is generally female moths that produce pheromones to call males from some distance away, in a few species the roles are reversed. In both the Wax moth, *Galleria mellonella*, and the Lesser Wax moth, *Achroia grisella*, it is the males that produce pheromones and females assemble to them.

Obviously, the pheromone plumes produced by moths are usually not precise geometric cones. Many factors, such as variations in wind speed and direction, land topography, obstacles such as trees and buildings and the rate of pheromone production by females, will lead to distortions in the shape of the plume. The result is that males will frequently fly out of the plume. If this happens the males alter their strategy from the small changes in direction in their previous upwind flight, to longer traverses across the wind in an attempt to relocate the plume (David et al. 1983; David & Birch 1989). Once the concentration of the pheromonal signal received by males exceeds a critical threshold value because the male is very close to its source, the female, the male alights and starts to search for the female on foot.

Mate recognition

Once a male has found a calling female, he has to indicate to her that he is an appropriate mating partner. In this, he may have to indicate first that he is of her own species by use of some type of species recognition signal. Second, he may have to demonstrate that he is a male of sufficient calibre for her to allow her eggs to be fertilised by him. In most species of moth we have little information on the courtship behaviour that males and females indulge in at close quarters. It is likely, however, that some species have two-way recognition, whereas in other species, recognition is left to one sex alone. This will usually be the female as the cost to her of mistakenly mating with a partner of the wrong species will be far greater than it would be for a male: the male has far more opportunity to re-mate. In the Emperor moth at least, species recognition appears to be purely a female function. Male Emperors will attempt to copulate with almost any object as long as it is giving off a high concentration of the appropriate female pheromone.

We have little knowledge of the proportion of moths that use male or female synthesised species recognition signals. Studies in this area are urgently needed. The sexual pheromones produced by male moths that have been analysed are generally rather large stable molecules. This in itself is suggestive that they are used in close contact and not in the manner of the volatile, low molecular weight attractants produced by females to attract males from far away.

Interestingly, males of many species, but by no means all, have specialised organs for releasing pheromones. These are eversible structures. They may comprise brushes or sac-like structures that are inflated from glandular pockets on the legs or abdomen. There has been considerable speculation on the function of these eversible male structures, and they may not serve the same purpose in all species (see Birch 1979), but little experimental evidence exists in regard to their use. One possibility is that they produce pheromones allowing females to determine their producer's identity.

Not all species of moth have eversible structures and it is probable that in some species males do not give females any recognition signals. In the wild this is unlikely to lead to serious difficulties or high levels of hybridisation. The species specific nature of the cocktail of pheromones that females release means that only conspecific males are attracted by females. However, in captivity, the one-sided nature of species recognition in such species can be utilised to produce interspecific hybrids. For example, hybrids between the Poplar Hawk moth, *Laothoe populi*, and the Eyed Hawk moth, *Smerinthus ocellata*, are not too difficult to obtain if two male Eyed Hawks are enclosed in a cage with two virgin females, one of each species. The pheromonal signal of the female Eyed Hawk moth will excite both males, one of which will mate with her. The second male, in his heightened state of arousal, will mate with the only other female available, the female Poplar Hawk. The deception works in the other direction as well, although because the eggs of the Eyed Hawk are smaller than those of the Poplar Hawk, the hybrid embryos die due to lack of space for development. This fate can be circumvented if the fully developed embryos are carefully cut out of the eggshell with a needle scalpel at the appropriate time. The hybrids thus produced are intermediate in appearance between the two parents, are sterile and often are part male and part female.

The presence of eversible structures in males of some species and their absence from other closely related species suggests that if they have a function in species recognition, it is a reinforcing function, backing up some other feature, such as the cocktail of female pheromones that attract males. In some closely related species, there is evidence to suggest that such backups might be selectively advantageous in certain circumstances. For example, Sir Cyril Clark described an interesting incident when Japanese Vapourer moths 'assembled' to his luggage containing netting cages that had previously been used to house virgin female European Vapourers.

As an example of a species recognition backup, we might consider the plume moths *Platyptilia carduidactyla* and *Platyptilia williamsii*. These moths produce the same chemical scent attractant, and so run the risk of hybridisation. However, they are temporally separated, for *P. carduidactyla* calls only in the first half of the night, and *P. williamsii* in the second half.

Population sex ratios

As already described (p. 66), the primary sex ratio, that is the sex ratio produced at fertilisation, is 1:1 for most species. Yet the apparent sex ratio of adult moths often appears to be biased in favour of one sex. Furthermore, the bias may change during the flight season of a species, or may vary according to the methods by which samples are collected. For example, as already mentioned, most lepidopterists are aware that moth light traps attract far more males than females. The reason for this is simply that for most species males fly far more than females. Hunting for dusk-flying, or crepuscular, species with a net also tends to produce a male bias for the same reason. Pheromone traps, in which virgin females are hung up to attract males, obviously only attract one sex. Sugaring, by which a thick syrup cocktail is daubed onto substrates as a bait to attract moths, produces a more equitable balance of the sexes of many species. However, in some, females appear more attracted than males, presumably because they need nutrients to mature their eggs. Thus, most methods of sampling adult moths are liable to lead to sex ratio biases that do not accurately reflect adult population sex ratios. Sampling at other times of the life cycle, by searching, beating or sweeping for larvae or digging for pupae and then rearing through to adulthood are likely to produce sex ratios that are a far more accurate reflection of the population sex ratio of most species.

Many lepidopterists will have observed that males of a particular species often start to appear before females. The reason for this is adaptive. Females of many moth species have mature eggs, ready to be fertilised and laid as soon as the female ecloses. Because of the risks of predation, it is in the interests of these females to mate as soon after emergence as possible, and females of most species will mate in the first 24 hours of adult life. This is not true of all species. Some, such as the Large Yellow Underwing, *Noctua pronuba*, have to take in nutrients to mature their eggs (Plate 5d), yet females of this species still usually mate soon after emergence, and certainly well before their eggs are ready to be laid. However, it is true for the majority. The rapid mating of females after eclosion means that a male that hatches late in the flight season is unlikely to find any virgin females available to him. Consequently, selection will favour males that hatch early in the flight season. If males hatch too early they run the risk of dying before females begin to emerge. Thus, the timing of male emergence is a balance struck between emerging in advance of the females, to be ready and waiting, and not emerging too early because of the risks of death in the period before females appear. The result is usually a lag period of a few days between the appearance of the first male of a species and the appearance of the first female.

The consequence is that at the start of the flight period for most species, the adult population shows a marked male bias. As the season progresses this bias diminishes and eventually the population becomes female biased, sometimes severely so by the end of the season. This is true of the Magpie moths, *Abraxas grossulariata* (Plate 11f), that frequent the currant patch in my garden. The total number of individuals recorded by searching the currant bushes and surrounding plants and shrubs over the last nine years has been 253. Of these, the ratio of males to females in July has been 81 males to 49 females. Conversely, of the moths recorded in August, 92 have been female and only 31 male.

Female biased sex ratios

Although the sex ratios in most moth species are approximately 1:1, some do show a very significant female bias in the primary sex ratio. This occurs in two rather exceptional situations. The first is when a species, or some members of a species, have evolved the ability to reproduce asexually, as discussed earlier in this chapter (p. 90). As females that reproduce parthenogenetically produce only daughters, this sex predominates either partially or totally, depending on whether some females retain sexual reproduction.

The second situation occurs when highly specialised bacteria, called *Wolbachia*, that live inside the cells of some moths, manipulate the sex determination systems of their hosts to their own ends. These bacteria live in the cytoplasm of the hosts' cells. They can be passed from one generation to the next in the cytoplasm of eggs, but not in sperm, because sperm are virtually devoid of cytoplasm. The consequence of this unequal transmission is that the interests of the bacteria are served only by being in females. Some of these *Wolbachia* have thus evolved the ability to change genetic males into females. For some time, it has been known that this bacterium has the ability to feminise woodlouse species. More recently, it has been shown to cause feminisation in two species of moth, the Asian Corn Borer, *Ostrinia furnacalis*, and its close relative, the Adzuki Bean Borer, *O. scapulalis*. Populations of these moths effectively consist of three types of moth: normal males (ZZ sex chromosomes), normal females (ZW sex chromosomes) and feminised males (ZZ sex chromosomes + *Wolbachia*) (Kageyama et al. 1998, 2000). These feminised males behave functionally as females. They develop ovaries and eggs in the way of a normal female, mate with males and lay fertilised eggs in the normal way. The progeny of a feminised female are almost all females as the vertical transmission of the *Wolbachia* is generally high. Interestingly, if a *Wolbachia*-feminised female is cured of the bacterial infection by administration of antibiotics, 'she' will mate normally, but thereafter only produce males. As she carries two Z sex chromosomes, her femininity being a consequence of the *Wolbachia* she harbours, once the bacterium has been purged, her progeny will all carry two Z chromosomes, one from her and one from the normal male she mated with.

Mechanism of feminisation

The mechanism of feminisation in *Ostrinia* has yet to be fully examined. However, in the woodlouse *Armadillidium vulgare*, the difference between developing into a male or a female appears to depend on the activity of a single gene that blocks the expression of one or more genes that cause the differentiation of the androgenic gland (Legrand et al. 1987). This gland produces male hormones and, if its formation is suppressed, a female phenotype results. There is thus a fairly simple mechanism by which an inherited symbiont may feminise a genotypic male, for all it has to do is inhibit the differentiation of the androgenic gland. Although the precise molecular basis of this inhibition is not known, the symbiont does seem to mimic the action of 'female genes' carried on the W chromosome that inhibit androgenic gland differentiation in WZ individuals.

Sexual selection

It is now generally accepted that one of the fundamental outcomes of the difference between the sexes of most organisms is that males should fight and females should choose. This view was an integral part of Darwin's theory of evolution. In his observations of animals and plants, Darwin deduced that when characteristics other than the primary sex organs were different between the sexes or were limited to one sex, this implied that they were probably the result of sexual selection.

Male competition and female choice

Darwin's theory of evolution involved not only natural selection, the concept of the survival of the fittest: it also included sexual selection, by which those most successful in producing fit progeny would be most heavily represented in future generations. Darwin proposed two types of sexual selection, male competition, by which males compete with one another for matings with females, and female choice, where females will choose to mate with the males possessing specific characteristics. Both types of sexual selection have been shown to operate in a diverse array of organisms. In many cases the two types are not mutually exclusive and operate together.

The eversible structures found in some male moths are probably the result of sexual selection. They would both provide males with the opportunity to compete with other males over the strength of signal they can produce and they would serve to give the females a trait, in the form of the pheromones released from the eversible structures, by which to judge males and make a choice.

Darwin called male competition the 'law of battle', citing examples of violent conflicts between male mammals such as deer, musk oxen and elephant seals. However, in many cases, male competition involves far more subtle antagonistic interactions. Thus, males may compete for access to females and success in inducing females to mate using a wide array of traits other than weaponry. Scent, coloration, sound and touch are all used and there may be other sensory stimuli of which we are unaware. While scent is the most used trait among moths, some species use visual attraction, particularly those species whose females are attracted to males.

Lekking

Perhaps the most obvious example of visual mate attraction among the British moths is the Ghost moth, *Hepialus humuli*. The male is brilliant white (Fig. 4.5). At dusk male Ghost moths aggregate in groups of five to 50 at specific sites over grass meadows, marshes or reed beds. Here they hover with an unusual side-to-side swaying motion, referred to by Kettlewell (1973) as 'pendeculating'. This motion, coupled with their bright whiteness, which seems almost to shine, even in the low light at dusk, has given the species its common name. Aggregated males space themselves out a few metres apart as they hover over the lekking site. Females are attracted to these lekking sites and will select a male on the basis of the brightness of his coloration, his flight pattern and probably his position on the lek. Once a male has been picked out, the female, which is dull yellow-brown in colour, will either alight on foliage near to the male, or fly rapidly towards the male and crash into him, knocking both to the ground. If the female alights, the male will soon drop from his lekking flight and seek her, probably using her scent to find her.

Fig. 4.5 A male Ghost moth, *Hepialus humuli.*

This is the characteristic behaviour of Ghost moths throughout most of the British Isles. However, Kettlewell (1973) notes that in the Shetland Isles and the Faroes, the males lack the bright white coloration of the forewing, this being obscured by brown (Plate 15e). The reason for this change appears to be related to the latitude of these islands and predator pressure. The Ghost moth flies in July at northern latitudes. Here, because it remains light throughout the night during the midsummer months, displaying male Ghost moths would be visible to predators. Kettlewell records that two species of gull, the Common Gull and the Black-headed Gull, regularly fly inland in their hundreds on these islands to hunt for Ghost moths. He speculates that the bright white males of southern populations would be at a great disadvantage in these circumstances. Consequently, selection has favoured a reduction in the visual component of mate attraction and a consequent increase in the scent component in these populations. Interestingly, when the scent brushes are dissected out from the tarsus of the third pair of legs of northern males, these can be used to attract both males and females. It seems that the pheromones produced by these structures influence both the aggregation of males to lekking sites and the attraction of females to males.

The act of mating

Once a pair of moths has found one another they may copulate. Most moths mate back-to-back, resting on some substrate (Figs 4.6, 4.7 and 4.8 and Plates 4a and 13f). Mating is achieved when the male and female genitalia are brought and held together. The genitalia are situated on the final abdominal segment and are accompanied by claspers, which are used to help the pair maintain tight contact during the union. The detailed morphology of the genitalia varies considerably between different species, but within a species, the male and female genitalia are highly conserved and complementary to one another. This high level of interspecific variation and low level of intraspecific variation in the morphology of the genitalia makes these features of considerable use in taxonomic classification.

In moths, the transfer of sperm from males to females is independent from the act of fertilisation, which typically takes place just prior to eggs being laid. Males pass their sperm packaged in a structure called a spermatophore. This is passed directly from the male to the female during copulation. The spermatophore is a gelatinous capsule made largely of protein. It is manufactured by the male using secretions from his accessory glands.

The spermatophore of the male is deposited in the bursa copulatrix of the female, a muscular section of her reproductive tract. From here, contractions of the bursa drive sperm from the spermatophore into the female's spermatheca, where they are stored until needed for fertilisation.

Mate guarding

The length of copulation in moths varies tremendously between species. In some it lasts as little as ten minutes, in others it may last almost 24 hours. Whilst the shorter times may be seen as the minimum time necessary to form and pass a spermatophore, the reason for the long duration in other species is more difficult to fathom. In some nocturnal species, if mating is necessarily of a duration that means there is a risk of a pair being still *in copula* at dawn, it may be selectively advantageous to stay immobile and so together during the hours of

Fig. 4.6 (top left) Most moths, such as these Lime Hawk moths, *Mimas tiliae*, mate back-to-back.

Fig. 4.7 (above) A pair of Puss moths, *Cerura vinula*, mating at dusk.

Fig. 4.8 (left) Mating in the tortricoid *Cydia aurana*. Here, a fresh female is mating with a much older, worn male.

daylight as movement may attract the attention of a predator. Alternatively, as males of some Lepidoptera are known to contribute nutrients to females within the spermatophores that they pass, it may be that some species take longer to manufacture and fully resource their spermatophores. Another possibility is that males are increasing their probability of paternity by staying 'in' the female until she is ready to oviposit. Prolonged mating (more than 12 hours) has been observed in a wide variety of moth species, including many sphingids, arctiids, lymantriids, notodontids, noctuids and some geometrids.

Unfortunately, despite the enormous amount of moth breeding that has been conducted over the last century or more, we are still ignorant of many important facets of the act of copulation among moths. To give just a couple of examples, while we know that males pass sperm in a spermatophore, we do not know at what point during a copulation the spermatophore is transferred into the female in most species. Nor do we know whether the male or female in a pairing terminates contact.

Multiple mating

It is generally thought that while male moths may mate several times with different females, most female moths mate only once. It is certainly true that in captivity a single mating appears to be sufficient to allow females to lay their full egg load without the reduction in fertility that would be expected if females ran out of sperm. However, the single mating idea has been challenged by the finding that wild-caught females of some species contain the remnants of more than one spermatophore. The usual interpretation is that these females have received spermatophores from different matings. While this may be the case, this interpretation needs to be substantiated experimentally. It is now known that in some insects individual males have the capability of passing two or more spermatophores within a single copulation. For example, in the 2 spot ladybird, *Adalia bipunctata*, males pass one, two or three spermatophores during mating, the precise number depending on the state of the male, the population density and the sex ratio (Majerus in press).

If females do regularly mate with more than one male, the reason for this behaviour should be investigated. The act of copulating usually carries a cost (time, energy, vulnerability to attack, risk of infection by sexually transmitted diseases), so a female that mates with more than one male should gain a compensating advantage. One possibility is that, by mating with more than one male, a female promotes post-copulatory male competition in the form of sperm competition. This may increase her reproductive success. For example, if genetically fit males produce larger ejaculates, sperm from such males are likely to be proportionately over-represented in a female's stored sperm pool. Alternatively, if deleterious genes affect not only the fitness of the phenotype, but also the competitive ability of gametes, sperm lacking such genes would be more successful in fertilisation. A third possibility is that female promiscuity may be a bet-hedging strategy, operating to increase the chances that at least some of a female's offspring are fathered by fit males. Finally, if females can assess male fitness, they may be able to influence which sperm achieve fertilisation, thereby increasing their reproductive output through post-copulatory female choice, or what has been termed cryptic female choice.

Once mating has been completed and the pair has parted, the males and females will follow different paths. Males, perhaps after feeding to replenish nutrients, will seek other potential mates. Females on the other hand will generally either seek food, if nutrients are required to mature eggs, or, if the eggs are already mature, seek oviposition sites. These will usually be in the vicinity of larval food, for feeding is what moth larvae do best. It is to the subject of feeding, food and growth, in the context of moth habitats, that I turn in the next chapter.

5

Host Plants and Habitats

The need to feed

When a moth egg is laid, the embryo inside it is a single cell. This cell divides through the process of mitosis as the embryo grows. To do so the cell needs fuel in the form of nutrients. Initially these nutrients come from the provisions that the mother has laid down in the egg. However, soon after hatching, moth larvae have to fend for themselves. Most feed by chewing on plant material of one sort or another. The larvae feed to increase size and to lay down nutrient reserves to fuel the transformations that occur during the pupal stage. Most also lay down energy reserves for adult activity, and indeed, some adult moths cannot feed. However, many adult moths do feed. Most of the food of adult moths is also plant in origin, but is very different from the food of larvae, for most adults have a liquid diet.

The energy that moths require for the functions of their lives is obtained from the breakdown of food. Thus, while energy that moths need to function is necessary in all the life history stages, in most moths it is only obtained as food in two stages and, in some, only in the larval stage. Even in species in which both larvae and adults feed, intake in the adult stage is a much smaller component of the total energy budget than that obtained in the larval stage.

The earliest moths, the Micropterigidae, that first evolved about 135 million years ago, probably fed on bryophytes (mosses and liverworts) (Powell 1980). Thus the relationship between moths and plants is a long one. In general the interaction is positive for the moth, through gaining nutrients, and negative for the plant through loss of body mass. However, through adult feeding, some flowers gain benefit as moths act as pollinators. Furthermore, there are a few instances in which the roles are reversed, for some insectivorous plants may make a meal of a moth. Most fascinating are those close interrelationships in which pairs of moth and plant species have become totally dependent upon one another, so that the continued existence of one depends on the survival of the other.

In this chapter, I shall discuss moth feeding and investigate the interrelationship between moths and plants. Vegetation is a major feature of most natural habitats and for moths it is frequently the most important feature, for the presence of appropriate foodplants determines the habitat choices and limitations of many species. Thus, in the second half of this chapter I will move on from feeding and host plant preferences to consider the habitats and habitat preferences of moths more widely.

Egg provisioning

The first energetic requirement of an individual moth is that needed for embryonic development. These nutrients need to be of high quality to furnish the high levels of energy required for cell division and differentiation in the embryo. Furthermore, as the embryo has no access to other food until it has hatched from the egg and begun to feed on an external food source, the resources provided for it by its parents within the egg and eggshell are crucial to its survival. The parental care that moths contribute to their offspring is largely maternal and is confined to this provisioning of the eggs, to laying eggs in appropriate places, i.e. close to or on food for the larvae, and, in some species, providing some sort of defence for the egg in the form of positioning, defensive chemistry or covering with urticating hairs (p. 202).

Larval feeding

What do larvae eat?

The larval stage of most species of moth has the greatest energy intake. Although a small number of species are carnivorous and a few eat non-living parts of animals, such as fur or feathers, the vast majority of moth larvae feed on plants, lichens or fungi. As over 95% of species, both in Britain and world-wide, feed on plants, it is sensible to consider the interactions between larvae and plants first, before discussing the rather few exceptions.

Broadly plants comprise roots, stems, leaves, flowers and seeds. Each of these parts is attacked by the larvae of some moth species. The tissues that make up the various structures of plants vary greatly between species and different lar-vae have developed adaptations for feeding on these various tissue types. The majority of species of larvae feed on the leaves of plants, some chewing through the tissues from outside, while others live inside the leaf, consuming it from within. In Britain, according to Emmet (1991), 68% of moth larvae (1,577 species) feed on leaves. Much smaller numbers feed on other parts of plants. Thus, about 8% feed on seeds, 6% feed inside the stems on plants, including live wood, 4% feed on flowers, while roots, dead wood and decaying plant matter are each consumed by 4% or less.

The proportion of species that eat living material of higher plants is greater in the macrolepidoptera than among the microlepidoptera. Of the other types of food, all species that feed on the wood of dead trees or on dead animal material are micros. Mosses, fungi and decaying plant material are also eaten by far more species of micros than macros. The same cannot be said of lichens, for here one group of macros, the footman moths, all of which feed on lichens or algae, swell the numbers in the macro column. In addition, all three species that have predatory larvae are macrolepidoptera.

The distribution of diets of moths is not random when considered against a phylogenetic classification. Some genera or families specialise on particular types of food or particular parts of plants. The ghosts and swifts (Hepialidae) feed largely on the roots of plants. Most of the clearwings (Sesiidae) feed on wood. Species in the genus *Phyllonorycter* feed inside plants, forming blister mines. The larvae of many pugs (*Eupithecia* spp.) feed on flowers, while *Perizoma* spp. specialise on seeds. These specialisations of particular groups have probably existed for very long periods of time, for they may reflect ances-tral food preferences. Most families of moths evolved about 70 million years ago, with diversification into different species occurring subsequently. Group host plant specialisations thus suggest that the food preferred by the ancestral species of these families is the origin of the food choices we see in such groups today.

Not all groups comprise species that feed on similar foods. Thus, for example, the Noctuidae include leaf-eaters, stem-borers, root-feeders and flower-eaters. The Tineidae include some species that feed on lichens, others on fungi, some that feed on animal detritus in mammal and bird nests and, of course, some that feed on our clothes.

Nutrients

The critical nutrients that moth larvae gain from their food are largely similar, whatever the source of food. In brief, the larvae need to take in carbohydrates, nitrogenous compounds such as amino acids and some lipids, a variety of vitamins and trace elements and of course water. Of these, rates of nitrogen and water uptake probably have most influence on the rate of growth. Nitrogen in particular may be limiting, for most plant tissues contain rather low concentrations of this element. Larvae thus have to process a large amount of plant food to gain a sufficient supply of nitrogen. In doing so, they may take in more carbohydrate than they need, so they have to get rid of this excess and indeed the excrement, or frass, of most moth larvae is deficient in nitrogen, but contains appreciable amounts of carbohydrate and sometimes water.

The water content of different larval foods varies greatly. Larvae of species that feed on aquatic plants, such as the china-mark moths (Nymphulinae) (Fig. 5.1), do not have a difficulty taking in sufficient water with their food. Conversely, species that feed on dried stored foods or animal fibres need to retain as much fluid as they can. For moth larvae, water loss occurs through evaporation and through excretion of frass. Regulation of water content involves both the metabolism of the larva and its behaviour. When water is at a premium, the proportion of the amount taken in that is retained increases. Moreover, many larvae reduce evaporation by forming shelters in the form of leaf-rolls or leaf nests, feeding within the plant or simply moving from positions where they are exposed to high levels of airflow. Some larvae will drink water directly. Thus, the name of the Drinker moth, *Philudoria potatoria*, derives from the larva's reputed habit of drinking from dew drops or raindrops, a behaviour that I have observed on a number of occasions.

Fig. 5.1 A Brown China-mark moth, *Elophila nymphaeata*. Its larvae feed on aquatic plants from a floating case.

The nutrients mentioned above are not the only substances that moth larvae obtain from their food. Many of the components that are used by larvae in their defence derive from their food. These include some of the pigments that larvae use for camouflage and some of the compounds that chemically defended larvae use to make themselves poisonous or distasteful (p. 201).

Plant-feeders

Leaf-eaters

Leaf-eaters may feed exposed on the outside of the leaf, hidden within the leaf or among leaves that have been tied together or rolled up. Exposed leaf-eaters tend to be larger than those that feed inside leaves. This is partly a consequence of their requirement for large amounts of food. Most feed mainly at night. They tend to be highly cryptic, as in the case of many arbivorous, stick-like caterpillars (Fig. 5.2); defended by chemicals or irritant or stinging hairs (for example, Plate 12b); or to move from feeding sites on leaves to some more hidden location during daylight hours. Cryptic species tend to rest by day in a

Fig. 5.2 Many leaf-eating larvae are highly cryptic, often resembling twigs.

Fig. 5.3 Larvae of the Scalloped Hazel, *Odontoptera bidentata,* attach a silk thread to the substrate as a security measure.

characteristic position. For example, the larvae of many geometrids rest holding onto a twig by just their anal claspers, although they usually attach a silken strand to the twig from their mouth (Fig. 5.3). This acts as a security rope in the event that they are dislodged or have to get rapidly out of the way of a predator. Those with chemical or hair defences are often brightly coloured to advertise their unpalatability (p. 199). Larvae that feed largely at night, moving to the lower herbage layers or digging into soil during the day, tend to be dull colours, most usually dull greens, olives, greys or browns.

Leaf-miners

Larvae that feed on leaves in exposed positions tend to be cylindrical, with well-developed legs and prolegs and with a ring of strong hooks, or crotchets, on each proleg that help them to cling onto the substrate. Those that feed inside leaves, the leaf-miners (Fig. 5.4), tend to be severely flattened in shape. This is because the space in which they live is thin and restricted. Here then we have a lifestyle in which those that adopt it are truly vertically challenged. In addition to being flattened, leaf-miners often have reduced legs, prolegs and antennae. In some cases, the number of stemmata is also reduced and the mouthparts are somewhat modified. Most true leaf-miners belong to a fairly limited number of families or superfamilies of micro-lepidoptera (for example, Elaschistidae, Eriocranioidea, Gracillariidae, Incurvarioidea, Nepticuloidea and Tischerioidea). Mines are of varying types and the shape of a leaf mine is often diagnostic of the species (Fig. 5.5).

Fig. 5.4 (left) The trace of a leaf-mining larva.

Fig. 5.5 (below) Shapes of leaf mines are often diagnostic of species. a) The mine of the moth *Nepticula aurella* in a bramble leaf. b) The mines made in Hogweed by four fly larvae, *Phytomyza spondylii*. The central line down the centre of the mine in a) is the frass produced by the larva. The larva in b) scatters frass around the mine. (Drawn by Anne Bebbington, from photographs by Michael Tweedie.)

a

b

Leaf-tiers and rollers

Larvae of some small and some larger moths feed externally to the leaf, but do so within leaves. They are thus less restricted by living within the confines offered by the upper and lower surfaces of a leaf, but gain from being unexposed. These larvae either roll leaves up, preventing the leaves from unfurling by judicious use of silk, or they tie leaves around themselves with silk. The Mother of Pearl moth, *Pleuroptya ruralis*, is an admirable example of a roller. This pyralid rolls leaves of stinging nettles. If disturbed, the larva runs out of its tube, either forwards or backwards, and drops on a silken thread. The larvae of all three British species of the genus *Schoenobius* roll leaves of reeds and sedges, although they sometimes also feed within the stems or leaves of the foodplant. These larvae are remarkable for their habit of making rafts out of leaf fragments and then using these to float to fresh plants.

Leaf-tying is common in several families, such as the Tortricidae and the Geometridae. The Green Oak Tortrix, *Tortrix viridana*, usually ties just two leaves together, living between the upper surface of one and the lower surface of the other. Larvae of the Winter moth, *Operophtera brumata*, may tie several leaves together to form their feeding shelters. A feature common to most leaf-

Fig. 5.6 Some larvae live in family groups within large silken 'nests' that they construct among foliage.

rollers and tiers is an anal comb. This is a structure that looks somewhat like a short-toothed Afro-comb. Situated at the larva's tail, it is used to flick frass away from the area where the larva is feeding.

Net-makers

The larvae of some species of moth go further than individually making shelters to live and feed in, for some make family nests (Fig. 5.6). The best known of these are some of the lasiocampids and the small ermines (Yponomeutinae). In the case of the ermines, such as the Orchard Ermine, *Yponomeuta padella*, the larvae feed within a silken net spun over a section of foodplant. In the Lackey, *Malacosoma neustria*, and the Ground Lackey, *Malacosoma castrensis*, the larvae spin nests in very different situations, the former among the foliage of a variety of deciduous trees and the latter amongst saltmarsh vegetation. The young larvae leave these nests to forage, returning to rest communally (Fig. 5.7), and then deserting the nest in the final instar (Fig. 5.8).

Fig. 5.7 Nest-making larvae frequently return to their nests, resting on the outside of the webbing.

Fig. 5.8 Larvae of the Lackey, *Malacosoma neustria.*

Root-, stem- and wood-feeders

Leaf-miners are not the only type of larvae that feed within plants. Many species feed within the stems or roots of their host plants. Due to the greater thickness of stems and roots than of most leaves, size is not a limit for these larvae. In consequence, many of the species that feed inside the stems or roots of herbaceous plants, or in the trunks or branches of shrubs and trees, are relatively large. In Britain, they include a number of the wainscot moths, including the two largest species, the Large Wainscot, *Rhizedra lutosa* (Plate 7a), and the Bulrush moth, *Nonagria typhae*, which feed in the stems of Common Reed and Reed-mace respectively. Among the root-feeders the Ghost moth, *Hepialus humuli*, and several other swifts are included. Larvae may live inside or outside the roots, depending on the relative sizes of roots and the larva. For example, larvae of the Gold Swift, *Hepialus hecta*, feed within roots for their first four instars, only feeding externally in the final instar. Wood-borers include the Goat moth, *Cossus cossus*, which is one of our heaviest species, the Leopard moth, *Zeuzera pyrina*, and many of our clearwings (Sesiidae).

There are both advantages and disadvantages to feeding within roots, stems or wood. The main advantage is that the larvae are well sheltered from predators and parasitoids, although a few of the latter specialise on wood-boring larvae and woodpeckers are known to find and feed upon Goat moth larvae occasionally. The major disadvantage is that the stem and wood are less nutritious than leaves. Stem- and wood-feeding larvae thus have to process very large amounts of food to grow. This takes time, and wood-feeders, in particular, frequently take more than a year to develop (p. 41).

Flower-, seed- and fruit-eaters

The larvae of about 12% of British moths feed on the flowers, seeds or fruits of plants. In addition, some foliage feeders, such as the Spurge Hawk moth, *Hyles euphorbiae*, the Cinnabar, *Tyria jacobaeae*, and the Angleshades, *Phlogophora meticulosa* (Plate 15a), will feed on flowers as readily as they feed on leaves. Many, but not all, of the flower- and seed-feeders are relatively small, presumably because flowers and leaves comprise a smaller part of the mass of plants than do leaves.

A number of the smaller geometrids, including a high proportion of the pugs (*Eupithecia* spp.) and all the rivulets (*Perizoma* spp.) feed on flowers or seeds. Some, such as the Pretty Pinion, *Perizoma blandiata*, and the Small Rivulet, *Perizoma alchemillata*, feed on both. Those species that only feed on flowers gain both advantage and disadvantage by so doing. On the plus side is the fact that flowers, particularly in the pollen and ovules, contain much higher concentrations of nitrogen than other parts of plants. Another possible advantage for some is that flowers are often bright and obvious, so that ovipositing females may find them easy to locate, although many species oviposit in buds. On the negative side is that for most plants, the flowering season is short. This means that larvae that feed exclusively on flowers have to hatch within a very short window of opportunity and have to develop rapidly. Thus, for example, the Foxglove Pug, *Eupithecia pulchellata*, which feeds on the flowers of Foxgloves, completes its development in less than three weeks. Even then, the duration of the flowers is only just sufficient to allow the larvae to develop fully, and female Foxglove Pugs play their part by laying their eggs on the developing flower buds of the foodplant. Another limitation of flower feeding for many species that use only one type of host plant is that they can have only one generation per year. Some species have circumvented this problem by feeding on the flowers of different plants at different times of the year. For example, the White-spotted Pug, *Eupithecia tripunctaria*, feeds on Elder blossom and seeds in June and July, but larvae of its partial second brood feed on the flowers or seeds of Hogweed and Angelica.

Exclusive seed-eaters are not so time-restricted because seeds are available for longer than flowers. A number of larger moths are thus able to use seeds as their main diet. These include all the British members of the genus *Hadena*, with the exception of Barrett's Marbled Coronet, *Hadena luteago*, which feeds on roots and stems of Sea Campion and a few other coastal plants. Other members of this genus specialise on the seeds and seed capsules of members of the Caryophyllaceae, the campions and catchflies. When small the larvae feed within the bulbous seed capsules. However, as they grow they become too large to be fully accommodated within the capsule and they sit partially or completely outside it, feeding on the seeds within. Larvae frequently move from seed head to seed head as they consume resources and they seem to be equally able to feed on young green seeds as fully ripe and dry seeds.

Fruit-eaters attack a range of soft fruits. Perhaps the best known of these species in Britain is the Codling moth, *Cydia pomonella*, which attacks apples. Named after an old variety of apple, the codlin, or perhaps after the Saxon name of the quince, the cod-apple, this moth attacks both apples and quinces and will also attack pears and walnuts, although less frequently. The female moths fly in late May, when fruit has just set. She lays her eggs on the surface of the new fruit and the young larvae bore into it. The larvae feed on the flesh of the fruit as the fruit develops. Full-grown larvae exit the fruit before it falls and shelter in a crack in the bark of their host tree through the winter, before pupating and eclosing in the spring. Many other species of the same or closely related genera attack other types of fruit. For example, the Oriental Fruit moth, *Grapholita molesta*, attacks the fruit and shoots of peaches in Europe and other similar fruits elsewhere. Larvae of the Pea moth, *Cydia nigricana*, may be familiar to people who pod their own peas, for these larvae feed within the pods. Many species of *Cydia* are pests.

Aquatic larvae

Larvae of a few species of moth feed on the foliage of freshwater plants and have a range of adaptations for this way of life. These species, of which the china-mark moths and the Water Veneer, *Acentria ephemerella*, are best known, frequently feed below the water's surface, either by mining into their food-plant or by constructing a case or silken shelter to maintain their position on their food. These species are all members of the Pyralidae and as such have evolved from a terrestrial ancestry. Their greatest challenge is thus to obtain oxygen. Some do this by keeping an 'air store' trapped in the surface folds of their cuticle, or in hairs. Others absorb oxygen from the water directly through their cuticle. A third method is the development of tracheal gills, which may be simple or branched and which connect straight to the haemocoele. Finally the Small China-mark moth, *Cataclysta lemnata*, has slender filamentous gills running in two rows along the thoracic and abdominal segments. These do not contain tracheae and probably act as blood-gills (Scoble 1992).

The Water Veneer is unusual in several ways. Apart from having aquatic larvae that feed well below the water's surface, this is one species in which at least
the adult males do come close to fulfilling one common myth about moths,
that is that they live for only a day. In fact the males of this species may live for
two days, but rarely longer. The most remarkable feature of the species, however, concerns the females. These are of two kinds. One form is winged and
flies well. Winged females tend to embark on a dispersal flight as soon as they
have mated and before they have started to oviposit. The second form is wingless and lives, mates and oviposits in the water.

Host plant specificity

Having shown that different species of larvae feed on different parts of plants,
I now turn to the choice of plant. The larvae of some species feed in the wild
upon the leaves of just a single species of plant, as in the case of the Purple-
bordered Gold, *Idaea muricata*, which feeds on Marsh Cinquefoil, and the
Small Dark Yellow Underwing, *Anarta cordigera*, which eats Bearberry. The
same is true of some seed- or flower-feeders. Thus, the Valerian Pug, *Eupithecia
valerianata*, feeds on the seeds of Valerian, while Haworth's Pug, *E. haworthia-
ta*, feeds on the flower buds of Traveller's Joy. Others are restricted to just one
taxonomic group of plants. For example, the Diamond Back moth, *Plutella
xylostella*, is confined to the *Brassicas*. Species that exhibit these high degrees of
foodplant specificity are described as oligophagous. Such species may be compared with polyphagous moths that will feed on a wide variety of plants. Of the
British moths, the former species are much more numerous than the latter.

What determines the foodplant choices made by different species of moth?
The answer to this question is not simple, for a great many characteristics of
plants will influence their suitability as food for moth larvae. These factors
include:
i) nutritional value
ii) levels of plant defences against herbivory (such defences may be chemical,
or physical in the form of toughness or the presence of hairs or spines)
iii) size
iv) abundance and density
v) length of life
vi) distribution
vii) period of residence in a region
viii) predictability
ix) position of an individual plant in relation to other plants
x) potential to offer shelter
xi) the number of herbivores supported by the plant.

Factors iii to ix inclusive are sometimes together referred to as apparency.
Apparent plants are abundant, large, long-lived and widely distributed natives.
These will attract a greater number of herbivores than less apparent plants.
Trees are thus likely to host more moth larvae than herbs, with native species
that lack strong defences attracting most. Perhaps not surprisingly, in Britain,
the plants that support the greatest number of moth species are the native oaks
Quercus robur and *Quercus petraea*, followed by some of the birches (*Betula* spp.)
and sallows and willows (*Salix* spp.). These substantial, common, native trees
each host the larvae of over 100 species of moth in Britain. Undoubtedly, the
deciduous habit of these trees contributes to their attractiveness, for the need

Fig. 5.9 The larvae of the Pine Beauty, *Panolis flammea,* are needled conifer specialists.

to make new leaves quickly each year means that, at least initially, the new leaves are unlikely to be strongly defended chemically. It is no coincidence that the majority of larvae that feed on these trees do so when the leaves are young (p. 164). Coniferous trees, even a large common native species, such as the Scot's Pine, host a much smaller number of species (for Scot's Pine between 30 and 40). This is partly because the needles of this pine are retained on the tree for longer, so it is in the interests of the tree to allocate more defensive resources to its foliage. The structure of the pine needles may also have some defensive function, making them unattractive to some species, although some species specialise on them (Fig. 5.9).

These native species of tree can be contrasted with introduced species. The Sweet Chestnut and Horse Chestnut, which are large trees, similar in form and habit to oaks, and which have been widely planted in Britain, host less than a tenth as many species of moth as our native oaks. The Sycamore is a large, common and widespread introduced tree, which might be considered similar in some respects to birch. Yet it is host to the larvae of fewer than 20 species of moth in Britain, although the number is climbing, largely as additional polyphagous species are found feeding on it.

The role of defences in influencing herbivore numbers is best seen by considering two of our native trees, the Holly and the Yew. Holly, in addition to having long-lived and tough leaves, also has defensive spines. Only three species of British moth are known to feed on it and two of these, the Yellow-barred Brindle, *Acasis viretata* (Fig. 5.10), and the Double-striped Pug, *Gymnoscelis rufifasciata,* feed on the flowers, not the leaves. Yew is well known for its toxicity, which appears to be as effective against invertebrates as against many vertebrates, for only one species of moth, the polyphagous Willow Beauty, *Peribatodes rhomboidaria,* has managed to adapt to it.

Species of moth that feed on one or a small number of plants will, over time, become adapted to their host plants. These adaptations may take the form of chemical adaptations to the specific chemistry of their food, or adaptations to their life on a particular plant through the evolution of cryptic coloration and appropriate behaviours, or methods of dispersal upon or between plants. The more precise and sophisticated these adaptations, the less likely a species is to

Fig. 5.10 The
Yellow-barred
Brindle, *Acasis vire-
tata*, one of only
three species of
British moth that
feeds on Holly.

be able to adapt successfully and rapidly to alternative foods. When host-plant-specific moths do adopt a new foodplant, it is usually a closely related species.

Polyphagous moths are not expected to exhibit such precise adaptations as oligophagous moths. This is true to some extent. Many polyphagous noctuids, rather than having cryptic coloration that correlates precisely with their food-plant, have a more generalised disruptive coloration (p. 193) and move to unexposed situations in the lower herbage layers during the day. In addition, the digestive chemistry of some species does not appear to be adapted to the defensive chemistries of particular plants. However, many polyphagous species have a suite of characteristics that have evolved precisely to cope with their polyphagous habits. These characteristics may be grouped under the heading of phenotypic plasticity. What this means is that the traits developed by an individual may change depending on its circumstances. Two examples will suffice to illustrate the point.

A number of species that feed largely or exclusively on the foliage of decid-uous trees have what are commonly called 'stick caterpillars'. As Professor E.B. Poulton showed, in an exhaustive series of experiments in the late nineteenth century, the larvae of some species such as the Scalloped Hazel, *Odontoptera bidentata*, the Brimstone, *Opisthograptis luteolata*, and the Peppered moth, *Biston betularia*, varied according to the colour and form of their host plant (e.g. Poulton 1892). In all cases, the changes made the larvae resemble the host plant that they were fed upon (p. 190).

Much more recently, experiments investigating the possibility of genetically engineering crop plants to be resistant to pest species of moth larvae by inhibiting the action of specific digestive enzymes have shown that the larvae of some polyphagous species can circumvent the inhibitors. These larvae have the ability to manufacture additional and different enzymes that are not inhib-ited within two to four hours of feeding on transgenic food containing specif-ic inhibitors (p. 263). These results suggest that polyphagous species have a suite of genes that produce a variety of digestive enzymes and that different genes are switched on depending on the chemical characteristics of food taken in. Furthermore, it has been known for some time that polyphagous species are better at detoxifying food than oligophagous species (Krieger et al. 1971).

Foodplant predictability is an important factor in host plant choice. Many of our common annual weeds that spring up on disturbed ground, flourish for a short time and then disappear under the competition of more durable perennials are only eaten by polyphagous larvae. Thus, plants such as Shepherd's Purse, Poppy, Scarlet Pimpernel, Groundsel and Petty Spurge have no oligophagous species that are resident in Britain, although Groundsel and Petty Spurge are eaten by the migrant oligophages, the Gem, *Orthonama obstipata*, and the Spurge Hawk moth, *Hyles euphorbiae*, respectively.

One other factor is important in determining the suitability of a foodplant. That is the number of other herbivores that feed on the plant. Interspecific competition for resources is a major problem for most organisms. Selecting a host plant that is eaten by few other species would thus appear to be advantageous. However, as we have seen, the fact that few other species feed on a particular plant may be because the plant is well defended physically, or more usually chemically. There is thus likely to be a cost in adopting a host plant that is generally avoided. Yet the benefits in reduced competition seem to be sufficient to counterbalance these costs, at least for a few species. Thus, one of our most toxic plants, the Deadly Nightshade, is the host plant of a single species of British moth, *Acrolepia autumnitella*, which also feeds on Woody Nightshade. Other highly toxic plants, such as the Hemlock, Hemlock Water-dropwort and Yew are also eaten by just one or two species. A few toxic plants have rather more herbivores. Thus the Common Ragwort, which contains a range of toxic alkaloids, is eaten by 11 species, although most preferentially feed on the roots or stems or flowers and seeds, rather than the leaves.

The chemicals that plants use against herbivores are of two types: those that are highly toxic, even in small amounts (qualitative defences), and those in which the degree of defence depends upon the amount of chemical present (quantitative defences). Examples of the former include alkaloids, such as atropine found in Deadly Nightshade, taxine from Yew, and cyanogenic glucosides produced by a variety of clovers and vetches. Quantitative defensive chemicals include tougheners such as tannins that reduce the nutritive profitability of the food and make it difficult to chew and digest. Qualitative defences tend to be found in small, rather unapparent plants that grow rapidly, reproduce and then die, although there are exceptions as in the cases of taxine in Yew and cyanide in Cherry Laurel. Quantitative defences are found largely in apparent plants and particularly trees. They appear to work well once they have been laid down in sufficient quantity, but trees using such defences often suffer heavy levels of defoliation of young leaves to which little tannin has yet been allocated.

Those species of moth that have evolved to be able to feed on plants with qualitative defences cope with these very nasty defensive chemicals in one of three ways. Some chemicals are simply broken down during digestion by specialised enzymes. Others are effectively partitioned off from the rest of the food and excreted. This is the case with nicotine eaten in tobacco by the Tobacco Horn-worm, *Manduca sexta*. The third method is to sequester the chemicals, storing them as part of the larva's own defensive armoury (see p. 201).

It is interesting to note that foodplant specificity may vary in different parts of a species' range. In some cases this is purely a function of the distribution of different species of plant that larvae can use effectively. However, there are some species that may be considered polyphagous in parts of their range, but that are rather choosy in other locations. This is the case with the Scarlet Tiger moth, *Callimorpha dominula*. This species is found on a wide range of herbaceous plants on the Continent. However, in Britain, larvae in the wild are almost invariably found on Comfrey. If collected, these larvae are capable of feeding up without detriment on other plants, such as White Dead Nettle. Laurence Cook, who first researched the foodplant preferences of this species, has suggested that the Scarlet Tiger moth is on the edge of its range in Britain, and here, it uses a specific foodplant as an indicator of a high quality habitat (Cook 1961). This pattern of greater host plant or habitat specialisation towards the edge of a species' range is seen in many other species, although it has been researched in very few. Perhaps the best-known case among the British Lepidoptera is the Swallow-tail butterfly, *Papilio machaon*, which in Britain is confined to the lowland fens and broads of East Anglia, where it feeds almost exclusively on a single host plant, Milk-parsley. On the Continent, it is found at altitudes up to 2,000 metres and the larvae feed on the foliage of a wide range of umbelliferous plants.

Larvae that do not feed on living plants

As already mentioned, not all moth larvae feed on living plant material. Larvae of the incurvariid genus, *Nematopogon*, feed mainly on dead leaves. Many of the species in the subfamily Oecophorinae feed on dead and decaying wood. Several species of pyralid feed on human produce of plant origin. For example, the Gold Triangle, *Hypsopygia costalis*, feeds on almost any dry vegetable matter, while the Meal moth, *Pyralis farinalis*, and the Painted Meal moth, *Pyralis pictalis*, feed just on stored cereals and dry hay. Tineids of the genus *Nemapogon* normally feed on bracket fungi, although the Corn moth, *Nemapogon granella*, and the Cork moth, *Nemapogon cloacella*, will feed on stored vegetable produce. The larvae of other tineids feed on animal matter. Thus the Fur moth, *Monopis laevigella*, feeds on dead birds and mammals and may also be found feeding in the remnants of the prey of owls that are discarded in owl pellets. The larvae of several species of tineid will attack clothes made out of animal fibres. These include the Common Clothes moth, *Tineola bisselliella*, the Case-bearing Clothes moth, *Tinea pellionella*, and the Large Pale Clothes moth, *Tinea pallescentella*, all of which breed continuously indoors, but also occur outside, usually in mammal or birds' nests. Some tineids are highly specialised. Larvae of *Triaxomasia caprimulgella* are reputed to feed on dead insects caught in spiders' webs. The two species of *Ceratophaga* on the British list, both of which have been reported as very rare accidental introductions from southern Asia, both feed on the hooves and horns of dead animals.

The larvae of the Wax moth, *Galleria mellonella*, the Lesser Wax moth, *Achroia grisella*, and the Bee moth, *Aphomia sociella*, all feed on the honeycomb in nests of bees.

A small number of species of moth have predatory larvae. In Britain, most of these, which include species such as the Satellite, *Eupsilia transversa*, and the Dun-bar, *Cosmia trapezina*, feed both on leaves and on other larvae of their own or other species. This predatory habit is taken further by the larvae of the Silky Wainscot, *Chilodes maritimus*, which hunt, kill and feed on moth larvae and other insects in the stems of Common Reed.

The foods of adult moths

Blood, sweat and tears

Adult moths, if they feed at all, have a largely liquid diet. This liquid can take a wide variety of forms. Most commonly it is nectar from flowers, but many species will feed on tree sap or rotting fruit or vegetation, when these are available. More rarely, moths may suck up liquid from the ground, feed on the liquefying remains of dead animals or suck secretions from live animals. For example, *Lobocraspis griseifusa* sucks tears (or lachrymal fluid) from the eyes of mammals such as Water Buffalo. Dr Hans Bänziger (1983) has published photographs of groups of these lachryphagous (tear-feeding) moths clustered in orderly fashion around the eyes of various large mammals.

A few moths have a proboscis that is capable of piercing solid material. Perhaps the most well-known example in Britain is the Death's Head Hawk moth, *Acherontia atropos*, which enters bee nests and is then capable of using its rather short and thick proboscis to pierce the waxen cells to steal honey. Elsewhere, particularly in the tropics, some moths pierce plant or animal material to obtain food. Thus some moths of the family Noctuidae, such as *Calpe thalictri*, are known to thrust their proboscis through the skin of citrus fruits to suck juice from within (Bänziger 1970). Perhaps most spectacularly, some noctuids can pierce mammalian skin and suck blood. The moth *Calpe eustrigata*, a Southeast Asian species, is capable of piercing and feeding from animals generally considered to have very tough hides, such as the Indian Elephant and the Black Rhino (Bänziger 1975).

The proboscis of these fruit and mammal piercers is specifically adapted to its role. It is thicker, more heavily sclerotised, particularly at the tip, and has a range of hooks and barbs for tearing the skin and helping to stay embedded during feeding. In addition, the proboscis muscles are more numerous and stronger than those of species with other diets. As the moth feeds, it may withdraw the proboscis slightly and push it back in. The barbs lining the proboscis thus rend the flesh further, maintaining the flow of blood.

Nectar- and sap-suckers

Tear- and blood-drinking moths are exceptional. Most adult moths that feed take in nectar or other plant-derived fluids, such as sap. In some species this food is used largely to power flight, eggs already being fully resourced when females eclose. In others, adult feeding is essential to mature the eggs. Food is sucked up through the proboscis. The proboscises of different species are of different lengths, which imposes some limitation on the flowers that can be profitably visited. Flowers with long corolla tubes are only worth visiting for moths with long enough proboscises. Many moths hover in front of flowers to feed, inserting the proboscis while in flight (Plate 5b). Others steady themselves with just the front tarsal claws holding onto the lower petal of the flower. The majority, however, land on the flower to feed. Some remain with their wings held in a posture instantly ready for flight. Others, particularly the noctuids, close their wings down into the resting posture (Fig. 5.11).

Food is a major element in the biology of all organisms and in moths the availability of suitable food is a crucial factor in determining which species of moth are found where. As we have seen, some species are very picky about

Fig. 5.11 A Common Wainscot, *Mythimna pallens,* feeding at a Ragwort flower.

their choice of food, others are much more catholic in their diet. Host plant or other food specificity thus plays a critical role in habitat selection for many moths. Just as with food, some species of moth may be restricted to a single habitat type, while others will survive and reproduce in a wide variety of habitats. It is to the causes and consequences of the habitat choices made by moths that I now turn.

Habitat specificity

Many species of moth are strongly restricted to specific habitats. Other species are more wide ranging and appear to thrive in a diverse array of habitat types. Often habitat choice is determined by foodplant preferences and the availability of preferred food. Species that feed on just one or a small number of plant species tend to have more specialised habitat preferences than polyphagous species, which are more likely to be habitat generalists. However, this is not always the case and some polyphagous species are still restricted to rather precisely defined habitat types.

A classification of habitat types has always been problematic because the level of division into different habitat types is bound to be somewhat subjective. However, the major habitat types that might be considered in Britain are listed, with some subdivision, in Table 5.1. In this table, a brief description of the habitats is given, together with a small sample of species of moth that might be considered characteristic of the habitat. These lists of examples are not exhaustive, and some species could certainly be included as species that are characteristic of and common in more than one habitat type.

In Britain we have over 2,000 species of moth and if detailed enough criteria are used for division, an almost infinite variety of habitat types could be categorised. Thus even if the habitat descriptions given were rather coarse and only the main reasons underlying the habitat preference for each species (if known) were used, a comprehensive listing of the habitat preferences of the British moths and their reasons would be tremendously complex. The problem is that there are too many habitats, habitats are too complex and the perspective of a habitat is different for different species of organism.

Table 5.1 Major habitat types found in the British Isles with a small sample of moth species characteristic of each habitat type. (Major source of information, Heath 1976)

Habitat type and description (major divisions in bold: subdivisions in italics).	Example species
Uplands (including some lowland habitats in exposed situations in the extreme north of Scotland and on some of the northern islands) (Fig. 5.12): vegetation above the tree line is dominated by low-growing shrubs, such as Heather, Ling, Bilberry, Crowberry, Dwarf Birch, Least Sallow, Mountain Avens (Fig. 5.13) and various mat grasses and club rushes. Many of these habitats feature large areas of deep blanket bogs (Fig. 5.14).	Grey Mountain Carpet, *Entephria caesiata* (Fig. 5.15); Pretty Pinion, *Perizoma blandiata* (Fig. 5.16); Northern Dart, *Xestia alpicola*, (Fig. 5.17); Small Dark Yellow Underwing, *Anarta cordigera*; Broad-bordered White Underwing, *Anarta melanopa*.
Lowland peatlands a) *Acid peat bogs*: wet or waterlogged ground with acidic soils consisting largely of semi-decayed organic material under anaerobic conditions. Vegetation is a mosaic of sphagnum moss, heathers and grasses, with birch encroachment on drier areas.	Oak Eggar, *Lasiocampa quercus*; Emperor moth, *Saturnia pavonia*; Purple-bordered Gold, *Idaea muricata*; Clouded Buff, *Diacrisia sannio*; Marsh Oblique-barred, *Hypenodes humidalis*.
b) *Alkaline fenlands*: an alkaline soil habitat, now usually maintained by management, produced in the transition from open water to dry land by drainage. Dominated by Common Reed and Reed-mace (Fig. 5.18), often with Alder and sallow carr.	Marsh Carpet, *Perizoma sagittata;* Dotted Footman, *Pelosia muscerda*; Flame Wainscot, *Senta flammea*; Bulrush Wainscot, *Nonagria typhae*; Silver Barred, *Deltote bankiana*.
Heaths and grasslands a) *Chalk and limestone grassland*: grasslands, often maintained by grazing, on base-rich rock formations. Chalk grasslands occur mainly in South East England, while limestones occur more in the north and west, including the Burren in County Clare. Florally diverse.	Chalk Carpet, *Scotopteryx bipunctaria*; Pretty Chalk Carpet, *Melanthia procellata*; Straw Belle, *Aspitates gilvaria*; Light Feathered Rustic, *Agrotis cinerea*; Dusky Sallow, *Eremobia ochroleuca* (Fig. 5.19).
b) *Breckland heath*: an unusual grassland heath on lowland sandy soils, overlying chalk, with low rainfall and, for Britain, warm summers and cool winters (Fig. 5.20). Large areas of this East Anglian heath have been cultivated or forested, but about 8,000 hectares remain uncultivated.	Grey Carpet, *Lithostege griseata*; White-line Dart, *Euxoa tritici*; White colon, *Sideridis albicolon*; Viper's Bugloss, *Hadena irregularis*; The Mullein, *Cucullia verbasci* (Fig. 5.21).
c) *Acid heath*: dry lowland heaths on acidic soils, dominated by heather and ling, with encroachment by gorse, pines and birches (Fig. 5.22).	Horse Chestnut, *Pachycnemia hippocastanaria*; Bordered Grey, *Selidosema brunnearia*; Common Heath, *Ematurga atomaria*; True Lover's Knot, *Lycophotia porphyrea* (Fig. 5.23), Beautiful Yellow Underwing, *Anarta myrtilli* (Fig. 5.24).

Table 5.1 (cont.)

Habitat type and description (major divisions in bold: subdivisions in italics).	Example species
d) *Arable farmland*: Variable habitat characteristics depending on crop types, rotation and levels of fertilisation. Often with low floral diversity.	Brighton Wainscot, *Oria musculosa*; Barred Straw, *Eulithis pyraliata* (Fig. 5.25); Light Arches, *Apamea lithoxylaea*; Nutmeg, *Discea trifolii*; Turnip moth, *Agrotis segetum*.
e) *Hedgerows*: Variable floral composition, dominated by trees or shrubs that will tolerate regular cutting. Moths associated with hedgerows include species that may also frequent deciduous woodland, or species associated with the ground flora under the hedges.	Chinese Character, *Cilix glaucata*; Treble Brown Spot, *Idaea trigeminata*; Shoulder Stripe, *Anticlea badiata* (Fig. 5.26); Dark-barred Twin-spot Carpet, *Xanthorhoe ferrugata*, Yellow-tail, *Euproctis similis* (Fig. 5.27).
Scrublands: Habitats that develop over grassland as shrubs and small trees encroach and establish. Scrub composition varies, but may include species such as Privet, Elder, Hawthorn, Blackthorn, Buckthorn, Dogwood, Hazel, Box and Juniper and introduced species such as Buddleia. Most often occurs on sloping ground where the gradient and lack of soil depth prevent full woodland developing.	Lackey, *Malacosoma neustria*; Pinion-spotted Pug, *Eupithecia insigniata*; Yellow Shell, *Camptogramma bilineata* (Fig. 5.28); Brown-tail, *Euproctis chrysorrhoea*; Pale Tussock, *Calliteara pudibunda* (Fig. 5.29).
Woodlands a) *Deciduous woodland*: very variable as a result of differences in the tree species composition in different regions and on different soils with differing drainage characteristics. Very little ancient deciduous woodland remains (Fig. 5.30). Most has been planted or severely managed by man.	Pebble Hook-tip, *Drepana falcataria* (Fig. 5.31); Large Emerald, *Geometra papilionaria* (Fig. 5.32); Great Oak Beauty, *Boarmia roboraria*; Scarce Prominent, *Odontosia carmelita* (Fig. 5.33); Four-dotted Footman, *Cybosia mesomella* (Fig. 5.34).
b) *Coniferous woodland*: relict native pine forests in Scotland support a diverse array of species (Fig. 5.35). However, most conifer woodlands elsewhere are planted and involve non-native trees, which themselves support rather few moth species (Fig. 5.36). In close plantations, little ground flora is present. However, in more open woodlands and those with wide rides or firebreaks, the ground flora can support a diverse array of species.	Grey Pine Carpet, *Thera obeliscata* (Fig. 5.37); Tawny-barred Angle, *Semiothisa liturata*; Satin Beauty, *Deileptenia ribeata*; Pine Hawk moth, *Hyloicus pinastri*; Pine Beauty, *Panolis flammea*.

Table 5.1 (cont.)

Habitat type and description (major divisions in bold: subdivisions in italics).	Example species
Disturbed habitats (including domestic gardens, urban and suburban parklands, railway and road embankments etc.): highly variable, characterised by highly fertile soils, great floral diversity, including many non-native and exotic species, and often regular disturbance.	Common Swift, *Hepialus lupulinus*; Latticed Heath, *Semiothisa clathrata* (Fig. 5.38); Buff Ermine, *Spilosoma luteum*; Heart and Dart, *Agrotis exclamationis*; Varied Coronet, *Hadena compta* (Fig. 5.39).
Freshwater related habitats a) *Still and slow moving water bodies*: water bodies supporting freshwater aquatic vegetation may occur in most of the above habitats (Fig. 5.40). A few species of moth are associated specifically with these habitats as their larvae feed on submerged vegetation (p. 115).	Brown China-mark, *Elophila nymphaeata*; Beautiful China-mark, *Nymphula stagnata*; Ringed China-mark, *Parapoynx stratiotata*; Water Veneer, *Acentria ephemerella*.
b) *Unstable river shingles*: the edges of some fast-moving rivers support shifting shingle banks that provide an unusual habitat (Fig. 5.41). Several species of moth utilise the vegetation that colonises this habitat, although none of the species appears confined to this habitat.	Narrow-bordered Five-spot Burnet, *Zygaena lonicera* (Fig. 5.42); Shaded Broad-bar, *Scotopteryx chenopodiata*; Netted Pug, *Eupithecia venosata*; Cinnabar, *Tyria jacobaeae*; Shark, *Cucullia umbratica* (Fig. 5.43).
Coastlands a) *Saltmarshes*: flat lands on the edge of river estuaries and on sheltered bays. Characterised by a very specific flora.	Rivulet, *Perizoma affinitana*; Scarce Pug, *Eupithecia extensaria*; Ground Lackey, *Malacosoma castrensis*; Essex Emerald, *Thetidia smaragdaria*; Star-wort, *Cucullia asteris* (Fig. 5.44).
b) *Sand dunes*: areas of sand alternating hills and hollows. Dunes may be relatively stable or very unstable. Stability depends on exposure and the extent of root systems of the flora on the dunes. Hollows between dunes may give rise to wet slacks with a rich and diverse flora. (Fig. 5.45)	Coast Dart, *Euxoa cursoria*; Sand Dart, *Agrotis ripae*; Portland moth, *Ochropleura praecox*; Belted Beauty, *Lycia zonaria*; Yellow Belle, *Aspitates ochreararia*.
c) *Shingle beaches*: when shingle beaches support vegetation, they constitute an important specialised habitat that is generally rare in Europe. Few large areas of this type of habitat remain.	Sussex Emerald, *Thalera fimbrialis*; Grass Rivulet, *Perizoma albulata* (Fig. 5.46); Pygmy Footman, *Eilema pygmaeola*; White Spot, *Hadena albimacula*; Toadflax Brocade, *Calophasia lunula*.
d) *Cliffs*: high gradient cliffs provide a refuge from disturbance for some species of moth. Vegetation is often highly specialised, but depends on the geology of the cliff (Fig. 5.47).	Isle of Wight Wave, *Idaea humiliata*; Portland Riband Wave, *Idaea degeneraria*; Black-banded, *Polymixis xanthomista*; The Grey, *Hadena caesia*; Beautiful Gothic, *Leucochlaena oditis*.

Fig. 5.12 Uplands, above the tree line, Sutherland.

Fig. 5.13 Mountain Avens.

Fig. 5.14 An upland bog, Sutherland.

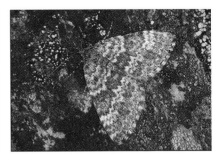

Fig. 5.15 The Grey Mountain Carpet, *Entephria caesiata.*

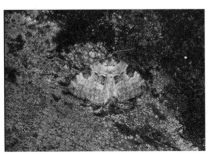

Fig. 5.16 The Pretty Pinion, *Perizoma blandiata.*

Fig. 5.17 The Northern Dart, *Xestia alpicola.*

Fig. 5.18 Common Reed and Reed-mace fen, Cambridgeshire.

Fig. 5.19 Dusky Sallow, *Eremobia ochroleuca.*

Fig. 5.20 Breckland heath, Suffolk.

Fig. 5.21 The Mullein, *Cucullia verbasci*.

Fig. 5.22 Acid heathland, Hampshire.

Fig. 5.23 True Lover's Knot, *Lycophotia porphyrea*.

Fig. 5.24 Larva of the Beautiful Yellow Underwing, *Anarta myrtilli*.

Fig. 5.25 The Barred Straw, *Eulithis pyraliata*.

Fig. 5.26 The Shoulder Stripe, *Anticlea badiata*.

Fig. 5.27 The Yellow-tail, *Euproctis similis*.

Fig. 5.28 The Yellow Shell, *Camptogramma bilineata.*

Fig. 5.29 The Pale Tussock, *Calliteara pudibunda.*

Fig. 5.30 A small, inaccessible piece of deciduous woodland in a coastal gully, Isle of Man.

Fig. 5.31 Pebble Hook-tip, *Drepana falcataria.*

Fig. 5.32 Large Emerald, *Geometra papilionaria.*

Fig. 5.33 The Scarce Prominent, *Odontosia carmelita.*

Fig. 5.34 Four-dotted Footman, *Cybosia mesomella.*

Fig. 5.35 Natural conifer forest in Rannoch Black Wood.

Fig. 5.36 A conifer plantation, Suffolk.

Fig. 5.37 Grey Pine Carpet, *Thera obeliscata.*

Fig. 5.38 Latticed Heath, *Semiothisa clathrata.*

Fig. 5.39 Varied Coronet, *Hadena compta.*

Fig. 5.40 An artificial lake, Surrey.

Fig. 5.41 Unstable river shingle, Dyfed.

Fig. 5.42 Narrow-bordered Five-spot Burnet, *Zygaena lonicera.*

Fig. 5.43 The Shark, *Cucullia umbratica.*

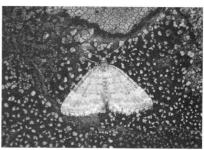

Fig. 5.44 (above) Larva of the Star-wort,
Cucullia asteris. (Courtesy John
Bebbington.)
Fig. 5.45 (top right) Sand dune, Sutherland.
Fig. 5.47 (middle right) Coastal cliffs on the
Isle of Man.
Fig. 5.46 (bottom right) Grass Rivulet, *Perizoma
albulata.*

Habitat favourability

Professor T.R.E. Southwood, appreciating the need for a simple classification
of habitats, considered the problem of extreme habitat diversity from the point
of view of any specified organism. He argued that a habitat could be either
favourable or unfavourable for a particular species. He defined favourable as
allowing reproduction and full development. He saw that a particular habitat
could then vary in favourability in both time and space.

Southwood (1977) recognised just four classes of habitat with respect to
time. These are constant habitats, which are always favourable; seasonal ones
in which favourable periods alternate regularly with unfavourable periods;
unpredictable ones where favourable periods of variable duration are interspersed with unfavourable conditions of variable length; and ephemeral ones
where a short favourable period is followed by an indeterminately long
unfavourable period. Notably, the periods of unfavourability in an unpredictable habitat are shorter than the period of time that the specified organism can survive in unfavourable conditions. Conversely, this length of time in
an ephemeral habitat is longer than a species can survive.

In terms of space, Southwood proposed just three classes. A continuous habitat was one in which the area of favourable habitat is more extensive than the dispersal range of the organism. A patchy habitat comprises a mosaic of areas of favourable habitat and areas of unfavourable habitat, with the favourable patches being close enough to each other for organisms to move from one to another. Finally, an isolated habitat involves a limited favourable area at a distance from the nearest other favourable patch greater than the dispersal range of the organism.

The four time and three space classes can be combined in any combination to give just 12 habitat classes (Box 5.1). It is not difficult to see that life cannot be sustained in two of these classes. Organisms in a continuous ephemeral habitat would flourish for a time, but once the habitat became unfavourable for a period longer than their lifespan, they would die out. Similarly, organisms in an isolated ephemeral habitat would suffer the same fate, as, by definition, they are too far away from the nearest favourable patch to reach it when their own natal patch becomes unfavourable. In the consideration of this type of classification, it is important to consider the whole of an organism's life cycle. For example, hot deserts, which may appear ephemeral habitats, may sustain life in species that produce at least one life history stage capable of becoming dormant for long periods. It is, for example, amazing to see an apparently sterile desert burst into flower when rains come as a result of the dormant seed bank that is catalysed into life by the coming of water.

This generalised type of habitat classification is very different from a descriptive habitat classification based on the pervading environmental factors (for example, hot desert) or the dominant species of organism present (for example, oak woodland), for it is based on the organism under consideration. It is of great value in assessing the nature of specific environments in respect of

---

Box 5.1 Southwood's habitat classification. Habitats are categorised in terms of their favourability, in time and space, to the organism under consideration.

In respect of time:
a) Constant: always favourable.
b) Seasonal: periods of favourable and unfavourable conditions alternate in a regular temporal pattern (for example, summer/winter, wet/dry).
c) Unpredictable: favourable periods are interspersed by periods of unfavourable conditions of variable length that are not longer than the organism's life cycle.
d) Ephemeral: favourable periods, often of short duration, are interspersed with unfavourable periods of varying lengths, some of which are longer than the organism's life cycle.

In respect of space:
i) Continuous: the area of favourable habitat is more extensive than the organism's dispersal range.
ii) Patchy: favourable patches, although divided by unfavourable habitats, are close enough to each other for organisms to move from one to another.
iii) Isolated: favourable patches are divided from each other by unfavourable habitat of greater extent than the dispersal range of the organism under consideration.

The temporal and spatial classes are combined to give 12 habitat classes, for example, constant patchy or unpredictable isolated. Two of these, ephemeral continuous and ephemeral isolated, cannot sustain an organism, leaving ten viable habitat classes that can support organisms.

particular species of moth and helps to simplify the way that we may think of and order the almost infinite variety of habitat divisions and subdivisions.

Moths in unfavourable habitats

Moths in winter

For many British moths the winter is generally unfavourable and has to be spent in some form of dormant state. Different species pass the winter in different stages (Table 5.2), and of course some species are active and reproduce during the winter.

Table 5.2 Number of species of British moths that overwinter in each life history stage. Macrolepidoptera are given by family. (Following Young (1997), the winter is taken as January.)

Taxonomic group	Overwinter as:			
	Eggs	Larvae	Pupae	Adults
Microlepidoptera	24	675	240	98
Hepialidae		5		
Cossidae		3		
Zygaenidae		10		
Sesiidae		14		
Lasiocampidae	5	4	2	
Saturniidae			1	
Endromidae			1	
Drepanidae			6	
Thyatiridae	1		8	
Geometridae	41	88	152	7
Sphingidae			9	
Notodontidae	2		21	
Lymantriidae	3	7	1	
Arctiidae		23	7	
Nolidae		4	1	
Noctuidae	71	139	94	16
Totals	**147**	**972**	**543**	**121**

Usually the relationship between a species and its habitat is investigated at times when conditions are broadly favourable and moths, at whatever stage, are active, feeding, metamorphosing, or reproducing. However, in Britain, conditions are unfavourable for most moths for a substantial proportion of the year, the winter.

Perhaps the biggest problem is that of subzero temperatures. Moths have a number of ways of coping with freezing temperatures. Some simply allow their body contents to be frozen. These species are said to be freeze tolerant. Others have evolved physiological or behavioural adaptations that prevent freezing. Typically these involve mechanisms that reduce the water content of cells, and/or the addition of antifreeze chemicals, such as glycerol, both of which serve to lower the freezing point well below 0°C. Behavioural adaptations involve selecting sites with relatively high temperatures, for example deep in the soil, or under a cover of snow. In freeze-avoiding species, physiological and behavioural mechanisms to prevent a species being exposed to temperatures below the freezing point of its cells generally act together.

The unfavourability of the winter derives largely from low temperatures and other adverse weather conditions, such as high winds, heavy rainfall and sometimes snow. In addition to low temperatures, winter is a problem because the larval and adult foods of many species of moth are scarce or absent in winter. Fewer plants flower in the winter than at other times of the year, so nectar will be in short supply. Similarly, deciduous trees and many other plants lose most or all of their foliage during the winter. These winter-brown plants will provide no food for leaf-eating larvae. It would seem probable, therefore, that the majority of moths would pass the winter in one of the non-feeding stages. However, this is not the case.

Over half British species pass the coldest month of the winter, January, as larvae, with two-thirds of the remainder overwintering as pupae. The numbers that overwinter as eggs and adults are roughly the same, comprising 8% and 7% of British species respectively. There are strong family biases in some cases. For example, all our resident hawk moths pass the winter as pupae, while all the zygaenids overwinter as larvae. Indeed, most families show some bias to one or two stages. The most dramatic example is that of the members of the Coleophoridae, of which all 101 British species, for which data are available, pass the winter as larvae. However, some groups buck this trend. Thus, the subfamily Cuculliinae contains species that overwinter in each stage (egg – 23 species, larvae – 8 species, pupae – 11 species and adult – 12 species).

There are two main factors to be considered when trying to fathom why a particular species passes the winter in a particular stage. First, we may ask in which stage it is most likely to be able to survive the winter. Second, we should consider whether there are constraints in respect of other parts of the life cycle, which determine that these stages should occur when conditions are favourable.

Overwintering as eggs

Species that overwinter as eggs are essentially of two kinds: those in which eggs are laid in the late summer or early autumn and do not hatch until the spring, and those in which the eggs are laid in the cold months of winter. The former group includes species such as the Rannoch Looper, *Semiothisa brunneata*, and the Minor Shoulder-knot, *Brachylomia viminalis*. Species showing this pattern must have two influences on embryonic development. First, some factor must prevent the embryos developing in the warmth of the summer. Second, there must be some cue that causes the embryos to begin developing after the winter. Tests on the Minor Shoulder-knot suggest that the eggs have to pass through a cold period before they will begin to develop. As yet, it is not known whether increased day length or increased temperature initiates embryonic development in the spring.

The second group of species that overwinter as eggs spends part of the winter as adults. This group includes the winter active geometrids and tortricoids. In these species, it seems probable that low temperatures in the winter are sufficient to arrest embryonic development, and the requirement is that the embryo should hatch precisely when food becomes available. For most species this is when deciduous trees begin to come into leaf. Early hatchers suffer losses from lack of food, while late hatchers may suffer intense competition and possible starvation in areas where there is considerable defoliation. Moreover, late hatchers may find the food less nutritious and more heavily defended by tannins and other defensive plant chemicals.

Larvae in winter

Of the species that overwinter as larvae, some do so within their food. This is the case for many stem- and root-borers. Most species that feed on decaying matter also overwinter as larvae. These species will frequently feed during warm periods in the winter. The same is true of a few exposed leaf-feeders. These species become quiescent during cold periods in winter, but retain the ability to become active if temperatures rise. The majority of species that overwinter as larvae, however, employ another strategy. They enter a period of diapause, in which the metabolic rate, initially lowered by a cue such as day length or temperature, remains low, even if temperatures increase. Diapausing species have the advantage of conserving energy reserves. In most species of British moth that have a winter diapause, this state is broken by day-length cues. Day-length cues have the advantage over temperature or other climatic cues of being more predictable. The precise day length that causes larvae to enter or break diapause varies between species and also within species, where it is frequently correlated with latitude.

The case-building larvae of the Coleophoridae all overwinter as larvae within their cases. These larvae, most of which feed on the leaves of deciduous trees or plants or on seeds, enter diapause in the late autumn. Some are fully fed when they enter diapause, while others feed again in the spring. That this family exclusively overwinters in the larval stage suggests that the case constructed by the larva gives it reasonable protection against the rigours of winter.

In other species that become fully fed in the autumn but do not pupate until the spring, the reason is not so obvious.

Pupae in winter

One obvious advantage of passing the winter in the pupal stage is that the adult moths may then be ready to emerge in the spring or early summer at favourable times when flowers and so nectar resources are most plentiful. Some species that overwinter as pupae eclose in the spring, taking advantage of nectar in sallow blossom (Plate 5f). This is particularly the case with members of the genus *Orthosia*, the Hebrew Character, *Orthosia gothica*, being a good example (Plate 5e). Eggs laid by these species hatch in the late spring or early summer and so larvae gain access to the young foliage of deciduous trees on which most feed. Other species that overwinter as pupae eclose somewhat later, in the early summer, when they are less likely to be affected by the high winds and heavy showers characteristic of March and April in Britain.

Many species that overwinter as pupae, including all the hawk moths that are resident in Britain, pupate in a subterranean cell. However, some species, such as the Emperor moth, *Saturnia pavonia*, and the Puss moth, *Cerura vinula*, overwinter above ground in protective cocoons spun on or amongst plant substrates.

Overwintering adults

Species that are adult in winter are of three types. First, there are those that eclose, mate, oviposit and die in the winter. These include a number of microlepidoptera and a number of geometrids. Many, but not all, of these geometrids have females lacking wings capable of flight. This adaptation and the habits of these species are discussed on page 195.

The second group that overwinters as adults comprises those that eclose in the autumn and then survive as adults through the winter before reproducing. Examples include the Red Sword-grass, *Xylena vetusta*, (Fig. 5.48), the Satellite, *Eupsilia transversa*, the Chestnut, *Conistra vaccinii*, and several other members of the subfamily Cuculliinae. Critically in these species, both males and females survive until the spring. Some species are known to feed on blossom and tree sap in mild spells during the winter. Most lay eggs in April, although the Dark Chestnut, *Conistra ligula*, and the Black-banded moth, *Polymixis xanthomista*, lay early, usually in March, and the Chestnut and the Orange Upperwing, *Jodia croceago*, typically do not oviposit until May. Exceptionally among moths in which both males and females overwinter as adults, in the Tissue moth, *Triphosa dubiata*, mating seems to occur exclusively in late autumn although eggs are not then laid until May (Morris & Collins 1991).

The third group comprises a small number of species that eclose in the autumn and mate. The males then die and it is only the females that survive the winter to oviposit in the early spring. Examples include the Brindled Ochre, *Dasypolia templi*, which lays its eggs in March, and the Autumn Green Carpet, *Chloroclysta miata*, which oviposits in May.

The locations where adults that do not oviposit in the middle of winter rest up during the dark months are diverse, but are generally sheltered, out-of-the-way places. Many species, particularly some of the small micros, squeeze into cracks in or under bark. Others reside in leaf litter or piles of fallen wood, generally selecting a fairly dry site. Some of the larger species overwinter in hollow trees, caves or unheated garden sheds or outhouses. Thus, for example, I have found Satellites, Chestnuts, Dark Chestnuts, Heralds, *Scoliopteryx libatrix*, and Tissue moths in such places, old underground ice-cellars being a particularly good place to find most of these species.

Migration: an alternative

Becoming specifically adapted to cope with conditions that are unfavourable to most other species may be beneficial as species that do so may avoid intense interspecific competition. Sitting out unfavourable conditions in an inactive or

Fig. 5.48 The Red Sword-grass, *Xylena vetusta*, overwinters as an adult.

dormant state is an alternative way of coping with harsh conditions. A third strategy is simply to disperse away from habitats that have become unfavourable. Seasonal migrations are a common and well-known feature of many species of bird. Many moths also move from unfavourable habitats, dispersal giving the possibility of finding more favourable conditions elsewhere. It is the subjects of dispersal and migration and the effects that these have on moth distributions that I will devote myself to in Chapter 6.

6

Flight, Dispersal and Distributions

To stay put or to move

In Chapter 5, the importance of habitat favourability was discussed. Most moth individuals, once in a favourable habitat, adopt a more or less stay-at-home attitude. Movement during life is restricted to larvae walking amongst plant material to find food, female adult moths flying short distances to find nectar and oviposition sites and males flying somewhat more to find nectar and mates. However, in many of these sedentary species, some individuals will disperse away from their favourable natal habitat patch. Other species are great dispersers, regularly engaging in long-distance migrations. For example, species such as the Convolvulus Hawk moth, *Agrius convolvuli*, the Silver Y, *Autographa gamma*, and the Diamond Back moth, *Plutella xylostella*, are regularly found on oil-drilling platforms in the North Sea (Young 1981). There is a complete gradation between these two extremes. In this chapter, migration into and out of populations, the second factor affecting population size, will be discussed. In doing so, the formal differences between dispersal and migration will be explained. The way that moths fly and navigate will be described. Finally, some of the factors that affect the geographic distributions of moths will be considered.

Dispersal versus migration

At the outset it is necessary to try to describe the difference between dispersal and migration. This is not easy because different types of biologist use the two words in different ways. Here, for simplicity, I will follow Douglas (1986) and take migration to mean movement in a specific direction and dispersal to mean undirected movement. Thus, the northerly flight of many of our regular immigrants from southern Europe may be considered migration, whereas the movement of larvae from plant to plant to find food would be considered dispersal. Yet in practice it is often difficult to decide where to draw the line between these two. For instance, does the directed flight of a male moth along a plume of pheromones produced by a female constitute migration or dispersal?

Johnson (1969) tried to define migration in a rather more conceptual manner. He saw migration as involving four elements. First, migration usually begins where adults emerge from pupae and terminates where they reproduce. In this way migration involves a journey between one breeding habitat and another. Second, the movement is active rather than accidental. Third, Johnson saw migration as a one-way journey for the individual. Once started on a migration, the individual would continue until it reached another suitable breeding habitat. It would not turn around to return to its starting point. Fourth, migration, because it involves moving from one breeding habitat to another, must involve females. It cannot simply be the movement of males to find females, even if this movement is directed.

Johnson's conceptual definition of migration is helpful, but it has its limitations. For example, anyone who has seen the mass movements of the larvae of species such as the Mediterranean Brocade, *Spodoptera littoralis*, or the Cosmopolitan, *Harpyia loreyi*, two of the notorious army worms of Africa and elsewhere, would certainly describe them as mass migrations. However, these difficulties over definitions should perhaps not delay us further. In most instances, whether movement is described as migration or dispersal matters less than the ecological consequences of the movement to the moth.

Methods of locomotion

Moths have three main ways of moving. First, the adults of most species can fly. Second, both adults and larvae can walk. Third, larvae can move by producing threads of silk. In most instances walking will involve movements over relatively short distances and need not detain us much in this chapter. Flight, on the other hand, may involve short-distance or long-distance movement.

The role of movement on threads of silk is more problematic. Some larvae that use this method to get from one location to another do so in three types of situation. First, they generate silk and attach a strand to the substrate as they feed or when at rest, so that if they are dislodged from their foodplant they have a safety line that they can climb back up to return to suitable food. Second, they may lower themselves from feeding sites in trees to the ground below before pupating on or under the ground. Most crucially in respect of dispersal, they may, when in the first instar, generate a strand of silk, hang from it, and then be transported away on the wind. By this method they may be dispersed considerable distances as part of the 'aerial plankton'. Usually, this strategy is adopted by larvae that are faced with a lack of appropriate food. The most common situation is when eggs are laid on twigs of deciduous trees and the eggs hatch before bud-burst. Larvae of species such as the winter moths *Operophtera brumata* and *Operophtera fagata*, the Dotted Border, *Agriopis marginaria*, the March moth, *Alsophila aescularia*, the autumnal and November moths of the genus *Epirrita* and the Mottled Umber, *Erannis defoliaria*, are frequently found as an element of the aerial plankton in late April and early May.

Flight

How do moths fly?

The ability to fly is the most important attribute of most moths with respect to dispersal. Moths fly largely by flapping their wings, although for some species gliding is a significant element of their flight pattern, particularly at higher speeds. The aerodynamics of moth flight are complex. Early attempts to explain moth flight in terms of the aerodynamic forces that had been analysed in respect of lift and drag from fixed wings, such as those of aeroplanes, were flawed. The forces generated were simply not great enough to allow most moths to fly. In particular, these forces could not support the body weight during the hovering flight seen in many species when feeding upon nectar (Plate 5b). Professor Charlie Ellington (1984) showed that additional forces resulting from the flapping action of the wings must play a crucial role in flight.

When a moth flaps its wings it continually changes the angle of the wings. The angle of the wings in relation to the direction of movement is known as the angle of attack. As this angle of attack changes, it causes turbulence or vortices in the flow of air around the wing. When the wing flaps, a vortex is created that forces air downwards, thereby creating lift. The vortices created by the movements of the wings and by the rotation of the angle of attack at the bottom of the downstroke and the top of the upstroke play a crucial role in the generation of the considerable forces needed for takeoff. During the upstroke the wings are held with the front margin pointing almost straight upwards. At the top of the upstroke the wings clap together and are either flung apart or peel apart and the wing then beats down through the air, forming a 'vortex ring' of turbulence around the moth.

The clap and fling mechanism produces sufficient uplift to allow some types of flight. However, analysis of the forces predicted by conventional aerodynamics and observed vortices showed disagreement with the lift forces measured in some moths. Therefore, some other force, at the time unknown, had to be present to explain flight. This additional force was discovered by Ellington and his research group in 1996. They studied the airflow around the wings of the Tobacco Horn-worm, *Manduca sexta*. Their initial methods involved tethering a moth in a wind tunnel (see Ellington et al. 1996 for full details). The rate of airflow was adjusted so that while flying strongly into the wind, the moth remained stationary. Smoke was added to the airflow to enable the flow of air around the wings to be seen. Then, by means of stereophotography, the three-dimensional flow of smoke around the moth was recorded. These studies revealed a strong vortex formed at the leading edge of the wings. However, the precise mechanism by which the vortex was created could not be determined because it was difficult to see the smoke-flow very close to the wings. To investigate this vortex in more detail, Ellington made a robot moth, which he named a 'flapper' (Plate 5a). This flapper was constructed to closely resemble the Tobacco Horn-worm in its wing movements. However, with a wingspan of 1.03 metres, it was about ten times larger than the Hawk moth on which it was modelled. The wing flap frequency was adjusted to take account of the greater wing area.

Using the flapper, Ellington and his team were able to show clearly that the creation of the leading edge vortex resulted from the rapid deceleration of the wing at the top of the upstroke and not from the rotation of the angle of attack at this point in the wing cycle. As Ellington put it, 'the vortex is created by dynamic stall, and not by rotational lift mechanisms'(Ellington et al. 1996). The leading edge vortex is maintained through the down stroke and increases in dimension during the down stroke and towards the wingtip. The result is a conical spiral expanding as it is swept along the wing during the down stroke.

These experiments have shown that the forces involved in insect flight are very much more complex than, for example, aeroplane flight. Not only are additional forces generated by the flapping action of the wings, but the wings also have much greater flexibility than those of a plane. Wootton (1987) has likened the wings of moths and butterflies to sails. Both lepidopteran wings and sails are composed of flexible membranes stretched over rigid supports, which limit the movement of the membranes. Furthermore, in both, the control of the membranes through the supports is essentially external. In the case of sails it is through the action of sailors on ropes and booms and in the case of a moth through the thoracic muscular connections with the wing veins.

The direction of flight

Having described the mechanics of moth flight as they are currently under-stood, we can move to the question of how moths direct their flight. Again at the outset we have to make a distinction between two terms: navigation and ori-entation. By navigation I mean the deliberate movement from one location to another specific location. By orientation I mean simply the maintenance of a specific direction. Most moth flight is either rather random or involves orien-tation, not navigation. For example, male moths that fly upwind following the pheromonal trails of females are not navigating. Displace a male away from the trail it is following and it will not 'know' where the female is. Rather the male will begin to search randomly to pick up another trail, whether this is from the same or a different female. Thus, in following such a trail, he is using the plume of pheromones to orientate towards the female. In essence then, ori-entation involves maintaining direction, while navigation may be thought of as involving some sort of internal map.

The question of whether moths ever navigate in the true sense of the word is a difficult one. There is no doubt that some territorial butterflies learn cer-tain features of their territory and use these when patrolling. Many have favourite vantage points that they use for perching to keep watch for females or incursions by other males. However, similar behaviour has not been record-ed for moths and there is no good scientific evidence that any moths have the ability to navigate (Young 1997). That said, my own impression from observa-tions of the feeding behaviour of marked Elephant Hawk moths, *Deilephila elpenor*, and Broad-bordered Bee Hawk moths, *Hemaris fuciformis*, in the New Forest, and from the feeding and basking behaviour of Zodiac moths, *Alicidis zodiaca*, in Australia, is that some moths do build up a mental map of suitable sites for some activities. For all three species, particular individual moths repeatedly foraged on the same plants or, in the case of the Zodiacs, used the same basking sites on several consecutive days (Fig. 6.1), with different moths showing different preferences. Given this latter point, it is difficult to attribute their behaviour purely to the attractiveness of particular feeding or basking sites, for then one would expect that different moths would use the sites on different days.

Fig. 6.1 A Zodiac moth, *Alicidis zodia-ca*, basking in the sunshine in the early morning. This butterfly was seen to use the same basking posi-tion on four consecutive mornings.

Even if moths do have the capacity to navigate over short distances, most directional moth flight involves orientation. What cues are used by moths in their orientation? Given that we do not have the senses of moths, much of the evidence for the cues used by moths to decide on a direction of flight is circumstantial and anecdotal. However, a wide variety of orientation cues have been suggested and in most cases some evidence for their role has been obtained. We have already discussed some of these cues. Chemical cues, in the form of sex pheromones, are used by male moths to fly towards females and, in the form of plant volatiles, by females to fly towards suitable oviposition sites. Undoubtedly, physical landmarks are used to help moths identify nectar-rich plants, oviposition sites or appropriate roosting sites. Visual cues may also be used by some day-flying or dusk-flying moths, such as the Six-spot Burnet, *Zygaena filipendulae*, and the Ghost moth, *Hepialus humuli*, to orientate towards mates. Even at night visual cues may be used by some species, for few nights are completely dark.

Orientation using chemical cues or landmarks is practical over short distances only. To orientate over longer distances, moths must use more sophisticated cues. A number have been proposed, ranging from the position of the sun, the moon and the stars, to the geomagnetic field of the Earth. Excellent research has been conducted upon the ways that Lepidoptera use celestial bodies in orientation. Working on the Small White butterfly, *Pieris rapae*, Baker showed that Lepidoptera have the ability to use the sun as an uncorrected compass (see Baker 1982). In the late spring and early summer, the butterflies were tracked as they flew during the day. The track of flight, generally in a northerly direction, actually described an arc, flying north-west in the morning and swinging through a straight northerly direction at midday to a north-easterly direction in the late afternoon. The butterflies are thus flying away from the sun. In the autumn the butterflies still use an undirected sun compass, but now fly towards the sun, bringing them back in a southerly direction. Although moths have not been shown to use a sun compass, it seems likely. Certainly some day-flying moths have the ability to detect the position of the sun in the sky, even when it is obscured by clouds, from the plane of polarised light (Wehner 1984).

Irrespective of whether moths can use a sun compass, it is known that they can orientate using the position of the moon or the stars. They use these bodies to help them fly in a straight line by maintaining a particular angle between their flight path and the direction of the moon or stars. This was demonstrated by Sotthibandhu & Baker (1979), who altered the apparent position of the moon by the use of mirrors and artificial moons. The moths used, Large Yellow Underwings, *Noctua pronuba*, changed the direction of their flight in response to the altered position of the 'moon'. Furthermore, Sotthibandhu and Baker showed that if the moon was not present in the night sky, moths were able to orientate using a cluster of stars near the Pole Star. This seems to be an inherent ability because it is possessed by moths that have been reared in captivity and so have no previous experience of the night sky.

Baker was also involved in the research that first showed that moths can use the Earth's magnetic field to orientate. He demonstrated, again using Large Yellow Underwings, that moths in a completely bare and dark box had a tendency to move to one side of the box. When the box was turned around through 180°, the moths moved to the other side of the box, orientating themselves with respect to their position in the outside world. By placing the box in an artificial electrical field, which effectively reversed the Earth's magnetic field, Baker & Mather (1982) were able to induce the moths to move to the other side of the box.

It thus seems that moths use a wide variety of cues to help them get around. Some of these cues are used by man to attract or trap moths. Thus in some pest monitoring and pest control programmes, pheromone traps are used to attract moths (p. 261). For amateur lepidopterists the reaction of moths to light has a special importance.

Moths and light

Second in the list of questions that I have most frequently been asked about moths, after 'what is the difference between a butterfly and a moth?' is 'why are moths attracted to light?' I have no really satisfactory answer to this question. The answer that is usually given is that moths mistake a strong point source of light for the moon. As I have already written, there is good evidence that moths use the position of the moon in orientation by maintaining a specific angle with its direction. This helps them to fly in a straight line at least over short periods because the moon is so far away. However, if moths use a close-at-hand, artificial light in the same way, to maintain the angle between the light and their flight path, they will have to keep changing direction to prevent themselves from flying past it. They will thus continually fly towards the light, coming towards the source following a spiral path of ever diminishing radius.

Although I learned this explanation nearly 40 years ago, I have never found it convincing. The problem has always been that most moths do not approach my moth traps following a spiral flight path. Many appear to come in along a straight line. Others fly around the light in haphazard fashion, often landing close to the light before taking flight again, then moving closer to the light or moving away. Still others fly directly past the light, apparently unaffected by its presence.

An alternative explanation was offered by Hsiao (1972), who argued that a bright point of light acting on the compound eye of a moth will so fire the ommatidia that receive the main stimulus, that other ommatidia will experience inhibition and the area around the point source of light will appear dark. A partial analogy is perhaps the dark spots that one tends to see after looking directly at a very bright light. Hsiao then argued that the moths, in an attempt to get out of the light, will fly towards these apparently dark areas peripheral to the light. Young (1997) says that as moths often settle in the shadows in and around light traps just out of the beam, this theory seems to bear some relationship to reality. I am not so sure, and again observations of moths in the vicinity of moth traps of a variety of models (Fig. 6.2) and other types of light are the source of my uncertainty. I am not convinced that the theory is sufficient to explain all the types of flight patterns of moths that I commonly see around my moth traps. Nor do I think that a very high proportion of the moths that come into the sphere of influence of a moth trap settle in shadows around the trap. I think that those that do settle in shadow may be inhibited from flight by the light, as they would be in daylight, and they then seek a site to rest of the type that they would normally seek. Of the moths that enter the trap, species that would normally secrete themselves away in dark places or shadows

Fig. 6.2 Four types of mercury vapour moth trap. a) A Robinson trap. b) A portable 'Heath' moth trap. c) A home-made 'dustbin' trap. d) A strip whiteboard trap.

'hide' under the egg boxes, while others that would rest in more open situations may rest more openly in the trap. More difficult to interpret in respect to this theory are the moths that come to a lighted window, settling on the pane of glass and usually remaining there for many hours until the light is turned off. It is difficult to see how these moths can be viewed as flying towards an apparent darkened point caused by stimulus overload.

I may be wrong in my interpretation of either or both of the theories outlined above. It is of course possible that some moths are attracted for one reason and others for the other. Certainly there is no reason to expect that all species of nocturnal moth should behave in precisely the same way. Indeed, as many lepidopterists know, some species of moth appear never to be attracted to light and other methods, such as 'sugaring' or 'assembling' to virgin females, have to be used to attract these species. In any case, until more convincing evidence is obtained, or a more convincing explanation is proposed, my response to the question 'why are moths attracted to light?' must remain 'I do not know'.

Immigration

The influx of moths into a population will influence the size of the population. Furthermore, it will influence the evolutionary course of the population. The climatic conditions in Britain, particularly in western regions, are somewhat different from those in continental Europe, being highly maritime and affected by the Gulf Stream. These conditions might lead populations of moths to become locally adapted, such that geographic races or subspecies that are recognisably different from those occurring anywhere else evolve. In some species this has undoubtedly happened. Indeed, there are a number of species of moth in which races confined to specific habitats or geographic subspecies unique to the British Isles or a part of the British Isles are recognised. For example, many species have distinctly darker or melanic races or forms in northern or western coastal regions (p. 243) (Fig. 6.3). However, in a great many species, such genetic divergence of British populations from continental populations due to local adaptation is prevented by the flow of genes from continental populations into Britain via migration. The level of migration does not have to be large to prevent divergence. Indeed, a single reproducing immigrant per generation will severely slow the rate of divergence between two otherwise isolated populations.

A great many species of moth are known to arrive in Britain as immigrants. The recording of arrivals has increased dramatically since the development of a variety of types of mercury vapour light moth traps and the instigation of Rothamsted Experimental Station's network of white light moth traps across the British Isles. The systematic collation of records of migrant moths for irregular periods over the last 50 years has allowed the status of many of our species to be assessed with some degree of confidence.

Resident and immigrant species

There are a considerable number of species of moth that are resident in Britain, and these are augmented on a fairly regular basis by immigrants from continental Europe. These moths include species such as the Large Yellow Underwing, the Angleshades, *Phlogophora meticulosa* (Fig. 6.4), the Diamond

Fig. 6.3 A single-brooded dark race, *borealis*, of the Ruby Tiger, *Phragmatobia fuliginosa*, occurs in Scotland. This is shown above the brighter nominate race.

Fig. 6.4 (left) The Angleshades moth, *Phlogophora meticulosa.*

Fig. 6.5 (above) The Great Brocade, *Eurois occulta.*

Back moth, the Scarce Silver Y, *Syngrapha interrogationis*, the Great Brocade, *Eurois occulta* (Fig. 6.5), the Rannoch Looper, *Semiothisa brunneata*, and the Flame Wainscot, *Senta flammea*. In some of these, such as the first three species named, immigrants mix freely with resident British populations and their genes become part of the 'British gene pool' for these species. In these, no difference between the immigrant individuals and residents is detectable and the status of some as immigrants is established by observations of arriving swarms.

In the Flame Wainscot, immigrants are also not distinguishable from residents. However, in this species it is the location of records that suggests immigrations. Until recently, resident populations of the Flame Wainscot centred on fenland habitats in Cambridgeshire, Norfolk and Suffolk. Occasional records from south-eastern counties, particularly Kent, Sussex and Essex, are considered to be of immigrant individuals, although the species has established as a resident in single locations in both East Sussex and Kent.

In other species, such as the Great Brocade, Scarce Silver Y and Rannoch Looper, immigrants appear somewhat different from resident individuals. In each of these, resident populations are more or less confined to more northerly or westerly locations, while immigrant records are predominantly from the south and east. It seems likely, from both the pattern of records of resident breeding populations and the discernible difference between residents and immigrants, that the immigrants do not often, if ever, exchange genes with the resident populations.

In the above cases, the arrival of immigrant individuals of resident species is well established, either from direct observation of arrivals, or from the distribution of records and knowledge of habitat specificity. However, I have no doubt that there are many resident species in which arrivals from the Continent play a significant role in both population demography and prevention of genetic divergence, yet such arrivals go unnoticed. As Bretherton (1983) notes, there are probably many other species in which immigrants regularly augment British resident populations.

Non-resident immigration

The majority of species that are known to arrive in Britain from other countries do not live here permanently. These can be divided into those that are recorded virtually every year; those that occur irregularly although sometimes in large numbers; those that might be considered scarce (Bretherton uses the criterion that fewer than about 100 have been recorded); and those that have been recorded fewer than ten times, which might be considered rare. These categories broadly follow those given by Bretherton (1983). Here I am considering species that have arrived in Britain without the aid of human transportation. Accidental or intentional introductions will be discussed later in this chapter.

Some species that are recorded almost every year arrive in such numbers that they are frequently considered as common. These include the Silver Y, the Dark Sword-grass, *Agrotis ipsilon*, and the Small Mottled Willow, *Spodoptera exigua*. Although these species breed in Britain, they are not capable of surviving sharp frosts with the result that they cannot establish here permanently. Three species of hawk moth also fit into this category. These are the Convolvulus Hawk moth, the Death's-head Hawk moth, *Acherontia atropos*, and the Humming-bird Hawk moth, *Macroglossum stellatarum* (Fig. 6.6). There may be some observer bias here, for these species are more notable than many smaller species, which may account for their regular presence in annual lists of immigrants.

Immigrants that arrive rather less regularly, but sometimes in large numbers, include the Bedstraw Hawk moth, *Hyles gallii* (Fig. 6.7), the Ni moth, *Trichoplusia ni*, the White-point, *Mythimna albipuncta*, the Delicate, *Mythimna vitellina*, the White-speck, *Mythimna unipuncta* and the Crimson Speckled,

Fig. 6.6 The Humming-bird Hawk moth, *Macroglossum stellatarum*. (Courtesy John Bebbington.)

Fig. 6.7 The Bedstraw Hawk moth, *Hyles gallii.*

Utetheisa pulchella. Also included should be some of the resident species that are augmented by immigration, such as the Large Yellow Underwing, the Great Brocade and the Four-spotted Footman, *Lithosia quadra.*

Some instances of immigrants augmenting resident species are also included in the category described by Bretherton as 'irregular, scarce'. Thus the White Satin, *Leucoma salicis,* the Rannoch Looper and the Golden-rod Brindle, *Lithomoia solidaginis,* among others, should be included. Non-resident species that are recorded in some years, but not in many others, include three of our more spectacular moths, the Oleander Hawk moth, *Daphnis nerii* (Fig. 6.8), the Silver-striped Hawk moth, *Hippotion celerio,* and the Spurge Hawk moth, *Hyles euphorbiae.* Larvae of all three species have been found in Britain, but our

Fig. 6.8 The Oleander Hawk moth, *Daphnis nerii.*

winters are too severe for the establishment of these species.

The largest category of immigrants in terms of number of species is that in which fewer than ten immigrant records exist. Again, some of the species on this list are species that are also resident in Britain. Furthermore, the list includes species, such as the Nonconformist, *Lithophane lamda*, the Scarce Dagger, *Acronicta auricoma*, and the Spotted Sulphur, *Emmelia trabealis*, which were previously recorded as probable or definite residents, but are now probably extinct in Britain.

For many of the species on this list, only one confirmed British record exists. In others records only exist for one year, while in still others, several individuals have been reported, separated by many decades. It must be remembered, however, that just because only one or a small number of individuals have been recorded in the British Isles, this does not mean that only one or a small number of individuals have ever reached our shores. The proportion of immigrants that are actually recorded by lepidopterists is small and the number of those records that become available to compilers of immigrant species is smaller still. It is probable that fewer than one in a thousand immigrant moths that reach Britain are ever observed by an entomologist, and even this estimate may be very over-optimistic. Over the last 50 years new species of moth, such as the Passenger, *Dysgonia algira* (Plate 16e), have been added to the British list as a result of occasional immigrants at the rate of about one a year. Other new arrivals have undoubtedly gone unnoticed. These unnoticed species would include some macrolepidoptera, but would undoubtedly be dominated by the micros, which receive so much less attention than their larger cousins. It should of course be remembered that the British list of moths is a list of the species that have been recorded in Britain. It is not a full list of the species that have occurred here.

Our knowledge of immigrant moths to Britain is nowhere near complete. Here is another area where amateur lepidopterists may make a significant contribution simply by making sure that their records of immigrants are published and so are freely available to those interested in them.

Three questions remain to be considered. First, where do our immigrants originate? Second, do any of those species that arrive in Britain but are unable to survive here ever undertake a return journey? Third, why do species undertake migrations or dispersals that take them to locations where they are unable to survive?

Where do our immigrants come from?

The moths that arrive in Britain from other parts of the world, unaided by human transportation, come from a wide range of localities. Not surprisingly, the majority come from relatively close parts of continental Europe, but the origins of arrivals are not simply a function of distance. Some directions of movement are more common than others. For example, in Europe, more species disperse from south to north than the reverse. Furthermore, changes in latitude are more common than changes in longitude. Also not surprising is the fact that arrival here is usually thought to be wind-assisted. It seems inconceivable that species that have their origins nearly 5,000 kilometres to the west-south-west in the southern United States could cross the Atlantic to arrive here without the aid of a favourable wind. It is probable that species that arrive from closer origins also only arrive if a tailwind aids their flight. Indeed, there is considerable evidence that arrivals from a variety of origins are temporally clustered and correlate closely with appropriate meteorological conditions.

I recall, for example, the 'red rain' of the night of 30 June/1 July 1968. On the morning after, the red spotting all over my parents' blue Ford Zephyr was very obvious. The cause was a fall of red soil picked up in the southern Sahara and carried to high altitude and northwards before being deposited. The extraordinary meteorological conditions that led to this event also aided moth movement northwards. Twenty immigrant species were recorded in the month following, with six of the usually rare migrants being numerous and one species new to the British list, the Southern Rustic, *Rhyacia lucipeta*, being recorded (French & Hurst 1969).

While most immigrant individuals probably arrive from north-west France, across the English Channel, many of these will not be recognised as immigrants as they will be of species resident in Britain. Unusual or non-resident species will be more noticed and frequently will have arrived from further afield.

Bretherton (1983) groups the locations of origins of immigrants to Britain into five categories as follows:

a) The Iberian Peninsula and the Atlantic islands, including Madeira, the Azores and the Canary Islands. Travel here is northwards or north-north-east, across the Atlantic and the Bay of Biscay, to arrive on the south coast of Britain.

b) Central and eastern parts of the Mediterranean region. Travel is in a north-north-west or north-westerly direction. Sometimes the progression of a species from its point of origin can be tracked as a result of the dates of records through central and western Europe prior to its arrival in Britain.

c) Central, eastern and north-eastern Europe and possibly western Asia. Travel is broadly in an easterly direction and records occur all the way up the eastern seaboard of Britain. Correlation of arrivals of such species with persistent (several days) hot summer winds from continental Europe is generally good. The irregularity of arrivals of species from these origins is probably a consequence of the irregularity of such sustained winds, which certainly do not occur every summer. The most obvious example of an immigrant species from this type of origin is the Great Brocade, but more rare species include Evermann's Rustic, *Ochropleura fennica*, and the Scarce Arches, *Luperina zollikoferi*. Evermann's Rustic occurs in Scandinavia and western Siberia, as well as North America, while the Scarce Arches is a resident of the extreme east of Europe and western Asia.

d) Arrivals from northern France and the Benelux countries, across the English Channel and southern North Sea. As mentioned previously, many arrivals from these locations may go unnoticed as the immigrants mix with resident populations. An interesting case involves the Figure of Eighty moth, *Tethea ocularis*, in which immigration was responsible for the arrival of melanism in this species in Britain in the 1930s (Fig. 6.9). The melanic allele subsequently spread to and through many populations in industrial regions of Britain. Some rare species also have their origins fairly close at hand across the Channel. An example is the Purple Cloud, *Actinotia polyodon*, which is widely distributed in Europe, including France and Belgium. Other species that come from such locations include many of the species that have arrived and established themselves temporarily or permanently as residents in recent years (p. 157).

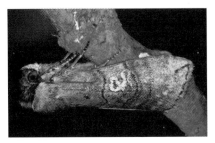

Fig. 6.9 The melanic form of the Figure of Eighty, *Tethea ocularis* (left), arrived in Britain by migration from the Continent, subsequently increasing in frequency at the expense of the non-melanic form (right).

e) North America, arriving on the western seaboard of Britain from across the Atlantic. Arrivals from such origins are rare. Most frequent is the Monarch butterfly, *Danaus plexippus*, a well-recognised long-distance migrant. Among moths, British records of Stephens's Gem, *Autographa biloba*, and the occurrence of a single Beautiful Utetheisa, *Utetheisa bella*, on Skokholm Island off the Welsh coast, probably represent examples.

Man-aided immigrants

Moths have been introduced into Britain by humans both on purpose and accidentally. Both categories should correctly be referred to as introductions rather than immigrants. Accidental introductions may be as incidental passengers on human transport, particularly ships, in timber, fruit, imported plants or other produce or packaging. Deliberate introduction may be for research, captive breeding or for fraudulent sale of rare species as 'British' specimens. Bretherton (1983) notes that fraudulent specimens of foreign origin that are passed off as British, for financial profit or kudos, were at one time rife, but have now diminished. Conversely, all other types of introduction have probably increased steadily over the last hundred years as the amounts of international travel and scientific research and the number of lepidopterists have increased.

The problem of accidental escapes of research organisms is particularly acute in the vicinity of a city such as Cambridge. I have twice in the last 15 years taken adults of the Tobacco Horn-worm, *Manduca sexta*, (Plate 16f) in mercury vapour light traps at the Department of Genetics Field Station on the outskirts of the city. I have no doubt that both were escapees from other research groups in the University that were using this large hawk moth in their studies.

Distinguishing immigrants from introductions may take a little research, but in any particular case the designation can usually be inferred with a high degree of probability if factors such as the non-British distribution, precise location, weather conditions and time of year are taken into account. Some species undoubtedly arrive both as accidental introductions and as natural immigrants. The Scarce Bordered Straw, *Helicoverpa armigera*, the Golden Twin-spot, *Chrysodeixis chalcites*, and the Mediterranean Brocade are cases in point. All these species have been reared in captivity from larvae found in imported plant material. However, adults of each of these species have also been taken in circumstances consistent with natural immigration.

Two-way migrations

There are various anecdotal reports that some species of moth fly north to our shores in the spring or summer, then return south in the autumn. Certainly, the Silver Y seems to have a weak southerly migration in the autumn for there are many records of moths flying across the south coast in September and October. In other parts of the world, more definite evidence of two-way dispersal has been obtained. For example, detailed studies of the Oriental Army Worm, *Mythimna separata*, in China, using mark–release–recapture techniques, has shown that moths fly north in the early summer months, returning south in August and September. In this case, the moths that move south are the progeny of those that move north. However, in one species of moth the same individuals are known to engage in return journeys. This is the Bogong moth, *Agrotis infusa*, of Australia (Common 1954). This species travels annually from the lowlands in New South Wales and Victoria, where it breeds and develops during the winter, to the mountains around Canberra, including the Bogong Mountains. Here it aggregates in large numbers in caves, rock crevices and rocky outcrops high up in the mountains to aestivate through the summer. In late summer, the same moths return to the lowlands to breed.

The mystery of moth migration

Since I became aware as a child that some of the largest of our moths, such as the Death's-head, Convolvulus and Oleander Hawk moths, arrived in Britain as migrants but were unable to survive here, I have always considered the plight of these moths, and others that behave in a similar way, to be both tragic and puzzling. The tragedy is undoubtedly an anthropomorphism that, as a scientist, I should try to curb. However, the puzzlement should be a spur to investigation. The mystery, which has been recognised by many other entomologists in the past, is that moths that regularly migrate on one-way journeys to localities where they cannot survive are effectively committing suicide. Given that suicide is not normally considered a successful evolutionary strategy, one would expect that selection would favour those individuals that dispersed less, thereby reducing the probability of moving into unfavourable climes or habitats.

That a considerable number of moths have not evolved strong 'stay-at-home' behaviours suggests that there must be some benefit to their dispersal habits. The most obvious benefit in moving will be to lower population density, thereby reducing intraspecific competition. There is considerable evidence to suggest that in some species dispersal rates increase as population density increases. The dispersal strategies of moths will thus be the result of the balance between the benefit of reducing intraspecific competition and the potential risk of dispersing too far. These two factors are probably those most generally involved in the evolution of dispersal and migratory strategies; however, they are not the only factors involved. For example, benefit may be gained by dispersers if in moving from their natal locality they move away from regions in which disease, parasitoids or predators have begun to accumulate.

Moth distributions

More is known about the distributions of moths, and the recent changes in those distributions, in Britain than in any other part of the world. This is partly the result of the tradition of moth-collecting we have in this country and partly the result of specific surveys aimed at mapping the distributions of our Lepidoptera. Yet even in Britain we are ignorant of the exact distributions of many moth species. This ignorance takes two forms, depending on one's perspective.

If asked whether the distribution of such-and-such a moth in Britain is known, for the larger moths, the macrolepidoptera, I would generally say yes, at least for most parts of our islands, although some parts of the Highlands and Islands are less well covered. However, that yes answer would hide a considerable difficulty in obtaining the information, for the detailed distributions of a great many species around different regions are scattered in the minds and logbooks of a great many lepidopterists around Britain. Each may know their own area and many may also know detailed information of some other areas that they visit regularly. However, attempts to collect and collate all this information into an accessible form have met with varying degrees of success.

Mapping projects

The various entomological journals and magazines that have been published in Britain since the nineteenth century contain an enormous amount of information on the distributions of the macrolepidoptera of Britain and a considerable amount of information on the distributions of microlepidoptera. Yet the coverage in such literature is severely biased to areas of high human population and towards rarer species. Furthermore, a number of published records are clearly fraudulent. Since the 1960s, when the Biological Records Centre was established at Monkswood Experimental Station, collection and collation of the distributions of many categories of the British fauna and flora has been more systematic. John Heath, one of the architects of the Biological Records Centre, instigated a mapping project for the larger British moths in the 1960s, recruiting many amateur entomologists as recorders. The first provisional maps, based on the 10 kilometre-square division of the national grid, were published under John Heath's authorship in 1970. Since this provisional atlas, many other maps have been published in the volumes of *The Moths and Butterflies of Great Britain and Ireland*, edited by A. Maitland Emmet and/or John Heath. Unfortunately, only seven of the proposed 11 volumes of this work have been published in the last 25 years. The volumes that await publication include those dealing with the Geometridae, for which distribution maps are still lacking. That said, the maps included cover the majority of the larger British moths and a considerable proportion of the micros. The maps are of two main types. For the macrolepidoptera, maps are based on the 10 kilometre-square system. For the micros, which are far less recorded, maps are based on presence or absence in British vice-counties as defined by Watson in the nineteenth century for recording the distribution of plants.

It is to be hoped that the remaining volumes of *The Moths and Butterflies of Great Britain and Ireland* will be published in due course so that a full set of maps of the known distributions of the British moths is available for future comparison. At a time when humans are influencing the environments of Britain more severely and in more varied ways than ever before, baseline data sets, against which future data can be compared, will be of inestimable importance. Those readers involved in conservation movements will already know that it is only when irrefutable statistical evidence is on the side of protection, that preservationists have any chance of success against the big financial and

Plate 1 The diversity of moths

a. Zodiac moth

b. Indian Moon moth

c. Scarlet Tiger moth

d. Elephant Hawk moth

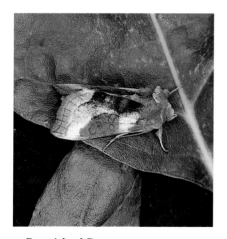

e. Burnished Brass

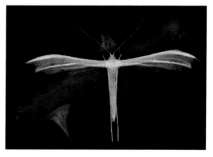

f. White Plume moth

Plate 2 Life history

a. Lead-coloured Drab ovipositing

b. Vapourer moth female with egg batch on her cocoon

c. Lime Hawk moth larva

d. Humming-bird Hawk moth larva

e. Green Silver-lines cocoon

f. Newly emerged Garden Tiger moth

Plate 3 Anatomical features

a. The forewing mark of the Figure of Eighty

b. Front view of the head of the Frosted Orange

c. Lateral view of head showing the curled proboscis

d. Lateral view of head and thorax of a Humming-bird Hawk moth

e. and f. Female (left) and male (right) antennae of the Drinker moth

Plate 4 Sex and Enemies

a. Mating Eyed Hawk moths

b. A sexual mosaic of the Emperor moth

c. and d. Sexual dimorphism in the Drinker moth, male (left) and female (right)

e. A spider eating a webbed Angleshades

f. Larvae of a parasitoid wasp exiting an Eyed Hawk moth larva

Plate 5 Flight and feeding

a. Giant robotic moth used
for study of moth flight. Flying
Manduca sexta are shown to scale

b. Broad-bordered Bee Hawk moth
hovering to feed

c. Elephant Hawk moth feeding of
honeysuckle

d. Female Large Yellow Underwing
glutted on oak sap

e. and f. Hebrew Character and Red Chestnut feeding on sallow blossom

Plate 6 Crypsis

a. Early Grey

b. July Highflyer

c. Merveille du Jour

d. Mottled Beauty

e. Small Waved Umber

f. Goat moth

Plate 7 Crypsis

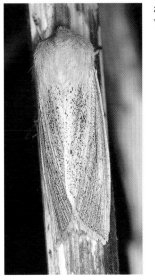

a. Large
Wainscot

b. Early
Thorn

c. Lappet moth

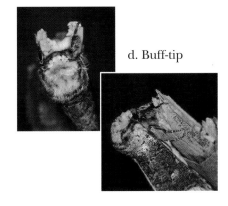

d. Buff-tip

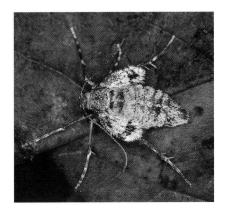

e. Female Winter moth

f. Three Mottled Umbers on
dead leaves

Plate 8 Disruptive patterns

a. The Streamer

b. Scalloped Oak

c. Green Carpet

d. Lime Hawk moth

e. Poplar Hawk moth

f. Lobster moth larva

Plate 9 Larval defense

a. Petiole-like larva of the Small Emerald

b. Disruptive patterning on a Dot moth larva

c. Lappet moth larva

d. Counter-shading on a Privet Hawk moth larva

e. and f. Puss moth larva in normal and alarm poses

Plate 10 Flash and startle patterns

a. Red Underwing at rest

b. Red Underwing flashing

c. Eyed Hawk moth at rest

d. Eyed
hawkmoth
flashing
(close-up of eye-spot inset)

e. and f. Elephant Hawk larvae
(brown and green forms)

Plate 11 Eye-spots and aposematic adults

a. Male Emperor moth

b. Close-up of Emperor moth eye-spot

c. Cinnabar moth

d. Leopard moth

e. Garden Tiger moth

f. Magpie moth

Plate 12 Aposematic larvae

a. Spurge Hawk moth

b. Pale Tussock

c. Garden Tiger moth

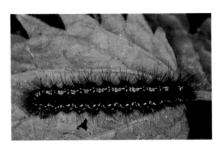

d. Scarlet Tiger moth

e. Sycamore moth

f. Aggregation of young Buff-tip larvae

Plate 13 Mimicry

a. Lime-speck Pug

b. Chinese Character

c. White Ermine

d. Buff Ermine

e. Currant Clearwing

f. Mating pair of Six-spot Burnets

Plate 14 Melanism

a. Black Mountain moth

b. Larvae of the Emperor moth

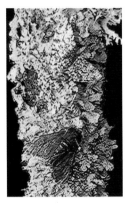

c. d. and e. Typical and *carbonaria* Peppered moths (c. at rest under a birch branch, d. on lichens under normal light, e. on lichens under UV light)

f. and g. Typical and melanic forms of the Green Brindled Crescent

Plate 15 Polymorphism

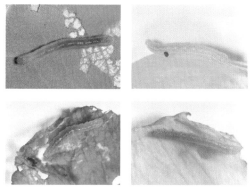

a. Third instar larvae of the Angleshades
fed on different foods

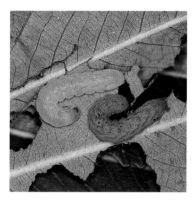

b. Green and brown forms of
Angleshades larvae (4th instar)

c. and d. normal and melanic larval forms of the Death's-head Hawk moth

e. Ghost moths, males (left) and females
(right) (top Cambridge; middle Orkney;
bottom Shetland)

f. Typical and yellow forms of
the Six-spot Burnet

Plate 16 New species, scarce species and vagrants

a. Blair's Shoulder-knot

b. The Wormwood

c. The Waved Black

d. The Burren Green

e. The Passenger

f. The Tobacco Horn-worm

political battalions on the side of development, change and 'progress'.

Distribution maps may be of value in more ways than just monitoring changes in our moth fauna resulting from man's influence on the environment. The distributions of moths are naturally dynamic. As already mentioned, species new to Britain are currently being recorded at a rate of about one per year. In addition, species are being lost from the British list through extinction. Furthermore, some species are known to have increased their range considerably over the last few decades, while the ranges of a much greater number of species have declined. Although such gains, losses, increases and decreases are probably occurring at a faster rate now than at any time in the last 20 millennia, changes in geographic distributions of this type have been taking place since moths first evolved. These changes are visible in speculations over the origins of our British moths.

The origins of British moths

We do not have to look too far back in history to investigate the origins of our British moth fauna. We need only look back to the last glaciation about ten millennia ago. Prior to this relatively recent warming of our climate, Britain was exposed to periods of ice ages, punctuated by warmer interstadials. The interstadials allowed the development of temperate fauna and flora. However, between these interstadials, long periods of intense cold saw two-thirds or more of the northern parts of Britain covered with an ice sheet and to the south of this a tundra-like landscape with an arctic fauna and flora (Fig. 6.10). At the height of the last great glacial phase, some 18,000 years ago, almost polar desert conditions would have prevailed over most of Britain. Very few species of moth would have existed in Britain at that time and, of the few that did, most will have subsequently moved northwards.

The present-day distributions of our moths are the result of four factors: the distributions of species in Europe, eastern Asia and North Africa about 10,000 years ago; climatic changes since the last glaciation; the dispersal abilities of different species of moth, and the activities of humans, which have so greatly affected habitats in Britain over this period.

Fig. 6.10 Glacial landscapes would have been a common feature of the British scenery in the last ice age.

During the last great glaciation, the moths that now frequent our islands would have existed elsewhere, mainly to the south of the great ice sheets, in southern Europe and North Africa. As the climate warmed and the ice sheet receded, moths will have moved northwards as their habitats expanded northwards and warming decreased the favourability of more southerly locations to species adapted specifically to temperate conditions. The movement north was relatively slow on an ecological scale and some minor adaptations may have occurred as environmental details, such as day length, altered with latitude. However, there is no reason to suppose that this period of climatic change saw rapid evolution of species adapting to climatic changes in their environments, for their environments on the whole did not change. Rather, mobile species, such as moths, that are adapted to particular climates, track these climates. They thus maintain environmental constancy, not geographic constancy (Majerus 1994). Movement, not adaptation, is the normal reaction to alterations in climate on the great landmasses, such as Eurasia with its connections into Africa. This pattern has been observed in other insect groups, such as the beetles, that are better represented in clay and silt deposits over the Quaternary period (Coope 1970, 1978).

This means that the majority of our moth fauna reached Britain between about 10,000 and 7,000 years ago, when the land bridge connecting Britain to continental Europe was severed. Although the majority of our moth species arrived before we became cut off from Europe, some species have arrived since. The existence of the English Channel for the last 7,000 years will have acted as something of a barrier to dispersal, but many moths can certainly fly across this relatively narrow band of water, as evidenced by the annual arrival of many migrants from the Continent described earlier in this chapter.

The climate within Britain, as well as other factors such as soil type, will have had a great influence on the distribution of the moths once they arrived. We describe the climate of the British Isles as temperate. However, that description blankets considerable diversity and the climate of our islands is significantly different from that of most other parts of Europe. Britain is in fact crisscrossed with gradients in climatic factors. Broadly, summer temperatures increase in a southerly and easterly direction, while winter temperatures increase southerly and westerly. In addition, some western coastal locations, particularly the coasts of Cornwall and Devon, the south-west coast of Ireland, and the west coast of Scotland, are strongly influenced by the warm Gulf Stream. Rainfall decreases eastwards. However, even in the East, the climate can be considered maritime or oceanic. Altitude also affects climate, with temperature decreasing and rainfall or snow increasing with altitude. Relatively high rainfall across the islands produces leaching of the soil and promotes acidic conditions. The high rainfall also promotes broad-leaved deciduous trees, and woodland of such trees is the natural climax vegetation for the majority of the British Isles.

Although deciduous woodland is the climax vegetation over much of Britain, the demands made on our country by humans means that this climax is achieved in only a tiny proportion of Britain. Much of the country is a mosaic of urban and suburban sprawl, agricultural land and commercial forest plantations. These provide new habitats, including chalk grassland with its highly diverse flora, hedgerows, fertile arable land and domestic gardens with high-nutrient soils and also great diversity of plant species, both native and exotic. As mentioned in Chapter 5, some of these have been exploited by species of moth, which have flourished as a consequence. Other specialised natural habitats still occur in patches, often in situations that have made development difficult or expensive. Thus habitats such as salt marshes, dunes, coastal cliffs, peat bogs, fen lands, sand heaths and uplands still occur, although often only as small remnants of much greater expanses that existed in the past. As described in Table 5.1 (p. 123), each of these, and others, has moths that are specially adapted to the conditions that it provides. The reduction in the areas of many of these habitats and the increasing distances between remaining patches of similar habitat are important for the future of many of these specialist moths.

The likelihood that a species originally arrived in Britain will obviously have depended partly on its dispersal abilities, particularly since the land bridge to continental Europe became submerged. However, dispersal ability cannot be seen in isolation from habitat specialisation. Species that are adapted to a wide range of habitats, yet are relatively sedentary, may have a much greater likelihood of establishing in Britain than much more dispersive species that can only survive in very specific habitats.

One of man's major influences on the distribution of the British moths is the fragmentation of habitats, such that habitat specialists become split into more or less isolated colonies that are prone to local extinction. If a species of moth becomes extinct in a patch of favourable habitat that is further from the nearest other favourable patch than the dispersal range of the moth, the likelihood of recolonisation becomes very low. Continued reduction and fragmentation of habitats may lead to a succession of local extinctions and eventually national extinction. This pattern has certainly been seen in some of the species we have lost over the last 200 years (p. 156).

Although human activities have certainly been responsible for the extinction of some species of moth in Britain, as already intimated, not all human activity since we arrived in Britain has been detrimental to moths. Through a variety of arable and animal agricultural practices, deforestation and forestry schemes and urbanisation, we have created many habitats that would not otherwise have existed in the British Isles.

Changes in the British moth fauna

The moth fauna of the British Isles is constantly changing in subtle, largely unnoticed ways. The gene pool of a species will change year on year as new genes are gained by mutation, or lost by drift or selection. The frequencies of existing genes will change through chance or as a result of selection due to changes in the environment. New combinations of alleles will be generated by recombination and sex. The most obvious changes involve visible morphological traits such as colour pattern, but many other genes will also be changing generation on generation. Population densities and distributions will also change little by little, year by year. In many cases such changes will be in response to relatively minor and directionless changes in both biotic and abiotic environments. Often these changes will be the result of a complex interaction of factors. Thus, for example, while an improvement in climate may benefit a particular species of moth through reduced development time or lowered winter mortality, the same climatic change may be even more beneficial to one of the moth's predators or parasitoids, so that overall the climatic change has a negative effect on the moth.

Changes in the British list of moth species

The total number of species on the British list of moths is about 2,500, including vagrants, occasional importations and extinct species. The most dramatic changes in moth distributions in Britain involve the loss or arrival of species. Since recording began, we have both lost and gained many species. Gains have come in two ways. First, the 'British list' has increased considerably over the last 100 years simply as a result of the discovery that one species was in fact two.

Taxonomic species splits

In my lifetime, such splits have occurred in several species of larger moth, notable examples being the splitting of Svensson's Copper Underwing, *Amphipyra berbera svenssoni,* from the Copper Underwing, *Amphipyra pyramidea,* and the division of the Common Rustic, *Mesapamea secalis,* into two species, the aforementioned and the Lesser Common Rustic, *Mesapamea secalella.* Rather more such splits have been recognised among the microlepidoptera, with some detailed taxonomic reconsiderations of particular genera or families sometimes generating several species new to Britain or new to science. Nowadays it is rare that individuals that have been considered as distinct species are merged into one, although such cases were quite commonplace in the early history of moth taxonomy when the sexes of sexually dimorphic species or seasonal forms or geographic variants were originally ascribed to different species.

Extinctions

More interesting perhaps are losses or gains that occur when a species is eradicated in Britain or when a species arrives for the first time. Losses in the last 200 years, of which there have been many, have resulted mainly from habitat destruction. The draining of the East Anglian fen lands saw the demise of species such as the Gypsy moth, *Lymantria dispar,* which disappeared in 1907, the Orache moth, *Trachea atriplicis,* last recorded in 1915 and the Reed Tussock, *Laelia coenosa,* which was last seen at Wicken Fen in 1879. The Spotted Sulphur, once locally common in the East Anglian Brecklands, has not been recorded since 1960. Another species that has disappeared from this location is the Viper's Bugloss, *Hadena irregularis,* which has not been recorded since the mid-1980s. It is presumed that the destruction of the characteristic steppe-like grasslands of the Brecklands, through cultivation and planting of conifers for timber, is responsible for the decline of these species.

Arrivals

Additions to the British list as a result of immigration are of several types. Some involve the reporting of species that arrive here under their own steam or as a result of particular weather conditions from North Africa, southern Europe or even occasionally America. These occur as very rare natural vagrants. Other rare vagrants arrive with accidental human help, transported in foodstuffs, timber or other goods. Of more significance than the rare individual vagrants are arrivals of one or more individuals of a species, usually from continental Europe, that lead to the temporary establishment of breeding colonies in Britain, which are later wiped out by adverse conditions. The third category is the most interesting, for this involves the new arrivals that establish and spread, suggesting that their colonisation is more permanent.

Vagrants and accidental importations

Vagrants and accidental importations are considered by most lepidopterists as interesting curios, worthy of note, but little more. However, each group has its own potential importance. Vagrants, which have arrived under their own steam, demonstrate that such species can disperse widely and may reach our islands occasionally. Such species, particularly those from Africa or the Mediterranean region, may be harbingers of the species that could colonise and establish in Britain as a consequence of climate changes due to global warming. The vagrants include species such as the Passenger, a southern European species that has been recorded in Britain fewer than a dozen times or the Geometrician, *Grammodes stolida*, another southern European and African species that has only been recorded in Britain once.

Species that are introduced accidentally by human activity include species that travel in the foodstuffs and other products that we move around the world. Some of these benefit from their association with man, feeding off stored products, and are considered economically important pests. They include many smaller moths and in Britain some, such as *Tinea translucens*, can only survive with man, because emanating from warmer climes, they are not able to survive out of doors in our climate. Among the accidental introductions are several species that feed on aquatic plants, which have been introduced with vegetation brought in for the tropical fish trade. Thus, of the 15 species of china-mark moths (Nymphulinae) on the British list compiled by Emmet (1991a), only four are found widely in natural situations. The others are six Far Eastern species, one Indo-Malaysian species, one Australian species and three American species.

Temporary residents

Immigrant species that are known or thought to have established as residents in Britain for short periods may be exemplified by the Lunar Double-stripe, *Minucia lunaris*. Colonies of this species have been recorded for periods from two to 17 years in several southern counties of England, the longest known colony enduring from 1942 to 1958 at Hamstreet in Kent. The Lunar Double-stripe is a rare migrant that has most often been reported as single individuals on the south and east coasts. Abroad its range is southern and Central Europe and North Africa. One of the more spectacular of the species in this category is the Bedstraw Hawk moth (Fig. 6.7). The larvae of this irregular migrant species feed on various bedstraws and willowherbs and have been found in some numbers following good years, such as 1870, 1888, 1955 and 1973. In parts of East Anglia, migrants that arrived in 1955 established and immature stages could be found without too much difficulty in some localities until 1958.

Established arrivals

While the majority of species that become temporary residents in Britain are moths that have a record as regular or irregular migrants, that is not the case for most of the species that have arrived in Britain in the last couple of hundred years and have become permanent residents here. Of course, one cannot predict the future fate of any species and permanent is a subjective description. However, for species that have established here and subsequently spread out from their original beachheads, it seems reasonable to believe that they will be with us for some years. Some of these species may be extending their range due to climate changes. For others, establishment may have resulted from a change in foodplant, or the planting in Britain of plant species that are not endemic to these islands. For still others, conditions may have been favourable for many years and lack of previous establishment was simply a result of not being able to breach the barrier of the English Channel. Here, increased human transport between Britain and other parts of the world may have been instrumental in initial introduction.

History is always a matter of interpretation and there are differences of opinion over whether lack of records of a species prior to a particular date is the result simply of the lack of recorders in the right place at the right time, or the true absence of the species prior to that date. Thus, for example, Feltwell (1984) records the Large Thorn, *Ennomos autumnaria*, as a new arrival, with its first record being in Kent in 1855. However, Bretherton (1983) does not list this species amongst those he considered to be 'now resident, probably as a result of immigration since 1850', and Skinner (1984) categorises it as a local resident probably reinforced by immigration.

This lack of certainty is a problem for all species that may have arrived and established more than about 100 years ago, simply because the number of lepidopterists and levels of recording were considerably lower in the nineteenth century than subsequently. One fairly definite arrival from the Victorian period is the Golden Plusia, *Polychrysia moneta*, which was unknown in Britain before 1890. Early records were from the south-east of England and East Anglia and the species subsequently spread to most parts of England and Wales and into Scotland as far as Aberdeen. The larvae feed on Delphiniums and the spread of this moth is undoubtedly a result of the great popularity of this plant as an ornamental for herbaceous borders and as cut flowers.

In the case of some new arrivals that have established, initial discovery in Britain has been in well-worked locations, making it unlikely that a species has been present, unnoticed, for any significant period before discovery. In others, discovery has been in more remote or inaccessible locations, so that a species may have been present for some time before its discovery. The Silurian, *Eriopygode imbecilla*, may be a case in point. This species was first discovered in Britain in 1972, on a mountainside in Monmouthshire. It has been recorded in the same location in most years since, sometimes coming commonly to light. Another example is the Burren Green, *Calamia tridens* (Plate 16d), which was first discovered on the Burren, County Clare, south-west Ireland in 1949. A second species that was found in County Clare in the twentieth century is the Irish Annulet, *Odontognophos dumetata*. Irish examples of this species are slightly different in colour from those found elsewhere, suggesting that the species has been established in Eire for some time and has adapted to local conditions (Forder 1993).

Uncertainty over the previous history of some apparently new species also occurs if the new species bears a close resemblance to another relatively common species, for the identity of a new species may not be correctly ascertained when it is encountered. This may have been the case with the Feathered Beauty, *Peribatodes secundaria*. The Feathered Beauty, which is easily mistaken for the Willow Beauty, *Peribatodes rhomboidaria*, was first identified in Britain from specimens caught in Hamstreet, Kent in 1981 (Skinner 1984). Here it appears to be well established and subsequently specimens have also been taken in Sussex.

Of course some species do not fall cleanly into any of these categories and the previous history of some species in Britain, such as the Southern Chestnut, *Agrochola haematidea*, discovered here for the first time in Sussex in the 1990s (Haggett & Smith 1993), remains a matter of speculation.

To the future

The origins of the present British moth fauna lie largely in the past. We can infer causes for the presence or absence of particular species, but we cannot know. Without very significant effort in terms of recording, the same is true of changes that are occurring in the distributions of our moths now.

Looking to the future, there can be no doubt that continued human interference with the environment at a national and international level will affect the distributions of many of our species over the next hundred years. I have little doubt that new species will arrive and establish in Britain from the south as the climate ameliorates under the influence of global warming. Fragmentation of specialised habitats, the homogenisation of our countryside and that in other parts of the world and the continual erosion or destruction of nature reserves and sites of special scientific interest (SSSIs) will put more and more pressure on our moths (see Chapter 10). Again, if we are to have any hope of minimising the destruction of many of our species, we require knowledge. That knowledge needs to extend to distributions, habitat preferences and other detailed ecological and behavioural data. Again I fear that little support for moths is likely to come from government, so the collection of such knowledge will fall on amateur entomologists. Only with such knowledge will we be able to make informed decisions over priorities, know what action needs to be taken and be able to make persuasive cases for conservation in the face of other interests.

Man, through the changes we are imposing on the environment both in Britain and globally, is the greatest enemy of moths. However, we are not the only enemies of moths. Moths suffer from the activities of a host of predators, parasites and pathogens, as well as being at risk from starvation and inclement weather. It is to the causes of moth death that I now turn.

7

The Deaths of Moths

Moth mortality

Moths have tremendous reproductive potential. Most species have the ability to lay from 200–500 eggs during their lives, although some, such as some species of hepialid, may lay many thousands. In the context of the population size equations (p. 89), this gives moths the potential for a very large intrinsic rate of natural increase. Although many species of moth are very common and population sizes do wax and wane, it is obvious that the majority of moth populations do not increase a hundredfold or more each generation. Thus, it is clear that most of a moth's progeny do not survive to reproduce. After all, it only requires that two survive to reproduce to maintain a constant population size. What factors then contribute to moth mortality? In this chapter, I will consider some of the many and varied ways that moths may die.

Life-table analysis

Most moth deaths occur before moths reach adulthood. To obtain a full picture of moth mortality within a particular population, the population must be monitored throughout the year, for a number of years. All stages in the life cycle must be considered so that a 'life-table' can be constructed.

A life-table is essentially a history of the fate of individuals from one generation through to the next. It records the number of reproducing adults, the number of progeny that they produce and the number of those offspring that die in each stage of the life cycle including the next adult generation. By calculating the level of mortality in each stage as a proportion of the number that survived the previous stage (known as k factors), the most significant mortality factors can be identified.

The case of the Winter moth

Rather few moth populations have been subjected to full life-table analysis. The major difficulty is the time-consuming nature of the monitoring that is involved. In the main, it is pest species that have been monitored in this way. The earliest thorough survey was the classic study carried out by Varley and his colleagues on the Winter moth, *Operophtera brumata*, in Wytham Wood near Oxford. This species was chosen for life-table analysis because it had a number of appropriate attributes. It is an abundant species, with discrete generations and an annual life cycle, and it is relatively easy to collect in various stages of development. The adult moths emerge from subterranean pupae from October to December. Males are fully winged (Fig. 7.1), but females have reduced wings and are unable to fly (Plate 7e). Newly emerged females climb the trunks of deciduous trees and attract males pheromonally. After mating, females continue to climb and lay eggs mainly in the higher canopy. Eggs hatch in early April and neonate larvae begin feeding if the leaf buds have

Fig. 7.1 A male Winter moth, *Operophtera bruma-ta* (*cf.* Plate 7e).

begun to burst. If food is unavailable, the young larvae suspend themselves on silken threads to be blown to other trees in which leaf development is further advanced. In late May, full-grown larvae drop to the ground on silken threads and burrow into the soil to pupate.

Varley and his group concentrated their data collection on just five mature oak trees in Wytham Wood. The life-table data were collected using a variety of different techniques, each one being appropriate to a different stage of the life cycle or to a different cause of death.

The adult population was estimated by setting traps for climbing, virgin females on the oak trunks. The proportion of each trunk's circumference that was trapped was used to obtain an estimate of the total number of virgin females climbing the five trees and, assuming a 1:1 sex ratio, the adult population size was estimated. Female fecundity was estimated by dissecting females and counting eggs. The population size of fully developed larvae was obtained by placing water traps of known area under the trees. The larvae that fell into these were counted and the total number of larvae was calculated by simple multiplication of the proportional area of the ground under the canopy of the five trees that was trapped. Levels of parasitism were obtained by dissecting the larvae that fell into the water traps. The pupal mortality rate was estimated by comparing the population densities of fully fed larvae and newly emerging adults. In addition, the proportions of various parasites present (in the fully developed larvae) that survived through to emergence from host pupae were estimated by assessing parasitoid prevalence in dropping larvae and proportional sampling of the adult parasites as they emerged from their subterranean hosts.

From these data, life-tables were constructed for the Winter moth and some of its parasitoids. The most important cause of mortality in terms of influencing Winter moth populations was found to be loss of first instar larvae that hatched before leaves were available (Varley & Gradwell, 1968). Pupal mortality, due to predatory beetles, small mammals and the parasitoid wasp *Cratichneumon culex*, was also found to be important (Varley & Gradwell 1963).

Varley's group collected similar data each year from 1950 to 1962. By identifying the key mortality factors from these data, they were able to construct a

Fig. 7.2 The key mortality factor of the Bordered White, *Bupalus pinaria*, a male of which is shown here, is the parasitoid wasp *Dusona oxyacanthae*.

model to predict future population changes, in the Winter moth and in two of its parasitoids. Data collection over subsequent years showed a relatively close correspondence between the predicted population fluctuations and those actually observed. This type of model thus has some biological veracity and similar analyses are now used routinely to monitor pest species around the world and help predict possible pest outbreaks before they occur.

Key mortality factors vary between species and sometimes between populations of a species. In addition, they vary within populations over time. As we have already seen, the highest k factor in the Winter moth in Wytham Wood is usually winter disappearance due to the starvation that results when Winter moth eggs hatch before the buds of their food trees have burst. In other species, parasitoids, disease, predation or dry season starvation may be the key factor, at least in some years. For example, work by Barbour (1985) and others has shown that the parasitoid wasp *Dusona oxyacanthae* is the key factor in regulating the Bordered White, *Bupalus piniaria* (Fig. 7.2), which can be a major pest of pine plantations.

Starvation

Larvae are the main feeding stage for most moths, so it is in this stage of the life cycle that mortality due to starvation is most influential. Female moths generally help to reduce the chance of starvation among their progeny by their choice of oviposition site, laying eggs on appropriate foodplants and in some cases selecting plants that do not already carry a high egg load. This latter strategy is known to occur in many heliconiid butterflies and some moths. For example, females of the European Corn-borer, *Ostrinia nubilalis*, can detect pheromones left by previous ovipositing females (Renwick & Chew 1994). Females then seek alternative oviposition sites. This behaviour benefits both the pheromone-producing female and the detecting female as it reduces the competition for the offspring of both.

As a result of these types of strategy, larval starvation is not a significant mortality factor for most species of moth. However, there are some circumstances that can produce high levels of larval starvation in some species, at least in some years. One of these has already been mentioned. In the case of the Winter moth and other species with eggs that overwinter on deciduous trees, lack of precise synchrony between egg hatch and bud-burst can leave neonate larvae without food.

Other situations that can lead to high larval starvation involve loss of food. This may be the result of high levels of herbivory, plant disease or inclement weather that adversely affects plants, such as drought or frost. Competition for food, either with other larvae of the same species, or with other herbivores that share the same foodplant, is a significant problem for some species, particularly those that specialise on just one or a small number of foodplants. For example, it is not uncommon to find individual plants or clusters of Common Ragwort eaten down to the stalks by larvae of the Cinnabar moth, *Tyria jacobaeae*, with the orange and black larvae (Fig. 7.3) wandering off across the soil or sand in search of less defoliated plants, often in vain.

High levels of herbivory may also occur when many different species attack the same foodplant. In Britain, the leaves of oak trees are eaten by the larvae

Fig. 7.3 Larvae of the Cinnabar moth, *Tyria jacobaea*, feeding on Common Ragwort.

of more species of moth than any other plant (p. 116). Most of these feed in the late spring and early summer. Several reasons have been suggested for this early glut of larvae on oaks. First, the water and nitrogen levels in oak leaves are highest early in the season. Second, the structural protein tannin, which contributes to the toughness of the leaves, is laid down only once the leaves have expanded to almost their full size. Feeny (1970) showed that this increased toughness of leaves later in the year severely reduces the rate at which nutrients can be taken up from oak leaves by the larvae of some species. Thus, larvae of the Winter moth feeding on oak collected in May produced adult moths that were nearly three times heavier than June-collected larvae. When Feeny ground up young and old leaves and fed these to the larvae, he obtained similar adult moth weights from both types of leaf. The deduction is that tannin makes leaves tougher and less digestible. A third advantage to the high density of larvae on oak in May is that the glut ensures that some survive the high levels of bird predation when birds are feeding their young. This is a more difficult reason to address because of a cause and effect identification difficulty. The question is whether birds breed in spring and early summer to take advantage of the high densities of moth larvae available at this time. They may do, but they may also have to breed in this season to allow their offspring to fledge and feed up sufficiently in the late summer to have a reasonable chance of surviving either long migrations or the rigours of winter. If the latter were the case, it seems unlikely that high larval density in spring could be purely to overwhelm bird predation levels, for any moth species that avoided this period of high predator activity would surely benefit.

Whatever the reason for the huge numbers of larvae of many species that feed on oak in May, their collective herbivory can produce almost total defoliation of oaks. I remember several occasions in the late 1970s when large tracts of oak woodland in Staffordshire were almost leafless due to the feeding activities of the Winter moth, the Northern Winter moth, *Operophtera fagata*, the Mottled Umber, *Erannis defoliaria*, the Dotted Border, *Agriopis marginaria*, the Scarce Umber, *Agriopis aurantiaria*, the Pale Brindled Beauty, *Apocheima pilosaria*, the Feathered Thorn, *Colotois pannaria*, the Early Thorn, *Selenia dentaria*, and the Green Oak Tortrix, *Tortrix viridana*. Pupae collected in these defoliated areas tended to produce unusually small adults, suggesting that food had become limiting. In addition, huge numbers of larvae were found roaming around in the branches and trunks of the trees looking for food. Many starved!

Interestingly, oak trees have a response to this heavy loss of leafage in May and early June. Unusually for deciduous trees, oak may have a second bout of leaf development in midsummer, producing what is called Lammas growth once the majority of the moth larvae that feed on it have completed their development and pupated.

Unfavourable weather

The weather that may adversely affect moth survival can be thought of as either active weather or passive weather. By active weather, I mean weather that has direct physical force, such as strong winds or the impact potential of hail or large raindrops, or even the force of surface tension of a still water body. By passive weather, I refer to high or low temperatures or abnormal humidity levels.

It is not difficult to envisage the potentially disastrous effects that active weather may have. In high winds, larvae may be blown from their foodplants. Particularly in tree-feeding species in which egg hatch occurs around the time of bud-burst, young larvae that hatch prior to food being available will hang on silken threads to be carried by the wind hopefully to an earlier leafing tree. However, in strong winds, such larvae may be carried far from any appropriate food.

Heavy rain or hail may be a hazard for flying moths in two ways. First, the impact of heavy raindrops or hailstones may cause damage. Second, such impacts may knock the moths to the ground where there is the risk of landing in puddles or on wet substrates where the surface tension in the large area of contact between water and wing surfaces may be too great for the moth to pull away from. After heavy storms on warm summer nights, examination of puddles in the morning often reveals a considerable array of dead or dying moths stuck on the surface.

Given the risk of flying during heavy rainstorms one might suppose that moths would seek shelter and rest up during downpours. However, this is certainly not the case for many species. In 1992, due to timetabling constraints of a field course, I had occasion to set up six Robinson mercury vapour moth traps behind a dune system near Wells-next-the-Sea on the Norfolk coast, on a night (22 July) when thunderstorms were forecast. The traps, run off portable Honda generators, were operated from 9 p.m. until just after midnight. The storm that arrived was not a run-of-the-mill storm. In just over three hours we had 37 millimetres of rain and, at the height of the storm, lightning flashes were coming at the rate of 14 per minute. Yet, amazingly, many species of moth were flying in good numbers. The full list of the catch from the six traps is given in Table 7.1. That several large species were flying is perhaps not surprising. Pine Hawk moths, *Hyloicus pinastri*, Oak Eggars, *Lasiocampus quercus*, and Drinker moths, *Philudoria potatoria* (Plates 4c and 4d), together with some of the more robust noctuids, would probably have the size and power to shrug off the wind and water. However, I was amazed that many geometrids were also flying, even during the strongest rain. Although some of the smallest geometrids were neither seen nor caught, suggesting that some species, such as the pugs and smaller waves, were deterred from flight, the results suggest that rain is not a flight-limiting factor for most species of larger moth.

Other types of inclement weather can take a heavy toll on moths, with different species or groups of species suffering depending on the nature of the adverse conditions. Thus, high winds may blow moths out to sea or onto the surface of water bodies where they get trapped by the surface tension. Severe flooding may cause heavy mortality of larvae that feed or overwinter in low herbage or within reed stems. Long periods of low night temperatures, particularly in early winter, may prevent or reduce mating and oviposition in those species that are adult at this time. High rainfall and humidity, particularly in the late winter and early spring, may lead to an increase in mortality of larvae and pupae from fungal attack.

Table 7.1 Lepidoptera taken during three hours of torrential rain, at Wells-next-the-Sea, Norfolk, on 20 July 1992. (Data from Majerus 1993.)

Species	Approx. no.	Species	Approx. no.
Oak Eggar *Lasiocampa quercus*	13	Flame Shoulder *Ochropleura plecta*	>10
Lackey *Malacosoma neustria*	>20	The Flame *Axylia putris*	>10
Drinker moth *Philudoria potatoria*	4	Large Yellow Underwing *Noctua pronuba*	>10
Oak Hook-tip *Drepana binaria*	12	Lesser Broad-bordered Yellow Underwing *Noctua janthina*	>10
Pebble Hook-tip *Drapana falcatoria*	4	Broad-bordered Yellow Underwing *Noctua fimbriata*	>10
Scalloped Hook-tip *Falcaria lacertinaria*	>20	True Lover's Knot *Lycophotia porphyrea*	1
Blood-vein *Timandra griseata*	10–15	Ingrailed Cay *Diarsia mendica*	>10
Riband Wave *Idaea aversata*	5	Small Square-spot *Diarsia rubi*	>10
Yellow Shell *Camptogramma bilineata*	3	Setaceous Hebrew Character *Xestria c-nigrum*	8
Barred Straw *Eulithis pyraliata*	4	Double Square-spot *Xestria triangulum*	4
Grey Pine Carpet *Thera obeliscata*	5	The Nutmeg *Discestra trifolii*	>10
July Highflyer *Hydriomena furcata*	2	The Shears *Hada nana*	3
Magpie *Abraxas grossulariata*	7	Tawny Shears *Hadena perplexa*	2
Brimstone moth *Opisthograptis luteolata*	6	The Clay *Mythimna ferrago*	>10
Clouded Border *Lomaspilis marginata*	9	Smoky Wainscot *Mythimna impura*	>10
Tawny-barred Angle *Semiothesa litura*	42	Common Wainscot *Mythimna pallens*	>10
Swallow-tailed moth *Ourapteryx sambucaria*	2	The Miller *Acronicta leporina*	2
Purple Thorn *Selenia tetralunaria*	3	The Sycamore *Acronicta aceris*	3
Early Thorn *Selenia dentaria*	3	Knot Grass *Acronicta rumicis*	3
Peppered moth *Biston betularia*	12	Dark Arches *Apamea monoglypha*	>10
Willow Beauty *Peribatodes rhomboidaria*	16	Slender Brindle *Apamea scolopacina*	1
Mottled Beauty *Alcis repandata*	3	Marbled Minor *Oligia strigilis*	2
Bordered White *Bupalus piniaria*	5	Common Rustic *Mesapamea secalis*	>40
Iron Prominent *Notodonta dromedarius*	4	Ear moth *Amphipoea oculea*	>40
Ruby Tiger *Phragmatobia fuliginosa*	9	Mottled Rustic *Caradina morpheus*	>10

Table 7.1 (cont.)

Species	Approx. no.	Species	Approx. no.
Sand Dart	>10	The Uncertain	7
Agrotis ripae		*Hoplodrina alsines*	
The Rustic	>10	Common White Wave	5
Hoplodrina blanda		*Cabera pusaria*	
Silver Y	>10	Pine Hawk moth	8
Autographa gamma		*Hyloicus pinastri*	
Black Arches	>10	Buff-tip	2
Lymantaria monarcha		*Phalera bucephala*	
Buff Footman	4	Pebble Prominent	1
Eilema deplana		*Eligmodonta ziczac*	
Common Footman	>30	Coxcomb Prominent	3
Eilema lurideola		*Ptilodon capucina*	
Garden Tiger	2	Yellow-tail	>20
Arctia caja		*Euproctus similis*	
		Holly Blue butterfly	1
		Celastrina argiolus	

Disease pathogens

Moths suffer from many types of disease. All the main groups of pathogenic microorganism, viruses, bacteria, fungi and protozoa, are known to cause disease in the Lepidoptera, with larvae most commonly being infected. Most entomologists who have tried to breed and rear moths will have experienced the disappointment of losing a complete batch to disease. Yet despite the common occurrence of disease, particularly when large numbers of larvae are reared together, rather little is known about the pathogens of many species and undoubtedly many species of pathogen remain unidentified. The task of characterising and identifying microorganisms is specialised, requiring considerable microbiological training and equipment outside the scope of most amateur entomologists. I will thus confine this discussion to more general points concerning the symptoms produced by the main groups, their transmission and the ways that breeders can minimise risk of infection.

Viruses

Viruses are extraordinary organisms. These minute creatures, which can only be seen by electron microscopy, are composed of a protein shell enclosing genetic instructions encoded in either RNA or DNA. The genetic material directs the production of new virus particles. However, viruses do not contain the biochemical machinery for producing proteins or manufacturing new RNA or DNA molecules themselves. Rather, they coopt the machinery of the host cells that they infect. Viruses can thus only replicate within another cell, where they use the host's enzymes and proteins for their own DNA and RNA replication. Newly synthesised viral particles are released from host cells, often killing the cells in the process. Released viral particles can then be transmitted to other host cells via almost any medium. Many are waterborne or are transmitted only by contact with an infected host, as in the case of the HIV virus. However, because of their small size, many are also airborne, as witnessed by the outbreak of foot-and-mouth disease in Britain in 2001.

Viruses are probably the most important pathogens of moths. The symptoms produced by viral infections of larvae include sluggish movement, reduced feeding rate, a liquid discharge from both the mouth and anus and sometimes a bloated appearance. The corpses of larvae that have recently died from a viral infection do not smell bad, unlike those that have been killed by bacteria. Furthermore, the skin colour rarely changes prior to death, although the skin does become rather fragile and is easily ruptured.

The most common group of viruses includes the polyhedrosis viruses. In these, virus particles are contained within a crystal-like structure called a polyhedron. These polyhedra may form in different parts of the host's cells, so both nuclear polyhedrosis and cytoplasmic polyhedrosis viruses are known. In the former, the virus particles tend to be rod-shaped and contain DNA, while in the latter, particles are spherical and contain RNA. Given that the nucleus of the host cell contains most of its DNA, while the cytoplasm is RNA-rich, this differentiation in the genetic content of nuclear and cytoplasmic viruses is not coincidental.

Members of the third group of crystal-forming viruses are known as the granulosis viruses. These are somewhat similar to the nuclear polyhedrosis viruses, but the minute crystals formed each contain just a single virus particle.

The symptoms caused by these viruses aid their transmission. In both the nuclear polyhedrosis and granulosis viruses, replication of virus particles takes place in a variety of tissues, including the fat body (a mass of fatty tisue in the abdominal cavity), haemolymph and tracheae (Rivers 1964). Replication can be extremely fast, and a single larva may contain hundreds of millions of virus particles before it dies. The dying larva characteristically climbs upwards on the foodplant before it dies. This larval behaviour induced by the pathogen is adaptive for the virus, but not for its host. On death, the larva is liquefied, its body contents dripping out of the corpse onto vegetation below. All that is left is the skin, hanging down from the substrate, still attached by the hooks on its prolegs. Each drop of liquid dripping from the corpse contains millions of virus particles in their crystals. These dry onto the foliage on which they land. Here they may remain alive for long periods of time. Polyhedra have been known to remain infectious for over 25 years outside their host if kept at 3°C. Transmission to a new host occurs when another larva ingests the plant material carrying the polyhedra. The crystals containing the virus particles are broken down in the larva's gut and the virus then migrates to cells in which it can replicate.

Cytoplasmic polyhedrosis viruses mainly infect the cells lining the gut. Larvae infected with these viruses are often small and have a starved appearance because build-up of virus numbers interferes with digestion. The polyhedra are passed out of the host in pale-coloured faecal pellets for some days before the larva dies. It is these faecal pellets that contaminate foliage, promoting transmission. The larval corpse itself plays little part in the transmission of its killer because larvae infected with this type of virus generally become weak and drop off their foodplant some time before they die.

Many other types of virus have been reported from Lepidoptera. These include entomopox virus, picorna virus, several parvoviruses and so-called iridescent viruses, which give infected tissues a bluish colour that can be seen through the body wall. Although some of these viruses have a wide host range, including in some cases vertebrate hosts, none appear very common in the Lepidoptera and epidemics have not been recorded.

Bacteria

Bacteria are single-celled organisms that reproduce asexually by simple division, or fission. Bacteria that cause the death of moths are of two main types: those that are always pathogenic, and those that only become pathogenic under particular conditions. The second group results because many species of bacteria are found in the gut of moth larvae, where they aid digestion. However, when their host is threatened as a result of starvation or infection by another disease agent, these bacteria may turn nasty. Under host stress, the bacteria pass through the gut wall and begin to multiply rapidly in the host's haemocoele. They are then transmitted via rectal or oral discharges from their host, or after the decay of their host's corpse. In contrast to hosts killed by viruses, larvae infected with disease bacteria become darker, soft and shapeless, the skin remains relatively strong rather than fragile, and the corpse smells badly.

A range of different types of bacteria have been found in moths. These include Bacillaceae, Bacteriaceae, Enterobacteriaceae, Lactobacteriaceae, Micrococcaceae and Pseudomonadaceae. As with viruses, identification of different bacteria is a job for the specialist using sophisticated microscopic and staining techniques, and it is complicated by the common occurrence of secondary infections. Indeed, secondary infections are an important factor in the pathogenicity of many bacteria. Thus, for example, the small rod-shaped bacterium *Serratia marcescens* only becomes pathogenic when associated with fungi such as *Beauveria bassiana*. Larvae of the Garden Tiger moth, once very abundant in the vineyards of southern France, were almost wiped out by the action of the bacterium *Coccobacillus cajae*, in conjunction with the fungus *Entomophthora ulicae*.

Some bacteria have been used extensively in biological control. The best known of these is *Bacillus thuringiensis*, which is highly lethal to moth larvae. The use of this disease in pest control programmes will be further discussed in Chapter 10.

Ultra-selfish symbionts

Most pathogenic microorganisms are transmitted to new hosts by contagious infection. Some microorganisms, however, are transmitted vertically, usually in the cytoplasm of eggs. These microorganisms are effectively inherited, being passed from mother to offspring. Such microbes are symbionts. Scientifically, symbiosis means simply living together. Symbionts can thus be harmful or neutral to their host, or in some cases, such as those bacteria that aid digestion, actually beneficial. In the case of harmful, i.e. parasitic, symbionts that are transmitted vertically, there is a general expectation that the cost imposed on a host by the symbiont should gradually diminish over evolutionary time. As the symbiont relies on the wellbeing of its host for its transmission and so its continued existence through time, individuals that harm their host least will gain a selective advantage. However, there are some symbionts that contravene this expectation. These are the so-called ultra-selfish inherited symbionts that gain advantage by adopting strategies that interfere with their hosts' reproduction, increasing the proportion of hosts that carry and transmit them. Ultra-selfish symbionts are inherited in the cytoplasm of eggs, so their transmission is from female parents to offspring only. Males do not transmit the symbiont to future generations because the sperm of the vast majority of species do not contribute cytoplasm to their offspring. Selective advantage may be gained by a symbiont if it decreases the fitness of uninfected hosts, or if it increases the proportion of the population that can transmit it, biasing the population sex ratio in favour of females. Four rather different manipulations of host reproduction are known to be performed by these ultra-selfish bacteria. One of these, a phenomenon known as cytoplasmic incompatibility (CI), reduces the fitness of uninfected hosts. The other three, feminisation, induction of asexual reproduction and male-killing, all lead to female-biased population sex ratios.

In respect of moths, there is as yet no known case of asexual reproduction being induced by an inherited microorganism. However, examples of cytoplasmic incompatibility, feminisation and male-killing involving moth hosts are known and may prove to be common.

Cytoplasmic incompatibility

Cytoplasmic incompatibility is caused by bacteria of one widespread genus called *Wolbachia*. If an infected male mates with an uninfected female, the female is rendered sterile thereafter. Other mating combinations are not affected (Fig. 7.4). First recorded in mosquitoes, CI has now been found in all the major orders of insects and in a variety of other invertebrates (see Hoffmann & Turelli 1997 for review). The first moth in which CI was recorded was the Almond moth, *Ephestia cautella* (Brower 1976). When moths from geographically isolated populations were crossed, these crosses failed when males were taken from one population, but not when males were drawn from the other. The compatibility could be restored by feeding larvae on antibiotics, suggesting that a bacterium was the cause of the incompatibility. Electron microscopy of testis tissue showed that the affected males were carrying a *Wolbachia*.

Fig. 7.4 The pattern of reproductive success resulting from matings between moths infected or uninfected with cytoplasmic incompatibility-inducing *Wolbachia*.

	Female infected	Female uninfected
Male infected	Reproduction normal	Female becomes sterile
Male uninfected	Reproduction normal	Reproduction normal

Subsequently, a variety of other moths have been shown to exhibit CI. The majority of these are pest species, such as the Flour moth, *Ephestia kuehniella*. This is not surprising. The advantage that infected females gain over uninfected females as a result of the sterility caused to uninfected females if they mate with an infected male means that CI *Wolbachia* rapidly spread through whole host populations once they invade. This means that CI is only likely to be detected if crosses are made between moths from geographically distant populations. Such crosses are most often conducted on pest species being intensively researched because of the damage that they cause.

Molecular genetic investigations of a wide range of insect species have shown that 10–20% of all insect species harbour *Wolbachia*. Not all these *Wolbachia* cause CI. Some cause sex ratio distortion while others appear neutral to their host. However, it is probable that CI is a common phenomenon in moths and that if appropriate crosses are made between individuals from different populations, many other cases await discovery.

In some cases, different populations of the same species carry different strains of *Wolbachia*. In this case, crosses between the populations fail in both directions, i.e. irrespective of which population a male comes from. This finding has led to the suggestion that CI *Wolbachia* may have played a significant role in speciation as such populations are effectively reproductively isolated from one another.

Feminisation

In addition to causing CI, *Wolbachia* may also cause feminisation. In two species of moth, the Asian Corn Borer, *Ostrinia furnacalis*, and the Adzuki Bean Borer, *Ostrinia scopulalis*, some females produce only daughters (Kageyama et al. 1998, 2000). Scrutiny of such families showed low levels of mortality during development suggesting that this was not a case of a sex-specific lethal gene. Furthermore, when larvae from these lines were treated with antibiotics, the resulting females surprisingly produced a strong male bias in progeny. This result can be understood if the sex determination system of Lepidoptera is considered. As discussed in Chapter 4, in most Lepidoptera females have ZW and males have ZZ sex chromosomes. If the females that produce just daughters are infected with a symbiont that feminises genetic males, such moths would have the sex chromosomes of a male, but would be reproductively female. These feminised ZZ males, when cured of the bacterium and mated by normal (ZZ) males, would only produce male offspring. Molecular genetic and microscopic analysis of the all-female lines again showed the presence of *Wolbachia* in both species of moth.

In an elegant experiment, Sasaki and colleagues (Sasaki et al. 2000) in Tokyo attempted to determine whether the strategy employed by *Wolbachia* in a particular host was under the control of the symbiont or the host. Taking body fluid infected with *Wolbachia* from the Adzuki Bean Borer, they injected this into embryos of *Ephestia kuehniella*. The *E. kuehniella* were from a line that had harboured a CI *Wolbachia*, but from which the bacteria had been removed by antibiotic treatment. If the trans-infected moths produced predominantly females, due to feminisation, this would indicate that the *Wolbachia* controlled the strategy it employed. Conversely, if the trans-infected moths exhibited CI when crossed to uninfected moths, it would suggest that the host controlled the strategy of the symbiont. As is so often the case in science, what actually happened was neither of the outcomes predicted, for the *Wolbachia* in the trans-infected moths exhibited a third strategy: male-killing. Although the moths did produce a strong female bias, this was shown to be due to the death of male offspring and not to the feminisation of genetic males.

Male-killing

Male-killing is the third of the ultra-selfish strategies shown by inherited symbionts in the Lepidoptera. However, unlike CI and feminisation, this strategy is not caused only by *Wolbachia*. In addition, other α-proteobacteria such as *Rickettsia*, γ-proteobacteria, flavobacteria and mycoplasmas have all been found to cause male-killing in insects. Male-killing has been reported from five orders of insects (Lepidoptera, Hemiptera, Coleoptera, Hymenoptera and Diptera), with nymphalid butterflies, milkweed bugs and ladybirds being known hotspots.

In the context of Darwinian evolution, male-killers are perhaps the strangest of the ultra-selfish inherited bacteria because in killing male hosts the bacteria that do the killing commit suicide. Suicide and the survival of the fittest seem somewhat contradictory. However, there is a sensible evolutionary reason behind this kamikaze behaviour.

For a male-killer to invade a host population, the death of males has to benefit infected females sufficiently to compensate for the death of the sons of an infected mother. Work on ladybirds has shown that, in some circumstances, infected females can benefit from the death of their brothers, which carry clonally identical bacteria. Ladybirds lay their eggs in batches, habitually eat any unhatched eggs in their clutch and feed on an ephemeral and often limited food: aphids. Typically, the death of males infected by bacterial male-killers occurs early in embryogenesis. The female larvae that hatch from a male-killed clutch of eggs have available for consumption the energy-rich contents of all their dead brothers. On average, this means that each female in such a clutch will have roughly twice the quantity of nutrients available prior to dispersing from the egg batch to seek aphid prey as a female larva from an uninfected clutch in which all eggs hatch. These additional resources give siblings of the dead males a tremendous fitness advantage, for they have up to twice as long to find their first aphid meal as a normal larva and they are larger when they disperse from the eggs, so they can catch and subdue larger prey (see Majerus & Hurst 1997 for review).

Other factors may promote male-killing. For example, it is commonly known that close inbreeding, such as between full siblings, is frequently deleterious as it leads to the expression of recessive deleterious alleles. Females that are infected by an efficient male-killer do not run the risk of copulating with full siblings if all their brothers are dead.

Male-killers have been found in several species of *Acraea* butterfly (Fig. 7.5), in the Common Tiger butterfly, *Danaus chrysippus,* the varied Eggfly, *Hypolimnas bolina,* and in the Gypsy moth, *Lymantria dispar.* They are also suspected in several other moths, including the army worm *Spodoptera littoralis,* the

Fig. 7.5 A female of *Acraea encedon*, a butterfly species showing sex role reversal due to high levels of prevalence of a male-killing bacterium.

Salt Marsh caterpillar, *Estigmene acrea,* and the Almond moth, although in these species the causal agent of male-killing has not been identified (see Majerus 2000 for review). Little work has been conducted on the factors that promote male-killers in Lepidoptera. However, it is notable that a great many species of moth lay their eggs in large batches and that in many the neonates indulge in the consumption of any unhatched eggs. Furthermore, in some species, the food for neonate larvae is limited either due to lack of availability at the necessary time or because it is too tough for the mandibles of neonate larvae. The conditions necessary for the invasion of male-killers probably exist in many species of moth. This then is an area in which amateur entomologists could make a very useful contribution. As explained in Chapter 3, the sex ratio of moths should be approximately 1:1. This is true within both populations and families. If moth rearers find sex ratios in families that differ significantly from equality, such observations should certainly be published or brought to the attention of a research scientist who works on insect sex ratios.

In species in which male-killers are known, population sex ratios are female biased, the extent of the bias being determined by the proportion of females infected and the efficiency of the male-killer's vertical transmission. The prevalence of male-killers varies from 1% to over 95%. The vertical transmission efficiency varies from just over 70% to almost 100%. Consequently, the sex ratios of populations containing male-killers range from almost equal numbers of the two sexes up to over 20 females for every male, as occurs in some populations of the Encedon Acraea, *Acraea encedon,* and Pierre's Acraea, *Acraea encedana,* butterflies. In the most female-biased populations, a variety of knock-on effects have been identified. These include reduced male investment in each copulation and full sex role reversal, with females competing for access to males and males choosing between females (Jiggins et al. 1999).

Fungi

Fungi of three main groups are disease agents of insects. Each of these groups, the Eumycetes, the Phycomycetes and the Zygomycetes, has different characteristics allowing identification at least to this level. Examination of the size and shape of the mycelium and fruiting bodies of fungi on the corpses of dead moth larvae or adults frequently permits identification to the genus and sometimes species level. Phycomycetes rarely infect moths. However, both Eumycetes and Zygomycetes infect many lepidopteran species and may cause high levels of mortality.

The Eumycetes includes fungi that produce a thick covering of thread-like hyphae and fruiting bodies (conidia) over the body of infected larvae. These are known as muscardine infections after the sugar-coated sweets common in many parts of continental Europe that the larvae resemble. Infection is mainly of larvae. Species living on low-growing vegetation or in the ground are most susceptible. A fungus enters when a spore germinates on the surface of the integument and sends a hypha into the body of the larva. The mycelium develops and eventually fills the body cavity of its host. Hyphae grow out covering the host and if conditions are favourable, conidiophores are produced. These release the spores, or conidia, into the air to complete the cycle. Because the development of many of these fungi is little affected by low temperature, they are most common in the winter when the development of their hosts is slowed due to low temperatures. Some species have only been reported from one or a small number of hosts. However, others have a very wide host range. For example, *Beauveria bassiana*, which causes a characteristic white cheese-like mass in and on the corpses of hosts, has been recorded from over 100 species of insect from a wide variety of orders.

The Zygomycetes include the Entomophthorales. The corpses of insects infected by species of this group may be recognised because they are attached to the substrate by a network of long hyphae covered with conidiophores. This type of fungus is most familiar to many people when it kills house flies, leaving the corpse of the fly attached to walls, ceilings or windows, with what looks like a misty halo surrounding the cadaver. Many moths are infected by fungi of this group, some species of fungi having a wide host range. Infection is usually of adults, the fungus entering via the joints, particularly in and around the legs. Again the mycelium develops in the body cavity and soft tissues.

The list of fungal pathogens of Lepidoptera and the range of species that each infects is very incomplete. Here again, amateur entomologists can make a useful contribution. Rather than discarding diseased larvae or adults, preservation of specimens in absolute ethanol may allow identification at a later date by an appropriate expert.

Protozoa

Protozoa are minute single-celled animals, such as *Amoeba*, with which most people who have been taught biology at school will be familiar. These microscopic organisms reproduce mainly by binary fission, in effect simply splitting in two. Although reproduction is simple, many species have complicated life cycles involving dormant stages as spores within cysts. All the major classes of Protozoa have members that are pathogenic to insects. In most cases, the disease has a slow development, with lethargy and reduced fecundity, rather than death, being common symptoms.

Many of the pathogenic protozoa are initially ingested by a new host in the form of spores on food. Infection thus starts in the gut, from which it may spread to other tissues; the Malpighian tubules, fat bodies, other adipose tissues and gonads being targets for different types of protozoa. Release of spores for transmission to new hosts may be with faeces, but some protozoans are also vertically transmitted in eggs. Most famous of these is the microsporidian *Nosema bombycis*, which had a devastating effect on the silk industry in the second half of the nineteenth century (p. 257). The problems posed by this disease, which became known as pebrine disease, were so acute that Louis Pasteur was asked to investigate. He discovered that the microsporidian was transmitted in the cytoplasm of the egg of the Silk Worm, *Bombyx mori*. His recommendations (Pasteur 1870), which successfully eliminated the disease, were that breeding moths should be caged as single pairs and that all adults should be examined microscopically for microsporidian spores before the eggs hatched, only eggs from infection-free pairs being retained.

Although a diverse array of protozoans infect moths, the microsporidia are undoubtedly the most important. In some pest species of moth, such as the Gypsy moth, and the Brown-tail, *Euproctis chrysorrhoea*, the microsporidian *Plistophora schubergi* is considered to be one of the most important pathogens controlling population size.

The finding that some microsporidians are inherited in the cytoplasm of eggs of their host raises the possibility that they would evolve ultra-selfish strategies such as feminisation or male-killing, thereby distorting the sex ratio of hosts in favour of females through which they may be transmitted. Although microsporidia employing these strategies have not been recorded in Lepidoptera, they are known to cause male-killing in many species of mosquito and feminisation in a number of crustaceans. If sex ratio biases are recorded in Lepidoptera, it would be valuable to assay for microsporidia as well as bacteria when seeking the causative agent.

Disease transmission and control

Some understanding of the transmission of moth diseases is needed both for the professional entomologist with an interest in methods of controlling pest species and for the moth breeder who wishes to minimise losses from disease. Locally, many diseases are transmitted by ingestion of contaminated food, or by contact with infected insects. However, these are not the only methods of local transmission and they contribute little to long-range transmission. As we have already seen, some bacteria and protozoans are transmitted down the generations in the eggs of their hosts. The same is true of some of the polyhedrosis and granulosis viruses. In some cases, viruses are transmitted both vertically in eggs from female hosts, and horizontally from males to females during mating.

Local transmission may also result from cannibalism. Many Lepidoptera indulge in cannibalism in the larval stage. In some cases this cannibalism involves the consumption of eggs of the same batch. In other cases, larvae cannibalise other larvae when at high density or when food becomes scarce. In a few species, cannibalism between larvae is habitual, as some sources of food are only sufficient to allow the development of a single larva. Although most moth pathogens have some stage in their life cycle that is capable of long-term survival outside a host, there are some viruses and bacteria, such as members of the Rickettsiaceae, that can only survive for a few hours in the open environment. Consequently, these pathogens are probably transmitted directly into new hosts. Interestingly, the larvae of some moth genera, such as *Spodoptera*, *Mamestra* and *Melanchra*, are attracted to fresh corpses of virus-killed conspecifics when the integument ruptures. It is thought that the ruptured corpses smell strongly of the foodplant and this attracts other larvae, which then feed on the liquified remains thereby imbibing a huge dose of the pathogen.

Various factors have been implicated in both long-distance transmission and new disease outbreaks. Wind, rain and water movement after substantial rains all play a role in dispersing spores and viruses over considerable distances. Although little systematic work has been conducted on the contents of the 'aerial plankton' specifically as it pertains to the diseases of insects, fungi, fungal spores and bacteria have all been recorded at altitudes over 6,000 metres in the atmosphere. Should thermal air currents carry disease particles to high altitude, high winds at these altitudes may then disperse the particles over very great distances.

Both predators and parasitoids of moths also play a role in disease transmission. Predatory bats, birds, bugs, beetles, ants and mites have all been shown to be capable of vectoring viral polyhedra. In some cases, when feeding on an infected caterpillar, the predator ingests the virus, passing it out some time later and some distance away when it defecates. Predators such as wasps may carry bits of or entire infected larvae some distance to nests or food stores. Scavengers that feed on the remnants of decaying corpses may transmit bacterial and viral insect pathogens, just as flies are known to transmit some vertebrate pathogens.

Parasitoids

Parasitoids are insects that feed as larvae entirely in or on other living insects, which are eventually killed as a result of the parasitoids' actions. The adults are free-living. The parasitoids of British moths are confined to two orders of insects, the Hymenoptera and the Diptera. Many families of Hymenoptera are represented among the parasitoids of British moths, while all dipterous parasitoids belong to one family, the Tachinidae. The larvae of most parasitoids live inside their hosts and are said to be endophagous. However, some are ectophagous, living on the surface of the host, feeding through a lesion in the host's skin.

All immature stages of the moth's life cycle are attacked by parasitoids. Many Hymenoptera lay their eggs inside the host by use of a piercing ovipositor. In some cases, the egg-laying equipment is exceedingly strong and sophisticated and has the ability to pierce plant material, including wood, to reach the larvae of leaf-mining, stem-boring or wood-boring moths. Where parasitoid eggs are laid on the surface of the host, the resulting larvae are either ectophagous or eat their way into the host. Tachinids do not have a piercing ovipositor. Many lay eggs on foliage, often close to feeding larvae. In some species, the eggs do not hatch unless they are eaten by appropriate larvae. Others hatch into robust and active larvae, which seek out host larvae and can survive for some time searching for potential hosts.

Some parasitoids develop fully in the stage of the host in which they are laid, emerging from this stage when they have completed their development. Others remain in their host for more than a single stage. For example, many Trichogrammatidae and Mymaridae oviposit into the eggs of moths and the minute, fully developed wasps emerge from these eggs. Conversely, Encyrtidae and some Braconidae, which also oviposit in moth eggs, do not emerge from their hosts until the hosts have reached the final larval instar (Plate 4f).

There is no doubt that the reaction of many lepidopterists to the appearance of parasitoids in their breeding stock is one of frustration, for parasitoids invariably cause the death of the desired host. However, as with insect diseases, our knowledge of parasitoids is remarkably poor, and here again those that breed moths may contribute considerably to scientific knowledge. All that is required is to keep the parasitoids, the cocoons that they emerged from if these are evident, and the remnants of their hosts together with normal data label details. As most parasitoids are difficult to classify down to species level, the specimens may then be passed on to a specialist in the field. Most museums that house decent insect collections keep lists of appropriate experts.

Further than this, an appreciation of the varied life histories of parasitoids and the extraordinary array of strategies they use to overcome the problems that they face may reduce the disappointment felt when weeks or months of care and attention result in a wasp or fly, rather than a moth.

Most of the parasitoids of Lepidoptera reproduce sexually. In the Diptera, the sex ratio is usually close to 1:1. However, in many of the Hymenoptera, females outnumber males to a very marked extent. Such ratios appear to contradict Darwin's and Fisher's explanation of the 1:1 sex ratio seen in most species. Bill Hamilton (1967), in trying to explain 'extraordinary sex ratios' in a variety of insects, formulated the idea of local mate competition. This theory was based on two observations that Hamilton knew to be true. First, the sex ratios of many hymenopterous parasitoids are strongly female biased. Second, in many of these species brother–sister matings occur commonly. The essence of local mate competition is that if there is more intense competition among siblings of one sex than among siblings of the other sex, the fitness of the more competing sex will, on average, be lower than that of the less competing sex. Selection will then act on the parental generation to produce more of the sex that has higher fitness because it suffers less competition.

This idea can be illustrated by thinking of a hymenopterous parasitoid that lays clutches of eggs in individual hosts. The Hymenoptera are haplo-diploid. Females are diploid as a result of normal fertilisation, while males are haploid, developing from unfertilised eggs. This means that female wasps have greater control over the sex of the progeny that they produce than do females of normal diploid species, for here sex is determined simply by whether or not a female wasp fertilises each egg before laying it. Furthermore, inbreeding depression, which is the reduced fitness that results from breeding with close relatives due to the expression of harmful recessive alleles, is generally low. The reason that it is low is simply that it has to be, for in the haploid males, deleterious recessive genes would always be expressed as there can be only one copy of each gene. They are thus selected out of the population as there is no chance of a second, dominant allele being present on a homologous chromosome to mask their effects. Given the lack of inbreeding depression in hymenopterous parasitoids, mating with relatives is no longer a problem. Here then, when a female wasp lays a batch of eggs in a moth larva, as long as males have the ability to mate many times there is little reason to produce more than one male. If the one male emerges from the host and becomes adult before any of his female sisters, he will be in a position to mate sequentially with each of his sisters as they emerge. This is the pattern seen in many of the parasitoids of moths that deposit many eggs in each host.

Female-biased sex ratios also occur in some species of parasitoid in which only one egg is laid per host. Because the fitness of male insects is less dependent upon size than the fitness of females, some female wasps lay unfertilised eggs in small hosts and fertilised eggs in large hosts.

The most female-biased parasitoids are those that reproduce parthenogenetically. In such species males are unknown or occur exceedingly rarely. In some cases, including many of the Trichogrammatidae, this type of parthenogenesis, in which females produce females in the absence of sex (thelytokous parthenogenesis), is induced by the presence of inherited bacteria of the genus *Wolbachia* (see p. 170). The parasitoids of moths vary greatly in their habits. Some species attack a wide variety of hosts: others just hosts of a single family or genus, or occasionally just of a single species. Those that attack just one or a small number of related species usually respond to a specific cue. For example, the ichneumonid *Venturia canescens*, which parasitises moths of the genus *Ephestia*, responds to a specific secretion from the mandibular glands of larvae. Host specificity has the benefit that a parasitoid species can become extremely well adapted to the conditions provided by the host. Thus the most sophisticated host detection systems and anti-immunity systems are found in parasitoids with high levels of host specificity. However, using a very limited range of hosts also bears a risk if that particular host species or group becomes unavailable. Polyphagous parasitoids avoid this risk, but tend to show less subtle and elegant adaptations to any particular host.

There are a number of differences between parasitoid Hymenoptera and Diptera. One obvious difference is genetic, in that the Hymenoptera are haplodiploid, while Diptera have diploid females and males. Another difference is that most hymenopterous endoparasites eat almost the entire contents of their host's body, while dipterous endoparasitoids frequently leave a portion of the host uneaten. Shaw & Askew (1976) argue that this may be a consequence of the ability of many Hymenoptera to retain waste products internally until they stop feeding. Only then is a connection between the middle and hind portions of the gut opened. This means that the host's body is not contaminated by the parasitoid's waste products and all is palatable. Another difference between Hymenoptera and Diptera is that, at a general level, the latter are less sophisticated in their ability to appraise some aspects of the quality of potential hosts. For example, they appear less able to detect whether a host already contains a parasitoid of their own or a different species.

The feeding of endoparasites is often rather precise. Most do not feed on the tissues of their host indiscriminately. Rather they concentrate initially on replaceable resources, such as the fat body. In this way the parasitoids avoid the risk of killing their host before they have fully developed and they allow the host to continue to take in nutrients that they can utilise.

Superparasitism, multiparasitism and hyperparasitism

Some parasitoids are strictly solitary. In these, a single host frequently only contains enough nutrients for the development of one wasp or fly. Such species frequently have mechanisms for searching inside their host for conspecifics, which if found are destroyed. Usually this results when more than one female has laid an egg in the same host, for in these solitary species, females lay just one egg at a time.

The laying of more than one egg in a host individual is termed superparasitism (Plate 4f), whether this be the result of one female laying several eggs in a host or several females of the same species laying one or more eggs in a host. The term multiparasitism is used for the situation in which females of two or more species lay eggs in the same host. The outcome is usually the death of all but one of the parasites. However, the remaining parasite does not eat the ones that die. Should that be the case, the term hyperparasitism could be used, for this covers precisely the situation in which one parasite develops on another parasite rather than on the primary host (Shaw & Askew 1976). Hyperparasitism is thus sometimes referred to as secondary parasitism.

In the Hymenoptera, the risk of multiparasitism has led to the evolution of chemical detection systems that allow females to discern whether a potential host has already been parasitised by another female. As it is usually the younger parasite that dies in cases of multiparasitism, this strategy is adaptive for a female wasp. Diptera parasitoids do not appear to have evolved this ability (Shaw & Askew 1976), although it would obviously be beneficial to them if they did so.

The division between multiparasitism and hyperparasitism is not always clear cut. For example, some chalcids can develop equally well on leaf-mining lepidopteran larvae or on other chalcid larvae that are devouring such larvae.

Predators

A wide array of predatory animals kill and eat Lepidoptera. Some of these specialise on one or more specific stages of a moth's life cycle, although many will eat any stage if they can catch and kill it and if it is profitable to do so. The amount of research that has been devoted to different types of predators varies tremendously. Thus, birds and bats have received a great deal of attention, while most invertebrates have been largely ignored.

Invertebrate predators

A huge range of invertebrates will attack and eat moths. Small predatory bugs, beetles, lacewings and earwigs will eat moth eggs if they encounter them. Many wasps, hornets and ants will kill moth larvae, often carrying the corpses back to their nests to be butchered and fed to the brood. Some solitary wasps specialise on caterpillars (for example, *Ammophila, Eumenes*), but not, except in a local glut, on one species. Predatory beetles and true bugs will also eat any immature stage if they encounter it. In most of these cases the predators do not specialise on a particular species of moth. Indeed most do not specialise on moths at all: they just attack them if they come across them.

The range of invertebrates that attack adult moths is rather smaller simply because adult moths have a greater ability to escape through flight. However, some invertebrates do catch and eat adult moths. Most of these catch their prey on the wing, either, as in the case of dragonflies and some robberflies, by grabbing them by claw or mouth in midair, or by snaring them as many spiders do (Fig. 7.6). A few groups of predators catch adult moths by stealth, and this is the case for some mantids and crab spiders that lie in wait on or below nectar flowers, waiting for these to be visited by a foraging moth that is then caught.

It is difficult to assess the relative levels of mortality imposed on moths by

Fig. 7.6 Police Car moths, *Gnophaela vermiculata*, in a spider's web, Alberta, Canada.

different types of invertebrate predator. Certainly levels will vary between species of moth. Thus, while small and delicate species of moth are at high risk from spiders' webs, in which they are easily ensnared, the larger noctuids and sphingids in Britain are only rarely trapped in any but the strongest spiders' webs (Plate 4e) simply because they tend to fly straight through them. I have often seen this with Large Yellow Underwings, *Noctua pronuba*, trying to find a way out of cobwebbed outhouses, the cobwebs ending in tatters by the time the moth makes its escape.

Given the very limited amount of information that we have on the types of invertebrate predators that eat moths, the species that they eat and the overall levels of mortality imposed on moth populations, here is another area in which enthusiasts can make their mark.

Amphibians and reptiles

As with the invertebrate predators, almost nothing is known about the impact of frogs, toads, newts, snakes or lizards on populations of British moths. Some work has been conducted on the palatability of brightly coloured moths or their larvae to amphibians and reptiles, but virtually no field work has been carried out on which of these groups eat which moths. Laboratory experiments and occasional field records do show that all these groups can and do eat moths. Indeed, I observed in Queensland, Australia, that cane toads would congregate around lights in the evening and many times I saw them take moths among the other insect visitors to the lights.

Again I suspect that predation of moths by all these groups is largely dependent on encounter rate and most of these predators will eat moths or their larvae if they see them and can catch them. Consequently, I suspect that some species of moth are more prone to attack than others. For example, I suspect that some of the species that fly and oviposit close to water or in reed beds are more prone to amphibian attack than others.

Birds

Birds are major predators of moths. Their impact is particularly severe on adult moths and on larvae, but small birds will also eat moth eggs and many birds will eat moth pupae if they find them. Most birds find moths by sight, using binocular colour vision. However, night-hunting birds, such as owls and nightjars, also catch moths and probably use hearing to detect the rustle of their wings.

Work on the predation of moths by birds has followed a variety of courses. Some has concentrated on questions related to the colour patterns of moths, with experiments showing that birds can learn to attack some species and avoid others, depending on the level of palatability of the moth. This type of research has demonstrated that birds vary in their ability to both learn and retain the memory of palatable and unpalatable prey. This variation is not just between species, but also within species, so, just as in ourselves, some birds have long memories while others forget very quickly. Indeed there are records of some captive birds that have been trained to avoid moths of a particular colour rejecting these after a year, with no experience of food of this colour in the interval. Conversely, some trained birds while rejecting certain prey on the day of training, try the same prey on the following day.

Different species of bird hunt moths in different situations and in different ways. However, most appear to have the ability to vary their hunting patterns depending on the availability of different types of prey that they encounter. For example, many have the ability to form searching images, retaining for a time an image of prey types that they have encountered commonly so that they actively search for prey that fit the image (p. 74).

Mammals

Many mammals will feed on moths. Small mammals inflict significant mortality on moth pupae in or on the ground, detecting them with an acute sense of smell. These small mammals will also eat many moth larvae that feed or hide in the lower herbage layers. Indeed, some larger mammals, such as foxes and badgers, will eat moth larvae as well, particularly when other food is scarce. In the winter of 1977–8, Dr Steve Harris presented me with the stomach contents of a road-killed fox. The recent diet of this fox, identified by head capsule analysis (over 250 head capsules present), turned out to be almost entirely noctuid larvae, with larvae of the Large Yellow Underwing among the most numerous. Gut content analysis has shown that lepidopteran larvae are a significant part of the diet of many mammals, including shrews, mice, rats, hedgehogs, foxes and badgers. However, as with most of the other predators mentioned above, the level of impact has not been accurately appraised.

Bats

Along with the birds, one group of mammals probably ranks as the most important in terms of the mortality rate that it inflicts on moths worldwide. These are the bats. In Britain, because bats, particularly the medium and larger species that tend to specialise on moths, occur at much lower densities than birds, the latter group certainly contribute more to moth mortality. However, in other parts of the world bats take huge numbers of moths when these are flying at dusk or under cover of darkness.

Bats find moths using a sophisticated echolocation system. They have the ability to produce very high-pitched squeaks from their mouths or noses, which are adapted to produce and project these ultrasonic beams. The sound, if it hits an object, whether this be a static object or a flying moth, bounces off it. Some of the echoing sound will return to the bat, which detects these very small sounds with incredibly sensitive forward-facing ears.

Bats emit sounds that vary in both intensity and pitch. To most of these sounds we are deaf, for their frequency is usually greater than 20kHz and above that of our hearing range. In most species, however, a small element is emitted at the high edge of our hearing and by listening very carefully, high-pitched squeaks can be heard. A few bats use sounds of lower frequency and some emit sounds that are not only within our hearing, but are very loud, sounding like some sort of car alarm or smoke alarm.

When flying to and from feeding grounds, bats will emit sound at a rate of about three to 10 pulses per second. This rate is continued when they reach the feeding ground until they detect a potential prey item. Then they increase their rate of sound production tremendously, accelerating almost instantaneously more than tenfold, and, during feeding, rates may be as high as 200 sounds per second. This increased sound emission rate gives bats great differentiation ability. Such ability is needed in many situations, for example when bats are hunting in woodlands where they will be flying among many complex shapes and where they will be assailed by moving echoes from leaves shaking in any breeze. The level of discrimination is such that some bats are capable of taking moths that are resting on leaves, while others, such as the Greater Horseshoe Bat, *Rhinolophus ferrumequinum*, can even distinguish between geometrids and noctuids on the wing (Schnitzler 1987).

Man

Finally, in dealing with the enemies of moths and moth mortality, we should not forget our own species. Unfortunately, man, through changes in land usage, habitat fragmentation and destruction, the use of pesticides of all sorts, and general pollution, has had a more severe detrimental effect on moth populations than any other species on Earth. I shall discuss our relationship with moths in the final chapter of this book.

Only two left, but two is enough!

A female moth lays hundreds of eggs. From the moment they are laid, their number starts to diminish. Some, through failure of fertilisation, do not begin to develop. Some die during embryo development. Many of the larvae that do hatch starve to death, particularly in the first instar. Predators, parasitoids and diseases each take a further toll during larval and pupal development. Inclement weather or other unfavourable environmental factors may also cause significant mortality before any of the siblings reach the adult stage. Once adult, there is further risk of predation, particularly by spiders, birds and bats. Throughout their lives, the moths are also at risk from one or more man-made obstacles, ranging from habitat destruction to the use of chemical insecticides and the allure of electric lights (p. 265). Finally, some adults, even if they avoid all of these causes of mortality, may simply fail to breed because they do not find a mate, or fail to induce another moth to mate with them. With all these jeopardies, it is perhaps not surprising that on average only about two of the eggs laid by a female will succeed in reproducing themselves. But two is enough. Furthermore, one may look at the situation the other way round. Given all the risks to which moths are exposed, it is amazing that as many as two do survive. It is with the strategies that moths have evolved to avoid some of their enemies that I will deal in the next chapter.

8

Moth Defences

Evolutionary arms races

As described in Chapter 7, moths face a tremendous array of enemies. In this chapter I will discuss some of the defences that moths have evolved to avoid being eaten, parasitised or killed in some other way. The array of defences that moths employ is as diverse as their array of enemies. Their ability to fly, the nocturnal activity of the majority of species, their chemistry, their habitat selectivity and their morphology, both when adult and in their immature stages, all contribute to defence in some instances.

The Red Queen

Antagonistic interactions between moths and their enemies seem rather one-sided affairs. If the predator or parasite (whether parasitoid or pathogen) wins, the moth dies. If the moth wins, the enemy often will simply go hungry for a while as it seeks another victim. This is called the life-dinner principle (the moth loses its life, whereas the predator loses only its dinner) and is one of several reasons suggested to explain why predators rarely drive their prey to extinction. However, in evolutionary terms, we often view both predator-prey and host-parasite interactions more equitably. The protagonists, prey/hosts on one side and predators/parasites on the other, are involved in evolutionary arms races. Prey/host species will evolve defences against their major enemies. When such defences become efficient, the predators or parasites have to turn to other types of victim or have to evolve measures to counter their prey's defences. In turn the victims will be selected to evolve countermeasures to their enemies' countermeasures and so on. This never ending struggle for supremacy has been termed the Red Queen hypothesis, in reference to the Red Queen from Lewis Carroll's *Alice Through the Looking Glass and What She Found There*. The Red Queen says to Alice, '… here you see, it takes all the running you can do to keep in the same place. If you want to get somewhere else, you must run at least twice as fast as that.'

Moths use different defences against different enemies. They will flee from some predators, hide from others. Many have evolved immunity to some parasitoids and pathogens. Some have the ability to encapsulate the eggs of parasitoids, thus killing them. An array of immunological defences to disease organisms has evolved, including encapsulation, inactivation, digestion and mechanisms to reduce pathogen transmission. Some moths have evolved, particularly in their larvae, an array of physical defences against predators in the form of sharp spines or barbed hairs. Others have coopted chemistry into their defence, so many are toxic or at least distasteful and some have stinging hairs (Fig. 8.1) or spit acid. Advantage is taken of these chemically defended species by others that just pretend to have such defences. Many of the defences of moths involve their internal chemistry and metabolism, and as such have to be

Fig. 8.1 The larvae of
Leucanella leucane have
stinging hairs.

studied using sophisticated techniques and equipment. However, many of
these defensive strategies have obvious physical manifestations in the external
morphology of the moth.

Considering for the present just the predators of moths, we can divide the
act of hunting into a series of components as listed in Table 8.1. For each of
these components we can imagine a variety of ways in which the predators can
improve their hunting skills. Furthermore, if we consider the chemistry, morphology and behaviour of moths for each of these predator activities, it is not
hard to think of examples of defensive countermeasures employed by at least
some species of moth during some part of their lives.

Table 8.1 Predator and prey adaptations and countermeasures resulting from evolutionary
arms races. (Adapted from Krebs & Davies 1981.)

Predator behaviour	Predator adaptations or counter-adaptations	Prey defence
Searching for prey	Good vision or other senses	Camouflage Disruptive patterns
	Search image formation	Polymorphism Flash patterns
	Area restricted search in areas of high prey density	Spacing out
Recognition of prey	Memory	Resemblance of inedible object (e.g. bird dropping) Müllerian mimicry Batesian mimicry
Subduing prey	Handling dexterity	Unexpected movement, rapid escape
Assessment of prey	Cautious attack Smelling and tasting	Resistance to injury Volatile unpleasant scent
Handling and consuming prey	Strong beak, tearing skills, disarming skills Immunity to stings and infection Disarming or detoxification skills	Spines, hairs, tough exoskeleton Barbed, urticating or stinging hairs or spines Toxins

It has been one of the greatest fascinations of my life to try to understand why the insects I encounter in the field have come to be the way they are and to speculate on the evolutionary pathways involved. I believe that I can explain many of the characteristics of many of the moths that I encounter, but there are multitudes of others that make me feel that I am struggling in the dark. Indeed, there are many moth mysteries I doubt will ever be solved satisfactorily. The problems faced by anyone seeking explanations are considerable.

First, many of the strategies employed are costly in terms of either energy or time. Both of these resources are required for many other aspects of life. For a moth, the optimal amount of time and energy that should be put into defence is the result of a complex trial and error calculation involving the need for time and energy to do all other important activities: feeding, growing, metamorphosing, finding a mate and reproducing. Genetic variation arising through mutation, recombination and sex creates the trials, and adaptive evolution selects only those trials that are close to the optimum. Our ignorance of the detail of most facets of the lives of most moths means that we rarely have the knowledge to undertake the complex cost-benefit analysis at the root of moth defences.

Second, we are not insects or birds or bats or bacteria. We do not perceive the world as other organisms do. Our senses are different. Compared with some animals, some of our senses appear more acute, but in many cases our sensory capabilities are inferior. How, for example, can we perceive the world at night, when most moths fly, as an insectivorous bat, 'seeing' with its sonar, does? Research over the last 30 years has even shown that perhaps the best of our senses, sight, is not as good as that of some of the enemies of moths. For many years birds were used in experiments on the defensive colour patterns of insects because it was believed that bird vision was similar to our own colour vision. However, it is now known that most birds have good vision in the ultraviolet spectrum to which we are virtually blind (Burkhardt & Maier 1989, Maier 1992, Bennett & Cuthill 1994). This lack of an ultraviolet dimension in our perception of the colour patterns of moths means that the patterns that we see may be somewhat different from those seen by birds.

Rates of evolution in arms races

There is one obvious difference between predator/prey and host/parasite arms races as they relate to moths. The reproductive rate of moths is greater than that of many of their predators. As a consequence, novel genetic variants will be generated more rapidly among moths than among their predators. The evolution of variants that are more efficient at avoiding predators is likely to be more rapid than the evolution of increase in predatory efficiency. This may be one of the reasons, but not the only reason, why prey species are rarely hunted to extinction by predation. Conversely, many of the parasitoids of moths are at least as fecund as moths and most of the pathogenic parasites, such as viruses, bacteria, protozoa and fungi, reproduce much faster than moths. Some enemies will thus evolve as fast as or faster than moths. Others will evolve more slowly, because they are asexual and so generate new genetic combinations more slowly. Thus in the case of host/parasite systems, it is more difficult to predict the likely course of evolution, except on a case-by-case basis.

Adaptive colour patterns of moths

The colours and patterns of moths are the product of evolution and as such, may be adaptive. There is probably no sphere that better illustrates the adaptive elegance and subtlety that may be produced by evolution than the colour patterns of the Lepidoptera. A variety of factors may influence this evolution, the most obvious being thermoregulation, species recognition, sexual selection and defence against predators. However, for many moths, only the last of these seems likely to have played a significant role in the colour pattern evolution of the majority of species. As we have already seen, because most moths are active under cover of darkness, they have adopted the use of pheromones to find, recognise and assess quality in potential mates. This is in contrast to most species of butterfly, in which the colour patterns, particularly of males, are crucial in securing acquiescence from females to copulate.

Thermoregulation has undoubtedly been influential in the evolution of adult colour patterns of many moth species, particularly day-flying species. In many day-active insects, including some moths, the extent of dark coloration is inversely correlated with environmental temperature. As dark surfaces absorb and radiate heat more rapidly than light ones, there is a general tendency for increased darkness in cooler climates. For example, in many butterfly and hoverfly species, individuals from high altitude or high latitude populations are darker than those from warmer climes. This is true of some moths, and here, the colour patterns are usually not constrained by having to look a certain way to be recognised by potential conspecific mating partners. For example, the Black Mountain moth, *Psodos coracina*, and the Netted Mountain moth, *Semiothisa carbonaria*, northern day-flying species of mountain tops, habitually open their dark-coloured wings and orientate them at right angles to the sun early in the morning to increase the rate at which they can attain efficient flight temperature (Plate 14a, Fig. 8.2). This 'thermal melanism' is one of the reasons why a disproportionately large number of species are dark in cool habitats, such as those at high altitude or latitude. However, as the main variable in colour pattern induced by thermoregulatory influences is simply how dark the colour pattern is, or to put it another way, the quantity of melanic pigments laid down, this aspect of colour pattern will be discussed in the next chapter in a more general discussion of melanism in moths.

Fig. 8.2 Netted Mountain moth, *Semiothisa carbonaria.*

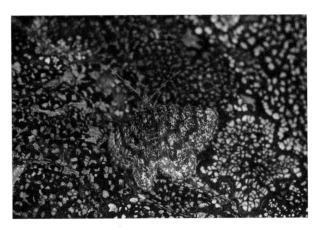

The fourth function of moth colour patterns, that of avoiding predation, has been the most influential in the majority of species. There is a wide array of ways that colour patterns can be used as a defensive measure. They may make the moth difficult to see, or difficult to recognise as food, or they may advertise some unpleasant quality of the moth. Consequently moths provide many of the most beautiful and often startling illustrative examples of camouflage, warning coloration and other types of defensive colour patterns.

Defensive colour patterns

Our interpretations of the various ways that the colour patterns of different species work defensively, are simply that: interpretations. We are not major predators of moths: birds, bats and other insects are. As I have already pointed out, our visual perception is not the same as that of insects or of birds. It differs in many ways, some of which we do not fully understand. For example, our virtual blindness to light in the ultraviolet (UV) spectrum (wavelength less than 400 nanometres), which most birds see well (Burkhardt & Maier 1989), is because while we have three types of colour sensitive cells, or cones, in our retinas, these being sensitive to blue, green and red, most birds have a fourth type of cone, which has a peak sensitivity in the UV (at around 360 nanometres) (Chen & Goldsmith 1986). Thus, while we may attempt to interpret the defensive strategies that may derive from the colour patterns of moths, we need to remain aware that our interpretation may be flawed unless supported by stringently controlled objective experimental results.

That said, our visual perception is sufficiently similar to that of birds that we can make some interpretation of the 'anti-bird' role of moth colour patterns. Although moths use a wide array of different defensive colour pattern strategies, at the most basic level these strategies can be split into just two groups: those that make moths difficult to see, and those that make moths easy to see. Each of these categories can be subdivided several times. For example, among the difficult-to-see strategies are a range of different types of camouflage, or crypsis, while in the easy-to-see group are those that have true warning colours, those that mimic unpalatable species, and those that mimic unpalatable objects, such as bird droppings. In addition, there are a few species that use both obvious and obscure patterns at different times, or in different situations, as parts of their defensive strategy.

Hard-to-see colour patterns

Crypsis or camouflage

Cryptic literally means hidden. A cryptic insect merges into its background. The use of cryptic colour patterns is one of the most common strategies employed by British moths against predators that hunt by sight. Crypsis is employed by all the different life history stages. The array of examples is huge, from the delicate green coloration of some of the emerald moths, which rest on the underside of leaves, to the complex patterns of species such as the Marbled Green, *Cryphia muralis*, (Fig. 8.3), that resemble pieces of lichen. In many instances, the strategy is only effective if the insect has strong resting-site preferences. For example, the stripy pale buff coloration of the forewings and thorax of many of the wainscot moths is only effective if the moths preferentially rest with correct orientation along dead grass or reed leaves or stems

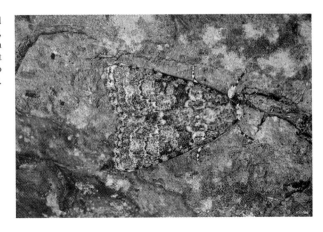

(Plate 7a).

Almost every solid substrate in the natural environment acts as a template for the colour pattern of some species of moth. Many moths are bark-resters, with specific adaptations to the bark of particular trees or to bark supporting a specific flora of lichens, mosses, algae or liverworts. This can be seen by comparing the colour patterns of the Early Grey, *Xylocampa areola* (Plate 6a), the July Highflier, *Hyriomena furcata* (Plate 6b), the Merveille du Jour, *Dichonia aprilina* (Plate 6c), and the Mottled Beauty, *Alcis repandata* (Plate 6d). Others, such as the Early Thorn, *Selenia dentaria* (Plate 7b), and the Lappet, *Gastropacha quercifolia* (Plate 7c), resemble dead leaves, although in rather different ways.

The basic strategy of blending into the background adopted by the examples given above is perhaps the simplest type of crypsis. However, there are many variations on this theme with varying levels of sophistication.

Adorning oneself

One effective method of resembling elements of the immediate environment is to adorn oneself with bits of the environment. This is practised by those larvae that include bits of bark or leaf in the cocoon. It is taken further by the larvae of the Psychidae, which are known as the bagworms. The larvae construct larval cases or bags of silk into which materials such as twigs, leaf debris, sand grains, particles of soil or pine needles are incorporated (Fig. 8.4). In some species, the females retain a larval appearance, even when adult, and spend their whole lives within the bag.

Fig. 8.4 The larvae of the bagworm moths construct a silken case and adorn themselves with bits of plant material or soil. (Drawing by Anne Bebbington.)

Countershading

A common problem for camouflaged organisms is that their bodies cast a shadow, making them stand out from their background. Many adult moths counteract this problem by resting on relatively flat substrates, clamping their wings against the substrate and using the fringes of hairs along the outer margins to produce a good, shadow-free contact. Many, but not all, moth larvae that are broadly cylindrical in shape share this problem of casting a shadow. Some avoid the problem by resembling a part of the plant that should cast a shadow. Thus, the larva of the Small Emerald, *Hemistola chrysoprasaria* (Plate 9a), in common with many other geometrid larvae, resembles a twig or petiole. Others, such as the larvae of the Lappet moth, use a similar technique to adult 'clamping' to reduce shadows. These larvae have a row of hairs and protuberances along the lower lateral edges that make shadow-free contact with the twigs or branches on which the larvae rest (Plate 9c).

However, the larvae of many other species have evolved a colour pattern that directly reduces the revealing effects of shadow. These colour patterns are known as countershading. In essence, such patterns involve a darkening of the surface of the body that is most often directed towards the light (Fig. 8.5). In many species this is the upper or dorsal surface. However, in species such as the Privet Hawk moth, *Sphinx ligustri*, whose larvae habitually rest upside down on their foodplant (Plate 9d), it is the ventral surface that is darkened.

Appropriate behaviour

The upside-down behaviour of Privet Hawk moth larvae highlights the importance of behaving in a manner appropriate to your colour pattern. It is of little use resembling a reed stem and then resting on a tree trunk. This means that selection will favour the evolution of resting-site preferences and associated behaviours. Species such as the Goat moth, *Cossus cossus* (Plate 6f), and the Buff-tip, *Phalera bucephala*, look like a broken branch stump or twig and behave in an appropriate manner. I have only found three Buff-tips resting in the wild

Fig. 8.5 A larva of the Mother Shipton, *Callistege mi*, showing typical countershading with the ventral part of the body lighter than the dorsal part. (Courtesy John Bebbington.)

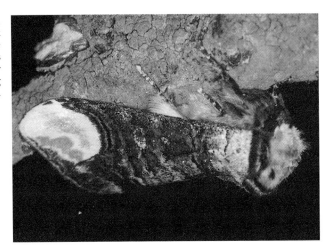

Fig. 8.6 A Buff-tip,
Phalera bucephala, at
rest showing the
cryptic value of its
colourful anterior
end and forewing
tips.

and in all three cases they were sitting on the ends of broken oak twigs (Plate 7d, Fig. 8.6).

Changing colour

One of the most superb exhibitions of camouflage is seen in a predator of moths from the tropics and subtropics, the chameleon. Chameleons achieve their fame in respect of camouflage because they have the ability to change colour rapidly. Light sensitive cells in their skin mediate a response in the epidermal cells by which pigment granules migrate in these cells so that a high degree of background matching is achieved. Although moths cannot change colour so rapidly, the larvae of many species can change colour over a period. Changes are of several types. In many larvae and some pupae, the colour is determined by the conditions that a larva is exposed to at a certain critical period in development. The critical period for the colour of late instar larvae is usually during the first, second or third larval instar. For pupae, the critical period is later, and usually during the final larval stage. Many workers, starting with Professor E.B. Poulton in the late nineteenth century, have shown that larvae of many geometrids will be different colours if reared in boxes covered with different coloured papers. Thus, Figure 8.7 shows three larval types of the Scalloped Hazel, *Odontopera bidentata,* produced in this way. Adding screwed up bits of black and white paper to the boxes produced the speckled form. This form occurs naturally in the wild if the twigs and branches that larvae are feeding amongst are covered in pale-coloured lichens.

In many other species, the colour is influenced by the colour of food ingested. In the larvae of the Angleshades, *Phlogophora meticulosa,* this can be demonstrated in a dramatic manner. Larvae of the Angleshades are highly polyphagous and feed readily on the flowers of many plants, although leaves of herbaceous plants are their more normal diet. Thus, all that is needed is to feed young larvae on petals of different colours to produce an array of differently coloured larvae (Plate 15a). This really is a case of 'you are what you eat'. The outer layers of the larvae are almost transparent, so what is seen is simply the gut contents showing through these outer layers. This only works for first, second and some third instar larvae. As the larva grows larger, this crypsis

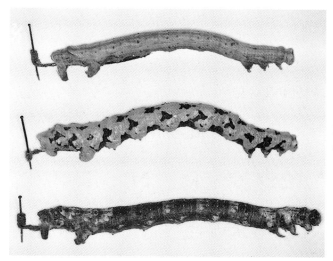

Fig. 8.7 Larvae of the Scalloped Hazel, *Odontopera bidentata*. The colour and patterning of these larvae depends on the colour of the surrounding vegetation in the early larval instars.

becomes inefficient as the larva starts to cast shadows, because the mechanism of camouflage does not entertain any form of countershading. Consequently, the larvae, which up to this point remain on their foodplant by day, start to move into the lower herbage layers during the day and only come up higher to feed at night. This switch in behaviour coincides with a switch in the control of colour of the larva, which now comes under full genetic control with virtually no dietary influence (see Box 8.1).

The larva of the Alder moth, *Acronicta alni*, changes its defensive strategy as it develops in an even more dramatic manner. In its early instars, the larva of this moth is an exceedingly good bird-dropping mimic. However, at its fourth larval ecdysis, it sheds this deceptive disguise and takes on a bright aposematic livery of black and yellow bands for its final instar (Fig. 8.8). The Miller, *Acronicta leporina*, follows a similar strategy, resembling a bird dropping when small. However, in its final instar, it becomes exceedingly hairy and usually a

Fig. 8.8 Larvae of the Alder moth, *Acronicta alni*. a) In the early instars the larva resembles a bird dropping. b) In the final instar, the larva becomes yellow and black and aposematic. ((a) courtesy John Bebbington.)

a   b

Box 8.1 The control of larval colour variation in the Angleshades moth, *Phlogophora meticulosa*. (Adapted from Majerus 1983.)

Instar	Colour	Method of control
First	Any colour, but usually green	Environmental control, determined by the colour of food ingested
Second	Any colour, but usually green	Environmental control, determined by the colour of food ingested
Third	i) Any colour: usually green	i) Environmental control, determined by the colour of food ingested (Plate 15a). Requires c^+ to be present.
	ii) Green	ii) Produced when c' and *b*' are both homozygous and either d^+ and/or e^+ are present.
	iii) Olive	iii) Requires c' to be homozygous, b' and b^o to be heterozygous and either d^+ and/or e^+ to be present.
	iv) Brown	iv) Requires c' and b^o to be homozygous and either d^+ and/or e^+ to be present.
	v) Plain yellow	v) Produced in one of three ways, all of which require c' and d' to be homozygous. If, in addition, e' and e^o are present, or both e' and b' are homozygous, or both e^o and b^o are homozygous, plain yellow will result.
	vi) Yellow-green	vi) Produced when c', d' and e^o are homozygous and b' is present.
	vii) Yellow-brown	vii) Produced when c', d' and e' are homozygous and b^o is present.
Fourth	i) Green	i) Produced when b' is homozygous and either d^+ and/or e^+ are present.
	ii) Olive	ii) Produced when b' and b^o are heterozygous and either d^+ and/or e^+ are present.
	iii) Brown	iii) Produced when b^o is homozygous and either d^+ and/or e^+ are present.
	iv) Plain yellow	iv) Produced in one of three ways, all of which require d' to be homozygous. If, in addition, e' and e^o are present, or when d', e' and b' are homozygous, or when d', e^o and b^o are homozygous, plain yellow will result.
	v) Yellow-green	v) Produced when d' and e^o are homozygous and b' is present.
	vi) Yellow-brown	vi) Produced when d' and e' are homozygous and b^o is present.
Fifth	i) Green	i) Produced when b' and a' are homozygous and either d^+ and/or e^+ are present.
	ii) Olive	ii) Produced when a' is homozygous, b' and b^o are heterozygous and either d^+ and/or e^+ are present.
	iii) Brown	iii) Produced when a^+ is present and/or b^o is homozygous, if either d^+ and/or e^+ are present.
	iv) Plain yellow	iv) Produced in one of three ways: when d is homozygous for either allele and e' and e^o are both present, when d', e' and b' are all homozygous, or when d', e^o and b^o are homozygous.
or	v) Yellow-green	v) Produced when d' and e^o and b' are homozygous.
	vi) Yellow-brown	vi) Produced when d' and e' are homozygous and b^o and/or a^+ are present.

Legend of alleles:

a⁺: acts in 5th instar, produces brown pigment. Dominant to a'.

a': acts in 5th instar, leaves colour under control of gene B. Recessive to a⁺.

b': acts in 3rd, 4th and/or 5th instar, produces green pigment. Co-dominant to b⁰.

b⁰: acts in 3rd, 4th and/or 5th instar, produces brown pigment. Co-dominant to b'.

c⁺: acts in 3rd instar, causing larval colour to be foodplant dependent. Dominant to c'.

c': acts in 3rd instar, causing 4th instar larval colour (genetically controlled) to be expressed in the 3rd instar. Recessive to c⁺.

d⁺: acts in 3rd, 4th and/or 5th instar, causing colour to be determined by alleles of genes A, B and C. Dominant to d'.

d': acts in 3rd, 4th and/or 5th instar, may cause yellow pigment to be produced. Recessive to d⁺.

e⁺: acts in 3rd, 4th and/or 5th instar, causing colour to be determined by alleles of genes A, B and C. Dominant to e' and e⁰.

e': acts in 3rd, 4th and/or 5th instar, preventing the expression of b'. Co-recessive with e⁰ to e⁺.

e⁰: acts in 3rd, 4th and/or 5th instar, preventing the expression of b⁰. Co-recessive with e' to e⁺.

In addition, there are a number of interactions between some of the alleles of the various genes.

pale blue-green colour. This larva is, I think, cryptic, a view that has added weight because melanic larvae are also known (Fig. 8.9).

Disruptive patterns

While countershading acts to reduce shadow effects, flattening the body outline, other colour patterns act to disguise the body outline completely. If cer-

Fig. 8.9 Larvae of the Miller, *Acronicta leporina*. In the early instars (a) the larva has some similarity to a bird dropping. In its final instar the larva becomes cryptic, and may be either green (b) or melanic (c).

a

b   c

Fig. 8.10 The disruptive patterning of the Beautiful Snout, *Hypena crassalis.*

tain predators commonly prey upon moths, it is likely that they will actively seek prey items of a particular basic shape: broadly triangular. To counteract this very generalised predator searching image, some species of moth, such as the Streamer, *Anticlea derivata* (Plate 8a), the Beautiful Snout, *Hypena crassalis* (Fig. 8.10), the Scalloped Oak, *Crocallis elinguaria* (Plate 8b), and the Green Carpet, *Colostygia pectinataria* (Plate 8c), have evolved patterns that disrupt their wing outline. Other species achieve the same end result by having unusually structured wings, as in the plume moths (Plate 1f), or by holding their wings so that the familiar moth-shaped triangle is not formed. The Poplar Hawk moth, *Lathoe populi* (Plate 8e), holds its wings out from the body with the hindwing protruding in front of the forewing. The Lime Hawk moth, *Mimas tiliae* (Plate 8d), manages to combine both types of disruptive strategy, holding its wings out away from its body and sporting a bold disruptive green bar across the forewings. The larvae of many moths also have disruptive patterns, often involving oblique lateral lines or crosshatching (Fig. 8.11).

Fig. 8.11 The larva of the Merveille du Jour, *Dichonia aprilina*, with crosshatch markings giving a disruptive pattern.

Becoming small

While the wings of moths are an essential feature of their locomotory system, in cryptic species they are also a liability, for these large anatomical structures have to be concealed in some way. In the females of some species the advantage of having wings for flight appears to have been outweighed by the cost of wings in terms of detection by predators. The result is that the wings of some females have been severely reduced in size or lost completely. Two examples are the Vapourer moth, *Orygia antiqua*, and its congener the Scarce Vapourer, *Orygia recens*, in which males are fully winged, while females are little more than egg bags. By dispensing with wings, female Vapourers have forgone adult dispersal entirely. When a female Vapourer emerges from her cocoon, she remains clinging to the outer surface of it. She attracts males pheromonally, sometimes from considerable distances, and mates. Still hanging onto her cocoon, she lays her eggs on its surface (Plate 2.1).

The Vapourer moth has its adult season from July to September, while the Scarce Vapourer is adult a little earlier, in June and July. However, the majority of species with 'wingless' females emerge as adults during the winter. Perhaps the most obvious examples are the winter moths, *Operophtera brumata* and *Operophtera fagata,* but females have forgone flight wings in 11 other species of geometrid that emerge when deciduous trees are bare of leaves. Most of these species have larvae that feed on a range of deciduous trees and pupate in the ground below the trees, reaching the ground by lowering themselves on silken threads when fully fed. Females, when they emerge from their pupae, crawl out of the ground, locate a tree and climb it. In the early evening of their first favourable adult night, they disperse pheromones from glands on their abdomens to attract males and usually mate on that first night. Thereafter, they climb further up the tree and oviposit on twigs, typically in cracks in the bark or at the base of leaf buds. The eggs hatch at about the time of leaf burst and so have young leaves to start consuming close by.

It is notable that in these winter species, eggs are at an advanced state of maturity when female moths eclose. In addition to reduced size as an antipredator device, it is possible that the wing reduction has resulted from a trade-off between the need to be mobile and the benefit of putting high levels of resources into egg maturation. Having eggs that may be laid quickly after eclosion and mating may be crucial, given the unpredictability of the weather in the winter and the risk that time for egg maturation may not be available before the onset of harsh conditions.

Females of these wingless species are much more difficult to detect than their male counterparts, simply because of their greatly reduced size. The question that needs to be asked is: why does such a high proportion of species that have evolved this strategy emerge in winter? There are two possibilities. First, the loss of wings may have evolved once in the past in an ancestral species that has subsequently speciated into all the winter-emerging species that now have the reduced wing trait. Alternatively, the conditions in winter may be such that the trade-off between the advantage of having wings for flight and the benefit in losing wings for predator avoidance is tilted towards the latter and the trait has evolved independently a number of times. Analysis of the evolutionary relationships between the winter-emerging species that have wingless females does not support the flightless female ancestor hypothesis, for while all the species concerned are geometrids, they are not all closely related. Furthermore, there are other geometrids that are closely related to some of the species in question, which fly in the summer and have fully-winged females. It thus seems more likely that the wing loss is the result of winter conditions, possibly in terms of the scarcity of other food for predators and the lack of foliage in deciduous woodlands to hide amongst or the extra energetic cost of flight at low temperature.

Polymorphism

As already mentioned (p. 181), many predators form what are known as searching images of prey items that they find commonly. Many experiments have been conducted on both captive and wild birds to show that this is the case. Some species of moth appear to have evolved a countermeasure that entails simply having lots of different forms within a population. By evolving high levels of colour pattern polymorphism these species disguise their true population density by spreading their appearance across a range of colours and patterns. Predators then can either only form rather vague and gener-alised size and shape searching images for a species, or have to form and remember a variety of different specific colour pattern searching images. Either way, being variable pays selective dividends.

Perhaps not surprisingly, many of the cryptic species that exhibit high colour pattern polymorphism are among the most common species of moth. This makes sense, for it will only be profitable for predators to form searching images of high density prey, and it will only be in these species that the anti-searching image response of increased variability will be selectively favoured. Examples of species in which such selection has probably occurred include the Clouded Drab, *Orthosia incerta*, the Large Yellow Underwing, *Noctua pronuba*, the Mottled Umber, *Erannis defoliaria* (Plate 7f), the Beaded Chestnut, *Agrochola lychnidis*, the Lunar Underwing, *Omphaloscelis lunosa*, the Spring Usher, *Agriopis leucophaeria*, and the Dotted Border, *Agriopis marginaria* (Fig. 8.12), all common species that occur locally at high densities.

Similar arguments can be made in respect of the larvae of some species. For example, the larvae of the Angleshades moth have evolved a considerable range of colour patterns with a highly sophisticated set of changes in their colours as they pass through their five larval instars. The environmental and later, genetic control of these different colour forms is complex. However, experimental evidence suggests that crypsis and searching image avoidance strategies have both played a role in the evolution of this complicated system (see p. 190 and Box 8.1)

Flash and startle patterns

Perhaps the most sophisticated defences among essentially cryptic moths involve those species that have hidden defensive assets behind their crypsis. Disturb a resting Eyed Hawk moth, *Smerinthus ocellata*, or a Large Yellow Underwing and each will reveal an unexpected feature, the former exposing a pair of large eyespots on its hindwings, the latter displaying, albeit briefly, bright contrasting colours on its hindwings. These two cases are classical exam-ples of startle patterns and flash patterns respectively. In both, the way that the moth behaves is an integral part of its defence.

In the case of the Eyed Hawk moth (Plate 10c), disturbance leads the moth

Fig. 8.12 Forms of
the Dotted Border,
Agriopis marginaria.
Both males and
females exhibit dif-
ferent colouring.

to move its cryptically patterned forewings forward sharply, thus exposing the
large eyespots on the hindwings (Plate 10d). These eyes are of a size and distance apart to suggest that they are the eyes of a fairly large vertebrate. The
moth moves as if 'hunching its shoulders', thereby exaggerating the suddenly-
exposed feature. Experiments have shown that this 'startle' strategy can be
effective in causing birds as large as Scrub Jays to take flight.

   As with most defensive strategies employed by adult moths, some larvae
employ the same device. The larvae of the Elephant Hawk moth, *Deilephila
elpenor,* and the Small Elephant Hawk moth, *Deilephila porcellus,* both sport large
eyespots on the 4th and 5th segments, a little way behind the head (Plate 10e
and 10f). If larvae of these species are disturbed, they retract their front segments into the 4th and 5th segments, causing these to enlarge, thus accentu-
ating the eyespots. This theme is taken to extremes in some tropical hawk
moths in which eyes are coupled with scale markings, turning the larvae into
superb snake mimics.

   The startle eyespots of the Eyed and Elephant Hawk moths are fairly coarse
mimics of vertebrate eyes (Plate 10d inset). They are effective because they are
likely to be encountered in relatively low light levels under foliage. However,
experiments by Tinbergen (1974) showed that the more eye-like a fake eye is,
the greater its benefit in deterring predators. He placed mealworms on papers
from which different shapes had been cut out. The papers were set on a light

switch pad of a light box so that if a bird pecked at the mealworm, the light in the box was switched on shining through the cut-out shapes either side of the mealworm. Using Great Tits as predators, he demonstrated that open circles were more efficient as frighteners than were crosses, and that rings were more efficient than open circles. The most efficient spot was a sophisticated pattern mimicking the iris and pupil of a vertebrate eye and with a small reflection segment on the eye as one will always see if one looks into such an eye.

This level of sophistication is achieved in the eyespots on the wings of the Emperor moth, *Saturnia pavonia* (Plate 11a). This species flies in the open during the day. Thus, to be effective the eye spots must closely resemble those of vertebrates, and indeed they do, with a series of differently coloured rings and a remarkable curved line of black and white scales resembling a reflection mark on a fluid-covered eye (Plate 11b).

A startle effect is also part of the strategy of the red underwing and yellow underwing moths. These species rely on crypsis as their first line of defence (Plate 10a). However, if this defence is breached, they reveal the bright contrasting colours of their hindwings, which may startle predators giving time for escape (Plate 10b). The combination of red and black or yellow and black may act as a deterrent if the predator has experience of unpalatable prey sporting these colours, such as ladybirds or wasps. However, the bright colours serve a further purpose. These combinations of bright colours are highly memorable. When disturbed these moths take flight readily, flying fast to some new resting site, flashing their bright hindwings as they go. When they land, the hindwings are immediately covered up by the cryptic forewings. Should the predator try to chase the moth to follow up its initial attack, there is a considerable probability that it will seek the brightly coloured insect that just evaded it, rather than the dull brown moth that is now all that might be found.

On a personal note, I well remember walks in the dry scrubland habitats in the foothills of the Alpes Maritimes in southern France when I was a boy. As I walked, flashes of bright blue, orange, red, yellow or green preceded me with almost every step as large grasshoppers leapt out of my path. The repeated frustration and fascination of not being able to find these radiant insects once they landed and concealed their striking hindwings remains with me to this day.

Colour patterns that make moths easy to see

From moths that have evolved colour patterns that make them difficult to see, as a first line of defence, we can move to those that are easily seen. The first such strategy is a little difficult to place because it must surely be thought of alongside crypsis. This strategy involves a resemblance to common inedible objects within most habitats where birds occur: bird droppings.

Bird-dropping mimicry

Anyone who regularly runs a mercury vapour moth trap overnight in the same place will be familiar with the fact that unless it is attended to soon after dawn, birds quickly learn of its location and that an easy meal may be had around the trap in the form of those moths that have been attracted to the light, but have not entered the trap. The evidence is a scattering of the discarded wings of the moths that the birds have consumed. However, in the summer months, among these remnants will be some intact moths alive. For example, Chinese

Fig. 8.13 Bird-dropping mimicry by the Scorched Carpet, *Ligdia adustata*. (Courtesy John Bebbington.)

Characters, *Cilix glaucata* (Plate 13a), Lime-speck Pugs, *Eupithecia centaureata* (Plate 13b), and several species of carpet moth (Fig. 8.13) frequently adorn the collar of my 'Robinson' trap, or may be found on foliage close by. It is very rare to find discarded wings of these species.

This scene around a moth trap is not difficult to interpret. As some of the birds that make a meal of moths around and on the trap sit on the trap while they consume their meal, they defecate here. The top of the trap is thus dotted with their droppings and the similarity in colour and shape of these droppings to species such as the Chinese Character or Lime-speck Pug resting alongside could hardly be missed.

As with most other types of colour pattern adopted by adult moths, some larvae employ bird-dropping mimicry, the previously mentioned Alder moth and Miller being examples.

Aposematism: true warning coloration

I have already mentioned on a number of occasions that many moths are brightly coloured. Various reasons exist for these bright colours. In some cases, bright colouring is a part of a defensive ploy used only when attacked by a predator as in flash and startle patterns. In others, particularly day-flying species, bright colours may serve in mate attraction or recognition. But by far the most common reason that moths have bright colours is to advertise that they are inedible as a result of some otherwise not obvious defensive capability. In some cases, this advertisement is a sham, as with the Batesian mimics discussed below (p. 206). When the bright colours are not a sham but are genuinely linked to some form of hidden defence, the moth is said to show aposematic coloration. In moths, the hidden defence is most commonly chemical in nature.

Aposematic colours are frequently called warning colours. I dislike this term for it seems to suggest that the most commonly employed colours, reds, yellow, black, are themselves a warning. This is obviously not the case. Many plants produce berries of these colours specifically to attract the attention of birds. The berries are eaten by birds, which then disperse the seeds within the berries by excreting the seeds in their faeces, usually some distance from the parent

Fig. 8.14 (top left) The aposematic larva of the Grey Dagger, *Acronicta psi*. (Courtesy John Bebbington.)
Fig. 8.15 (top right) The aposematic larva of the Toadflax Brocade, *Calophasia lunula*. (Courtesy John Bebbington.)
Fig. 8.16 (bottom left) When disturbed, the Leopard moth, *Zeuzera pyrina*, curls its abdomen revealing yellow stripes between the abdominal segments.
Fig. 8.17 (bottom right) The Hornet moth, *Sesia apiformis*, is a wonderful mimic of stinging Hymenoptera.

plant. In the commercial sector, we humans also use bright colours in advertising to attract the attention of consumers. Bright colours are thus not inherently a warning, but they are memorable, and may thus aid in recalling to a predator some previous unpleasant experience.

Many moths or their larvae have aposematic colour patterns. These include many of the tiger moths, the burnet moths and foresters, the larvae of some of the hawk moths, the larvae of many of the tussock moths, lasiocampids and a few noctuids (Figs 8.14 and 8.15) and the adults of a few of these species. In addition, the Leopard moth, *Zeuzera pyrina* (Plate 11d, Fig. 8.16), and a few species of geometrid, noctuid, and pyralid have aposematic larvae or adults or both. Finally, many members of the clearwing family (Sesiidae) and some hawk moths have conspicuous coloration (for example, Plates 5b, 13e, Fig. 8.17). However, it is not known whether these are palatable, and so they may be either aposematic or Batesian mimics.

The basic defences of aposematic British moths may be split into three categories: chemicals sequestered from food, chemicals manufactured by the moth and urticating hairs.

The Scarlet Tiger moth, *Callimorpha dominula*, sequesters pyrrolizidine alkaloids from its foodplant Comfrey and both larvae and adults are aposematic (Plates 1c and 12d). Similar chemicals are sequestered from other plants by other arctiids. Thus the White Ermine, *Spilosoma lubricipeda* (Plate 13c), and the Cinnabar (Plate 11c) can both sequester alkaloids from Ragwort, although the White Ermine only rarely feeds on this plant. Plants of the spurge family (Euphorbiaceae) contain a variety of defensive chemicals in their milky sap. Larvae of the Spurge Hawk moth, *Hyles euphobiae* (Plate 12a), sequester a number of these, including diterpenes (Rothschild 1985).

As an example of the second category, we can take the burnet moths (Plate 13f) and foresters of the family Zygaenidae. The burnet moths are coloured bright red and iridescent blue-black while the foresters are bright bronzy green moths. All occur in colonies and have a tendency to aggregate both as larvae and adults. Their unpalatability is based upon hydrogen cyanide, which is released from damaged tissues. These moths manufacture cyanogenic glycosides both as larvae and as adults. Many experiments conducted with burnet moths have shown that they are extremely repellent to vertebrate predators. The Five-spot Burnet, *Zygaena trifolii* (Fig. 8.18), is considered the most toxic moth on the British list and, as far as is known, none of its defensive chemicals are derived from its food (Rothschild 1985).

In many cases, moths combine both sequestered and manufactured chemicals. Thus, for example, the Garden Tiger moth, *Arctia caja* (Plate 11e), is known to sequester cardiac glucosides from Foxgloves, but it also manufactures acrylylcholine, choline esters and histamines.

Fig. 8.18 The Five-spot Burnet, *Zygaena trifolii*, is the most toxic species on the British list.

Urticating hairs

Many larvae are hairy (Plates 12b–e). Some of these hairs may simply make the larvae unappetising, or increase the handling time of predators. However, others have a more active defensive role. Many of these hairs are said to be urticating because the rash that they cause resembles that induced by the Stinging Nettle, *Urtica dioica*. Some of these hairs have a poison gland at their base; others do not. Larvae with both types of hair may produce a rash on vertebrate skin. The hairs of those without associated chemical defence are often sharp and barbed and lodge in skin, causing an irritation. The tips of these hairs are usually brittle so that they snap if attempts are made to brush them off. In those that inject a chemical, this is usually a protein, although some inject histamines. The effect is usually slower than that of a Stinging Nettle sting. Rashes produced are usually mild, but the severity varies both with larval species and with the susceptibility of the recipient of the hairs. Some species, such as the Brown-tail, *Euproctis similis*, and the Gypsy moth, *Lymantria dispar*, may produce severe dermatitis. In some individuals, urticating hairs may cause anaphylactic shock, convulsions and internal haemorrhaging. However, such reactions are rare. Some species of saturniid have stinging spines, as in *Leucanella leucane* (Fig. 8.1). The larva of the South American silk moth *Lonomia achelos* injects a strong anticoagulant from its spines and may cause severe internal bleeding in humans.

Many species that have larvae with urticating hairs are warningly coloured or aposematic, and some of the larvae with this type of defence are truly spectacular (see Plate 12e).

I have always been somewhat cautious when handling hairy caterpillars. This caution dates from when I was ten. My parents visited Minorca bringing back, in a shoe box, as a present for me, a 'nest' of caterpillars collected for them the day before their return by one of the hotel attendants. Ignorant of the potential dangers, I opened the box and lifted out the nest. Within an hour, my hands and lower arms had swollen to an extraordinary extent, causing tremendous pain. The nest was of the Pine Processionary moth, *Thaumetopoea processionea*. Wirtz (1984) estimates that one of these larvae carries about 600,000 urticating hairs, and there were over 150 larvae in the nest. In common with many aposematic insects the larvae of this species are highly gregarious (see Plate 12f). Some years after my first encounter with them, I heard of an experiment involving the 'follow-my-leader' behaviour of larvae of this species when they venture out of their nest to forage. The experimenter had guided the lead larva onto the edge of a bowl, allowing larvae to follow until the rim was full, the first larva joining up to follow the last larva. With no leader, the larvae continued to walk around the rim until they starved to death!

The evolution of aposematism

It is not easy to envisage how aposematism evolves. The problem is that two different characteristics, bright coloration and unpalatability, apparently have to evolve together to produce an effective defence.

Many theories have been proposed for the evolution of aposematism. These can be split into those in which unpalatability evolves first with warning coloration evolving secondarily; those in which the order of evolution of the two components is reversed; and those in which the two evolve simultaneously. In my view, all the following evolutionary scenarios are possible, and all will have operated in some cases, although not with equal frequency.

First unpalatable, then conspicuous

The way I like to think of this theory is by imagining a natural scenario. A cryptic species of moth that can feed on a number of species of plant is threatened with extinction by the competition from other species that feed on these plants. Accidentally, a female lays eggs on a species of plant that is well defended chemically, for example Common Ragwort. The larvae that result can feed on this plant, but have to cope with its chemical defence. There is a cost to this detoxification in the form of slower food processing and development. However, because the chemically defended plant is eaten by few other animals, these larvae have greater fitness than those that feed on other non-defended plants where there is severe competition from other species. During the detoxification process, the chemicals produced by the plant are sequestered by the caterpillars, making their new owners unpalatable. We now have a rationale for the evolution of the first stage of aposematism. From here, we need only increase the efficiency of the defence. Advertising one's distasteful qualities would seem to be sensible. However, there is a problem. If a mutation arose that made a cryptic species conspicuous, it would attract the attention of a predator that could have no previous experience of it and so would not know that it was chemically defended. In the ensuing attack, the mutant might be fatally injured and the mutation lost. Sir Ronald Fisher (1930) recognised this difficulty and invoked kin selection (p. 85) to overcome it. Suppose our moth laid a large clutch of eggs together. Then the new mutant with its conspicuous coloration would not be alone. Many of its brothers or sisters would have the same mutant phenotype. Then, although a predator might attack and kill one, the unpleasant experience of so doing would deter it from attacking others that looked the same. Crucially here, producing progeny within a small area may lead to a local abundance of conspicuous and distasteful individuals.

Other characteristics associated with aposematism, such as further aggregative behaviour, giving off nasty smells by use of volatile secretions and resistance to injury, may then evolve to further increase the efficiency of the defence. The White Ermine, *Spilosoma luricipeda*, for example, has specialised eversible structures (structures that can be turned outward) called coremata for distributing volatile anti-predator pheromones (Fig. 8.19).

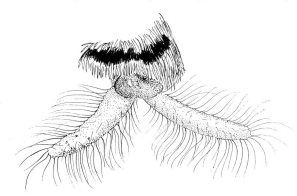

Fig. 8.19 The coremata of the White Ermine, *Spilosoma luricipeda*. (Drawn by Anne Bebbington from a photograph in Rothschild 1985.)

Conspicuous first, then unpalatable

Intuitively, it seems more likely that in the evolution of aposematism, unpalatability would evolve before conspicuousness simply because a conspicuous moth that was palatable would presumably be seen and eaten. However, there are two possible scenarios in which unpalatability might evolve secondarily to conspicuous coloration.

First, defence is not the only evolutionary reason for evolving bright and obvious colour patterns. Conspicuous displays are part of the courtship displays of many organisms, including many Lepidoptera. Although bright visual sex-related displays are perhaps more associated with butterflies than moths, examples among the latter do occur. One has only to think of the lekking displays of male Ghost moths, *Hepialus humuli*, or the sexual dimorphisms in some of the day-flying silk moths, including the Emperor moth (Fig. 8.20). Should bright coloration evolve for reasons other than defence, the fact that a species would then be at high risk from predators that hunt by sight could impose a selection pressure to evolve unpalatability thereafter.

An alternative evolutionary pathway could begin with Batesian mimicry (p. 208). A Batesian mimic is palatable, but gains protection from predation by closely resembling an aposematic species. As we shall see, one of the critical factors that influences the efficiency of such a system is the density of the mimic compared with that of its model. The mimic gains greatest protection when it is comparatively rare and its model is common. Now consider the possible fates of a Batesian mimic whose model has become extinct. There appear to be four possibilities. First, the mimic might become extinct through predation pressure and its lack of any effective defence in the absence of unpalatable models. Second, it might evolve a resemblance to another unpalatable species, thereby changing its model. Third, it might lose its fake warning coloration, becoming cryptic. Finally, it might become unpalatable itself, thereby transforming from a Batesian mimic into an aposematic species. Although I know of no proven case in which this evolutionary pathway has been followed, I have often wondered whether the reputed unpalatability of the Hornet Clearwing moth, *Sesia apiformis* (Rothschild 1985), has not evolved along these lines (see p. 209).

Fig. 8.20 The Emperor moth, *Saturnia pavonia*, shows considerable sexual dimorphism. Left - male; right - female.

Conspicuous and unpalatable together

Perhaps the least likely pathway to the evolution of aposematism is that in which both arise together. Given the rarity of genetic mutation, it seems improbable that what are likely to be discrete mutations, one involving a trait that makes a species unpalatable, the other causing it to become conspicuous, should arise concurrently. But unlikely is not the same as impossible, and this avenue should not be totally discounted. One way in which the concurrent creation of both types of trait may be made more likely is if the two were bio-chemically related. For example, it is feasible that following a foodplant shift as described above, the detoxification of food gave rise not only to distasteful-ness as toxins were sequestered from the food, but also to a new pigment as a waste product of the detoxification process. Again I know of no examples of this type, but the pathway appears possible.

Crypsis, aposematism and longevity

The selective rationales behind the evolution of crypsis and aposematism are rather different. The former relies on the predator not seeing or not recog-nising a moth as potential prey. The latter relies on the moth being seen and being remembered. These differences may have had an evolutionary effect on the relative life spans of cryptic and aposematic species. For a cryptic species, selection pressure from predators that hunt by sight and form searching images should reduce life span. The argument is that, as related individuals will often occur within the foraging ranges of the same predators, an individ-ual moth, once adult, should reproduce as fast as possible and then die. The quicker it dies once it is reproductively played out the better, because it reduces the chance that it will be found by a predator that then forms a search-ing image of it, putting the moth's relatives in jeopardy.

For an aposematic species, the opposite rationale applies. As the defence relies on the learning and memory of predators, an aposematic moth that sur-vives for a time, even once it has finished reproducing, may benefit similar rel-atives. Its presence increases the number of targets for naive predators to learn the unpalatability to be associated with a particular colour pattern. The chance of a relative, which has not finished reproducing, being attacked by a naive predator is then reduced.

The conclusion is that aposematic species should, other factors being equal, live longer than cryptic species. As far as I am aware, this idea has never been tested experimentally. However, the moths would be an eminently suitable group on which to test the suggestion by means of comparative analysis.

Mimicry

Biological mimicry is traditionally defined as the resemblance of an organism, or part of an organism, to another species for defensive or, more rarely, aggressive purposes. This definition has been the subject of some debate for two reasons. First, some workers include crypsis. Following the formal definition, when crypsis involves resembling say a piece of tree bark or lichen or a leaf, they are, strictly speaking, correct. However, in practical terms, I find it difficult to concede that a bark-resembling species should be regarded as a mimic when a stone-resembling species should not.

The second area of difficulty involves specific cryptic mimics, such as bird-dropping mimics, which are included in discussions of mimicry by some and excluded by others. Here the mimicry is with an inanimate object and thus should fall outside the normal definition of mimicry. I regard the copying of bird faeces in the colours and patterns of some moths as an extension of crypsis, the moth effectively looking like an inedible part of the environment. Thus, in this discussion, I will confine myself to the two major classes of mimicry, Batesian and Müllerian mimicry.

Before dealing with specific cases of Batesian and Müllerian mimicry, a number of general points should be made in respect of these two classes. Batesian mimicry involves an association in which the members play different roles. The model is a species possessing some form of inherent protection. Its mimics, of which there may be one or more, gain protection by resembling the model. Predators that learn to avoid the model also avoid the mimic.

Müllerian mimicry involves resemblances between a number of species, all of which have some inherent protective device. All members of a Müllerian mimicry complex benefit, for the loss due to inexperienced predators learning to avoid a particular colour pattern is spread across many species.

Conventionally, in Batesian mimicry, the model loses what the mimic gains in protection from predators, whereas Müllerian mimics all gain from the resemblance.

A number of different points may be expected in examples of each of these two types of mimicry. These are tabulated in Table 8.2.

How do these mimetic resemblances evolve? The evolutionary pathways of Batesian and Müllerian mimicry are rather different. The latter is the simpler and so I shall deal with it first.

The evolution of Müllerian mimicry

The evolutionary pathway that would lead to the production of a Müllerian mimicry complex is simple. Suppose two differently patterned protected species occur in the same region. One species is common (for example, population size, N = 10,000), the other is rare (for example, N = 100). If an inexperienced predator takes ten attempts to learn that each colour pattern should be avoided, the rarer species suffers proportionately more than the common. Consequently, if a mutation occurs that makes an individual of the rare species resemble the common species, it will gain an advantage by being one of many rather that one of a few. Thus the rare species will come to resemble the common species. Unless a mutation arises that gives its bearer an appearance that is intermediate between both species, so that predators that have learnt to avoid either species avoid it, the common species will not evolve towards the rare species at all.

This is a very simple evolutionary pathway. In reality a number of factors may complicate the evolution of a Müllerian complex. Some changes in appearance may be more likely to evolve than others. For example, it is easier to lose a trait than to gain a specific trait. Thus, in a gene that causes the production of yellow pigment, many chance changes in the nucleotide sequence are likely to simply shut the gene down, so that the yellow pigment is not produced, leaving a blank or white area of patterning. In the same gene, relatively few and possibly only one specific change in the code might lead to the production of red pigment rather than yellow pigment. Here then, a change from yellow to

Table 8.2 Expected features in cases of Batesian and Müllerian mimicry

Batesian mimicry	Müllerian mimicry
The model must be relatively inedible or otherwise protected.	Some defensive feature, such as a sting, bite, irritating hairs, nasty taste or toxicity, protects each of the species involved.
The model must have some conspicuous feature, most usually a warning colour pattern.	All the species will be relatively conspicuous.
The model must be common compared with the mimic. This condition is obviously necessary because, should the model be rare, the predator will have little chance of learning its harmful properties, and will therefore not avoid the mimic. Indeed, if the mimic is much more abundant than its model, naive predators are likely to come across the palatable mimic first and may come to associate its colour pattern with edibility.	All species may be equally common, but the abundance of any one species will not be limited by its mimicry.
Both model and mimic must be found together at the same time, or the model may precede the mimic.	Species involved may be found together at the same time or they may enter the environment sequentially.
The mimic, unlike the model, will not be particularly resistant to injury. As the mimic is palatable and has no nasty taste to reveal, once caught, it is likely to be consumed. There is thus little benefit in expending resources on strengthening to survive the initial attack of a predator that is unlikely to let go.	The species are likely to be relatively resistant to injury during initial attack.
The mimic should bear a very close resemblance to the model. Selection will act on predators to increase their discriminatory abilities. Concomitantly, selection will also act on the mimic to increase its resemblance to the model, because the closer it is, the less chance a predator has of distinguishing between the model and the mimic.	The resemblance between species need not be very exact, but must simply involve a feature that reminds a potential predator of an unpleasant previous experience.
The resemblance between a Batesian mimic and its model is only likely to extend to visible structures, colour patterns, behaviours, scents, sounds or other criteria by which a predator may identify prey. It will not extend to basic anatomical make-up, development processes, metabolism or biochemistry.	

white may occur far more easily than one from yellow to red.

Evidence for the evolution of Müllerian mimicry comes from extensive work on various species of heliconiid butterflies, particularly *Heliconius melpomene* and *Heliconius erato*, which are both known to be highly distasteful to birds. These two South American species show great variation in their colour patterns. However, in any one place the patterns in the two species are strikingly similar and there is usually only one form. Polymorphism does occur, but it is found in narrow hybrid zones between monomorphic races. Furthermore, genetic investigations have shown that several different genes control the differences between the various patterns suggesting that the differences must have evolved gradually. This is exactly what the theory of the evolution of Müllerian mimicry would predict.

There is considerable evidence, from the distribution of other organisms, that the present-day Amazonian rain forest was reduced to a number of small isolated pockets of forest during dry periods in the Pleistocene. It was probably in these forest refuges that the distinct mimetic races of the two species evolved. The species composition with respect to many butterflies, moths and possibly some other insects, as well as their relative abundance, is likely to have been different in each isolated forest. Since the advantage of a particular pattern depends not only on the degree of inedibility of a species, but also its abundance, the most advantageous pattern is likely to have been different in each refuge, thus leading to the evolutionary divergence we see today. The subsequent spreading of the forest, during wet periods, would lead to the presence of polymorphic hybrid zones where the races, evolved in isolation, subsequently met.

Many cases of Müllerian mimicry are known among moths. In the tropics, arctiid moths form Müllerian complexes with pierid and heliconiid butterflies. In Britain, the burnet moths (Zygaenidae) and the Cinnabar have superficially similar colour regimes and all are chemically defended. The larvae of the Cinnabar moth, with their orange and black ring markings (Fig. 7.3), are Müllerian mimics of stinging Hymenoptera.

The paradox of polymorphic Batesian mimicry

The evolution of Batesian mimicry is more difficult to explain. However, it is worth considering in some detail as the uncovering of the evolutionary mechanism involved has been of great importance in the development of evolutionary genetic thinking and proved to be of unexpected medical benefit to mankind. The reason that evolutionists found instances of Batesian mimicry of particular fascination was partly because the phenomenon provided workers with a view of the optimum outcome of an evolutionary process: the mimic should look like the model. In addition, Batesian mimicry was of interest because some species were polymorphic. Early studies of these polymorphic Batesian mimics confronted evolutionists with what appeared to be two contradictory facts. On the one hand, the resemblances of the mimics to the models were very exact, often involving several pigment changes, the distribution of pigments, overall wing morphology and some behavioural traits. On the other hand, the differences between forms of a species appeared to be controlled by a multiple allelomorphic series of a single gene. The main problem was, therefore, whether the multifaceted resemblance of the mimic to its model could have arisen and have been perfected gradually, as proposed by Darwinian evolution, if just a single genetic change was involved in the difference between different mimetic forms, as seemed to be the case.

The palatability spectrum

Before considering how this problem was resolved, it is perhaps pertinent to point out that the dividing line between Müllerian and Batesian mimicry is not as clearly defined in the natural world as we tend to suggest when discussing these two phenomena in print. Palatability involves a complete spectrum from very nice to very nasty. It must, therefore, be realised that what is nasty to one predator may be edible to another. So a species that is a Müllerian mimic in the presence of one predator may be a Batesian mimic in the presence of another. It is also worth noting that an individual predator may accept, when hungry, prey that it would reject when well fed, bringing into question experimental work on mimicry using captive animals, which have to be well treated and well fed. Certainly, field and laboratory observations of the reactions of birds to some brightly coloured moths, such as the Hornet Clearwing, and many ladybirds, are not consistent. In the main, captive or tame birds are much choosier over their food than wild birds.

The evolution of polymorphic Batesian mimicry

Because of its influence in evolutionary biology, we will consider the evolution of polymorphic Batesian mimicry before considering the British examples of Batesian mimics.

The existence of polymorphic Batesian mimics, with the different forms of a species apparently controlled by alleles of a single gene, poses two problems for Darwinian evolutionists. First, as already mentioned, Darwin did not see a role for selection in the maintenance of polymorphisms (p. 65). Following the Darwinian idea of the survival of the fittest, Darwinists in the early part of the twentieth century found it difficult to conceive that two very different forms of a butterfly could have precisely the same fitness and so both be maintained. Second, if Batesian mimics did evolve to resemble unpalatable species, it seemed impossible that this could have happened gradually if just a single genetic change were involved.

Much of the early work on the evolution of Batesian mimicry revolved around a small number of species of butterfly, such as the tropical swallowtails, *Papilio dardanus*, *P. polytes* and *P. memnon*. It was Sir Ronald Fisher (1927) who first realised that the frequency of a novel mimetic form would affect its fitness. Imagine that in a non-mimetic species, a new form that mimics an aposematic species arises by mutation. Initially this form may be fitter than the non-mimetic form due to its mimicry, and so it will increase in frequency. However, as it increases in frequency, becoming commoner relative to its model, its fitness will slowly decline as the probability that naive predators come across it before they have experienced and learned the unpalatability of the model increases. If the fitness of the mimetic form declines to that of the non-mimetic form before the mimic has completely replaced the non-mimic, the two forms will be maintained in the population at specific frequencies through the negative frequency dependence in the fitness of the mimetic form. If, for some reason, this form becomes rarer, it will become fitter than the mimic and so start to increase in frequency again. Conversely, if it becomes commoner so that its frequency exceeds the equilibrium frequency, it will be less fit than the non-mimetic form and so decline back to the equilibrium frequency. Should another novel form that resembles a different aposematic species arise, the process would be repeated.

The negative frequency dependence of the fitness of mimetic forms allows two or more forms to be maintained in a population, thus solving the difficulty of trying to envisage very different forms having precisely the same survival value. Fisher also addressed and solved the second problem. He recognised that the observation of the multiple traits involved in producing a precise mimetic form being controlled by a single gene might be more apparent than real. He argued that two genetic mechanisms could lead to a range of genes, each one controlling a different character of the mimic, appearing as though they were a single gene. These two mechanisms were termed the switch gene and supergene mechanisms. A switch gene is a gene that controls the expression of other genes. A supergene is in fact a number of genes that lie very close together on the same chromosome so that they are inherited together.

Fisher suggested that the evolution of a novel mimetic form would start with a single mutation that produced some resemblance to a potential model. Even if the resemblance was very coarse, say just a similarity in coloration, it would begin to spread if some predators were deceived by its resemblance to its model. Selection would then favour any increase in the accuracy of the mimicry, as long as the genetic factors that were being selected were only expressed with the initial mutation. This limitation of expression could be achieved if either the initial mutation acted as a switch gene, switching on the expression of a series of modifiers, or if additional genes that improved the mimicry were all tightly linked to the initial mutation. Both of these mechanisms have been shown to occur in some cases of polymorphic Batesian mimicry. In *Papilio dardanus*, different mimetic forms are controlled by alleles of the *h* locus, which is a switch gene. In *P. memnon*, the characters involved in producing the different mimetic forms are controlled by eight genes, of which six are tightly linked on the same chromosome into a supergene so that recombination between any of these genes occurs only very rarely.

Fisher's theoretical resolution of the problems posed by the existence of polymorphic Batesian mimicry, and the elegant experimental work of Sir Cyril Clarke and Professor Philip Sheppard that demonstrated the existence of switch genes and supergenes, are among the most elegant pieces of evolutionary detective work of the last century. These cases were rightly given a very high profile: a profile that was heightened further when Sir Cyril Clarke perceived similarities between the genetics of mimicry in *P. dardanus* and the rhesus blood group system. Identification of these similarities led to a breakthrough in the understanding of rhesus babies and the development of the rhesus jab, which has saved millions of lives. However, the high profile of the work on polymorphic Batesian mimics has led to one misconception, for most texts on the subject state that the expected outcome of Batesian mimicry is polymorphism. This is not true.

Monomorphic Batesian mimicry

In most instances natural selection will lead Batesian mimics to be monomorphic. Indeed this is the case with all the British species of moth that may be

Batesian mimics. Unfortunately, there is rather little evidence relating to the palatability of many of these species. Here I am thinking of species such as the Bee Hawk moths, *Hemaris tityus* and *H. fuciformis*, and many of the clearwing moths (Sesiidae). There is some suggestion that some predators reject some of these species, at least in captivity. However, I have seen both Broad-bordered and Narrow-bordered Bee Hawk moths taken by birds on the Continent, and I have seen Magpies eat Currant Clearwings, *Synanthedon tipuliformis* (Plate 13e) in the New Forest. It is notable that all these species are monomorphic.

Leaving aside the relative palatabilities of each of these species, there is a number of reasons why polymorphism does not evolve in most cases of Batesian mimicry. First, the models of most Batesian mimics are themselves components of Müllerian mimic complexes. This means that the effective population size of models may be the sum total of all the species in the Müllerian complex. Thus, in most cases, before the population density of a Batesian mimic can increase enough for its advantage to be lost, because it is too common relative to the model, other factors, such as food availability, will limit its population size. The mimic therefore spreads through the whole population, completely replacing the original non-mimetic form. Additional genes that improve the mimicry will spread in the same way, although here there is no pressure for a switch gene or supergene to evolve as the first mutation will have spread through the whole population. Second, the number of species of potential models may be limited. There may simply not be another potential aposematic species available for a potential mimic to evolve resemblance to. Third, there is some evidence that some predators have innate avoidance behaviours towards some warning patterns, such as the yellow and black coloration of many stinging Hymenoptera. In this situation the frequency dependent selection necessary for the evolution of mimetic polymorphism will be irrelevant. Fourth, the complex genetic systems (switch genes or supergenes) that are necessary for the evolution of polymorphism will arise only rarely.

That most Batesian mimics are monomorphic may be easily appreciated if the assemblage of yellow and black insects in Britain is considered. In addition to the Bee Hawk moths and clearwings, these include bees, wasps, hoverflies, robber flies, beetles and some moth larvae. Many of these are Batesian mimics and all are monomorphic in respect of those elements of their colour patterns that are involved in mimicry. The only cases of polymorphic Batesian mimicry that I can find among the British moths are both rather tenuous. The first concerns the Buff Ermine, *Spilosoma luteum*, which is reportedly much less unpalatable than the White Ermine, of which it is possibly a Batesian mimic (Rothschild 1985). The Buff Ermine is polymorphic in a few coastal populations where it has secondarily evolved a cryptic colour pattern (p. 249). The second case involves larvae of the Death's-head Hawk moth, *Acherontia atropos*. Larvae of this species are usually yellow with dark oblique stripes on the sides (Plate 15c). However, a brown form of larva also occurs (Plate 15d) and, with some imagination, this could be seen to have some resemblance to a snake, making these larvae Batesian mimics.

The number of cases of polymorphic Batesian mimicry is rather small. Only in a few species have the basic requirements for the evolution of polymorphism been met. These spectacular cases are the ones that have attracted attention and because a biological paradox exhibited by these has been explained, the fact that these are rare special cases has been obscured.

Defences against bats

In many parts of the world, bats are the most important predators of night-active moths. In consequence, moths have evolved the ability to detect bats. Most moths have hearing organs that are analogous to our ears. The proportion with 'ears' is greater in nocturnal species than in diurnal species. The ears, which should more correctly be called tympanal organs, may be located at the base of the wings or on the legs, but are most often on the first abdominal segment. Analysis of the frequency of sounds to which the ears of moths are sensitive has shown that they cover the range of ultrasounds usually produced by hunting bats. Indeed, a comparative study of moth hearing from different locations has shown that moths in habitats supporting a high bat density overall have better hearing than those in places where bats are scarce (Fullard 1982).

Because the two ears of a moth will receive the sound of a bat at fractionally different moments, a moth is able to judge the direction of the bat's approach. The general reaction of most moths that detect the sound of a bat some distance away is to fly away from the bat. This is effective, because moths seem able to detect foraging bats that are emitting their ultrasounds at a greater distance (about 30 metres) than a bat can detect a moth (up to about 20 metres). However, if a bat is detected at closer range, i.e. when the intensity of the ultrasounds from the bat is high, the moth's response is different. Bats fly faster than moths, so attempting to fly away from the bat is unlikely to be successful. Instead, most species of moth appear to drop out of the sky, making for the ground either by furling their wings and using the force of gravity, or more actively in a strong powered dive.

This behaviour is easy to observe in the summer. Bats are quick to learn that street lamps, or moth traps that are run regularly in one place, lead to a high density of potential prey. I have often watched bats chasing moths above one of my moth traps, and the dropping reaction of moths in the flight path of a bat is a regular sight in the light of the mercury vapour bulb. This response is often, but not always, successful, for bats are agile fliers and will follow moths down, catching the moth in their mouths in mid-dive, or more often scooping the moth out of the air in the crook of a curved wing that pulls the moth to the bat's mouth. I have been told that bats sometimes catch moths in midair with their feet. However, I have never observed this myself. On rare occasions, the dive of a bat after a diving moth over a moth trap may lead to disaster for the bat, for I have three times found dead pipistrelle bats in moth traps. It seems likely that in these cases the bats, while following moths down, have been preoccupied with their pursuit and have followed their prey into the trap, thereafter becoming disorientated and dying of shock.

Not all moths use evasion as their primary defence against bats. Some have more sophisticated defences that rely on sounds that they themselves make and that may be heard by bats. A study carried out in Canada supports this view. Fullard & Barclay (1980) looked at the proportion of spring and summer arctiid moths that produced clicking ultrasounds and related these to the levels of bat predation of moths in the two seasons. They found that bats ate fewer moths in the spring than in the summer. The reasons were that actively foraging bats were scarcer in the spring than in the summer. Furthermore, in the spring, most of the bats foraged over water, feeding on midges and mayflies. Conversely, in the summer, when many female bats had to feed heavily to make milk for their offspring, they tended to stay close to their roosts and young. The summer density of foraging bats was also increased when the young began to fly and hunt, but these also tended to remain close to the roost and took a high proportion of moths. In respect of the spring and summer moths, Fullard & Barclay found that the spring-flying species could detect the sounds made by bats, but did not produce clicks. The summer-active species could detect the sounds of bats and make also their own clicking sounds in response. The clicking sounds made by the summer arctiids were interpreted as an adaptive response to the higher levels of predation imposed by lactating female bats and their young at this time of year.

There are three ways in which sounds made by the tymbal organs of some moths may give them protection against bat predation. First, in aposematic species, sound may act as an indication of unpalatability. This is probably the case in many of the Arctiidae. As already described, many of these chemically defended moths have bright contrasting colour patterns that are easily remembered by predators that hunt by sight. A specific sound emitted by chemically defended moths could have the same function for predators that do not hunt by sight. In experimental conditions it was found that when bats had been trained to avoid arctiid moths that emitted a specific clicking sound, they thereafter avoided arctiids that emitted substantially different clicking patterns (Dunning 1968). This was interpreted by Dunning as a case of Müllerian sound mimicry.

The second mode of sound defence follows from the first. If bats can learn to avoid a distasteful moth on the basis of the sound it makes, this gives palatable moths scope to evolve false warning sounds. Thus Dunning (1968) has interpreted the clicking sounds made by moths of the genus *Pyrrharctia*, which are relatively palatable, as Batesian mimetic sounds.

The third possible sound defence entails that the clicks made by some moths interfere with the bat's echolocation system (Dunning & Roeder 1965). Several lines of evidence support this idea. First, Fullard found that the ultrasounds made by the small arctiid *Cycnia tenera* mimic the sound made by the bat *Eptesicus fuscus*, as it approaches its prey (Fullard et al. 1979). This is an unusual type of mimicry, for here the moth, by mirroring the bat's own sound, may confuse the bat into believing that it is receiving the echo of its own emission bouncing off a solid surface, and so itself take evasive action.

It is possible that in some instances the sound defence goes one step further. Scoble (1992) notes that although most bats modulate the frequency of their transmissions, some, such as the Horseshoe bats, emit sounds with a constant frequency. He speculates that moths may thus be able to produce ultrasounds at precisely the frequency necessary to jam these bats' sonar.

How do arms races begin?

In this chapter, we have looked at a variety of adaptations that moths appear to have evolved to avoid predation. The Darwinian thesis for the evolution of these adaptations is that they will have arisen and become perfected gradually, with selection favouring a series of small improvements in an adaptive character. Critics of Darwinian evolution have questioned this gradual evolution, asking what use is it to look just 5% like a twig or a piece of bark or a bird dropping. The dilemma is that the initial resemblance of say an ancestor of the Merveille du Jour to a piece of lichen-covered bark must have been very remote, yet the Merveille du Jour is now remarkably cryptic against this type of substrate (Plate 6c). If the ancestral moth were such a poor match for its resting substrate, it would only gain an advantage if the predators of its time had remarkably poor vision. Yet, as the resemblance now is so good, it seems to follow that the predators whose selective predation put the finishing touches to the evolution of the colour patterning of the Merveille du Jour must have had very good vision indeed.

Three hypotheses have been put forward to explain this contradiction. The first proposes that predator vision has been improving over the same evolutionary timescale as insect camouflage. The second suggests that different predators have been responsible for the different elements in the complex colour patterns that contribute to the amazing crypsis of so many moths and other insects. The third argues that under particular conditions, even predators with extremely good vision may have more difficulty detecting a moth that looked a little bit like the substrate that it was resting on than one that bore no resemblance at all. Most evolutionary biologists favour this third explanation.

To illustrate this point, I would now like to invite the reader to try a little experiment with a member of the family or a friend as a helper. Figure 8.21 (opposite) is a black-and-white photograph of a moth. This moth is sitting on an inappropriate background, for it is adapted to rest on lichen-encrusted rocks. I show it on the wrong background, on which it is very obvious, to allow you to get your eye in. At the top of p. 271 and the following two right hand pages you will find further black and white photographs. Do not look at them yet!

Now show the moth on this page to your helper. Once they have seen the moth for a few moments, turn to p. 271 and turn the following pages at about three-second intervals until you have turned four pages. You should now be on p. 277 (with no picture). Ask your helper how many moths he or she saw. (Please do the experiment before reading on.)

I think that you will frequently find that they only see moths in Figures 8.22 and 8.23. The last photograph (Fig. 8.24) is I admit a bit of a cheat because the moth is not sited in the centre of the photograph, as it would usually be. Normally, the main subject is more or less at the centre of a photograph, so we know where to look. Moreover, the moths in the photograph are in focus, so you know where to focus your eyes. But a foraging bird does not know where to look, or where to focus. I could have made things worse by having one of the moths out of focus, or perhaps underexposed. Often a bird would be hunting at dawn or dusk, or under a woodland canopy in low light conditions. The point I am making is that even a predator with good sight might miss an ancestral insect with a slight resemblance to its background more often than one that bore no resemblance. Even if the predator would normally be able to distinguish our slightly cryptic moth from its background most of the time, this time the slight resemblance means that the bird does not notice it and so bring its focus onto precisely 'that bit of rock'. The next time it flies past, it sees our moth, but between the two passes, our moth has laid a batch of eggs. In that batch of eggs is the selective advantage that starts the evolution of crypsis and the arms race.

In the next chapter, I will continue the theme of the evolution of crypsis in moths, examining a phenomenon that has provided some of the best evidence supporting the theory of evolution by natural selection: the phenomenon of melanism in moths.

Fig. 8.21 The Poplar Grey, *Acronicta megacephala*, here shown on an inappropriate background (see text opposite).

9

Melanism in Moths

Introduction

Moths have had a considerable influence on the way biologists think about evolution. The phenomenon of melanism has been particularly influential.

Bernard Kettlewell (1973) defined melanism as: 'The occurrence in a population of a species, of some individuals which are darker than the typical form due to an increase in the epidermis of certain polymerised products of tyrosin substances which produce the complex of pigments collectively known as the melanins.'

Examples of melanism have been known and discussed since the middle of the nineteenth century. In particular, increases in the proportion of melanic forms of many moths in industrial regions have been hailed as demonstrations of the central mechanism of Darwin's theory of evolution: natural selection. The case of one of these species, the Peppered moth, *Biston betularia*, has perhaps been cited in more textbooks, newspaper, magazine and research journal articles, than any other as an example of evolution in action. Yet this case is still controversial as shown by recent newspaper articles and commentaries in entomological and other magazines (see, for example, Coyne 1998; Matthews 1998). In this chapter, I shall describe a variety of cases of melanism in moths and discuss whether or not the rise and subsequent fall in the proportion of melanic forms in many species stand as evidence for Darwinian evolution.

Melanism is a very widespread phenomenon in the animal kingdom, examples having been described from most phyla. Melanic forms have been recorded in over 200 species of British moth. At the outset, I want to stress that the rise and fall of melanism in the Peppered moth is rather unusual, even among the British moths. Few other species have shown the same pattern of evolution of melanism and there is a considerable array of reasons for the existence of melanic forms among other moths (p. 235). However, most research has focused on the single case of the Peppered moth. This case has become an icon for Darwinian evolution. The reasons for the prominent position of this case history are easy to appreciate. First, the change was rapid and visually dramatic. A relatively invariant species of white and black moth became black in many populations over a period of just 50 years. Second, the change was seen to be associated with a specific environmental factor, the darkening of tree bark due to air pollution. Third, a single easily understood factor, bird predation, appeared sufficient to account for differences in the fitnesses of the melanic and non-melanic forms in different locations and so to explain the evolutionary changes observed. Fourth, the rapidity of the increase in the melanic form bespoke selective differences of far greater magnitude than those envisaged by early Darwinists. Finally, the change was witnessed. As Sewall Wright (1978) wrote, the case of the Peppered moth is: 'the clearest case in which a conspicuous evolutionary process has been actually observed'.

Industrial melanism in the Peppered moth

The basic story of the Peppered moth cited in most school and undergraduate texts is simple. The typical form of this species has whitish wings, speckled with black (Fig. 3.10, Plate 14c). In 1848, a black form, named *carbonaria* (Fig. 3.10, Plate 14c), was recorded in Manchester (Edleston 1864). The *carbonaria* form increased in frequency rapidly, so that by 1895, 98% of Mancunian Peppered moths were black. The melanic form spread to many other parts of Britain. By examination of old collections, Steward (1977a) mapped the spread of *carbonaria*, concluding that all British *carbonaria* probably derived from a single mutation.

In 1896, J.W. Tutt gave a reasoned explanation for the increase in *carbonaria*. He suggested that the ancestral typical form (*typica*) would have been well camouflaged when at rest on surfaces covered by foliose lichens. However, such surfaces had become rarer in regions affected by industrialisation since the Industrial Revolution. The major causes of these changes were two pollutants: sulphur dioxide, which kills foliose lichens, making surfaces more uniform in colour, and soot fallout, which blackens the surfaces denuded of their lichen flora. Tutt stated that on these surfaces *carbonaria* would be better camouflaged than *typica* and so it was natural selection, augmented by 'hereditary tendency', that had led to an increase in the frequency of melanics.

Resistance to this suggestion was based on the view, held by most entomologists and ornithologists of the day, that birds are not major predators of cryptic day-resting moths. Consequently, during the first half of the twentieth century, a variety of other explanations of the evolution of industrial melanism were put forward. These included the suggestion that some of the pollutants were mutagenic agents; the idea that the heterozygote between *carbonaria* and *typica* was fitter than either of the homozygotes; and the possibility that Lamarckian inheritance was involved. The theory of Lamarckian inheritance proposes that traits developed during life may be passed on to offspring and so is often referred to as the inheritance of acquired characteristics. None of these explanations appeared completely convincing, but it was not until the second half of the twentieth century that Tutt's differential predation hypothesis was tested experimentally.

One important advance during the first half of the twentieth century was the calculation of the fitness of *carbonaria* relative to *typica* that would be necessary to explain the rise in *carbonaria* frequency in Manchester. Haldane (1924) calculated that *carbonaria* would have had to have been about half as fit again as *typica* to explain the rapidity of its rise. This estimate was criticised on a number of counts. For example, Haldane assumed that the frequency of *carbonaria* only reached 98% in 1895. Yet there is some evidence to suggest that the rise may have been even more rapid. Thus Edleston (1864), in the paper in which he reports the first finding of *carbonaria*, writes:

'I placed some of the virgin females in my garden in order to attract the males, and was not a little surprised to find that most of the visitors were the "negro" aberration: if this goes on for a few years the original type of *A. betularia* [*Biston betulara* was previously assigned to the genus *Amphidasys*] will be extinct in this locality.'

This suggests that *carbonaria* was already in the majority in Manchester by 1864. If this were the case, Haldane's calculation would underestimate the fitness differences between the two forms necessary to account for the change. Thus, the main point of Haldane's findings – that fitness differences between forms could be much higher than most evolutionary biologists had previously supposed – was not undermined.

In the 1950s, Bernard Kettlewell began his now classical work on the Peppered moth. Using direct observation of predation of moths from tree trunks and mark–release–recapture techniques in two populations, one in a polluted and the other in an unpolluted oak woodland, he obtained strong evidence to support Tutt's differential predation hypothesis (Tables 9.1 and 9.2). Kettlewell also showed that there was a good correlation between the frequency of melanic Peppered moths and areas of high sulphur dioxide and atmospheric soot pollution. The correlation between high melanic frequencies and high levels of pollutants has been reinforced by the finding that following the instigation of anti-pollution and smoke control legislation in Britain since the mid 1950s, pollution levels have declined, as has the frequency of *carbonaria* (p. 223).

Table 9.1 Direct observation on predation of Peppered moths, *Biston betularia*, by wild birds. The numbers are of *typica* and *carbonaria* forms observed to be eaten. On all occasions, observations commenced with three live moths of each phenotype being released onto a tree trunk. When all three of one type had been taken, any remaining of the other type were removed and six new moths were released onto the trunk. (a) Data from the Christopher Cadbury Bird Reserve, Birmingham, 1955; (b) Data from Deanend Wood, Dorset, 1955. (Observations by N. Tinbergen and H.B.D. Kettlewell.) (Adapted from Kettlewell 1956.)

(a) Predation by Redstarts

	typica	*carbonaria*	Total
19 July a.m.	12	3	15
20 July a.m.	14	3	17
20 July p.m.	17	9	26
Total	**43**	**15**	**58**

(b) Predation by five species of wild bird

	typica	*carbonaria*	Totals
Spotted Flycatcher	8	46	52
	1	35	36
Nuthatch	8	22	30
	0 (first day)	9	9 (first day)
	3 (second day)	9	12 (second day)
Yellow Hammer	0	8	8
	0	12	12
Robin	2	12	14
Song Thrush	4	11	15
Total predation observed	**26**	**164**	**190**

Table 9.2 Recovery rates of marked *typica* and *carbonaria* forms of the Peppered moth, *Biston betularia*, released in unpolluted Dorset and polluted Birmingham woodlands. The recapture rate for *typica* in the unpolluted woodland is approximately double that of *carbonaria*. The reverse is true in the polluted woodland. (Data from Kettlewell 1955a, 1956.)

		typica	*carbonaria*	Total
Dorset, 1955	Released	496	473	969
	Recaptured	62	30	92
	% of releases recaught	12.5	6.3	
Birmingham, 1953	Released	137	447	584
	Recaptured	18	123	141
	% of releases recaught	13.1	27.5	
Birmingham, 1955	Released	64	154	218
	Recaptured	16	82	98
	% of releases recaught	25.0	52.3	

The textbook story of the Peppered moth

The components of the basic Peppered moth story, as it is usually related in textbooks, are given in Table 9.3.

Table 9.3 Components of the basic 'Peppered moth story' as related in most textbooks (Based upon Majerus 1989.)

i   The Peppered moth has two distinct forms.
ii   These forms are genetically controlled.
iii   Peppered moths rest by day on tree trunks.
iv   Birds find Peppered moths on tree trunks and eat them.
v   The likelihood of a moth being found by a bird depends on its degree of crypsis.
vi   Non-melanic Peppered moths are better camouflaged than melanics on lichen-covered tree trunks in rural areas. Melanic Peppered moths are better camouflaged than non-melanics in industrial areas where tree trunks have been denuded of lichens and blackened by soot fallout.
vii   The frequencies of melanic and non-melanic moths in a particular area are dependent on the level of bird predation of each form and the rate of migration of moths into the area from adjacent districts in which the form frequencies of the moth are different.

Recent criticisms of Kettlewell's experimental methods have been used to cast doubt on the case of melanism in the Peppered moth as a valid example demonstrating Darwinian selection. Thus, for example, *The Sunday Telegraph* (14 March 1999), carried an article by Robert Matthews with the headline 'Scientists pick holes in Darwin moth theory', beginning the article with the following:

'Evolution experts are quietly admitting that one of their most cherished examples of Darwin's theory, the rise and fall of the peppered moth, is based on a series of scientific blunders.
   Experiments using the moth in the Fifties and long believed to prove the truth of natural selection are now thought to be worthless, having been designed to come up with the "right" answer.'

This article came as something of a surprise to me. I know most of the scientists who have done significant experimental research on the Peppered moth and I do not know any who would subscribe to the view put forward by Matthews. Moreover, if evidence were available that seriously undermined the qualitative accuracy of the basic story, it would be of such importance that I cannot imagine any scientist speaking of it quietly. Rather, it would be publicised loudly in scientific journals and at conferences, for a scientist could gain a considerable reputation as a result of such evidence.

Leaving aside the many scientific inaccuracies and the misquotations attributed to reputable scientists, the message of Matthews' article needs to be addressed because it has become widely quoted on Web pages of creationist organisations, particularly in America, aiming to undermine Darwin's theory.

Assessing the validity of the Peppered moth story

We can begin to address the validity of the case by appraising the components of the basic story, and then consider some of the additional factors that are rarely addressed in general textbooks.

The Peppered moth has two distinct forms

As many lepidopterists who regularly operate moth traps will know, the Peppered moth does not have just two forms. A third form, called *insularia*, occurs (Fig. 9.1). This form is intermediate between *typica* and *carbonaria* and is itself very variable, being a complex of three genetically discrete forms. It is quite common in some regions, comprising at present about 15% of the Cambridge population, and having long had frequencies of around 25% in industrial areas of South Wales, where occasionally it may be the commonest form. Little research has been conducted on the *insularia* forms apart from working out their pattern of inheritance.

The genetics of melanism in the Peppered moth

The inheritance of the *carbonaria* and *typica* forms is controlled by two alleles of a single gene, the *carbonaria* allele now being completely dominant to the *typica* allele. Genetically, the *insularia* form is a complex of forms controlled by three additional alleles at the same locus. In general, dominance increases with darkness (Fig. 9.2). There is evidence that modifier genes, which influence the expression of the alleles of the main colour pattern gene when two

Fig. 9.1 The *insularia* complex of forms of the Peppered moth, *Biston betularia*, is controlled by at least three different alleles. Two of these forms are shown here.

different alleles are present together, affect this progression of dominance. Some of this evidence was obtained by Kettlewell through the examination of Victorian specimens of *carbonaria*. Many of the earliest specimens bear a fine dusting of white scales, particularly on the hindwings. Kettlewell conjectured that this could be a case of the evolution of genetic dominance through selection as proposed by Fisher (1928). Fisher's idea was that if a new advantageous mutant allele arose, it would be unlikely to be fully dominant to the old allele when the mutant first arose. As this new mutation while initially rare would most often be coupled with an old allele (i.e. in a heterozygous individual), selection would act to promote the alleles of any other genes in the genome that increase the expression of the advantageous mutation in heterozygotes. Arguing that dominance modifier genes that increased the expression of the *carbonaria* allele would only have been selectively favoured in industrial regions, Kettlewell then performed a series of crosses between *carbonaria* from industrial areas and *typica* moths from both Cornwall and Canada. He was able to show not only that the genetic dominance of *carbonaria* over *typica* could be broken down, but that thereafter, by artificial selection, it could be recreated. This evidence, therefore, supports the view that *carbonaria* was not fully dominant to *typica* when it first arose in the nineteenth century and that full dominance evolved as a result of selection acting upon polygenic dominance modifier systems.

Fig. 9.2 The inheritance of the *typica*, *carbonaria* and *insularia* forms of the Peppered moth. The inheritance involves five alleles of a single gene. Dominance follows a hierarchy correlated with increasing melanisation. Dominance is not entirely complete, as indicated by vertical arrows showing that a genotype may occasionally have the phenotype to which the arrow points. (Adapted by Majerus 1998 from Lees 1981: based upon Lees & Creed 1977; Steward 1977b; Clarke 1979; with additional data from Majerus (unpublished).)

Phenotypes in decreasing order of melanisation	Allele	Genotypes
carbonaria	C	CC, CI^3, CI^2, CI^1, CT
		$\uparrow \qquad \downarrow \uparrow$
insularia 3	I^3	$I^3I^3, I^3I^2, I^3I^1, I^3T$
insularia 2	I^2	I^2I^2, I^2I^1, I^2T
		$\uparrow$
insularia 1	I^1	I^1I^1, I^1T
typica	T	TT

The Peppered moth rests by day on tree trunks

This is not true. In his predation experiments, Kettlewell placed live moths out on tree trunks, allowing them to walk up the trunks and choose their own place to clamp down. He did this for practical reasons. With the moths in exposed positions on tree trunks, he would be able to observe any predation. Furthermore, because of the resistance of birdwatchers and entomologists to the idea that birds are major predators of cryptic adult moths, he wanted to film the predation from a hide, which he accomplished in 1955 with the help of Niko Tinbergen (see Kettlewell 1973).

In fact, Kettlewell was fully aware that Peppered moths do not usually rest in exposed positions on tree trunks. In an article in the *Entomologist* (Kettlewell 1958), he wrote:

> '... whilst undertaking large-scale release of both forms (*typica* and *carbonaria*) in the wild at early dawn, I have on many occasions been able to watch this species taking up its normal resting position which is underneath the larger boughs of trees, less commonly on trunks'.

Unfortunately, most evolutionary biologists do not read the *Entomologist*. The majority of scientists who have repeated Kettlewell's predation experiments have also placed moths (either alive or dead) out on tree trunks. Estimates of the relative fitnesses of *carbonaria* and *typica* have been obtained in this way at many sites. The quantitative accuracy of these fitness estimates must be questionable simply because Peppered moths in the wild rarely rest in exposed positions on tree trunks.

So where do Peppered moths usually rest up through the day? Data sets on the natural resting sites of Peppered moths are pitifully scarce. For example, Sir Cyril Clarke and his co-workers, writing in 1985, make the extraordinary admission that:

> '... in 25 years we have only found two *betularia* on the tree trunks or walls adjacent to our traps, and none elsewhere.'

The largest data set on the natural resting positions of wild Peppered moths that I am aware of is my own. This comprises just 52 moths found in the wild in situations not affected by artificial lights (for example, moth traps, streetlights) over a period of 37 years (Table 9.4). These data, other data from observed resting sites close to artificial light (Majerus 1998) and experimental work by Mikkola (1984) and Liebert & Brakefield (1987), suggest that Kettlewell's 1958 observation is essentially correct. Peppered moths generally rest by day on the underside of lateral branches and twigs in the canopy (Figs 9.3 and 9.4, Plate 14c), or if they rest upon trunks, they select a position in shadow below where a branch joins the trunk.

Table 9.4 The resting positions of Peppered moths, *Biston betularia*, found in the wild between 1964 and 2000. All forms in the *insularia* complex are combined. (Adapted, with additional data, from Howlett & Majerus 1987.)

	typica	*insularia*	*carbonaria*
Exposed trunk	3	1	2
Unexposed trunk	2	1	3
Trunk/branch joint	10	4	7
Branches	8	4	7

Birds find Peppered moths at rest during the day and eat them

Despite the agreement of most ornithologists and entomologists in the first half of the twentieth century that birds are not major predators of day-resting adult moths, evidence to the contrary has been steadily accumulating since

Fig. 9.3 A typical Peppered moth, *Biston betularia*, in a natural resting position, under a hazel twig.

Fig. 9.4 A Peppered moth, *Biston betularia*, of the *carbonaria* form, at rest on the underside of a birch branch.

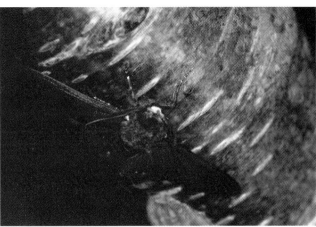

Kettlewell's pioneering experiments. In addition to Kettlewell's own filming of the act, many workers who have conducted predation experiments on Peppered moths and other species of moth have witnessed this behaviour. In addition, several data sets relating to the food brought back by foraging parent birds to their nestlings include adult day-resting moths among the prey delivered.

The likelihood of a moth being found by a bird depends on its crypsis

This is the central component of the Peppered moth story. The results of the predation experiments of Kettlewell and other workers strongly suggest that the likelihood of a moth being eaten by a bird will increase in environments where it is less likely to find a resting situation in which it is well camouflaged. Yet, a formal experiment, involving a variety of artificial backgrounds upon which Peppered moths of different forms can be offered to birds, has never been conducted. It should not be beyond the bounds of possibility to produce artificial backgrounds with known reflectance characteristics that would allow predictions of the relative crypsis of the *carbonaria* and *typica* forms to be constructed. This type of experiment would certainly be timely and might lay to rest some of the criticisms currently directed at the case of the Peppered moth.

Carbonaria is more cryptic in polluted habitats, *typica* in unpolluted habitats

The reciprocal nature of the results of Kettlewell's mark–release–recapture experiments in Birmingham and Dorset provides strong evidence to support the contention that the forms have different fitnesses in polluted and unpolluted environments. Other workers have reported similar differences in fitness. Of particular note is Jim Bishop's work on a transect running from Liverpool into rural North Wales. Bishop (1972) obtained form frequency data at many sites in this region and fitness data from predation experiments at seven sites along the cline. In obtaining these predation rates, Bishop placed dead moths on trees in what he called life-like positions that maximised their crypsis to his eye. He also obtained information about the life history of the moth, including how quickly moths lay their eggs, their fecundity and fertility and migration rates for both forms. Bishop then calculated the proportional contribution of each form to the next generation, combining the fecundity and oviposition rates with the relative survival values from his predation experiments. He then simulated, using a computer model, the rise and spread of *carbonaria* along this cline, assuming that at some time in the early nineteenth century the frequency of *carbonaria* was close to the mutation rate. He included in the model migration rates obtained from field investigations and a variable level of heterozygote advantage, which was still thought to play some role at that time. A 54-kilometre transect, running from Liverpool into North Wales, was divided into 27 two-kilometre blocks and migration was allowed between adjacent blocks. The model was then cycled for 160 generations.

The simulated frequencies of *carbonaria* along the transect were compared with observed natural frequencies (Fig. 9.5). The fit was not good for two reasons. First, the predicted position of decline of *carbonaria* was much closer to Liverpool than that actually observed. Second, the predicted rate of decline was much less abrupt than observed. The fit of the model to the observed data can be substantially improved if non-visual fitness differences favouring *carbonaria* are introduced into the model (Mani 1982). Support for the incorpo-

Fig. 9.5 Results of the computer simulation of the decrease in the *carbonaria* form of the Peppered moth with distance from Liverpool (solid line). The points represent the actual frequencies of *carbonaria* from field sampling. (After Bishop 1972.)

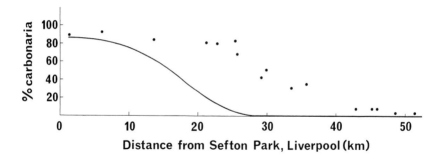

ration of such fitness differences has been based on the results of deviations from expected ratios in segregating broods of laboratory-bred Peppered moths. However, Howlett & Majerus (1987) have challenged the values used by Mani to produce his best fit. They suggested instead that the poorness of fit of Bishop's simulation to observed frequencies results from quantitative errors in estimates of the survival values of the forms along the transect as a result of placing moths in unnatural positions.

To support their case Howlett & Majerus give the results of a predation experiment in which *typica* and *carbonaria* were placed in two different types of situation, either exposed on tree trunks, or on the trunk five centimetres below the junction with a major branch. The experiments were carried out in two oak woodland sites, one in the Potteries (polluted): the other on the western edge of the New Forest (relatively unpolluted). The results (Table 9.5) showed, as expected, that predation of *carbonaria* was lower than that of *typica* in Stoke, but higher in the New Forest. The level of predation of moths of both forms was lower on moths that were situated below branch/trunk junctions than on moths placed in exposed positions on trunks in all cases. Most significantly, this decrease was greater for *carbonaria* than for *typica* and greatest for *carbonaria* in the rural environment. This seems intuitively sensible, because a black moth is likely to benefit more from being in shadow than is a pale moth (see Majerus 1998).

Table 9.5 The results of predation experiments to investigate the effect of resting position on predation of the *typica* and *carbonaria* forms of the Peppered moth, *Biston betularia*, in a polluted woodland (Stoke-on-Trent) and an unpolluted woodland (New Forest). (From Howlett & Majerus 1987.)

	typica		*carbonaria*	
	Eaten	Not eaten	Eaten	Not eaten
Stoke-on-Trent				
Exposed trunk	29	21	20	30
Trunk/branch joint	25	25	14	36
New Forest				
Exposed trunk	16	34	31	19
Trunk/branch joint	13	37	20	30

This result may explain part of the lack of fit of Bishop's model, for it suggests that the fitness estimates Bishop obtained for *carbonaria* are too low, particularly along the unpolluted part of the transect. Increasing the fitness of *carbonaria* in this region to more realistic levels will have the result of pushing the position of Bishop's predicted decline in *carbonaria* away from Liverpool.

The frequencies of the forms of the Peppered moth depend on a selection–migration balance

Despite the finding that *carbonaria* has a substantial selective advantage over *typica* in many highly polluted regions, in no population has the *carbonaria* allele become fixed. This is partly because of the slow rate at which disadvantageous recessive alleles are eradicated from a population. Once the *typica* allele becomes rare in a population, it will generally be present with a dominant *carbonaria* allele in heterozygotes. For example, when the *typica* allele has a frequency of 10%, only two out of every 20 *typica* alleles will be in *typica* homozygotes that express this allele. The other 90% are in heterozygotes, which, because of the dominance of *carbonaria* over *typica*, are not being selected against. If the *typica* allele drops in frequency to 1%, then only 1% of the *typica* alleles will be in homozygotes and so exposed to selection.

The second factor that led to *typica* being retained in all populations is migration. More rural areas where *typica* retained a high frequency surrounded areas of high pollution. Continual migration from these regions ensured that *typica* retained a presence even in highly industrial areas. Similarly, *carbonaria* would have migrated from industrial areas into rural areas. Here it would have been at a selective disadvantage. The result would be that selective elimination of the unfit form from the population is balanced by migration of that form into the population from surrounding areas. Comparison of the abruptness of changes in morph frequencies with migration rates in different species of moth with melanic forms, such as the Scalloped Hazel, *Odontoptera bidentata* (Fig. 9.6), and the Pale Brindled Beauty, *Phigalia pilosaria* (Fig. 9.7), as well as Bishop's work on Peppered moth clines lends support to the selection–migration balance hypothesis.

The Peppered moth story extended

From the analysis of the components of the Peppered moth story, it is evident that there are some oversimplifications in the story when compared with the

Fig. 9.6 Non-melanic and melanic forms of the Scalloped Hazel, *Odontoptera bidentata.*

Fig. 9.7 Typical and melanic (f. *monacharia*) forms of the Pale Brindled Beauty, *Phigalia pilosaria.*

real situation. Furthermore, there are certainly some valid criticisms that may be made of some of the experimental designs used by various workers, myself included. Thus, it may be reasonable to challenge the quantitative accuracy of some of the fitness estimates obtained from these experiments. However, I can find nothing in the considerable literature on this case that undermines the basic thrust of Tutt's differential predation hypothesis or Kettlewell's qualitative interpretation of his experiments in the 1950s. The increase in *carbonaria* in polluted regions of Britain occurred because this form was more cryptic than *typica* in such regions.

Since Kettlewell's work on selective predation, several other factors have been added to the Peppered moth story. These include the moth's resting behaviour, its mating behaviour and the way that birds see. In addition, over the last three decades the frequency of the melanic form has declined very significantly. An understanding of these additional features aids in the appraisal of the validity of the case. Again, I will consider each of these additional elements in turn.

Resting-site selection

Kettlewell suggested that the different forms of the Peppered moth choose resting positions that maximise their crypsis. He conducted experiments in which moths of both main forms were placed in old barrels lined with equal amounts of black or white cloth and covered with glass. Each morning, the numbers of each type of moth on each background were recorded. His results, shown in Table 9.6, show that *carbonaria* preferentially rested on the black card, while most *typica* chose to rest on the white.

Table 9.6 The resting preferences of the *typica* and *carbonaria* forms of the Peppered moth, *Biston betularia*, in Kettlewell's barrel experiments. The moths were presented with a choice of black and white surfaces of equal area. (After Kettlewell 1955b.)

	typica	*carbonaria*	Totals
Black background	20	38	58
White background	39	21	60
Totals	**59**	**59**	**118**

The idea that the different forms will vary in behaviour in this way is intuitively seductive, for it would be promoted by selection. However, further investigations to obtain evidence in support of such morph-specific resting-site preferences have produced contradictory results. Other workers, who have replicated Kettlewell's experiments in some form, have either found that the moths show no preference, or that all the moths select the same type of background, irrespective of their own colour pattern (for example, Howlett & Majerus 1987; Table 9.7).

Table 9.7 The resting preferences of the *typica, carbonaria* and *insularia* forms of the Peppered moth, *Biston betularia*, when presented with a choice of black and white surfaces of equal area in cylinders. (From Howlett & Majerus 1987.)

	typica	*insularia*	*carbonaria*	Totals
Black surface	58	30	70	158
White surface	20	7	14	41
Floor	21	5	36	62
Totals	**99**	**42**	**120**	**261**

Howlett & Majerus (1987) have questioned the initial premise of the resting-site selection argument. At the root of their criticism were measurements of light reflected from the wings of Peppered moths. These revealed that both forms are closer to pure black than pure white.

Leaving aside whether the forms do select appropriate resting sites, we can ask how such sites might be chosen. Two hypotheses have been suggested. Kettlewell put forward a hypothesis that he called contrast–conflict. In basic terms, the moths attempt to match the colour of background they choose to rest upon to the colour of the scales (circumocular scales) below their eyes. When settling to rest in the early light, if the colour of the circumocular scales contrasts too greatly with the colour of the substrate beneath, the moth is in a state of mental conflict and moves until the contrast has been reduced before it clamps down.

Ted Sargent (1968) attempted to test this hypothesis by manipulating the colour of circumocular scales of moths. He was unable to produce any evidence to support the contrast–conflict hypothesis, proposing, as an alternative hypothesis, that the ability to select appropriate resting sites is genetically determined. The pertinence of Sargent's experiments to the Peppered moth may, however, be questioned, because, inexplicably, he used two species of noctuid moth, rather than Peppered moths, in his experiments.

There are two theoretical problems with the intuitively persuasive verbal argument that morph-specific resting-site selection behaviour should evolve in industrial melanic Lepidoptera. First, an efficient resting-site selection mechanism would reduce the importance of differential visual selection in the maintenance of the polymorphism. At least some dark homogeneous and some pale heterogeneous surfaces are present in almost all woodland habitats, whether these be in polluted or unpolluted regions. As Peppered moths rarely occur at very high density, sufficient appropriate resting sites are likely to be available to all moths, irrespective of their colour pattern. All would then have a high degree of crypsis and could, potentially, have the same fitness with respect to bird predation.

Second, unless a resting-site selection system did operate along contrast–conflict lines, it is difficult to see how it could evolve in the short time available since the frequency of *carbonaria* became appreciable in the middle of the nineteenth century. Indeed, computer model simulations have shown that unless the resting-site preferences genes are the same as the colour pattern genes, or are very tightly linked to them on the same chromosome, morph-specific behaviours of the type demonstrated by Kettlewell could not evolve in 200 generations or fewer. The essential problem with the model is a difficulty in producing an association between a particular form and a particular behaviour.

One may assume that prior to industrialisation, Peppered moths (mainly *typica* and a small proportion of *insularia*) rested on pale heterogeneous surfaces. If a new mutation, which gave moths a preference to rest on dark homogeneous surfaces, is introduced into a population in which *carbonaria* is increasing in frequency following industrialisation, the expected result is either that it fails to increase, or that it increases relatively rapidly to fixation. Which fate occurs depends largely on the frequency of forms in the population in which the new behavioural mutation occurs. If *carbonaria* is rare, the new mutation, even if it first arose in a *carbonaria* individual, will, through the process of sex and independent assortment of genes, most commonly be found in the commoner morph, i.e. *typica*. The tendency to rest on dark homogeneous surfaces would obviously be maladaptive for a *typica* moth and the behaviour would rapidly be selected out of the population. Conversely, if the mutation occurred once *carbonaria* had spread to become the commonest form in a population, the new behaviour would be appropriate for the majority and would spread. The old behaviour, which would be maladaptive for the now common *carbonaria*, would be eradicated. Consequently, this model predicts three types of population.

a) Populations in which a dark-preference allele has never spread, so that all moths have the ancestral resting behaviour.

b) Populations in which a dark-preference allele has arisen and is in a state of transient polymorphism as it spreads towards fixation or annihilation, depending on whether the frequency of *carbonaria* is increasing or decreasing. In these populations some moths will prefer pale backgrounds, others dark ones, but preferences will not be strongly morph-specific.

c) Populations in which a dark-preference allele has become fixed, so that all moths prefer dark surfaces.

Evidence supporting the existence of Peppered moth populations that differ with respect to their resting-site preferences comes from tests showing inter-population differences in levels of preference for dark and light backgrounds. Using a 'dawn box' (Fig. 9.8), with dimmer operated lights, that enabled four dawns to be simulated within a 24-hour period, replicate tests were performed on both individual moths and large samples from various populations (see Majerus 1998 for review). In general, populations from industrial regions showed higher levels of preference for dark backgrounds, and although individual moths had strong preferences for dark or light surfaces, there was no evidence of morph-specific resting-site preferences (Jones 1993). This latter point is important as the proposed evolutionary scheme does not predict that strong morph-specific resting-site behaviours would evolve. Furthermore, a balanced polymorphism is never promoted unless the behavioural gene and the melanism gene are tightly linked.

Given these possibilities, the apparently contradictory background-choice experimental data might be explained. I have argued elsewhere (Majerus 1989) that if Kettlewell used moths from different populations, for example

Fig. 9.8 The dawn box used to get four repeated resting choices of the Peppered moth, *Biston betularia*, within a single day: inside, with cylinder and outside shown.

typica from rural (type a) populations and *carbonaria* from industrial (type c) populations, the observed preference of *typica* for white and *carbonaria* for black resting sites in his tests would be explained. Unfortunately, despite exhaustive enquiries, the origin of the moths Kettlewell used in his barrel experiments is not known. However, as this work was conducted when Kettlewell was working in the Birmingham and Dorset woodlands, it is possible that the *typica* and *carbonaria* moths he used in his barrels came from unpolluted and polluted woodlands respectively. The same theory can be used to explain other results of resting-site selection data.

Resting-site preferences are crucial to the interpretation of other experimental results in the Peppered moth. For example, the levels of selective elimination of *typica* in Birmingham and *carbonaria* in Dorset in Kettlewell's mark–release–recapture experiments would be unnatural if the moths released were from populations with different resting-site preferences. As Kettlewell recorded *carbonaria* to be absent from his experimental site in Dorset, the *carbonaria* he used there at least must have come from elsewhere.

The idea that different populations may contain moths that have different behaviours may explain the second inconsistency between the observed and simulated frequencies of *carbonaria* along the Liverpool/North Wales cline in Bishop's research. The rate of decline in *carbonaria* frequency with distance away from Liverpool was less abrupt in the model simulation than in the observed data. Suppose then that a dark-preference allele has become fixed in the Liverpool population, but has failed to spread in rural North Wales, where *carbonaria* is rare. In this circumstance the rarer morphs at each end of the transect will behave in a manner inappropriate to their coloration. The *typica* form at the Liverpool end of the cline will preferentially rest on dark homogeneous surfaces. Conversely, the *carbonaria* in North Wales will choose pale heterogeneous backgrounds. Where they are rare, both forms will thus be exposed to exaggerated levels of selective predation as a result of their inappropriate behaviour. This increased elimination of rarer morphs at each end of the cline must have the effect of making the cline in frequencies more abrupt than that predicted by Bishop's model.

The effect of mating on selective predation

The adult life span of the Peppered moth is short. Estimates of average longevity range from two to seven days. As pairs stay *in copula*, or at least close together, for nearly 24 hours, this represents a considerable proportion of the time that adult Peppered moths are exposed to predation. Whether mating moths are exposed to different levels of predation is therefore important to the dynamics of the system. Considering just the *typica* and *carbonaria* forms, there are three mating combinations. It has been suggested that a pair of mating *typica* resembles a patch of foliose lichen more closely than does a single moth. It has also been argued that a mating pair of *carbonaria* would be less 'moth-shaped' than a single *carbonaria*. Professor Paul Brakefield (1987) has thus argued that both similar mating combinations may be associated with reduced predation. However, against this must be placed the increased target size and the fact that, if detected, two moths will be eaten.

More importantly, the third mating combination, *typica* x *carbonaria*, is likely to be at an overall disadvantage relative to either of the other two combinations as in nearly all habitats, one of the forms will be poorly camouflaged. The levels of predation on moths that form hybrid pairs between the two forms are thus likely to be higher than those on moths that choose partners of their own form. If this is so, one might expect an assortative mating preference to evolve. If such assortative mating were to be detected, it would be of great significance in respect of general evolutionary theory, for it would represent evidence for the first step of speciation through disruptive selection. Furthermore, such evidence would show that mating barriers could evolve in the absence of any great degree of genetic divergence or geographic isolation. No evidence of preferential mating in the Peppered moth with respect to morph has been sought. Given the short period since *carbonaria* first spread, it is unlikely that such mating preferences have had sufficient time to evolve.

The visual acuity of birds in the ultraviolet

A critical part of Kettlewell's early work on predation of the Peppered moth involved the evaluation of the relative crypsis of *typica* and *carbonaria* forms on tree trunks showing different levels of pollution. Kettlewell obtained cryptic indices by placing Peppered moths of either *typica* or *carbonaria* forms on oak trunks and measuring the distance from the trunks that observers found them indistinguishable from their background. In many later experiments on the predation of moths by birds, the assumption was made that birds had similar vision to humans. For example, in many Peppered moth experiments moths were put out in what were described as 'life-like positions in situations where their crypsis was maximised'. However, birds do not see as we do. They have greater discriminatory prowess due to the presence of oil droplets in their cone cells that act as filters (Bowmaker 1991). More significantly, birds have acute vision in the ultraviolet to which we are virtually blind (p. 187). The exact way in which birds use their UV-sensitive cones is not known. However, their vision is probably tetrachromatic (i.e. the image is a result of their four types of cone used in concert) (Chen & Goldsmith 1986). The question is, could this extra element to bird vision change their assessment of the crypsis of the different forms of the Peppered moth in various natural situations? The answer is yes.

Jim Stalker, Clair Brunton and I measured the UV reflectance of *typica*, *insularia* and *carbonaria*, together with that of six lichen species from seven types of tree. We found that the black scales and hairs of all forms of the Peppered moth absorb UV wavelengths, while the white scales reflect UV strongly. Of the lichens assessed, the foliose green lichens, for example, *Hypogymnia* and *Evernia* spp., absorb UV. On the other hand, crustose grey lichens, such as *Lecanora* spp., have some parts that absorb UV and other portions that reflect it, giving these lichens an overall speckled appearance in pure UV.

The tests showed that while *carbonaria* was much more conspicuous than *typica* in the human visible spectrum against foliose lichens on bark, the reverse was true in the UV spectrum (Plate 14d and 14e). Conversely, when set against bark covered with *Lecanora conizaeoides*, *carbonaria* was easier to see than *typica* in both human visible and UV wavelengths (Majerus et al. 2000).

These results suggest that experiments that have involved some element of human assessment of the crypsis of Peppered moths may be flawed. More crucially, it suggests that the resting site to which Peppered moths were adapted ancestrally is likely to have been crustose lichen-covered tree bark, not foliose lichen-covered bark as stated in most texts. If this is the case, it supports the contention that the most usual day-time resting site for the Peppered moth is under horizontal branches, which, at least in unpolluted regions, are largely coated with crustose lichens. The upper surfaces of branches would not be appropriate resting sites as these usually support a rich foliose lichen flora (Liebert & Brakefield 1987).

Melanism in the Peppered moth outside Britain

Melanic polymorphism in the Peppered moth is not confined to Britain. In Holland, *carbonaria* was first recorded in 1867 (Haylearts 1870). By 1900 it was widespread and the full range of *insularia* forms was also present. Comparisons of the frequencies of *carbonaria* with industrialisation and epiphytic flora show correlations similar to those in Britain. However, the frequency of *carbonaria* in Holland has not reached the highest levels recorded in Britain, never exceeding 75%, and *insularia* is generally commoner in Holland than in Britain (Brakefield 1990). In the 1970s, in Luxembourg, *carbonaria* comprised over 70% of populations in southern industrial districts, but only 30% in the Ardennes. By 1989–1993, the frequency of *carbonaria* had declined significantly in both regions (Majerus 1998). Both *carbonaria* and *insularia* are common in industrial regions of Belgium and northern France, and in Germany *carbonaria* was already common in industrial regions by 1900. High melanic frequencies have also been reported in industrial regions of Denmark, Sweden, Finland and the Czech Republic.

Industrial melanism has also been recorded in the American subspecies, *Biston betularia cognataria*. The full melanic form, f. *swettaria*, is indistinguishable from *carbonaria*, and is also controlled by a dominant allele of a single gene. Form *swettaria* was first recorded in 1906 near Philadelphia (Owen 1961). In parts of Michigan, the frequency of *swettaria* rose to over 90% by 1960 (Owen 1961, 1962). Elsewhere in North America, *swettaria* has been recorded from Illinois, Massachusetts, Delaware, Montreal, Toronto and southern Ontario. A third subspecies of the Peppered moth, *Biston betularia parva*, occurs in Japan. Melanism has not evolved in this subspecies as it does not occur in regions affected by industrial pollution to any significant degree (Asami & Grant 1995).

Industrial melanism in reverse

In the 1950s, smokeless zones and other anti-pollution legislation were introduced in Britain. This legislation led to declines in the levels of both sulphur dioxide and soot pollution. After a lag period, the frequencies of *carbonaria* began to decline throughout Britain. Time taken for new unpolluted growth on trees, for pollutants to wash or wear off old trees and for the recolonisation of bark by lichens is thought to be responsible for the lag in response. Subsequently, the frequencies of the melanic forms have continued to decline, so that now no population is known in Britain in which the frequency of *carbonaria* exceeds 30%. Unlike the rise in *carbonaria*, this decline has been well monitored at several locations. The frequencies of *carbonaria* between 1960 and 2000, for two sites in England, are given in Table 9.8. The pattern of decline accords well with expectation. In Britain, the current rates of decline are broadly in line with theoretical predictions from computer simulations. If *carbonaria* continues to decline at the predicted rate, it will be reduced to a frequency of less than 1% throughout Britain by 2020.

Table 9.8 The decline in melanism in the Peppered moth, *Biston betularia*, since anti-pollution legislation. Figures given are the percentage *carbonaria* in samples at two sites in England and one in America. Data are for each fifth year, or nearest equivalent (indicated by asterisk). More detailed data are given in Majerus 1998 and Grant et al. 1996.

Year	Caldy Common, West Kirby, north-west England	Cambridge, England	George Reserve Michigan, USA
1960/1961*	94.2	94.8	91.7*
1965	90.2	–	–
1970	90.8	75.0	–
1975	86.6	64.7	–
1980/1981*	76.9	45.9*	–
1985	53.5	39.5	–
1990	33.1	22.2	–
1995	17.6	19.2	20.0
1998*/2000	11.5*	15.1	

Similar reductions in *carbonaria* frequencies have been reported in the Netherlands and the United States. In the Netherlands, *carbonaria* is being replaced by both *typica* and the darkest of the *insularia* forms. In Michigan, the decline in the frequency of *swettaria* closely parallels the decline in *carbonaria* on the Wirral. In both cases the decline has been from over 90% to less than 20% (Table 9.8).

Professor Bruce Grant, commenting on the declines in melanics on the Wirral and in Michigan, showed that these correlate well with reductions in sulphur dioxide and soot pollution. However, he also reports that the increase in *typica* does not appear to be correlated with an appreciable increase in the lichens on trees. This latter statement should be regarded with some caution for several reasons. First, the assessments of lichens were anecdotal, rather than systematic. Second, the lichen flora in the woodland canopy, where the Peppered moth rests by day, was not appraised. Third, a number of other authors have recorded substantial increases in lichens following anti-pollution legislation (for example, Cook et al. 1990).

The observed declines of the melanic forms, *carbonaria* in Britain and *swettaria* in America, hold a three-fold importance. First, they indicate that biological evolution is not a one-way process. If the selective factors that lead to evolutionary changes are reversed, the changes may be reversed. Second, the observations from Britain and America are essentially replicate natural experiments. The consistency in the patterns of increase and decrease in the melanic forms and the correlation of melanic frequencies with pollution levels add weight to the selective explanation of the changes observed. Third, the accord between decreases in the observed melanic frequencies and the changes predicted on the basis of computer simulations argues that the main factors affecting this case have been identified and that these are broadly correct.

Kettlewell's work on the Peppered moth had a considerable influence on evolutionary biology, for it shifted the primary perceived mechanism of biological evolution from theory to fact. The recent reversal in the fortunes of *carbonaria* has offered an opportunity to fill a major gap in scientific knowledge. Although it is often said of the Peppered moth that we witnessed the evolution of melanism, in fact very little accurate information on the increase in the frequencies of *carbonaria* in the nineteenth and early twentieth centuries exists. By the time scientists began looking at the case in detail, most of the increases had happened. The decline in *carbonaria* following the clean air acts has raised the potential to at least monitor the demise of a genetic form in the wild.

Classes of melanism

Early in this chapter I pointed out that the Peppered moth is something of a special case. Although a few species show a similar pattern with respect to the evolution of melanism, such cases are a small minority of those British moths known to have melanic forms. The other causes of melanism in adult British Lepidoptera are many and varied. In 1998, a classification of melanism in the Lepidoptera, based upon and extended from that of Kettlewell (1973), was published (Majerus 1998). This classification is given with minor amendments in Table 9.9. Three main categories are identified: industrial melanism, non-industrial melanism and melanism in conspicuous species. Each of these has a number of subdivisions.

Industrial melanism

Industrial melanism is the proportional increase of melanic pigments in members of a population, whether this be as a result of an increase in the frequencies of distinct melanic forms, or as a result of a general darkening of some or all forms within a population, where this increase is associated with the effects of industrialisation. The class can be split into three categories as follows:

i) *Full industrial melanic polymorphism*: melanic forms have reached significant frequencies only since and as a consequence of industrialisation.

ii) *Partial industrial melanic polymorphism*: melanic forms that were present prior to industrialisation have spread geographically, or increased in frequency since and as a consequence of industrialisation.

iii) *Polygenic industrial melanism*: the average ground colour of some populations has darkened gradually as a consequence of the effects of industrialisation on the environment.

Table 9.9 A classification of melanism in the Lepidoptera. Main classes are given in bold. Subclasses are given in italics. (Adapted from Kettlewell 1973 and Majerus 1998.)

Class	Definition and selective rationale	Example
Industrial melanism	Increase in frequency of melanism associated with the effects of industrialisation. Relative crypsis and differential bird predation.	
Full industrial melanic polymorphism	Distinct melanic forms have reached frequencies > 1% only since and as a result of industrialisation. Relative crypsis and differential bird predation.	Peppered moth, *Biston betularia*
Partial industrial melanic polymorphism	Distinct melanic forms that existed prior to the Industrial Revolution have spread and increased in frequency since and as a result of industrialisation. Relative crypsis and differential bird predation.	Pale Brindled Beauty, *Phigalia pilosaria*
Polygenic industrial melanism	Gradual increase in the tone of the average ground colour in a population as a result of the effects of industrialisation. Relative crypsis and differential bird predation.	Scalloped Hazel, *Odontoptera bidentata*, in Birmingham
Non-industrial melanism	Any melanism in a non-conspicuous species that appears to be independent of the direct or indirect effects of industrialisation.	
Thermal melanism	Melanism is favoured in cool climes because of the thermal properties of dark compared with light surfaces. Increased melanisation allows faster warming, leading to greater activity.	Black Mountain moth, *Psodos coracina*
Rural or background choice melanism	The occurrence of melanic forms in heterogeneous habitats, which present both dark and pale potential resting sites. Different morphs may choose resting sites appropriate to their colour patterns. Increased crypsis on dark resting substrates.	Clouded-bordered Brindle, *Apamea crenata*
High latitude melanism	Increased melanisation at high latitude. May result from cool climate, diffuse sunlight or the lack of darkness at night in the summer months. Fitness affected by thermal characteristics and differential predation of moths both when at rest and/or when in flight.	Hebrew Character, *Orthosia gothica*; Ghost moth, *Hepialus humuli*
Western coastline melanism	Melanism occurring in populations close to western coasts. Selective factors not known, but increased crypsis may be involved.	Marbled Coronet, *Hadena confusa*
Pluvial melanism	Melanism associated with very high rainfall and humidity in forest habitats. Selective factors not known, but increased crypsis assumed to be involved.	Various Noctuidae and Geometridae

Table 9.9 (cont.)

Class	Definition and selective rationale	Example
Melanism associated with fire	Melanism associated with cycles of burning and regeneration. Relative crypsis and differential bird predation.	Horse Chestnut moth, *Pachycnemia hippocastanaria*
Ancient conifer melanism (relict melanism)	Melanic forms occur in ancient conifer woodlands. Reduced predation by birds when in flight under dense canopies during the day.	Mottled Beauty, *Alcis repandata*
Anti-search image melanism	Distinct melanic forms occur in abundant species. Acts as a defence against predators that form searching images for common prey items.	Mottled Umber, *Erannis defoliaria*
Melanism in conspicuous Lepidoptera	Melanism in Lepidoptera that have bright colour patterns.	
Aposematic melanism	Rare melanics that arise as a result of mutation in aposematic species. Usually selectively disadvantageous.	Six-spot Burnet, *Zygaena filipendulae*
Mimetic melanism	Increased melanisation as a result of the evolution of a mimetic resemblance to a species that has a large dark component in its colour pattern.	Some forms of *Papilio dardanus*
Sexual melanism	Melanic frequencies increase or are maintained at specific levels because some individuals have preferences to mate with melanic partners.	Scarlet Tiger moth, *Callimorpha dominula*

Full industrial melanic polymorphism

The case of the Peppered moth is the most obvious example of full industrial melanic polymorphism. This case is not unique. A small number of other species fall into this category. In the Lobster moth, *Stauropus fagi*, as in most of these cases, the melanic form (Fig. 9.9) is controlled by the dominant allele of a single gene. The Brindled Beauty, *Lycia hirtaria* (Fig. 9.10), is an exception in this respect for the melanic form *nigra* is the result of a recessive allele. It is not coincidental that most recent melanic forms are genetically dominant. If a new mutation is dominant when it first arises, it is immediately fully expressed and so exposed to selection. If at an advantage over the original form, it will be favoured and begin to spread. Recessive mutations, on the other hand, would not be exposed to selection until they attained a sufficient frequency to occur in homozygotes, in which they would be expressed. The third possibility, that the heterozygotes between the new melanic and the old non-melanic alleles were intermediate between the two homozygotes, could lead to the evolution of dominance if the darkest form were most favoured. This is what is thought to have happened in the case of the Peppered moth (p. 221).

In some species showing full industrial melanic polymorphism, such as the Poplar Grey, *Apatele megacephala*, a melanic form, *nigra*, arose about the same time as *carbonaria* appeared in the Peppered moth. In others, industrial melanism has developed much more recently, as in the Sprawler, *Brachionycha*

Fig. 9.9 Non-melanic and melanic forms of the Lobster moth, *Stauropus fagi*.

Fig. 9.10 Non-melanic and melanic forms of the Brindled Beauty, *Lycia hirtaria*.

Fig. 9.11 The Oak
Beauty moth,
Biston strataria.

sphinx, the Early Grey, *Xylocampa areola*, and the Red Underwing, *Catocala nupta*. In these species industrial melanism developed only in the second half of the twentieth century, probably because an appropriate melanic mutation simply did not arise earlier in a suitable location.

The variation in the initial occurrence of industrial melanics between species emphasises one important feature of natural selection. Natural selection can only cause change if it has genetic variation that is expressed phenotypically to act upon. The Peppered moth's closest British relative, the Oak Beauty, *Biston strataria* (Fig. 9.11), is a wonderful illustration of this. This moth has a melanic form, *melanaria*, which is common as an industrial melanic in Holland. However, *melanaria* has only been recorded as a rare mutation in Britain. The ecology, behaviour and distribution of the Oak Beauty are similar to those of the Peppered moth. However, the *melanaria* mutation seems not to have occurred in Britain in a population in which industrial factors would have caused it to spread. Furthermore, because of the relatively sedentary habits of this moth, the *melanaria* form has not migrated into Britain from continental Europe.

The lack of melanism in the Oak Beauty in Britain can be compared with the case of the Figure of Eighty, *Tethea ocularis*. This moth has a melanic form, *fusca*, which was known to occur in Belgium and Holland, but not in Britain, early in the twentieth century (Fig. 6.9). Form *fusca* arrived in England, by migration, in the mid-1940s, the first recorded individual being captured in 1945. Thereafter, *fusca* increased in frequency rapidly, spreading to many industrial parts of Britain, although it is now declining again as pollution levels decrease.

In a way I am saddened by the current declines in melanism seen in those moths that truly represent examples of full industrial melanic polymorphism. I have gained great enjoyment from monitoring the frequencies of the various melanic forms of these species in my moth traps since 1964. Yet the fact that these species did not have melanic forms prior to the Industrial Revolution suggests that if pollution levels continue to decrease, as we all surely hope that they will, these forms are doomed. With a little luck, I would hope to live out at least my quota of three score years and ten; maybe more. That should give me at least until 2024. By that time, the full industrial melanic polymorphisms

may all be gone from the country in which they have been most closely scrutinised.

Partial industrial melanic polymorphism

Melanic forms of many species of moth are independent of industrialisation.
These have been discussed in detail by Kettlewell (1973) and Majerus (1998)
and are considered briefly towards the end of this chapter. Their relevance to
industrial melanism is that the presence of melanic forms prior to, and independently from, industrialisation provided a repository of melanic variants
that were favoured as pollution levels increased. Examples where such melanic forms are inherited and distinct from non-melanic forms represent cases of
partial industrial melanic polymorphism. The majority of moths that exhibit
industrial melanic polymorphism had melanic forms prior to the Industrial
Revolution.

The distinction between partial and full industrial melanic polymorphism is
well illustrated by the case of the Willow Beauty, *Peribatodes rhomboidaria*. This
species has two melanic forms. One, f. *perfumaria*, existed as a non-industrial
melanic prior to the Industrial Revolution. Following industrialisation, the frequency of *perfumaria* increased in industrial regions in response to the darkening of resting sites. In the twentieth century, *perfumaria*, which still occurs at
low frequency in some rural areas, particularly in Scotland, was displaced in
polluted regions by a new and even darker form, f. *rebeli*. The *perfumaria* thus
fits the definition of a partial industrial melanic, while *rebeli* is a full industrial
melanic.

There are many probable instances of partial industrial melanic polymorphism, but rather few that have been investigated in any depth. The result is
that were a list of all the cases that fall into this class to be drawn up, it would
be largely a matter of conjecture because very few specimens from before the
Industrial Revolution still remain. Allocation of a species to this category thus
depends on the finding of melanic forms now existing at appreciable frequencies in unpolluted regions rather than firm evidence that the melanic
forms were present before pollution caused changes to the environment. Thus
comparison of the frequencies of the melanic form, *monacharia*, of the Pale
Brindled Beauty, shows that melanics occur in non-industrial regions of
Scotland and Wales, and at inflated frequencies in industrial regions of
England. For example, the melanic form *monacharia* comprised between
11.8% and 32.5% of samples from four sites in Perthshire (where the *carbonaria* form of the Peppered moth is absent), and 33.8% to 80.0% at 12 sites
across Lancashire, Cheshire, Staffordshire and Yorkshire, during the late
1960s. Melanic forms of the Mottled Beauty, *Alcis repandata*, the Satin Beauty,
Deileptenia ribeata, the Green Brindled Crescent, *Allophyes oxyacanthae* (Plate 14f
and 14g), the Clouded-bordered Brindle, *Apamea crenata* (Fig. 9.12), and the
Dark Arches, *Apamea monoglypha*, show similar patterns. In each case the
increase in melanics in industrial regions has been attributed to increased
crypsis.

Some of these species show morph-specific habitat preferences. Morph-specific habitat preferences in Lepidoptera showing melanic polymorphism were
first suggested to explain abrupt differences in melanic frequencies of the
Mottled Beauty and the Tawny-barred Angle, *Semiothisa liturata*, in moth trap
catches either side of sharp habitat boundaries (Table 9.10) (Kearns & Majerus

Fig. 9.12 Typical and melanic forms of the Clouded-
bordered Brindle, *Apamea
crenata.*

1987). Such differences have subsequently been recorded in 14 species of 20
tested (Majerus 1998). In all cases, melanics had higher frequencies in woodland with dense canopies than in adjacent more open habitats.

Table 9.10 Details of the numbers of different forms of Mottled Beauty, *Alcis repandata*, and
Tawny-barred Angle, *Semiothisa liturata*, taken from Heath moth traps (see Fig. 6.2b) in different habitats, on 12 July 1984, at Ynys-Hir, Dyfed. Trap 1 was set up in mixed deciduous
woodland, trap 2 in a Douglas fir plantation. The traps were set 20 yards apart. (From data
in Kearns & Majerus 1987.)

	Trap 1	Trap 2	Totals
Mottled Beauty			
typica	41	45	86
conversaria	0	11	11
nigricata/nigra	0	2	2
Totals	**41**	**58**	**99**
Tawny-barred Angle			
typica	8	16	24
nigrofulvata	1	20	21
Totals	**9**	**36**	**45**

I have speculated that in many species now showing industrial melanism,
melanic forms first arose and spread in specific ecological circumstances long
before industrialisation (Table 9.11; Majerus 1998). Pointing to the existence
of melanic polymorphism in several species in unpolluted ancient coniferous
forests, such as Rannoch Black Wood in Scotland, I argued that such habitats
would have been far more widespread in the past, as would the melanic forms
that their particular ecologies supported. Such melanic forms would only have

occurred in habitats to which they were suited. Those that migrated from areas with the specific ecological criteria favouring melanism would have been eliminated. Consequently, the melanics, over time, would have evolved behaviours that restricted them to these specific habitats.

Table 9.11 Suggested evolutionary scenario to explain morph-specific habitat preferences in species exhibiting partial industrial melanic polymorphism (Based on Majerus 1989.)

(a) In the long past, typical forms of relevant species had patterns that maximised their crypsis in their normal habitats.
(b) Melanic (or dark-banded) morphs evolved in specific ecological circumstances, such as in the great conifer forests that periodically covered large areas of Europe over the last 100,000 years and more.
(c) Melanic (or dark-banded) forms were at a selective disadvantage if they moved from areas in which the specific ecological circumstances persisted.
(d) Consequently these forms evolved behaviours that restricted them to habitats where they were not at a disadvantage. Indeed, as habitat types moved up and down across the map of Europe, with successive changes in climate during the cycles of ice ages and interstadials, the moths would have moved, albeit passively, with suitable habitats.
(e) Recent changes in forestry, land usage and increases in pollution in more recent times, have provided new habitats (for example, conifer plantations and woodland areas with high pollution levels and lacking lichens) in which the ecological conditions favoured melanic forms. This does not imply that the typical forms were, or are, necessarily less fit in such habitats than these forms were, or are, in other habitats.

Over the last millennium, changes in forestry and land usage and, more recently, increases in pollution, have created novel ecological circumstances that favour melanics. The melanics have, in consequence, spread out of their original habitats into these new environments and have risen in frequency, producing examples of partial industrial melanic polymorphism, yet they have retained their morph-specific habitat preferences.

Polygenic industrial melanism

Of all categories of industrial melanism, that involving the gradual darkening of the ground colour due to directional selection acting on polygenic systems has been least considered. Examination of specimens collected over the last century and a half suggests that many species have experienced a darkening of the colours and consequent obscuring of patterning in industrial regions. Museum specimens fade with age. Consequently, the lighter colour of old specimens may be partly due to their age. However, it is difficult to ascribe all of the differences between old and recent specimens to this cause. Indeed, a comparison of series of specimens of six species collected between 1880 and 1914, from rural and industrial regions, with those collected between 1992 and 1996, showed that the ground colour had darkened more in industrial regions than in the rural areas (Majerus, unpublished data).

Although practically no work has been conducted specifically on polygenic industrial melanics, some data exist for species that also show industrial melanic polymorphism. For example, in the Scalloped Hazel, a full industrial melanic polymorphism, f. *nigra*, exists, occurring at high frequency in Liverpool, Manchester, Leeds and the Potteries. This form does not, however, occur in Birmingham. Yet in Birmingham, individuals of this species are considerably darker than those found in rural regions to the south and west. The darkening of the ground colour of the Birmingham moths is due to many genes. If Birmingham moths are crossed with paler individuals from Exmoor or Aberystwyth, the progeny are generally intermediate in colour between the parents. In the following generation, a complete spread in colour tone, between that characteristic of Birmingham and that found in rural populations, results. Kettlewell (1973) reports a similar situation for the Sprawler. In this species, full industrial melanic polymorphism only developed in the 1960s. However, prior to this, continuous variation in ground colour tone, correlated with industrialisation, was known. This continuous variation is probably controlled by a polygenic system, although no breeding experiments have been conducted to confirm this.

The situation in which small variations in the colour patterns of many species are controlled by many genes, each having a small effect, is common in the Lepidoptera. The selective predation of lighter, and thus less cryptic, forms in regions affected by soot will lead to an increase in those alleles that produce darker morphs. It is difficult to see how the past increase in the tone of moths can be experimentally tested. However, the recent decrease in pollution should produce a reversal in this trend, with selection favouring paler ground colours and patterning becoming more clearly defined. The development of new digital cameras and instruments for measuring the spectral reflectance of surfaces, coupled with computer storage of data, should allow comparisons of material over long periods of time without reliance on museum specimens or photographic prints, both of which may fade with time.

Non-industrial melanism

The prominence of the case of the Peppered moth in biological texts has tended to obscure the fact that most British moths that now have melanic forms had such forms prior to the Industrial Revolution. Some of these are featured as examples of partial industrial melanic polymorphic species. However, in many species melanism is entirely independent of industrialisation.

The reasons for the existence of melanic forms independently of pollution are diverse. In species that rely largely on crypsis for their defence, eight subclasses have been recognised. This classification is based on the geographic characteristics of populations showing melanism, or on the selective factors considered most likely to account for the melanism (Table 9.9).

Thermal melanism

In some organisms, melanism is not a defence against predators, but is purely a result of the thermal properties of dark compared with light surfaces. Heavily melanised Lepidoptera warm up more quickly than their lighter counterparts. The reverse is also true, for melanics radiate heat more rapidly, losing heat more quickly after dusk. In Arctic or temperate climes, melanised forms of day-flying species may gain a significant advantage if they can warm up and become active when non-melanics cannot.

Examples are most common among species occurring at high latitudes and high altitudes, because of the usually low ambient temperatures. Comparative analysis of butterflies of the genus *Colias* has shown that Arctic species have increased melanisation, particularly in the basal third of the wings, allowing the butterflies to heat up more rapidly. In the white butterfly, *Pieris protodice* ssp. *occidentalis*, melanism varies with season, the spring generation being darker than the summer generation for thermoregulatory reasons. The adaptive involvement of thermoregulation in the occurrence of melanic forms has been suggested or demonstrated in many other Lepidoptera (for example, James 1986). Thus for example, the dark coloration of the Black Mountain moth, *Psodos coracina* (Plate 14a), and the Netted Mountain moth, *Semiothisa carbonaria* (Fig. 8.2), has a thermal dimension. Both species are found at high altitude and are day-flying. They move out of their night-time retreats in the morning on sunny days and take up a vantage point in the full sun, opening their wings and holding them at right angles to the sun's rays to absorb heat as rapidly as possible.

Kettlewell (1973) asserts that thermal melanism is confined to day-flying Lepidoptera. However, some thermal advantage probably accrues indirectly to night-flying moths that have specific habitat preferences. For example, the melanic forms of many night-flying British moths have a strong habitat preference for dense canopied woodlands (p. 239). In such woodlands, temperature drops more slowly after dusk than in the open. It is probable that the morph-specific habitat preferences shown by these moths have evolved primarily for predator avoidance. However, the disadvantage of being melanic, in terms of heat loss for a night-active species, may be reduced for species that confine themselves to such woodlands.

The primary reasons for the evolution of melanism in the other classes are all based on predation levels in particular circumstances. However, in some classes (for example, northern melanism, western coastline melanism), thermal melanism may also play a part. Certainly the various selective explanations suggested are rarely mutually exclusive.

Rural or background choice melanism

Many habitats are heterogeneous and contain both dark and pale potential resting sites. In many species, melanic forms have evolved in response to this habitat heterogeneity. Variation in the colour of potential resting sites may be within a habitat leading to polymorphism and morph-specific resting-site preferences, as in the Pine Beauty moth, *Panolis flammea* (Majerus 1982). Alternatively it may be on a wider geographic scale, with local races resulting, as seen in the Annulet, *Gnophos obscuratus*, the White-line Dart, *Euxoa tritici*, Archer's Dart, *Agrotis vestigialis*, the Feathered Rustic, *Agrotis cinerea*, and the Sand Dart, *Agrotis ripae*, in each of which the degree of melanism is correlated with soil colour.

High latitude melanism

Kettlewell (1973) referred to this class of melanism as Northern melanism. I have changed the name so that it includes examples showing the same phenomenon in the southern hemisphere. It simply involves the common incidence of melanic forms at high latitudes (Fig. 9.13). The selective reasons why melanism is favoured at high latitudes are varied. Obviously, as has already been described, thermoregulation may play a part. In addition, disruptive patterns may be ineffective when the angle of incidence of the sun is low (Kettlewell 1973) obscuring such patterns as occur in the Hebrew Character, *Orthosia gothica* (Fig. 9.14), and the Scalloped Oak, *Crocallis elinguaria*, in northern Scotland. Thirdly, and perhaps most importantly, summer-flying species

Fig. 9.13 Typical and melanic forms of the Ingrailed
Clay, *Diarsia mendica*, which
exhibits high latitude
melanism.

cannot fly under the cover of darkness at high latitude because the sun does
not set (Fig. 9.15). Anyone who has tried to collect crepuscular species as dusk
approaches will be aware that dark moths are harder to see on the wing than
are pale ones, particularly in poor light.

Studies of Lepidoptera in the Shetland Islands, where moths suffer high predation levels from gulls and crows, have shown a high prevalence of melanism
on these islands. In some cases, such as the Ingrailed Clay, *Diarsia mendica* (Fig.

Fig. 9.14 The
northern form of
the Hebrew
Character, *Orthosia
gothica* f. *gothicina*,
in which the nor-
mal black marks
around the orbicu-
lar stigma have
been lost.

Fig. 9.15 Midnight of 23 July in Swedish Lapland.

9.13), the Netted Pug, *Eupithecia venosata*, and the Marbled Coronet, *Hadena confusa*, the melanics comprise more or less monomorphic geographic races. In others, such as the Autumnal Rustic, *Paradiarsia glareosa* (Fig. 9.16), the Square-spot Rustic, *Xestia xanthographa*, and the Northern Spinach, *Eulithis testata* (Fig. 9.17), polymorphism has resulted.

The case of the Ghost moth, *Hepialus humuli*, is of particular interest. In southern populations of this species, the males fly over lekking grounds at dusk, attracting females to them by dint of their startling white wings (p. 103). However, on Uist, males lack the stark white coloration, with the emphasis of mate attraction being shifted from the visual to a pheromonal system because the bright shining wings are too costly for males in the face of bird predation during the hours of the 'midnight sun' (Kettlewell 1973) (p. 104) (Plate 15e).

Fig. 9.16 Melanic polymorphism in the Autumnal Rustic, *Paradiarsia glareosa*, from Shetland.

Fig. 9.17 Southern and northern forms of the Northern Spinach, *Eulithis testata*.

Western coastline melanism

This is perhaps the most perplexing of the classes of non-industrial melanism. This class encompasses a small number of species in which melanic forms are found in Northern Europe along western coastlines, with the darkness then diminishing inland to the east. In all British species showing this phenomenon, melanism appears to be controlled polygenically. Examples include the Tawny Shears, *Hadena perplexa*, the Yellow Shell, *Camptogramma bilineata*, and the Marbled Coronet. In the Tawny Shears, the usual pale forms of eastern and central England are replaced by mid-brown forms in western Wales, Devon and Cornwall. On western coasts of Ireland, the nominate subspecies is replaced by *Hadena perplexa capsophila*. Kettlewell (1973) suggests that in some related species, melanic forms found along western coasts have experienced full speciation. Indeed, several species of dark-coloured noctuid, such as the Grey, *Hadena caesia* ssp. *mananii*, and the Black-banded, *Polymixis xanthomista* ssp. *statices*, are confined to western coastal habitats. It is likely that the phenomenon occurs in many Palearctic regions where conditions are similar.

The reasons underlying western coastline melanism are unclear, with several alternatives having been suggested. First, as cloud cover is high in coastal regions facing the prevailing wind, there may be a thermal advantage to being dark in such locations (Majerus 1998). Second, the protective qualities of melanic pigments against abrasion may reduce wear on wings from sand blasting (Majerus 1998). Third, the darkening of moths along western coasts may be an anti-predator device, increasing crypsis when moths rest on rocks darkened by sea spray or by the high rainfall in such regions (Tutt 1896). Finally, dark forms may have greater tolerance to salt than paler forms (Kettlewell

1973). Experimental work on species exhibiting western coastal melanism is clearly needed.

Pluvial melanism

This class of melanism may be related to the previous one. It concerns species occurring in forested regions, which have very high rainfall. These very wet habitats are found in South Island, New Zealand, the Himalayas, in the Olympic Mountains in north-west USA and in parts of the great Andes range in South America, where rainfall can exceed 500 centimetres per annum. In these forests light intensity is low and the backgrounds are dark because of repeated wetting. Melanism is common in these situations (Hudson 1928). Although virtually no experimental work has been conducted on pluvial melanism and possible evolutionary causes remain untested, increased crypsis on wet darkened surfaces and thermal melanism are likely to be involved.

Melanism associated with fire

In habitats where a cycle of burning and regeneration is the norm, the ratio of dark to light resting sites will change cyclically. Here melanic forms may increase rapidly after burning, only to begin to decline again as the vegetation regenerates. For example, in forests composed of fire-resistant trees, such as those in the eastern pine forests of North America, several species of 'underwing' moth, *Catocala* spp., show melanic polymorphisms (for example, *Catocala cerogama*, with its melanic form, f. *ruperti*). Similarly, the moth *Cleora tulbaghata* shows melanic polymorphism in South Africa, where *Acacia cyclops*, a fire-resistant tree introduced from Australia, grows. In Britain, the Horse Chestnut moth, *Pachycnemia hippocastanaria*, has a melanic form, *nigricans*, that is found locally on heather and ling heathland. The frequency of *nigricans* is positively correlated with the quantity of burnt heathland, resulting from accidental fires (Majerus 1981).

Ancient conifer melanism (relict melanism)

Melanism has high prevalence in indigenous coniferous forest such as the relict Caledonian pine forests in Scotland and many parts of Canada and Siberia. In Britain, species such as the Mottled Beauty, the Willow Beauty, the Satin Beauty and the Tawny-barred Angle (Fig. 9.18) all have melanic forms because, in the dim light conditions under the canopy, they are less visible on the wing than the non-melanics. The reason that these species are on the wing in such forests during daylight hours is that they get disturbed from their resting sites on the trunks and branches of trees by foraging wood ants (Kettlewell 1973).

Anti-search image melanism

In some abundant species it has been conjectured that melanism has evolved simply because the species occurs at high density. It is known that many predators that hunt by sight, including birds, form searching images for prey items that they encounter commonly. These predators then tend to concentrate their efforts on looking for these types of prey (p. 74). The evolutionary rationale behind anti-search image melanism is simply that by producing additional forms, levels of predation by birds that form searching images will be decreased because predators will have more colour patterns to learn and

Fig. 9.18 Non-melanic and
melanic forms of the
Tawny-barred Angle,
Semiothisa liturata.

remember. Here then the existence of melanic forms has less to do with being black or dark as it has to do with being different from previously existing forms.

This class of melanism has also been called apostatic melanism, following Bryan Clarke's (1962) use of the term apostatic selection, to describe a situation in which a rare form was favoured by selection as a result of its rarity.

Probable examples of anti-search image melanism include the Common Marbled Carpet, *Chloroclysta truncata*, the Grey Pine Carpet, *Thera obeliscata*, the July Highflyer, *Hydriomena furcata*, the Mottled Umber, the Large Yellow Underwing, *Noctua pronuba*, the Clouded Drab, *Orthosia incerta*, the Beaded Chestnut, *Agrochola lychnidis*, the Dunbar, *Cosmia trapezina*, the Common Rustic, *Mesapamea secalis*, and the Lesser Common Rustic, *Mesapamea secalella*. In all of these abundant species melanic forms occur in non-industrial regions. However, most of these species have higher melanic frequencies in industrial regions than elsewhere. This fits expectation because the likelihood of a predator forming a searching image for a particular prey type depends on the apparent abundance of the prey to the bird, which in turn is a function of both the real abundance and crypsis of the prey.

The understanding of the evolution and genetics of non-industrial melanism may be crucially important to research into industrial melanism, for in many instances the source of industrial melanic forms may have been melanics that evolved long ago, independently of the effects of industrialisation.

Finally, it should be noted that the larvae of many moths exhibit melanic polymorphism, as in the case of the Miller, *Acronicta leporina* (Fig. 8. 9c), or continuous variation in their extent of melanisation, as in the Emperor moth, *Saturnia pavonia* (Plate 14b). Very little research has been conducted on the causes of melanism in larvae of moths. Only in one species, the Oak Eggar, *Lasiocampa quercus*, is there good evidence that differential bird predation has a role to play in the maintenance of a melanic form of larva (Kettlewell 1973).

Melanism in conspicuous Lepidoptera

Melanism occurs most commonly in moths that rest up during the day and depend upon camouflage for their defence against predators that hunt by sight. However, Kettlewell (1973) notes that some day-flying species of Lepidoptera, which have bright and conspicuous colour patterns, also have melanic forms. He lists three subclasses.

Aposematic melanism

In many aposematic species in which black is present as a component of the colour pattern, genetically controlled melanic forms occur. Usually the inheritance of these melanics depends on the recessive alleles of single genes. Examples are known from several species of Zygaenidae (Fig. 9.19) and Arctiidae. Such melanic forms are generally maladaptive and are rapidly selected out of the population when they arise. Consequently, in most aposematic species, melanic forms of this type only occur as rare mutations.

One exceptional case concerns the Buff Ermine, *Spilosoma luteum*. Typically, this moth has a yellow ground colour with a patterning of dark brown or black spots, is known to be unpalatable and may therefore be considered aposematic

Fig. 9.19 Typical and melanic forms of the Five-spot Burnet, *Zygaena trifolii*.

(Rothschild 1963). In sand dune habitats in Yorkshire and Lancashire and on continental coasts in north-west Europe, a melanic form *zatima* occurs as a polymorphism. In this form the patterning is considerably extended so that the greater part of the wings is dark (Fig. 9.20). The *zatima* form is inherited as an incomplete dominant with a rather variable heterozygote. Where it is polymorphic, the Buff Ermine represents a rare evolutionary phenomenon: the change from aposematism to cryptic coloration. On the sand hills where it occurs, it rests on the trunks and branches of Elder, upon which it is well camouflaged.

Mimetic melanism

Some palatable Lepidoptera are Batesian mimics of non-palatable species (p. 206). When the model of one of these mimics is dark, the mimic will show increased melanism compared with non-mimetic or ancestral forms. Similarly, in the evolution of a Müllerian mimetic complex (p. 206), the colour pattern that the complex converges upon may have a large black component, so that some species become darker than they were ancestrally. The evolution of such forms through either type of mimicry may be said to involve the evolution of mimetic melanism.

Sexual melanism

Some aposematic insects exhibit melanic polymorphism. This is unexpected as the general theory of aposematism should favour monomorphism (p. 199). In those cases that have been studied closely, mating preferences, which are necessarily frequency dependent, have been implicated in the maintenance of the melanic polymorphism. The best studied case involves the Two-spot Ladybird, *Adalia bipunctata*, in which some females have a preference to mate with melanic males, irrespective of their own colour pattern. Other examples include

Fig. 9.20 The typical and *zatima* forms of the Buff Ermine, *Spilosoma luteum.*

Arctic Skuas, Snow Geese and the Scarlet Tiger moth, *Callimorpha dominula*, in which the melanic forms *medionigra* and *bimacula* are maintained by disassortative mating (p. 70).

Conclusion

Cases of the evolution of industrial melanism in the Lepidoptera generally, and in the Peppered moth in particular, are the most cited examples of evolution in action. Recent studies on wild populations in England and America have revealed that similar evolutionary changes have occurred in the Peppered moth at two independent sites, effectively providing replicate natural experiments. In both populations, melanic forms arose following environmental changes resulting from industrial pollution. The frequencies of the melanics peaked at over 90% around 1960 and have subsequently declined to below 20%, following enactment of anti-pollution legislation. The primary selective cause of the rise of melanism in the Peppered moth, first postulated by Tutt over a century ago and confirmed by experiments by Kettlewell in the 1950s and many others subsequently, was differential bird predation. In industrial regions, melanic forms became more cryptic than non-melanics on their lichen-denuded, soot-blackened resting sites in trees, while non-melanics remained more cryptic in rural locales where trees retained their lichen flora. The significance of the Peppered moth to evolutionary biology should not be understated. Not only has it provided one of the best observed examples of an evolutionary change due to natural selection, but it showed that selection could be a strong force, the melanic form *carbonaria* having to be half as fit again as the non-melanic *typica* form to account for the rapidity of its initial rise. Furthermore, evolution has now been demonstrated to be reversible and replicable.

In this chapter I have described a great variety of factors that may promote melanism in moths. In many cases the various factors are not mutually exclusive and several factors may act in concert with the proportional contribution of different factors varying between cases. It must therefore be dangerous to extrapolate from one species to another. Even within one class of melanism, the relative influence of different aspects of a species' biology will vary from one species to another. Each species that has evolved melanic forms will have done so in the presence of a variety of different intrinsic and extrinsic circumstances. Furthermore, as different populations are exposed to different environments, it may be wrong to extrapolate from one population to another, at least in respect of certain details of behaviour and ecology.

Melanism has been closely studied in only a few species of the great many that exhibit the phenomenon. Those species that have been closely scrutinised suggest that many different factors play a part in the evolution and maintenance of melanism. The different parts played by factors such as selective predation, migration, thermal dynamics, mating preferences and a variety of types of non-visual selection, even in the few well-studied species, show that there is still enormous scope for original research into this phenomenon.

Knowledge advances very unevenly. Great bounds forward resulting from a novel insight, or the development of a new technique, are punctuated by smaller advances as details are examined and refined. In many cases ideas are added to or amended. Such additions or amendment to the detail do not invalidate previous work: they endorse it. Thus, while Albert Einstein's view of the universe was more correct than Sir Isaac Newton's, we still revere the latter. More recently, Professor Stephen Hawking has refined and corrected some of Einstein's ideas. This is as it should be, and I have no doubt that our current understanding of the mechanisms and processes of biological evolution will be amended and added to in the future. But this does not mean that our current perceptions are wholly wrong, they are just, as yet, not complete or wholly right.

Recent scientific writings in respect of the Peppered moth, which have examined the detail of this classical case and have identified some of the weaknesses in experimental techniques in Kettlewell's work, have been taken by the anti-Darwinian lobby to suggest that the rise and fall of melanism in the Peppered moth does not provide supportive evidence of evolution by natural selection. This lobby has been extremely vocal in the media and on the Web. The arguments used are highly subjective and based on false premises, on data drawn very selectively from that available and on misquotations. It is relevant to point out here that every scientist I know who has worked on melanism in the Peppered moth in the field still regards differential predation of the morphs in different habitats as of prime importance in the case. The critics of work on this case and those who cast doubt on its validity are, without exception, persons who have, as far as I know, never bred the moth and never conducted an experiment on it. In most cases they have probably never seen a live Peppered moth in the wild. Perhaps those who have the most intimate knowledge of this moth are the scientists who have bred it, watched it and studied it, in both the laboratory and the wild. These include, among others, the late Sir Cyril Clarke, Professors Paul Brakefield, Laurence Cook, Bruce Grant, K. Mikkola, Drs Rory Howlett, Carys Jones, David Lees, John Muggleton and myself. I believe that, without exception, it is our view that the case of melanism in the Peppered moth still stands as one of the best examples of evolution, by natural selection, in action.

10

Of Moths and Men

Interactions between moths and man

Moths are common insects. They occur in an enormous variety of terrestrial habitats and have tremendous reproductive potential. Not surprisingly, these abundant insects interact with the species that dominates the terrestrial world, humans, in a variety of ways. From a human perspective, these interactions may be categorised as harmful or beneficial to us. In addition, humans, having the greatest impact on the terrestrial and most other environments on Earth of any species, have an enormous influence on moths. Sadly, the division of the role of man in the lives of moths, from the moth's point of view, is not into the beneficial and deleterious: it is into the purposely deleterious and the accidentally deleterious. In this final chapter, I will consider the impacts that moths have on humans and then the impacts that humans have on moths. In the last section I will discuss briefly the role that moth enthusiasts and less specialised naturalists may have in helping moths in the future.

Moths of benefit to man

Although generally considered deleterious insects, moths can also be beneficial in a number of ways. Some of these benefits have already been mentioned in passing in previous chapters. However, it may be helpful to draw the full list together here.

Pollinators

Moths take nectar from a tremendous variety of flowers, including many fruit trees and crop plants. In this way they are beneficial to farmers and gardeners. Most moths are adapted with a long proboscis to gain access to nectar by probing down the flower's corolla tube. By so doing they have to pass the anthers and stigma of the flowers. Pollen picked up from the anthers may thus be transferred to the stigma of another flower. Moths thus tend to be honest pollinators. Nectar stealing, whereby access is gained to nectar through a hole near the base of the corolla tube made by the robber or a previous visitor, is rare in this order, although some moths may be classed as thieves if they remove nectar without pollinating the flower, or if they damage it.

The range of plants that are sometimes moth pollinated is enormous. However, many of these plants would suffer little if moths did not exist, for they have many other potential pollinators. This is not true of all plants, and moth pollination is most important for those plant species whose flowers are specifically adapted for pollination by moths. Such adaptations are most obvious in species with very long corolla tubes that occur in places where some moths have very long proboscises. This is the case in many tropical and subtropical regions. Flowers of the genus *Nicotiana* are often pollinated mainly by long-tongued moths such as sphingids. One of the most famous examples, which was mentioned by Darwin, concerns the exceptional corolla tube length of the Madagascan orchid *Angraecum sesquipedale*, which is pollinated almost exclusively by the moth *Xanthopan morgani*.

The correlation between the orchid's corolla tube length and the moth's proboscis length is an example of tight coevolution. However, the two are not totally interdependent. If one of the members in this partnership were to become extinct, the other would not follow. Yet examples of total reliance do exist. For example, the flowers of the yucca and some species of yucca moth, *Tegeticula* spp., are completely dependent upon one another. In this case, the seeds of the flower provide food for the moth larvae, while the moths are the only pollinators of the flowers. These moths carry pollen on special palps, and stuff it onto the stigma.

Biological control agents

I have already noted the spectacular success of the use of the pyralid moth *Cactobastis cactorum* in Australia as a control agent of the Prickly Pear Cactus. There are many other examples of moths as biological control agents, but in few others has the success been as great, and there have been plenty of failures. Generally, failures have resulted simply from a lack of establishment of the control species in the target area. Few moths that have been used in biological control have caused problems themselves by adapting to and becoming a pest on non-target species. However, this is certainly possible, and a full cost-benefit appraisal of any potential control species ought to be carried out before it is adopted for widespread use.

Although generally of use in the control of weeds, a few moths may also be considered beneficial because they attack pest animals. For example, a number of microlepidoptera are predators or parasites of various crop pests, such as cicadellids, psyllids and coccids. The best known of these micros are those of the family Epipyroidae from tropical Asia and Australasia. However, some momphid and pyralid species also fit into this category, as do a few macros of the family Noctuidae.

Environmental and pollution indicators

Man's impact on the environment is enormous. We are changing natural ecosystems at a truly alarming rate. In the long term, many of the changes for which we are responsible may have a detrimental impact on ourselves through our health and quality of life. This is well recognised, although politicians tend to give only lip service to the problems that modern technology and lifestyles are throwing up. Few politicians appear to be able to see further than the next election. However, when environmental change is shown to be having a strong short-term impact on, for example, public health, steps are taken. That was the case with atmospheric pollution in the mid-twentieth century. Regular winter smogs associated with increases in chronic bronchial conditions led to the introduction of anti-pollution legislation. The legislation, aimed primarily at soot fallout and sulphur dioxide emissions, had the desired effect. That the legislation did have the desired effect is shown by the reversal in the fortunes of the melanic form, *carbonaria*, of the Peppered moth, *Biston betularia*, and the decline in melanic forms of many other species in industrial areas over the last two or three decades (Grant et al. 1996, Majerus 1998). These species may thus be thought of as biological indicators.

The health of particular ecosystems on a more global scale could also be monitored by use of a range of species, each chosen because it is specifically adapted to a narrow ecological niche provided by a particular ecosystem. Once suitable species have been identified, they may be used to monitor ecosystem movement, shrinkage, expansion or degradation. This will be of benefit to humanity whether the need for ecosystem maintenance is to allow sustainable crop development or to preserve, as well as is feasible, the biodiversity of our planet.

Almost any organism might be used as a biological indicator. However, the most useful would be those species that will respond quickly to relatively small changes in an ecosystem and are relatively easy to monitor. Moths fulfil both of these criteria. Many species of moth are ecosystem specialists. Furthermore, they produce large numbers of offspring, have short generation times and are known to be subject to strong levels of selective elimination. In addition, they are easily caught for monitoring using light traps or pheromone traps and their taxonomy has been more fully studied than that of most other groups of terrestrial invertebrates.

I suspect that as the Earth becomes increasingly affected by global warming and it is finally accepted in the highest political circles that the climatic zones on Earth are shifting position, the need for biological indicators as a means for tracking ecosystem changes will increase. I have no doubt that moths will be in the forefront of the indicators used.

Producers of silk

Moths have two roles to play in the textile industry and both have considerable commercial value. The first, which has undoubtedly reduced in recent decades, derives from larval feeding habits of a rather small minority of species that are known in the vernacular as clothes moths. These moths have undoubtedly contributed to manufacturing turnover by the destruction of otherwise completely serviceable woollen, cotton or fur garments. The second contribution is through the silk industry. Although silk is produced by many moths as well as spiders, over 99% of silk used by the textile industry derives from just a single species, the Silk Worm, *Bombyx mori*. This moth may be considered an entirely domesticated animal, for it is no longer found in the wild. The Silk Worm first came into domestication about 5,000 years ago, probably in China. Artificial selection for traits including high reproductive output, reduced mobility by both adults and larvae and, most particularly, high quality silk, has produced a moth unable to fly, with larvae that rarely stray far from their food-plant and which have a high output of silk. Indeed, due to the relatively short generation time of Silk Worms relative to other domesticated animals, it may be argued that artificial selection has been conducted for more generations in silk moths than in any other domesticated animal.

In BC 2640 the Lady of Si-ling, Empress and wife of Emperor Huang-ti, is known to have become involved personally in sericulture. She reared Silk Worms, encouraged the planting of White Mulberry trees and is reputed to have invented the loom. Ancient Chinese literature testifies to the close association between families of high office and the silk industry. The arts of Silk Worm breeding and more particularly the production and manufacture of silken materials seem to have been carefully guarded by the Chinese. It was not until the third century AD that the secrets of sericulture reached Japan, probably via Korea. Some time afterwards, silk production and a knowledge of the working of silk reached India. Legend has it that both eggs of the moth and seeds of its foodplant were carried to India by a Chinese princess in the linings of her headdress.

Although raw silk materials were certainly transported from the East to Europe by the beginning of Christianity, this raw material and the products made from it were exceptionally expensive. The Roman Emperor Aurelian (270–275 AD), who neither used silk himself, nor would allow his wife to possess it, reported silk to be worth its weight in gold. A breeding stock of Silk Worms was not established in Europe until around 550 AD. This stock derived from eggs smuggled to Constantinople in a hollow cane by two Persian monks. The monks, who had previously lived in China for some period, gaining a full knowledge of the techniques for rearing Silk Worms, were instructed to obtain this stock by the Emperor Justinian. These stocks, which included a variety of different strains, were the progenitors of all silk production in the West for over 1,200 years.

In England, silk manufacture was introduced during the reign of Henry VI. James I attempted to increase production for economic reasons in the early seventeenth century. He ordered the planting of Black Mulberry trees in many locations. The introduction was not a commercial success. However, many of the Black Mulberry trees planted at that time are still alive. Just one of a number planted on Parker's Piece in the centre of Cambridge still stands today. Silk Worms are reared in Britain now largely for educational or research purposes. Indeed, I have three weeping White Mulberries growing in the grounds of the Department of Genetics Field Station specifically to provide food for Silk Worms. The British silk industry is almost but not quite non-existent. The Lullingworth Silk Farm, in Dorset, is a going concern, partly through its silk production and partly as a tourist and educational attraction. In 1981, this silk farm achieved wide recognition for producing the silk for Diana, Princess of Wales's wedding gown.

The silk that is used in manufacture is derived from the cocoon. The larva constructs its cocoon from a single strand of silk, laid down in a figure of eight motion. When the adult moth exits its cocoon, it breaks through the silk, thus breaking the strand. This makes it unusable, for the cocoon cannot then be reeled (unwound). This means that the pupa must be killed before the moth inside emerges. This is usually done by placing the cocoons in hot air dryers at around 90°C for about 12 hours. This not only kills the pupa, but also dries it out so that the pupa will not putrefy in stored cocoons.

Cocoons are sorted into perfect and various degrees of imperfect cocoons. The process of reeling involves the bringing together of a number of silken strands from separate cocoons. Usually five or six strands are woven together to produce a single filament. In some cases as many as 20 strands may be used. The unwinding of cocoons is done with the cocoons floating in hot water and involves a variety of techniques to find the main filaments, twist them together and skein them. The twisted filaments are then reeled and because the fibres produced are still very fine and delicate, they are then usually doubled into a more substantial yarn. After reeling, the silk is checked and cleaned before spinning. Because silk has such a high value, waste products from all stages in the process are retained and used if possible.

Although the vast majority of commercial silk comes from the Silk Worm,

Bombyx mori, a small amount of so-called wild silk has also been produced. This was particularly the case in the mid- and late nineteenth century, when breeding stocks of the Silk Worm came under severe attack from a disease known as pebrine, caused by a microsporidian, which threatened the entire industry (p. 174). Investigations at that time and thereafter showed that some silk moths produce silk of sufficient quality and manageability to be of at least minor commercial value. Species that have been used include several other species of *Bombyx,* as well as *Antheraea pernyi, Antheraea assama* and *Antheraea mylitta,* which produce tussur silk.

Because of its economic importance and the fact that it has long been reared in captivity, the Silk Worm has been characterised genetically more completely than any other moth or butterfly. Very large numbers of genes have been identified, covering a wide range of traits, from simple silk colour genes to multigene families, such as the chorion genes that are involved in the characteristics of the eggshell, and genes that confer immunity to disease.

Silk Worms feed only on the leaves of mulberry trees, the White Mulberry being preferred over Black Mulberry. The centres of silk production are still in South and Eastern Asia, although some is produced in other parts of the tropics and subtropics.

The deleterious effects of moths

Worldwide impact

It is through their feeding habits that moths most frequently come into conflict with human interests. As noted in Chapter 5, the majority of moths feed on the foliage of plants and it is in the destruction of leaf matter that moths are most usually considered pests. However, other types of feeding can produce damage if moths reach high density and their target is a commercially important crop.

Almost all the major families of moths have species that are regularly or irregularly considered pests. Furthermore, almost all major crop plants have one or more species of pest moth associated with them. A comprehensive listing of crops and their moth pests is outside the scope of this book. However, even a few examples of some of the more important species on a global scale will show the diversity of the species involved.

Rice, the most important food crop, is attacked by numerous moths. Several pyralids, including *Cnaphalocrocis medinalis,* cause leaf-roll. Other pyralids, such as *Chilo polychrysa,* feed within the stems of rice, hollowing them out and causing wilting, while *Chilo auricilia* causes stems to snap where the larva bites into it. Rice stem-borers also include *Maliarpha separatella* from the tropics in Africa and Asia and various species of the genus *Scirpophaga.* Maize is attacked by *Chilo partellus,* which is also a stem-borer.

Wood-borers of great economic importance include several members of the family Cossidae and a number of hepialids. Shrubs and trees can be affected and coffee, mango and a variety of timber trees can be badly affected by such species and by larvae of some Noctuidae.

Flower-feeders include *Pectinophora gossypiella,* which is a major pest of cotton flowers and bolls around the world. Cotton also suffers leaf-roll caused by the pyralid *Syllepie derogata* throughout the tropics of Africa and Asia. Seeds are also attacked by many species, with *Etiella zinckenella,* a pest of legume seeds, being one of the most important economically. Fruits such as apples, pears, peaches and various types of citrus are attacked by a variety of moths, especially members of the Tortricidae.

Finally, a legion of species, too numerous to mention specifically, eat leaves and can lead to total defoliation of some crops, or to lesser damage that is still sufficient to be detrimental to yields. Damage may be to almost any type of plant, from the largest trees to the smallest herbs and grasses. Although it is difficult to generalise about the economic effects of defoliators, it does appear that the most detrimental outbreaks tend to occur where the same crop is grown for many years without rotation, and that monoculture crops are more prone than natural vegetation or mixed species crops.

Pest species in Britain

In Britain, over 160 species of moth have been listed as being pests (Holloway et al. 1987). Damage is done to roots, stems, leaves, flowers and seeds.

Root-eaters

The worst of the root-feeders are probably the common hepialids, such as the Common Swift, *Hepialus lupulinus*, and the Ghost moth, *Hepialus humuli*. Edwards (1964) reports that densities of the latter commonly reach 10,000 larvae per acre and may reach as high as five times this density. These species feed on a variety of plants, causing damage to grasses, including cereal crops, almost any root vegetable, flower bulbs, strawberries, raspberries and many herbaceous plants. They feed largely on or in the roots and may also burrow into stems below ground level.

Stem-borers and cutworms

The larvae of moths that attack the stems of their host plants can conveniently be split into those that attack woody-stemmed plants and those that attack plants with rather softer, more succulent stems. The larvae of noctuids dominate the latter group. The cutworms, which include larvae of the Large Yellow Underwing, *Noctua pronuba*, Turnip moth, *Agrotis segetum*, the Heart and Dart, *Agrotis exclamationis*, and the Garden Dart, *Euxoa nigricans*, among others, derive their collective name from their habit of biting through the stems of plants, thus felling them. Again they attack a very wide variety of crop and ornamental plants, although they rarely do serious damage to cereal crops or pasture grasses. Apart from cutting through the stems of plants, these larvae will also burrow into subterranean stems and roots and will feed on foliage higher up during the night, returning to ground level, where they hide in the soil surface, by day.

Other species of noctuid that do damage to stems include the Antler moth, *Cerapteryx graminis*, whose larvae attack the stems of grasses and cereals at ground level. The Common Rustic, *Mesapamea secalis*, and its sibling species the Lesser Common Rustic, *Mesapamea secalella*, attack cereal crops and some wild grasses, usually feeding in the central shoot. The Rosy Rustic, *Hydraecia micacea*, also attacks cereals, but it is more important as a minor stem-boring pest of potatoes, rhubarb and raspberries. The Cabbage moth, *Mamestra brassicae*, tunnels into the heads of cabbages, often burrowing right to the heart. The tunnels that it forms in the stems and through the tightly packed foliage as it burrows are fouled by its frass. This fouling, as much as the actual consumption of stem and foliage, lowers the value of attacked cabbages.

In the past, when reeds were grown commercially on a wider scale than they are today, for thatch and a variety of other uses, the stem-boring larvae of a number of wainscots did considerable damage. Important species in this regard included the Large Wainscot, *Rhizedra lutosa*, the Fen Wainscot, *Arenostola phragmitidis*, the Twin-spotted Wainscot, *Archanara geminipuncta* and the Brown-veined Wainscot, *Archanara dissoluta*. Nowadays, these species are of less economic importance. However, as over 75% of reed beds in Britain are now protected by conservation organisations, the detrimental effects of these moths on the dominant plants of such habitats are sometimes of concern to environmentalists.

Outside the noctuids, some grass moths (Crambidae) feed in the stems of grasses and cereals, occasionally causing economic damage on a local scale. The Leek moth, *Acrolepiopsis assectella*, a member of the family Yponomeutidae, burrows in the tightly packed leaves and stems of leeks. This species was first recorded in Britain in 1943 and now causes occasional damage through the rotting of the tissues around the tunnels.

Leaf-feeders

In Britain, as elsewhere, leaf-feeders comprise the majority of species that cause economic damage. The damage caused by some is easy to assess because it has a direct effect on a crop. However, in many cases, the impact of loss of leaf to crop yield is less easy to assess because plants vary in their ability to compensate for leaf loss. Examples in which the economic costs of leaf-eating larvae are reasonable easy to assess, include damage to members of the cabbage family due to the Diamond Back moth, *Plutella xylostella* (Fig. 10.1), loss of

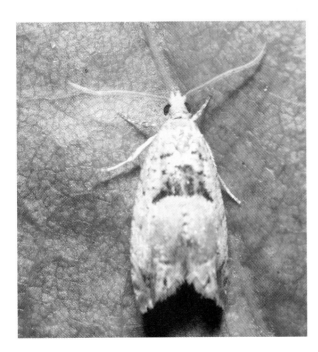

Fig. 10.1 The Diamond Back moth, *Plutella xylostella*.

berry yield in currants attacked by Magpie moths, *Abraxas grossulariata*, and loss of timber resulting from the Bordered White (also called the Pine Looper), *Bupalus piniaria*, and subsequent attack by the Pine Shoot Beetle.

Much more difficult to quantify are the losses of fruit or timber from the defoliation caused by geometrid and tortricoid moths on fruit trees. The moths that do the greatest damage to fruit yields are those that attack leaves early in the season, including a number of those that have 'wingless' females (p. 195), and the tortricoid moths that have leaf-rolling larvae. Although larvae that feed on deciduous timber trees rarely do sufficient damage to kill the trees, high levels of defoliation will lead to reduced rate of growth (Varley & Gradwell 1960). There is also some evidence that trees that have been heavily defoliated are more vulnerable to disease.

The larvae of some species live together in 'nests'. These nests are composed of silk webbing, produced by the larvae. Larvae of some species, such as the Lackey, *Malacosoma neustria*, make compact nests, venturing out of the nests to feed and returning for shelter. Other larvae make much larger nests, extending them as they feed. Some of the small ermine moths (subfamily Yponomeutinae) (Fig. 10.2) reach high density on fruit trees and can do damage.

Fig. 10.2 Small ermine moths.

Other problems

Moths can be detrimental in other ways, particularly if they occur at high density. In the Sydney Olympics of 2000, the stadium lights attracted huge numbers of moths that were something of a hazard to athletes and audiences alike. In Africa, there have been reports going back for over a century of trains sliding to a halt when movements of army worms across the tracks have, through dint of their squashed bodies on the rails, reduced friction so that the wheels could not gain sufficient traction. Even the moths that feed on the tear secretions of mammals (p. 121) can be a problem, for these can vector diseases and so be of veterinary importance.

Turning to the detrimental impact that humans have on moths, it is difficult to know where to start. Because some moths are pests, we do take direct action against some species. However, it is through indirect action that we probably do much more damage to many species.

Humans: moths' greatest enemy

Direct anti-moth action

A range of products and techniques are used for the destruction of pest species of moth. These include chemical insecticide sprays, biological control using bacterial and viral diseases, genetically modified crops containing insecticide genes and pheromone traps usually to catch males. Some control methods do not involve the destruction of moths per se. Thus, the release of radioactively sterilised males does not lead to the death of the females that these males mate with. However, females thus mated lay inviable eggs. Genetically modified crops containing anti-insect genes, which deter larvae from feeding on the crop rather than killing the larvae directly, are being developed. I have no doubt that this type of genetic modification will extend to the transposition of genes that will deter female moths from laying eggs on crops in the near future.

Some of the techniques used are highly target-specific and, assuming they have been fully risk-assessed, these seem to me to be the most environmentally friendly techniques available. The baculoviruses offer a particularly fertile field for development of target-specific biological control agents. In preference, these techniques should be used in the field alongside monitoring programmes and should only be employed when a pest species approaches densities at which it threatens economic damage. Such an approach makes good scientific sense as well as environmental sense, for the intermittent, rather than continual, use of any particular technique will slow the rate at which the pest will evolve tolerance, immunity or circumventory strategies against the control technique. Moreover, some alternation of control strategies, as occur in many integrated pest management programmes, is beneficial for the same reason.

Moths and genetically modified crops

The human population is increasing at an alarming rate. If the current rate continues, by 2040 there will be between nine and ten billion people on Earth. My first memory of the world's population, from my school days, was about three billion. I have at least some chance of surviving to see 2040. It is staggering to realise that we will have trebled our numbers in my lifetime. The task of feeding this enormous population falls to farmers. The amount of land available to agriculture is not increasing at this rate. Thus year on year there is less land available to feed each person. There appear to be two options available to us. First, we could reduce our population growth. Although this has been advanced as a major aim of humanity for as long as I can remember, as yet, we seem to be making very little progress globally. Second, we may increase the efficiency of our use of agricultural land. Of the food we grow, about 60% is ultimately consumed by humans. The remaining 40% is eaten by insects or destroyed by disease or weeds. The loss to insects is just over 14% of the total production. The problem that insects pose for humans and the efforts that we put in to eradicating them are reflected in the ten billion dollars we spend on chemical insecticides in a year. Chemical insecticides are not the only tools we use against crop pests. As I have already explained, there have been many successful examples of natural enemies being used in biological pest control programmes. Furthermore, almost since humans began to cultivate crops for food and other purposes, we have used natural resistances by selecting strains that were more resistant to pest attacks than the norm. This selective breeding is a form of genetic engineering. However, with the development of new recombinant DNA technology, our ability to improve plants genetically has increased to a remarkable extent, for we can now transfer genes from one species of organism into another.

In many parts of the world, the approach to pest control is through integrated pest management schemes. These schemes incorporate biological, chemical and genetic approaches. Where the genetic approaches involve crops that have one or more genes from another organism incorporated into their own genetic make-up, the crops are said to be transgenic and the crops are classed as genetically modified organisms. The question that must be addressed is whether we should employ this new technology.

A tremendous amount of rubbish is talked about genetically modified (GM) crops. In this short discourse on the potential use of GM crops and their use against pest moths, I will try not to add to this. I hope that readers will consider GM crops objectively and come to their own answer, for too often I have found that those on either side of the argument are highly subjective, their position on the matter being driven by faith, gut feelings or financial considerations rather than fact and logic.

One point should be stressed to start with. No gene that has been transferred from one organism to another has been found to be incorporated into a mammalian genome through eating the transgenic product. Indeed, on current genetical knowledge, one would have to conclude that such an event is mechanistically impossible.

Pest control GM crops have been used commercially since 1996. The majority have been transformed to be herbicide resistant. A much smaller proportion involves insect resistance and about 5% are both herbicide resistant and insect resistant. In 1999, the commercial value of GM crops was 2.25 million dollars, worldwide. This figure is predicted to increase tenfold by 2010. Most commercial GM crops are grown in the United States (72%), with Argentina, Canada and China also growing appreciable quantities.

The anti-insect genes used in GM crops have a diverse array of origins, some being bacterial, others being from plants or even other animals. The only ones to be used commercially are derived from a Gram-positive, spore-forming bacterium, *Bacillus thuringiensis* (Bt). Several thousand strains of this bacterium have been isolated, and genes from it have been shown to be effective against different groups of insects. Transgenic crops that express an anti-insect Bt gene produce a protoxin. When the plant is eaten by a target pest insect, this interacts with cell surface binding proteins, leading to damage to the insect's gut, and eventually death.

Transgenic Bt strains of cotton and maize are currently in commercial use, and similar strains of rice and various crucifers will be available in countries allowing their use in the next year or so. Use of Bt cotton in the United States is reported to have saved 99 million dollars in 1999. The transgenic strains of cotton and maize were both shown to produce higher yields than conventional strains. Tests in Australia showed that the use of Bt cotton allowed a reduction of 40–60% in the application of chemical insecticides.

It is perhaps worth pointing out here that the use of Bt genes is not as great an innovation as it may at first seem, for the organism that the genes are derived from has been used as a biological insecticide for over 60 years. Microbial pesticides were first used in 1938. They have been used extensively against lepidopteran forest pests, such as the Gypsy moth, *Lymantria dispar*. Different strains have been used. *Bacillus thuringiensis kurstaki* was used from around 1960, and this strain was largely replaced by *B. t. aizawai*, in 1980. These microbial pesticides are widely recognised as some of the least ecologically harmful pesticides in use.

Genes from plants that are currently under trial include lectin genes. Lectins are inhibitors of insect digestive proteins. Most of these genes are not so lethal to target insects. Although they do increase mortality, their main effect is in slowing development and depressing reproduction of the pest. Genes from other insects have also been used. These include genes that disrupt digestion (protease inhibitors) and those that break down chitin.

Protease-inhibiting transgenic crops are not yet in use commercially. Indeed, some problems have been identified relating to their efficiency in laboratory trials. For example, when a protease inhibitor was administered directly to the Bright-line Brown-eye moth, *Lacanobia oleracea*, a pest of tomatoes, it was found to be highly effective. However, when administered via a transgenic strain of tomatoes, the expected protein inhibition was not observed. Furthermore, work on the Scarce Bordered Straw, *Helicoverpa armigera*, showed that these insects could circumvent the protein inhibition by synthesising alternative digestive proteins that were insensitive to the transgene product. This switch in the digestive proteins synthesised in the gut of the larvae was incredibly rapid, taking only two to four hours. This rapid adaptive ability brings to mind the Borg, one of the alien species featured in *Star Trek, the Next Generation*. The Borg, who were all connected telepathically, had the ability to adapt their defences to any weapon used against them, and to retain the adaptation in their collective memory. The Scarce Bordered Straw is polyphagous, feeding on a huge range of herbaceous plants. Although in Britain it is known as a scarce immigrant or imported species, in southern Europe and North Africa it is a frequent and serious pest of many cultivated plants. Its catholic diet makes it likely that it will have adapted to the considerable range of plant defensive chemicals that it has encountered in the past by conserving within its genome a range of genes that may be switched on, i.e. expressed if triggered by the presence in food of a particular substance. It is thus not so strange that a larva faced with a plant defensive gene product when eating tomatoes that is normally not in tomatoes has the capacity to start synthesising sidestepping products.

Here then is one problem in the assessment of this type of GM crop. Full assessment of their value is only likely to be valid in field conditions.

Transgenic Bt crops do not suffer the same problems as the protein inhibitors. They seem to be far more efficient in killing their target groups of insect. The target groups vary depending on the defence strain that the transferred genes came from. Some are specific in their effect to beetles, others to hemipteran bugs and still others to Lepidoptera. However, Bt strains face another problem, for there is already evidence that some pests are evolving resistance to Bt crops. The Diamond Back moth, *Plutella xylostella* (Fig. 10.1), a major pest of *Brassicas* throughout the world, has up to 20 generations per year. Some populations already contain strains of moths that have become resistant to Bt through the loss of the Bt binding sites. Fortunately, there are many different strains of Bt so the evolution of resistance may be circumvented by rotating crop strains with genes from different Bt strains. Furthermore, because resistant genes are generally recessive and resistance generally carries a metabolic cost, if crops are planted with non-GM refugia in which non-resistant strains of insect will be at an advantage, the increase in resistance can be slowed very considerably.

There may be other problems. For example, work using a lectin gene from snowdrops transferred into potatoes has shown some promise of success in controlling the Bright-line Brown-eye. However, it is possible that the benefit of this control might be offset if the natural enemies of this moth are negatively affected by lectin obtained by feeding on the pest. As usual, the position is not clear cut. One enemy, the ectoparasitic wasp *Eulophus pennicornis*, appears to suffer no detrimental effect from intake of lectin. No increase in mortality or loss of fecundity or reproductive potential was found. Furthermore, the wasp showed no preference for attacking larvae that had fed on non-transformed potatoes compared with the lectin potatoes. Here then seems to be a viable integrated pest management strategy, involving use of a rotation of transgenic crop strains, the planting of non-GM refugia to slow the evolution of resistance and the use of an ectoparasitic wasp as a mop-up to keep damage to the crop to a minimum. Yet, on the reverse side is the effect of these same larvae on a predatory bug, *Podisus maculiventris*. In controlled experiments, bugs that fed on lectin potato-feeding larvae were smaller and produced fewer eggs.

These experiments were conducted in the laboratory or in climate-controlled greenhouses. Generally, a high level of food availability was maintained throughout the experimental treatments. Whether the effects or lack of effects recorded would be precisely the same in a field situation, where predators usually face a dearth of food and so are frequently starving, is currently open to speculation, for field tests on transgenic crops are currently very difficult to undertake.

If we are to improve agricultural efficiency, GM crops do seem to offer significant opportunities.

Human activities that have an inadvertently negative effect on moths

The array of human activities that are incidentally detrimental to moths is enormous, from habitat destruction to the use of phenomenal numbers of pollutants and from global warming to the metallic missiles in which we hurtle at speed through many environments as we transport ourselves from place to place. Examine the radiator of a car after a drive on a warm summer night, and the mortality rate that is imposed on moths just as a result of traffic is brought into sharp focus.

A wide variety of human activities has been discussed as detrimental to moths. However, good scientific evidence to show that a particular activity has been detrimental to a particular species is lacking in most cases. The cause and effect are thus usually a matter of interpretation and argument. Lack of evidence usually derives from lack of appropriate data. Even when we have data relating to both the human activity and the moth in question, comparative data on an untreated control situation are rarely available. This means that any correlations between a particular human factor and the decline in a moth population can at best be taken as circumstantial evidence of cause and effect. It is for these reasons that it is difficult to quote examples of species for which the cause of decline over the last two centuries is known and supported by good scientific evidence.

There is a range of human activities that reasoned logic would argue must have detrimental effects on moths, but for which we have no good case evidence for direct cause and effect. These include the use of chemical insecticides, general air pollution, thermal pollution in the form of global warming and collecting by entomologists. Mark Young includes an interesting and objective discussion of most of these factors in his excellent book *The Natural History of Moths* (Young 1997). Here I will discuss just one of these factors, light pollution, which has previously been largely ignored.

Light pollution

In 1999 I had the pleasure of conducting fieldwork in various parts of Russia. One stop involved staying for four nights in a very pleasant modern hotel near Novosibirsk, in a magnificent pine wood. The grounds of the hotel were latticed with paths through the woodland and these were lit by very strong arc lights. Before retiring on the first night there I went for a walk to look for moths attracted to the lights. Plenty were, the largest being seven Clifden Nonpareils, *Catocala fraxini*, that were sitting on pine trunks directly in the arc lights. The lights remained on until well after dawn and I was able to see the moths in the same positions as the night before, sitting on the pine trunks, although they certainly had to be looked for carefully, for against the bark they were very cryptic. This story has a point and it is a disturbing one. Over the next three nights and four days, six of the seven moths stayed in precisely the same place, normal movement being prevented by the lights during the night. Three further moths were also 'caught' by the lights on subsequent nights. Whether the seventh of the original moths managed to escape the lights or was found and eaten by a predator I do not know. However, the experience made me wonder how our electric lights impact on moths.

As far as I am aware, there has been no research conducted into the effect of electric lights, used at night, on moth populations. However, it seems likely that where strong lights are operated on a nightly basis, such as the arc lamps used to illuminate certain tourist attractions, work areas and of course roads, the normal activities of moths must be severely disturbed. I cannot conceive that such disturbance can be beneficial to moths.

While cause and effect evidence is lacking for most human activities, the same is not true for one factor.

Habitat destruction and fragmentation

In Britain, perhaps the most detrimental effect that we have on moths is simply the change of land usage through so-called development. The loss of many of the most species-rich habitats over the last 50 years has been enormous. Some 95% of Britain's flower-rich lowland meadows have been destroyed or extensively damaged since the Second World War. More than 80% of lowland chalk and Jurassic limestone grasslands has been lost to arable farming, or has been so enriched by fertilisation and reseeding that it has lost most of its wildlife diversity and interest. Peat extraction, drainage, and reclamation for afforestation, farmland and industrial or housing developments have accounted for over half the fens, mires and bogs in the last 50 years, and this is on top of the huge loss due to the drainage of the fenlands in the nineteenth century. By area, half of our ancient, broad-leaved deciduous woodland has been lost since 1947. The practice of rotational coppicing, which had such an influence on the maintenance of the floral and faunal diversity in these deciduous woodlands, has almost completely died out. A huge proportion of the lowland heaths have been destroyed, with, for example, over seven-eighths of the Dorset heathlands being lost since 1750, and the East Anglian Brecks, once covering 560 square kilometres, now reduced to about 8,000 hectares. The list makes depressing reading, and upland habitats are also coming under increasing threat.

Habitat destruction and loss has been responsible for the decline or extinction of many British moths. As already mentioned, drainage of lowland bogs, marshes and fenlands, particularly in East Anglia, has caused the extinction of species such as the Gypsy moth, *Lymantria dispar*, and the Reed Tussock, *Laelia coenosia*. Many other fenland species that occurred predominantly in wet lowlands in South-East England have also declined dramatically in distribution and numbers. Use of the Brecklands for farming and forestry has seen the decline and probable extinction of the Spotted Sulphur, *Emmelia trabealis*, and the Viper's Bugloss, *Hadena irregularis*. Loss of rabbit- and sheep-grazed chalk grassland in southern England has led to a massive reduction in many species that are adapted to this type of habitat, including the Small Waved Umber, *Horisme vitalbata* (Plate 6e), the Fern, *Horisme tersata*, the Pretty Chalk Carpet, *Melanthia porcellata* (Fig. 10.3), the Wood Tiger, *Parasemia plantaginis*, the Royal Mantle, *Catarhoe cuculata*, and the Lace Border, *Scopula ornata* (Fig. 10.4). Destruction of mature deciduous woodland has led to the decline of many species, including the Dark Crimson Underwing, *Catocala sponsa*. The list goes on and on. For each type of natural or semi-natural habitat that has been reduced due to human development and progress, a list of moths that have declined in consequence could be drawn up.

On the positive side over the last 40 years there have also been moves on 'nature's' behalf through government-led tree-planting schemes, set-aside schemes and the effects of the clean air acts and other anti-pollution legislation. There have also been various efforts over the last 40 years to systematise moth recording and the collation of records. Sadly, most of these have lacked sufficient long-term funding, which is essential if they are to produce results that have long-term value. Long-term funding is essential to allow monitoring to be continued for a sufficient period for trends in population size to be differen-

Fig. 10.3 (left) The Pretty Chalk Carpet, *Melanthia porcellata.*

Fig. 10.4 (right) The Lace Border, *Scopula ornata.* (Courtesy John Bebbington.)

tiated from background variation due to natural population size fluctuations.

Young (1997) describes the various schemes that have been instigated to monitor moth populations and distributions over the last 40 years. Most have come and gone, their demise usually being a result of lack of funding. A laudable current project is the National Moth Conservation Project. This project, arising largely out of the charity Butterfly Conservation, now has a list of 53 British moths that it suggests should be the focus of conservation efforts (Parsons et al. 2000). These species, called Biodiversity Action Plan (BAP) moths, are listed in Table 10.1. Reports of the action being taken in respect of these moths are a regular feature of Paul Waring's Wild Life Reports in the excellent magazine *British Wildlife*, edited by Andrew Branson. This scheme seems to have great merit for it has defined aims and focuses on a group of species that fit specific criteria. Although the aims are ambitious, they are not overambitious and this scheme, I believe, deserves unreserved support.

Table 10.1 The species of moth covered by the Moth Biodiversity Action Plan. (From Parsons et al. 2000).

English Name	Scientific name
Reddish Buff	*Acosmetia caliginosa*
Straw Belle	*Aspitates gilvaria*
Marsh moth	*Athetis pallustris*
Toadflax Brocade	*Calophasia lunula*
Light Crimson Underwing	*Catocala promissa*
Dark Crimson Underwing	*Catocala sponsa*
Basil Thyme Case-bearer	*Coleophora tricolor*
Speckled Footman	*Coscinia cribraria*
White-spotted Pinion	*Cosmia diffinis*
Dingy Mocha	*Cyclophora pendularia*
Heart moth	*Dicycla oo*
Dark Bordered Beauty	*Epione vespertaria*
Netted Carpet	*Eustroma reticulatum*
White Spot	*Hadena albimacula*
Bordered Gothic	*Heliophobus reticulata*
Narrow-bordered Bee Hawk moth	*Hemaris tityus*
Waved Carpet	*Hydrelia sylvata*
Marsh Mallow	*Hydraecia osseola*
Buttoned Snout	*Hypena rostralis*
Silky Wave	*Idaea dilutaria*
Bright Wave	*Idaea ochrata*
Orange Upperwing	*Jodia croceago*
Belted Beauty	*Lycia zonaria*
Scarce Blackneck	*Lygephila craccae*
Netted Mountain moth	*Macaria carbonaria*
Drab Looper	*Minoa murinata*
Scarce Merveille du Jour	*Moma alpium*
Double Line	*Mythimna turca*
Lunar Yellow Underwing	*Noctua orbona*
Brighton Wainscot	*Oria musculosa*
Clay Fan-foot	*Paracolax tristalis*
Cousin German	*Paradiarsia sobrina*
Barberry Carpet	*Pareulype berberata*
Common Fan-foot	*Pechipogo strigilata*
Small Lappet	*Phyllodesma ilicifolia*
Pale Shining Brown	*Polia bombycina*
Black-banded	*Polymixis xanthomista*
Fiery Clearwing	*Pyropteron chrysidiformis*
Argent and Sable	*Rheumaptera hastata*
White-line Snout	*Schrankia teanialis*
Chalk Carpet	*Scotopteryx bipunctaria*
Striped Lychnis	*Shargacucullia lychnitis*
Black-veined moth	*Siona lineata*
Essex Emerald	*Thetidia smaragdaria*
Barred Tooth-stripe	*Trichopteryx polycommata*
Olive Crescent	*Trisateles emortualis*
Four-spotted	*Tyta luctuosa*
Northern Dart	*Xestia alpicola*
Ashworth's Rustic	*Xestia ashworthii*
Square-spotted Clay	*Xestia rhomboidea*
Sword-grass	*Xylena exsoleta*
Slender Scotch Burnet	*Zygaena loti*
New Forest Burnet	*Zygaena viciae*

Moths now and in the future

The first National Moth Night was held in Britain on 17 July 1999. Volunteer recorders from the Channel Islands to the Shetlands were involved. On that single night, 798 species of moth, approximately a third of the species on the British list, were recorded. A similar event was held in September of 2000 and the organisers hope that it will become an annual event. Even if they serve no other purpose, such events will heighten the profile of moths, particularly if the media can be persuaded to give them good coverage.

Moths do not deserve the bad press that they have received. Humans should view these diverse and often beautiful insects more benignly. True, some are harmful through the damage that they do to crops, but the vast majority are of no economic consequence to us and some are beneficial. Furthermore, this group can bring both aesthetic pleasure and academic enlightenment. Moths, as I have already demonstrated, have played a central role in evolutionary studies and they have the potential to contribute as study material in many other areas, some of which is already being fulfilled. Some of the uses of moths in academic study result from their unique features. Others result from the similarity of systems throughout the invertebrates or animals or multicellular organisms. The understanding of the genetics and molecular biology of silk production, through the modification of salivary glands, is a feature unique to moths.

The wing patterns of the Lepidoptera provide a medium for the study of colour and pattern development that is unequalled in any other group. Work over the last two decades has produced considerable advances in our understanding of the way that pigments are laid down and patterns are formed, and of the relative roles played by genetic and environmental factors (see Nijhout 1991 for review).

Sex pheromones were first isolated from moths. Molecular biological analysis of these pheromones, coupled with studies of moth behaviour, examination of sensory morphology and detailed neurological analysis has led to a thorough understanding of the olfactory system of moths. This system represents one of the most completely known complex sensory systems of any organism and the findings are already being widely applied to increase understanding of other systems, including the olfactory systems of mammals.

Recent investigation of the responses of moths to invasion by microorganisms has revealed previously unsuspected parallels with mammalian systems in respect of a number of the proteins involved (Mulnix & Dunn 1995).

Less unique to the moths, but still with advantages not shared by many other groups, moths have proved to be of great use in studies of polymorphism, sex ratio, the hormonal systems that control metamorphosis, and as environmental indicators. Other opportunities will undoubtedly be revealed in the near future. For example, differences between systems in fruit flies and moths, concerning sex determination, the suppression of crossing over in one sex and the pattern of embryonic development, show that it may be very dangerous to base the majority of genetic work on just one small group of insects such as the fruit flies.

Yet I do not want to dwell too long on the pure or applied scientific benefits that the study of moths may bring to man. Certainly at the age of four I was not concerned with justifying why I had such a fascination with moths. Nor am I sure that I should be too preoccupied with such a justification now. Moths to me are, first and foremost, fascinating. Moreover, they are accessible. I can walk into my garden at any time of the year and expect to find some species of moth in some stage of its life cycle somewhere. Would that it will always be so. In 1998 I visited Uganda to work on *Acraea* butterflies with Frank Jiggins. One lasting impression that I had of Uganda was that outside National Parks and game reserves, I saw no mammals larger than a ground squirrel other than domesticated animals. While the parallel is a little stretched, I fear that it may soon be the case that many of our resident and habitat-specific British moths will be largely confined to nature reserves or sites that are conserved in some other way. This is already true for some species of moth, such as the Marsh Mallow moth, *Hydraecia osseola hucherardi*, and the Black Veined moth, *Siona lineata*. Sadly, despite the best efforts of a few, I can only see the situation worsening over the next few decades.

The fascination and beauty of moths has enriched my life. Through talks, articles and now this book, I hope I have introduced these delightful creatures to others, so that they may benefit as I have done. I realise that most of my readers will already have an interest in moths and many may share my passion. In this sense, I am probably preaching to the converted. To them in particular, I have one final message. Don't be shy! Tell people of your passion! Show your friends the next Privet Hawk moth caterpillar that you find and explain its coloration and countershading. Tell them that it is a common moth in southern Britain and may be found almost anywhere that Privet grows. Few non-entomologists will ever have seen an Eyed Hawk moth or a Peppered moth or a Magpie moth or a Garden Tiger or a Drinker or a Ghost. Yet each moth has a story to tell and it is rare to find a person who is not interested or delighted to hear and understand such stories if told. Only by changing the public perception of moths do we have a real chance of reversing the decline in moths' fortunes. So, show and tell your friends, colleagues and above all, your children of the delights of these 'butterflies of the night'.

Glossary

Abdomen: The hindmost of the three main body divisions of an insect.

Accessory glands: Glands that secrete substances involved in copulation, including the material that is used to form the spermatophore, but not sperm.

Adaptation: Any characteristic of an organism that enables it to better cope with conditions in its environment.

Aeropyles: Pores in the chorion of moth eggs allowing gaseous exchange.

Aestivation: Summer dormancy, when conditions become unfavourable.

Allele (Allelomorph): Form of a gene. Genes are considered alleles of one another when they occur in the same positions on the members of a chromosome pair (homologous chromosomes), have different effects in respect of a particular characteristic, and can mutate one to another.

Amino acids: The basic building blocks of proteins.

Fig. 8.22 The Poplar Grey is cryptic on lichen-encrusted rocks and stones (see text p. 214).

Anal claspers: The pair of prolegs on the hindmost abdominal segment of an insect lava.

Anal cremaster: A hook and suction structure on the rearmost abdominal segment of larvae (and pupae) that allows attachment to the substrate.

Androgen: Male hormone that produces secondary sex characteristics.

Angle of attack: The angle of the wings of a moth in relation to the direction of movement.

Antennae: Paired sensory appendages on the head of insects, sensitive to smell, touch and, in some species, sound.

Apolysis: The first stage in the shedding of the old skin as a larva moults, preceding ecdysis.

Aposematism: The phenomenon whereby unpalatable (distasteful, toxic or otherwise dangerous) organisms advertise the fact with bright coloration or other strong stimuli.

Apterous: Without wings.

Arbivorous: Feeding on trees.

Arms race: A coevolutionary pattern involving two or more interacting species (for example predator and prey or parasite and host), where evolutionary change in one party leads to the evolution of a counter-adaptation in the other.

Artificial selection: Human attempts to exaggerate natural traits by breeding selectively from those organisms that show these traits most strongly.

Assortative mating: The tendency for individuals showing similar traits to mate together.

Autosome: A chromosome other than a sex chromosome.

Axilla: Point of attachment of the thoracic muscles to the wings.

Balanced polymorphism (stable polymorphism): A genetic polymorphism in which the various forms are maintained in the population at constant frequencies, or their frequencies cycle in a more or less regular manner, and both alleles are maintained above a frequency that could be maintained by recurrent mutation.

Balancing selection: With reference to stable polymorphisms, the balance of advantages and disadvantages conferred by different forms that allows each to be maintained in equilibrium.

Basal: Concerning the base of a structure: that part nearest to the body.

Batesian mimicry: The resemblance shown by one species (the mimic) to another (the model) that is better protected by poisonous or distasteful qualities or active defence (sting, bite, etc.).

Bilateral mosaic: An individual in which one half displays one phenotype, the other half displaying a different phenotype.

Biological control: The control of pests by exploiting their natural enemies or by interfering with their life cycle.

Bursa copulatrix: The region of the female genitalia that receives the male intromittent organ and sperm during copulation. Its structure is often important in distinguishing closely related species.

Bursicon: One of the hormones in insects involved in moulting.

Carrying capacity: The maximum number of organisms of a species that a habitat can sustain.

Cerci: Paired appendages, probably sensory in function, at the end of the abdomen in many insects.

Chiasma (Plural: **chiasmata**): Regions of contact between homologous chromosomes during pairing in meiosis (from late prophase to anaphase I) at which crossing over takes place to effect the exchange of homologous sections of non-sister chromatids.

Chitin: The tough, horny material, chemically known as a nitrogenous polysaccharide, that makes up the bulk of the insect cuticle.

Chitinase: The enzyme that digests chitin.

Chloroplast: A green, membranous organelle in the cytoplasm of plant cells that contains chlorophyll and in which starch is synthesised using light energy.

Chorion: The outer shell of an insect's egg.

Chromatid: One of the two halves of a chromosome formed by longitudinal fission during meiosis or mitosis.

Chromosomes: Small elongated bodies, consisting largely of DNA and protein, in the nuclei of most cells, existing generally in a definite number of pairs for each species, and generally accepted to be the carriers of most hereditary qualities.

Chrysalis: The pre-adult stage in the life cycle of some insects, particularly butterflies; the pupa.

CI: see cytoplasmic incompatibility.

Circumocular scales: Scales or hairs of a moth situated around the compound eyes.

Claspers: A pair of processes at the posterior end of the abdomen of a male insect, used to grasp the female during copulation.

Cline: A gradual change, within an interbreeding population, in the frequencies of different genotypes, or phenotypes, of a species.

Coarse-grained environment: An environment comprising a mosaic of habitats. Individuals of a species are distributed randomly across the habitats at some point in their life cycle, but thereafter remain in the same habitat for the majority of their lives.

Cocoon: A protective covering for the pupa of some insects, particularly moths, constructed largely of silk secreted by the larva.

Fig. 8.23 The Poplar Grey is cryptic on lichen-encrusted rocks and stones (see text p. 214).

Competition: The interaction of individuals or species resulting from the use of limited resources.

Compound eye: An eye consisting of a number of separate lenses, each one contributing to the image produced.

Cone (of the eye): A colour-sensitive cell.

Conidia: Asexual haploid spores of a fungus, usually borne on an aerial hypha.

Conspecific: Of the same species.

Continuous variation: Variation in a trait in the individuals of a population or sample that give a continuous spectrum of values.

Countershading: Coloration that obscures shadows on the body of an organism by having the side usually towards the light darker than that away from it.

Coxa: Basal section of an insect's leg, joining the limb to the body.

Cremaster: A cluster of hooks at the posterior end of the abdomen of a pupa, used to anchor or support the pupa.

Crepuscular: Active during the period of twilight, either at dusk or dawn.

Crossing over: An interchange of groups of genes between the members of a homologous pair of chromosomes.

Cryptic coloration: The colours of an animal matching those of the environment in which it lives.

Cryptic female choice: The selective favouring, due to a female-controlled process or structure, of fertilisation of a female's eggs by conspecific males bearing a particular trait over other males that lack the trait when the female has copulated with both types of male.

Cuticle: Non-cellular outer layer secreted by the epidermis. In insects it is rigid enough to act as an external skeleton.

Cytoplasm: The living substance of the cell, excluding the organelles within it.

Cytoplasmic genes: Genes located in the cytoplasm of cells rather than in the nucleus, usually referring to those associated with mitochondria and chloroplasts.

Cytoplasmic incompatibility: Reproductive failure caused by elements inherited in the cytoplasm. If a female not bearing such an element mates with a male bearing an element, she is rendered partially or completely sterile.

Deoxyribonucleic acid (DNA): The principal heritable material of all cells. Chemically it is a polymer of nucleotides, each nucleotide subunit consisting of the pentose sugar 2-deoxy-D-ribose, phosphoric acid and one of the five nitrogenous bases adenine, cytosine, guanine, thymine or uracil.

Diapause: A resting or dormant period during the development of an insect.

Dimorphism: The presence of two different forms in a population, in respect of such characteristics as sex, coloration, size, etc.

Diploid: Having two sets of chromosomes, i.e. twice the haploid number.

Directional selection: Selection in which individuals at one end of the distribution of a trait showing continuous variation are at an advantage over other individuals.

Disassortative mating: A preference to mate with individuals having a different genotype from one's own.

Disjunct distribution: The discontinuous occurrence of a species over its geographical range.

Dispersal: Undirected locomotion.

Disruptive coloration: A colour pattern that serves to break up the body outline.

Disruptive selection: Selection in which individuals at both extremes of the distribution of a trait showing continuous variation are at an advantage over intermediate individuals.

DNA: see deoxyribonucleic acid.

DNA fingerprinting: The first genetic method capable of identifying individuals uniquely, based on minisatellite DNA sequences and invented by Professor Alec Jeffreys. Often used more loosely to refer to any genetic method that identifies individuals with high confidence.

Dominant: In a genetic sense, the opposite of recessive. The stronger of a pair of alleles, expressed as fully when present in a single dose (i.e. heterozygous) as it is when present in a double dose (i.e. homozygous).

Dorsal: Concerning the back or upperside of an animal.

Ecdysis: Following apolysis, the second part of the moulting process, by which an insect sheds its outer coat.

Ecdyson: One of the hormones involved in larval moulting.

Eclosion: The act of emerging from the pupa.

Ectoparasite: A parasite that lives on the outside of the body of its host.

Ectophagous: Feeding on the outside of a host.

Effective population size: The effective size of the population is the size of an ideal population that would exhibit equivalent properties with respect to genetic drift.

Egg tooth: A small projection on first instar larvae of some insects used to aid them in breaking out of the egg.

Electrophoresis: A technique used to detect differences in proteins and polypeptide chains based on differences in electrical charge of the molecules.

Elytra: The hard and horny front wings of a beetle (singular elytron).

Embryogenesis: The development and evolution of the embryo.

Endoparasite: A parasite that lives inside the body of its host.

Endophagous: Feeding on the inside of a host.

Endopterygota: Insects in which wings develop internally in the immature stages.

Endosymbiotic: Living within the cell or body of another.

Environmental heterogeneity: The differences that occur between environments, usually related to the fact that such differences will impose different selection pressures on the organisms that live there.

Enzyme: A protein that initiates or facilitates a chemical reaction between other substances.

Fig. 8.24 The Poplar Grey is cryptic on lichen-encrusted rocks and stones (see text p. 214).

Epidermis: The single layer of living cells that underlies and secretes the cuticle in an insect.

Epiphysis: A sclerotised projection of the legs of moths used to clean the antennae.

Eukaryote: Single or multicellular organism in which the cell(s) contain a well-defined nucleus containing multiple linear chromosomes and which is enclosed by a nuclear membrane.

Eversible structure: Structure that can be turned outward or inside out.

Evolution: A cumulative, heritable change in the organisms in a population.

Exoskeleton: The external skeleton of an insect, made of cuticle.

Exuvia (plural *exuviae):* The cast-off outer skin of an immature insect.

Exopterygota: Insects in which the wings develop externally in the immature stages.

F_1, F_2, etc.: First, or subsequent generation. Abbreviation for first filial generation, second filial generation, etc.

Fat body: A mass of fatty tissue that may occupy a large proportion of the abdominal cavity. The material stored in the fat body includes fats, glycogen and proteins and is used as a reserve for overwintering and metamorphosis.

Fecundity: The number of eggs or offspring produced by an organism.

Female choice: One of Darwin's two mechanisms of sexual selection. The phenomenon whereby females exercise choice over which of two or more available males they mate with.

Femur: The longest segment in the leg of a moth, between the trochanter and tibia.

Fine-grained environment: An environment comprising a mosaic of habitats. Individuals of a species are distributed randomly across the habitats throughout their lives.

Fisherian mechanism of sexual selection: The spread of a female choice gene because of genetic correlation with the preferred male trait, the spread initially being due to a naturally selected advantage, and later being associated with a sexually selected advantage,

Fission: The division of a cell or of a unicellular organism to form new cells.

Fitness: The relative ability of an organism to transmit its genes to the next generation.

Flagellum: All the antennal segments after the first two.

Founder effect: The effect on genetic variability of the small size of a colonising, or founding, population, which may comprise just one or a few individuals, and consequently contains only a small fraction of the genetic variation of the parental population.

Frass: Caterpillar faeces.

Frenulum: One or a group of bristles on the front margin of the hindwing of adult Lepidoptera, acting as part of the wing-coupling mechanism.

Frequency dependent selection: Selection in which the fitness of a genetic form is dependent on the frequency of that form in the population relative to others.

Galea: The apex or outer lobe of the maxilla of an insect.

Gamete: Reproductive cell.

Gene: An hereditary factor or heritable unit that can transmit a characteristic from one generation to the next. Composed of DNA and usually situated in the thread-like chromosomes in the nucleus.

Gene flow: Genetic exchange between populations resulting from the dispersal of gametes, zygotes or individuals.

Gene pool: The entire set of genes in a breeding population.

Genetics: The study of inheritance.

Genetic bottleneck: The reduction in genetic variability in a population resulting from a period of low population size.

Genetic drift: Random changes of the frequency of genes in populations.

Genetic linkage: The tendency for certain genes to be inherited together, instead of assorting independently, because they are situated close to one another on the same chromosome.

Genetic markers: Any allele (or sequence) that is used experimentally to identify a sequence, gene, chromosome or individual.

Genetically modified organism: Now generally used to mean an organism into which genes of another species have been incorporated artificially.

Genetic polymorphism: The occurrence together in the same population, at the same time, of two or more discontinuous, heritable forms of a species, the rarest of which is too frequent to be maintained merely by recurrent mutation.

Genome: The entire complement of genetic material in a cell. In eukaryotes this word is sometimes used in referring to the material in just a single set of chromosomes.

Genotype: The genetic make-up of an individual in respect of one genetic locus, a group of loci or even its total genetic complement.

Geographic race: A form of a species that occurs in one or more specific geographic regions and is distinct from forms that occur in other regions.

Germ cells: Those cells destined to become the reproductive cells.

Germ line: The sex cells (gametes) of an organism and the cells that give rise to them

GMO: see genetically modified organism.

Gonad: An organ in which gametes are produced: a testis or an ovary.

Good genes hypothesis: The theory whereby a female mating preference is selected because the preferred trait is carried by males whose genes confer greater than average fitness. Consequently, the gene for the preference tends to be inherited by progeny who will also carry 'good genes' and will spread.

Gradualists: Evolutionists who took the view that most evolutionary change resulted from the action of selection on heritable continuous variation exhibited by individuals in populations (cf. mutationists).

Group selection: Natural selection acting in favour of the survival of a group of individuals of a species, but not necessarily that of each individual.

Gynandromorph: An insect that has some cells that are phenotypically male and some that are phenotypically female: a sexual mosaic.

Habitat: The specific place and type of local environment that an organism lives in.

Habitat selection: Exhibited by an organism that preferentially resides in one type of habitat, rather than others.

Haemocoele: A large blood-filled cavity surrounding most of the organs in arthropods and many other invertebrates.

Haemolymph: Insect blood.

Haplo-diploid: Having one sex haploid and the other diploid. Based upon a sex-determining mechanism by which females develop from fertilised eggs and functional males from unfertilised eggs.

Haploid: Of cells (particularly gametes) or individuals: having a single set of chromosomes.

Hardy–Weinberg equilibrium: The state in which genotype frequencies in a population are in accord with expectations of the Hardy–Weinberg law.

Hardy–Weinberg law: A basic principle of population genetics that allows genotypic frequencies to be predicted from gene frequencies. The law states that in an effectively infinite population of sexually reproducing, randomly mating, diploid organisms containing a gene with two alleles having frequencies p and q, the frequencies of the homozygote genotypes will be p^2 and q^2 and that of the heterozygote will be *2pq* within a single generation, and will not change thereafter in the absence of mutation, migration and selection.

Hemimetabolous: Of insects that do not undergo a complete metamorphosis: exopterygotes.

Hermaphrodite: An individual that bears some tissues that are identifiably male and others that are female, and that can produce mature male and female gametes.

Heritability: The proportion of the total variation in a trait that is due to genetic rather than environmental factors.

Heterogametic sex: The sex that carries sex chromosomes of different types and thus produces gametes of two types with respect to the sex chromosome they carry. In humans, males are the heterogametic sex carrying one X and one Y chromosome. In moths, females are heterogametic carrying one W and one Z chromosome.

Heterogeneous: Variable. Thus a heterogeneously coloured surface is one that is not uniform in colour.

Heterozygote: An individual that bears different alleles of a particular gene, one from each parent.

Heterozygote advantage: The situation in which the fitness of heterozygous individuals exceeds that of either type of homozygote.

Holometabolous: Of insects that undergo a complete metamorphosis: endopterygotes.

Homogametic sex: The sex that carries sex chromosomes that are the same. In humans, females are the homogametic sex, carrying two X chromosomes. In moths, male are homogametic, carrying two Z chromosomes.

Homologous chromosomes: Chromosomes which, in normal diploid cells, occur in pairs with largely similar nucleotide sequences and gene sequences. These chromosomes pair up during cell division.

Homozygote: An individual that bears two copies of the same allele at a given gene locus.

Hormone: Chemical messenger effective within the body and responsible for the timing and regulation of metabolic, behavioural or other processes.

Host: An organism that is being attacked by a parasite or parasitoid.

Host plant: A plant that an animal feeds upon, or on or in which it resides.

Hybrid: Individual resulting from a mating between parents that are genetically dissimilar. Often used to describe the offspring of matings between the individuals of two different species.

Hyperparasite: A parasite that lives on or in another parasite.

Hyphae: Filaments of a fungal thallus.

Hypopharynx: One of the unpaired mouthparts of an insect, often carrying the salivary duct.

Imago: The adult stage in an insect's life.

Inbreeding: Reproduction between close relatives.

Inbreeding depression: The reduction in fitness of offspring from matings between close relatives, resulting from the increased likelihood of the same deleterious recessive genes being inherited from both parents and thus being expressed in their progeny.

Inclusive fitness: The fitness of an individual plus the effect that individual has on the fitness of other individuals, weighted by their relatedness to it.

Instar: The stage in an insect's life history between two moults. An insect that has recently hatched from an egg and that has not yet moulted is said to be a first instar nymph or larva.

Integument: The outer protective covering of an animal.

Intersex: An individual that appears to be intermediate between male and female, due to an abnormality of the sex chromosomes.

Interspecific: Between species.

Intraspecific: Within a species.

Introgression: The incorporation of genes of one species into the gene pool of another through hybridisation and backcrossing.

Inversion: Of a chromosome, a segment of the chromosome that has been reversed.

Invertebrate: An animal without a dorsal column or vertebrae: non-chordate metazoan.

Jugum: A lobe on the trailing edge of the wing membrane close to the thorax and separated from the outer part of the wing by a dorsal fold.

Juvenile hormone: A hormone in insects involved in development and moulting.

Karyotype: The chromosome complement, in terms of number, size and constitution, of a cell or an organism.

Keratin: Any of a group of nitrogenous substances that form the basis of hair, feathers, horns, nails, etc.

Kin selection: Selection acting on an individual in favour of survival not of that individual, but of its relatives which carry many of the same genes.

Labial palps: Appendages or feelers borne on the labium of an insect.

Labium: The lower lip of an insect.

Labrum: The upper lip of an insect.

Lachryphagous: Feeding on tears or other secertions from the lachrymal glands of vertebrates.

Lamarckian inheritance: The inheritance of characteristics of an organism acquired as a result of environmental influence on the organism, during the organism's lifetime.

Larva: The stage between the egg and the pupa in the life cycle of insects that undergo full metamorphosis.

Leaf-miner: An insect, usually a larva, that makes a tunnel between the upper and lower surfaces of a leaf.

Lek: A site where males of a species congregate in dense groups, and which is visited by females for the sole purpose of mating.

Locus: The position of a gene on a chromosome.

Macrolepidoptera: An arbitrary name given to moths and butterflies of super-families whose average size is large or medium, for example Geometroidea, Noctuoidea, Sesioidea, Sphingoidea.

Male competition: One of Darwin's two mechanisms of sexual selection. Males compete among themselves (for example by aggressive displays or fighting) to gain access to females.

Mandible: One of a pair of laterally-moving horny jaws of an insect.

Maxilla: One of a pair of laterally-moving mouthparts behind the mandibles in insects.

Meiosis: The process of two nuclear divisions and a single replication of the chromosome complement of a cell by which the number of chromosomes in resultant daughter cells is reduced to one half during gamete production.

Melanin: A complex of pigments, usually black, brown or yellow, derived from tyrosine.

Melanism: The possession of dark or black pigmentation.

Mendelian trait: A variable character, the forms of which are passed from parents to offspring according to Mendel's laws of inheritance.

Mesothorax: The second thoracic segment.

Metamorphosis: The change that takes place during an insect's life as it turns from a larva to an adult.

Metathorax: The third thoracic segment.

Microlepidoptera: An arbitrary name given to moths of superfamilies whose average size is small, for example Nepticuloidea, Pyraloidea, Tineoidea, Tortricoidea.

Micropyles: Pores in the eggshell, allowing entry of spermatozoa.

Microsatellite: A block of short tandemly-repeated motifs of nucleotide bases in DNA, in which the basic repeat unit is five or fewer bases in length.

Migration: Directed locomotion.

Mimicry: The resemblance shown by one organism to another for protective, or, more rarely, aggressive purposes.

Minisatellite: Any of a group of many dispersed arrays of short tandemly-repeated motifs of nucleotide bases in DNA. The family is to an extent unified by the presence of a so-called core sequence, possibly related to the bacterial recombination signal chi, in every repeat unit. Minisatellites can exhibit extreme length variation due to the frequent gain and loss of repeat units.

Mitochondria: Complex membranous organelles in the cytoplasm of eukaryotic cells. They are the sites of the majority of the energy-releasing biochemical processes within the cells. Usually inherited maternally, they have their own DNA and reproduce autonomously within cells.

Mitochondrial DNA: The circular, double-stranded genome of eukaryotic mitochondria.

Mitosis: The normal process of cell division in growth, involving the replication of chromosomes, and the division of the nucleus into two, each with the identical complement of chromosomes to the original cell.

Modifier genes: A series of genes, each with small effects, that influence the exact expression of a major gene.

Monogamy: Situation in which an individual has a single mating partner over a set time period.

Monomorphic: the opposite of polymorphic; a sequence, gene or organism in which all individuals in a given sample are indistinguishable.

Morph: Form.

Morphology: The form and structure of an organism.

Mosaic: The presence in an individual of areas of two genetically different patterns.

Motor neuron: A nerve conveying an impulse directly to a muscle, causing it to contract.

Müllerian mimicry: Resemblance of two or more species each of which has characteristics that are unpleasant to predators. The resemblance reduces the destruction of members of a Müllerian mimetic complex while inexperienced predators learn of their unpleasant properties.

Multiparasitism: The occurrence of parasites of two or more species within a single host.

Multiple alleles: A series of forms of a gene occurring at the same locus on a chromosome which have arisen by mutation.

Mutagenic: Of an environmental agent, whether physical or chemical, which is capable of causing mutations.

Mutation: A sudden change in the genetic material controlling a particular character or characters of an organism. Such a change may be due to a change in the number of chromosomes, to an alteration in the structure of a chromosome, or to a chemical or physical change in an individual gene.

Mutationists: Evolutionists who took the view that most adaptations and species arose as the result of mutations (cf. selectionists, gradualists).

Mycelium: The vegetative portion of a fungus, composed of a network of filaments called hyphae.

Natural selection: According to Charles Darwin, the main mechanism giving rise to evolution. The mechanism by which heritable traits that increase an organism's chances of survival and reproduction are more likely to be passed on to the next generation than less advantageous traits.

Navigation: Deliberate locomotion towards a specific destination.

Neo-Darwinian theory/Neo-Darwinian synthesis: A development of Darwin's evolutionary theory refined by incorporating modern biological knowledge, particularly Mendelian genetics, during the mid-twentieth century.

Neutral mutation: A mutation that is selectively neutral, i.e. it has no adaptive significance.

Neuron: A nerve cell with its axon and dendrites: the fundamental unit of the nervous system.

Normal distribution: The bell-shaped frequency distribution of measurements of a trait that falls symmetrically either side of the mean value.

Nucleotide base: The structural unit of a nucleic acid. The major nucleotide bases in DNA are the purines adenine and guanine and the pyrimidines cytosine and thymine, the last of which is replaced by uracil in RNA.

Nucleus: That portion of a cell that contains the chromosomes.

Nymph: An immature stage in the life cycle of hemimetabolous insects. The nymph resembles the adult insect except that the wings and reproductive organs are undeveloped.

Ocellus: A simple eye consisting of a few sensory cells and a single lens.

Oligophagous: Feeding on one or a limited range of foods.

Ommatidium: A single optical unit of the compound eye of an insect. Each ommatidium is a cone-shaped structure consisting of a lens, a crystalline cone and light sensitive retinulae.

Organelle: A complex structure of characteristic morphology and function within eukaryotic cells but outside the nucleus, such as a mitochondrion or chloroplast.

Orientation: Maintenance of a specific compass direction.

Ovary: The female reproductive organs, in which eggs are produced.

Oviposition: The act of laying eggs.

Ovipositor: The egg-laying apparatus of a female insect.

Palp: An elongated sensory appendage. Palps occur in pairs on the labium and the maxillae of insects.

Parasite: An organism that lives in or on another organism, its host, obtaining resources at the host's expense.

Parasitoid: An organism (usually an insect) that lays its eggs inside another insect species, where the parasitoid develops, ultimately killing its host.

Parthenogenesis: Reproduction in which eggs develop without fertilisation.

Pathogen: Any disease-causing organism, but most usually used for micro-organisms.

Pedicel: The second segment of the antenna of an insect.

Phenotype: The observable properties of an organism, resulting from the inter-action between the organism's genotype and the environment in which it develops.

Pheromone: Chemical substance which when released or secreted by an animal influences the behaviour or development of other individuals of the same species.

Phylogenetic: Relating to the pattern of evolutionary descent.

Phylogenetic tree: A diagrammatic representation of genetic distances between populations, species or higher taxa, the branching of which is said to resemble a tree.

Phytophagous: Feeding on plants.

Planiform: Resting with wings held flat either side of the body.

Pleiotropy: The situation in which a single gene affects two or more apparently unrelated phenotypic traits of an organism.

Polygamy: The situation in which an organism of either or both sexes has more than one mating partner within a single breeding season.

Polygenic trait: A character controlled polygenically is affected by a large number of genes each of which has a small effect.

Polymorphism: The occurrence of two or more distinctly different forms of a species in the same population.

Polyphagous: Feeding on a range of different types of foods.

Polyploid: Of individuals or cells having more than two complete chromosome sets (for example triploid = three sets, tetraploid = four sets, hexaploid = six sets, etc.).

Population: A group of organisms of the same species living and breeding together.

Post-zygotic reproductive isolation mechanism: Any characteristic of an organism that prevents gene flow between it and members of other species by causing sterility, decreased viability and/or decreased fitness in zygotes formed as a result of fertilisation between gametes of the organism and those of another species.

Prevalence: The proportion of a host population that is infected by a parasitoid or pathogen.

Pre-zygotic reproductive isolation mechanism: Any characteristic of an organism that prevents gene flow between it and members of other species by reducing the likelihood of zygote formation, usually by decreasing the likelihood of cop-ulation between the organism and a member of another species.

Primary sex organs: The gonads (testes and ovaries), their ducts and associated glands.

Primary sex ratio: The sex ratio at fertilisation or zygote formation.

Proboscis: The elongated mouthparts of many adult insects, including most Lepidoptera.

Prokaryote: Single-celled organisms that lack a membrane-bound nucleus or any membrane-bound organelles.

Proleg: One of the fleshy, unjointed legs on the abdomen of an insect larva. Sometimes called false legs to distinguish them from the true jointed legs that arise from the thoracic segments and are present in the adult insect.

Pronotum: The dorsal surface of the first thoracic segment.

Proteinase: An enzyme that breaks down proteins.

Proteins: Complex nitrogenous compounds whose molecules consist of numerous amino acid molecules linked together.

Prothorax: The first thoracic segment.

Protozoa: Single-celled animals.

Pseudoautosomal region: Of sex chromosomes: the region of homology between the Z chromosome and the W chromosome. Genes in this region behave in the same way as autosomal genes.

Pupa: The stage between larva and adult in the life history of insects undergoing complete metamorphosis, during which the larval body is rebuilt into that of the adult.

Puparium: The barrel-shaped case that encloses the pupae of some true flies (Diptera).

Quaternary period: The most recent two million years of geological time, up to and including the present day.

Random genetic drift: Fluctuation in the frequencies of neutral genes and neutral alleles in a population due to the fact that each generation is only a sample of the one it replaces.

Recessive: A recessive allele is not expressed phenotypically when present in a heterozygote, but only when in a homozygote. The opposite of dominant.

Recombination: The generation of new combinations of chromosomes and parts of chromosomes during meiosis both through crossing over and through the independent segregation of chromosomes.

Red Queen hypothesis: In *Alice in Wonderland*, the Red Queen states that one has to keep running in order to remain in the same place. Evolutionary arms races are regarded in the same way, in that there is no obvious end point to the competition, yet there is constant change.

Reflex bleeding: The defensive secretion produced by ladybirds (and some other insects) when threatened, from pores in the exoskeleton. The secretion consists of a bitter fluid, including haemolymph and noxious chemicals.

Replication: The duplication of genomic DNA, or RNA, as part of the processes of meiosis and mitosis.

Reproductive isolation: The situation in which individuals in a group of organisms breed with one another, but not with individuals of other groups. In sexually reproducing organisms true species are reproductively isolated from one another.

Retinaculum: A hook-like structure by which the forewing of a moth engages with a bristle or frenulum on the hindwing, thereby holding the wings together during flight.

Retinulae: Light-sensitive cells around the bases of the crystalline cones in the ommatidia of the compound eyes of many insects, including moths.

Sampling error: The random statistical deviations that occur when drawing measurement information from a sample that is supposedly representative of a larger set.

Scape: The largest, basal segment of the antenna.

Scent brushes: Tufts of modified scales with scent glands at their bases. Located in a variety of positions, they serve to distribute sex pheromones involved in the attraction and recognition of a mate.

Sclerites: Hard, dark chitinous plates separated by more flexible membranes in the exoskeleton of insects and other arthropods.

Sclerotin: A hard nitrogenous substance impermeable to water, found together with chitin in the cuticles of insects.

Seasonal varieties: Forms or varieties of a species that occur only in specific seasons.

Secondary sexual characters: Characters that differ between the sexes, excluding the primary sex organs.

Segregation: The separation from one another of the pairs of genes constituting allelomorphs, and their passage respectively into different reproductive cells.

Selection differential: The difference between the average value of a quantitative trait for a population and the average of those selected to be the parents of the next generation.

Selection response: The difference between the average value of a quantitative trait for a population and the average value of the progeny of a selected sample of the population used as parents.

Selectionists: Evolutionists who took the view that most evolutionary change resulted from the action of natural selection on small heritable differences between the individuals in populations (cf. mutationists).

Sensillum (plural sensilla): A small sense organ.

Sensory exploitation hypothesis: The theory that mate choice, particularly female choice, may evolve as a result of a pre-existing bias in the sensory biology of an organism.

Sericulture: The study and production of silk.

Sex chromosome: A chromosome that is present in a reproductive cell (or gamete) and that carries the factor for producing a male or female offspring. Such chromosomes are usually denoted by the letters X and Y, or Z and W. In humans, females carry two X chromosomes, and males carry one X and one Y chromosome. In most moths, males carry two copies of the same chromosome (ZZ) while females carry one Z and one W chromosome (ZW).

Sex limited inheritance: Inheritance due to genes, situated in any chromosome, which are expressed in one sex only, although transmitted by both.

Sex linkage: The association of characters with sex, because the genes controlling them are situated in the sex chromosomes.

Sex role reversal: The situation found in species in which the operational sex ratio is female biased, with the result that females compete for males and males choose between females.

Sexual dimorphism: The existence, within a species, of morphological diffe-rences between the sexes in traits other than the primary reproductive organs.

Sexual mosaic: An individual composed of a mosaic of tissues, some essentially male in character and some female.

Sexual selection: Selection that promotes traits that will increase an organism's success in mating and ensure that its gametes are successful in fertilisation. This is distinct from natural selection which acts simply on traits that influence fecundity and survival.

'Sexy sons': According to Fisher's theory of the evolution of female choice, females who choose to mate with males carrying a particular trait will produce 'sexy sons', progeny who tend to carry the preferred trait and so be attractive to other females with the same mating preference.

Sibling: Brother or sister.

Speciation: The evolution of new species.

Species: Groups of actually or potentially interbreeding natural populations which are reproductively isolated from other such groups.

Species selection: The theory that some evolution results from selection acting at the level of the species. It proposes that species with particular characteristics are more likely to go extinct than species with other characteristics. For example, the predominance of sexual reproduction compared with secondary asexual reproduction among higher organisms is attributed to the reduced likelihood that sexually reproducing species will go extinct in changing environments.

Spermatheca: A small, sack-like branch of the female reproductive tract (of insects and other arthropods) in which sperm may be stored.

Spermatophore: A packet containing sperm and sometimes also nutrients that contribute to the resourcing of eggs.

Sperm competition: The competition between sperm from two or more males, within a single female, for fertilisation of the ova.

Sperm exhaustion: Depletion of the sperm from previous copulations in an already mated female.

Spinneret: An organ in the hypopharynx of many moth larvae, used to spin silk produced by modified salivary glands.

Spiracle: The respiratory or tracheal apertures of insects, situated along the sides of the body.

Stabilising selection: Selection in which individuals that are intermediate in the distribution of a trait showing continuous variation are at an advantage over those towards the ends of the distribution.

Stable polymorphism: See balanced polymorphism.

Sugaring: A method of attracting moths by daubing a syrupy concoction, often involving black treacle, onto tree trunks or other substrates.

Supergene: A group of genes controlling a complex set of related traits and lying so close to each other on the same chromosome that they behave as a single unit.

Superparasitism: The occurrence together of individuals from more than one conspecific parent parasitoid within the body of a single host.

Suppresser: Any secondary mutation that completely or partly restores a function lost as a result of the presence of another gene or genetic element.

Sutures: Grooves along the junctions between skeletal sclerites.

Switch gene: Any gene that controls the expression of one or more other genes in an on or off manner.

Symbiont: An organism living in intimate association with another dissimilar organism. Symbiotic associations can be mutualistic, neutral or parasitic.

Symbiosis: The phenomenon of organisms of different species living together in an intimate association.

Tangled bank: A theory of the evolution of sex based on the advantages of diversity of offspring in an environment with many niches and strong competition for resources.

Tarsus: The part of a moth's leg immediately outside the tibia, and segmented.

Taxonomy: The study of the classification and naming of organisms.

Tectiform: In respect of the resting postures of moths: like a roof.

Tegulae: Small scale-like sclerites overlapping the bases of the wings in some moths.

Tentorium: The internal skeleton of the head of insects, comprising a number of chitinous struts connecting the exoskeleton to a transverse bar in the centre of the head.

Testis: The primary reproductive organ of males, producing spermatozoa.

Tetrachromatic vision: Having four types of light-sensitive cell, each being sensitive to light of different wavelength. The image seen is the product of the stimuli received by all four types acting in concert.

Tetraploid: Having a chromosome complement comprising four of each type of chromosome, rather than the more usual two (diploid).

Thelytokous parthenogenesis: The form of secondary asexual reproduction in which unfertilised eggs develop into females.

Thorax: The body region of an insect behind the head and in front of the abdomen, comprising three segments and bearing the legs and wings.

Tibia: The leg segment between the femur and tarsus.

Tracheae: The breathing tubes of insects, opening by spiracles situated along the sides of the body.

Transient polymorphism: Genetic polymorphism in which the forms are changing in frequency in a directed manner.

Translocation: A chromosomal mutation characterised by the change in position of chromosome segments within the chromosome complement.

Triploid: Containing three sets of chromosomes in the nucleus, thereby having three times the haploid number.

Trochanter: A short segment of an insect's leg between the coxa and the femur.

Tymbal organ: A sound-producing sclerite.

Tympanal organ: A sound-sensitive membrane, often positioned in a depression on the abdomen or thorax.

Tyrosine: An amino acid essential for the production of proteins by living organisms. Among other functions, it plays a part in the production of melanin pigments.

Ultra-selfish symbiont: Symbionts whose spread and maintenance occur despite and because of the fact that they cause damage to the host in which they occur.

Ultrasound: Sound waves of frequency higher than the audible limit of about 20,000 vibrations per second.

Urticating hairs: Irritating or stinging hairs.

Veliform: Resting with the wings held vertically above the back, as in most butterflies.

Ventral: Concerning the front or underside of an animal.

Vertical transmission: Transmission of genetic elements, including intracellular symbionts, from parents into progeny.

Viability: The ability of an organism to survive from zygote formation to reproductive maturity.

W chromosome: The partner of the Z chromosome in female Lepidoptera, birds and a few other groups of species.

X chromosome: The chromosome carrying genes concerned with sex determination in most organisms, but not Lepidoptera or birds. There are usually two X chromosomes in females and a single X chromosome in males.

Y chromosome: The partner of the X chromosome in males of most species, but not the Lepidoptera or birds.

Z chromosome: The chromosome carrying genes concerned with sex determination in Lepidoptera, birds and a few other groups of species. There are usually two Z chromosomes in male moths and a single Z chromosome in females.

Zygote: The first cell of a new organism resulting from the fusion of two gametes.

Bibliography

Allen, J.A. & Clarke, B. (1968). Evidence for apostatic selection by wild passerines. *Nature*, **220**, 501–2.

Asami, T. & Grant, B. (1995). Melanism has not evolved in Japanese *Biston betularia* (Geometridae). *Journal of the Lepidopterists' Society*, **49**, 88–91.

Baker, R.R. (1982). *Migration: Paths through Time and Space*. Hodder and Stoughton: London.

Baker, R.R. & Mather, J.G. (1982). Magnetic compass sense in the large yellow underwing moth, *Noctua pronuba*. *Anim. Behav.*, **30**, 543–548.

Bänziger, H. (1970). The piercing mechanism of the fruit-piercing moth *Calpe* [*Calyptra*] *thalictri* Bkh. (Noctuidae) with reference to the skin-piercing blood-sucking moth *C. eustrigata* Hmps. *Acta Trop.*, **27**, 54–88.

Bänziger, H. (1975). Skin-piercing blood-sucking moths I: ecological and ethological studies on *Calpe eustrigata* (Lepid., Noctuidae). *Acta Trop.*, **32**, 125–144.

Bänziger, H. (1983). Lachryphagous Lepidopera recorded for the first time in Laos and China. *Mitteilungen der schweizerischen entomologischen Gesellschaft* **56**, 73–82.

Barbour, D.A. (1985). Patterns of population fluctuations in the Pine Looper moth *Bupalus piniaria* L. in Britain. In *Site Characteristics and Population Dynamics of Lepidopteran and Hymenopteran Forest Pests*. Forestry Commission Research and Development Paper 135.

Barbour, D.A. (1990). Synchronous fluctuations in spatially separated populations of cyclic forest insects. In *Population Dynamics of Forest Insects* (Eds Watt, A.D., Leather, S.R., Hunter, M.D. & Kidd, N.A.C.). Intercept: Andover.

Bennett, A.T.D. & Cuthill, I.C. (1994). Ultraviolet vision in birds: what is its function? *Vision Research*, **34**, 1471–8.

Birch, M.C. (1979). Eversible brushes. In *The Moths and Butterflies of Great Britain and Ireland*, Vol. 9 (Eds Heath, J. & Emmet, A.M.). Curwen Books: London.

Bishop, J.A. (1972). An experimental study of the cline of industrial melanism in *Biston betularia* (L.) (*Lepidoptera*) between urban Liverpool and rural North Wales. *J. Anim. Ecol.*, **41**, 209–43.

Blair, K.G. (1952). *Lithophane (Grapholitha) lapidea* Huebner in Britain. *Entomologist*, **85**, 123–124.

Bowmaker, J.K. (1991). Photoreceptors, photopigments and oil droplets. In *Vision and Visual Dysfunction*. Vol 6. *Perception of Colour* (Ed. P. Gouras), Macmillan, London.

Bradley, J.D. (2000). *Checklist of Lepidoptera Recorded from the British Isles*. (2nd Edition). D. Bradtey: Fordingbridge, Hants.

Brakefield, P.M. (1987). Industrial melanism: do we have the answers? *Trends Ecol. Evol.* **2**, 117–22.

Brakefield, P.M. (1990). A decline of melanism in the peppered moth, *Biston betularia* in the Netherlands. *Biol. J. Linn. Soc.*, **39**, 327–34.

Bretherton, R.F. (1983). The incidence of migrant Lepidoptera in the British Isles. In *The Moths and Butterflies of Great Britain and Ireland*, Vol. 10 (Eds Heath, J. & Emmet, A.M.). Harley Books: Colchester, Essex.

Brower, J.H. (1976). Cytoplasmic incompatibility: occurrence in a stored product pest *Ephestia cautella. Annals Entomol. Soc. Am.,* **69**, 1011–1015.

Burkhardt, D. & Maier, E. (1989). The spectral sensitivity of a passerine bird is highest in the UV. *Naturwissenschaften,* **76**, 82–3.

Calvert, M.S. (1826). *Evolution of an English Town.*

Chen, D. & Goldsmith, T.H. (1986). Four spectral classes of cone in the retinas of birds. *J. Comp. Physiol., A,* **159**, 473–9.

Clarke, B. (1962). Natural selection in mixed populations of two polymorphic snails. *Heredity,* **17**, 319–45.

Clarke, C.A. (1979). *Biston betularia,* obligate f. *insularia* indistinguishable from f. *carbonaria* (Geometridae). *J. Lepid. Soc.,* **33**, 60–4.

Clarke, C.A., Mani, G.S. & Wynne, G. (1985). Evolution in reverse: clean air and the peppered moth. *Biol. J. Linn. Soc.,* **26**, 189–99.

Common, I.F.B. (1954). A study of the ecology of the adult Bogong moth, *Agrotis infusa* (Boisd.) (Lepidoptera: Noctuidae), with special reference to its behaviour during migration and aestivation. *Australian J. Zool.,* **2**, 223–263.

Cook, L.M. (1961). Food-plant specialisation in the moth *Panaxia dominula* L.. *Evolution,* **15**, 478–485.

Cook, L.M., Rigby, K.D. & Seaward, M.R.D. (1990). Melanic moths and changes in epiphytic vegetation in north-west England and north Wales. *Biol. J. Linn. Soc.,* **39**, 343–54.

Coope, G.R. (1970). Interpretation of Quaternary insect fossils. *Ann. Rev. Ent.,* **15**:97–120.

Coope, G.R. (1978). Constancy of insect species versus inconstancy of Quaternary environments. In *Diversity of Insect Faunas,* (Eds Mound, L.A. & Waloff, N.)

(*Symposium of the Roy. Ent. Soc. Lond.,* **9**). Blackwell: Oxford.

Coyne, J.A. (1998). Not black and white. *Nature,* **396**, 35–36.

Darwin, C.R. (1859). *On the Origin of Species by Means of Natural Selection, or the Preservation of Favoured Races in the Struggle for Life.* John Murray: London.

Darwin, C.R. (1871). *The Descent of Man, and Selection in Relation to Sex.* John Murray: London.

David, C.T. & Birch, M.C. (1989). In *Pheromones and Insect Behaviour.* (Eds Jutsum, A.R. & Gordon, R.F.S.). John Wiley and Sons: Chichester.

David, C.T., Kennedy, J.S. & Ludlow, A.R. (1983). Finding of a sex pheromone source by gypsy moths released in the field. *Nature,* **303**, 804–806.

Dawkins, R. (1976). *The Selfish Gene.* Oxford University Press: Oxford.

Dethier, V.G. (1963). *The Physiology of Insect Senses.* Methuen: London.

Douglas, M.M. (1986). *The Lives of Butterflies.* University of Michigan Press: Ann Arbor.

Duméril, A.M.C. (1823). *Considerations generales sur la classe des insects.* Leorault: Paris.

Dunning, D.C. (1968). Warning sounds of moths. *Zeitschrift für Tierpsychologie,* **25**, 129–138.

Dunning, D.C. & Roeder, K.D. (1965). Moth sounds and the insect-catching behaviour of bats. *Science,* **147**, 173–174.

Edleston, R.S. (1864). No title (first *carbonaria* melanic of moth *Biston betularia*). *Entomologist,* **2**, 150.

Edwards, C.A. (1964). The bionomics of swift moths. I. The ghost swift moth, *Hepialus humuli* (L.). *Bull. Ent. Res.,* **55**, 147–160.

Ellington, C.P. (1984). The aerodynamics of hovering flight (I-VI). *Phil. Trans. Roy. Soc. Lond.,* **305**, 1–181.

Ellington, C.P., van der Berg, C., Willmott, A.P. & Thomas, L.R. (1996). Leading-edge vortices in insect flight. *Nature,* **384**, 626–629.

Emmet, A. M. (1991a). Chart showing the life history and habits of the British Lepidoptera. In *The Moths and Butterflies of Great Britain and Ireland,* Vol. 7, part 2 (Eds Emmet, A.M. & Heath, J.). Harley Books: Colchester, Essex.

Emmet, A. M. (1991b). *The Scientific Names of the British Lepidoptera: Their History and Meaning.* Harley Books: Colchester, Essex.

Feeny, P. (1970). Seasonal changes in oak leaf tannins and nutrients as a cause of spring feeding by winter moth caterpillars. *Ecology,* **51**, 565–581.

Feltwell, J. (1984). *Field Guide to the Butterflies and other Insects of Britain.* Reader's Digest Association Ltd.: London

Fisher, R.A. (1922). On the dominance ratio. *Proc. Roy. Soc. Edinb.,* **42**, 321–41.

Fisher, R.A. (1927). On some objections to Mimicry Theory: Statistical and genetic. *Trans. Roy. Ent. Soc. Lond.,* **75**, 269–78.

Fisher, R.A. (1928). The possible modification of the response of the wild type to recurrent mutations. *Amer. Nat.,* **62**, 115–126.

Fisher, R.A. (1930). *The Genetical Theory of Natural Selection.* Oxford University Press: Oxford.

Fisher, R.A. & Ford, E.B. (1947). The spread of a gene in natural conditions in a colony of the moth *Panaxia dominula. Heredity,* **1**, 143–74.

Ford, E.B. (1940). Polymorphism and taxonomy. In *The New Systematics* (Ed. J.S. Huxley). Clarendon Press: Oxford.

Ford, E.B. (1945). *Butterflies,* No. 1, New Naturalist Series. Collins: London.

Ford, E.B. (1955). *Moths,* No. 30, New Naturalist Series. Collins: London.

Ford, E.B. (1964). *Ecological Genetics.* Methuen: London.

Ford, E.B. (1975). *Ecological Genetics.* (4th Edition) Chapman and Hall: London.

Ford, E.B. & Sheppard, P.M. (1969). The medionigra polymorphism of *Panaxia dominula. Heredity,* **24**, 112–134.

Forder, P. (1993). *Odonthognophos dumetata* Treitscke (Lep.: Geometridae) new to the British Isles with a description of a new form *hibernica* Forder ssp. nov.. *Ent. Rec. J. Var.,* **105**, 201–202.

French, R.A. & Hurst, G.W. (1969). Moth migrations in the British Isles in July 1968. *Entomologist's Gaz.,* **20**, 37–44.

Fullard, J.H. (1982). Echolocation assemblages and their effects on moth auditory systems. *Can. J. Zool.,* **60**, 2572–2576.

Fullard, J.H. & Barclay, R.M.R. (1980). Audition in spring species of arctiid moths as a possible response to differential levels of insectivorous bat predation. *Can. J. Zool.,* **58**, 1745–1750.

Fullard, J.H., Fenton, M.B. & Simmons, J.A. (1979). Jamming bat echolocation: the clicks of arctiid moths. *Can. J. Zool.,* **57**, 647–649.

Grant, B.S., Owen, D.F. & Clarke, C.A. (1996). Parallel rise and fall of melanic peppered moths in America and Britain. *J. Hered.* **87**, 351–357.

Haggett, G.M. & Smith, C. (1993). *Agrochola haematidea* Duponchel (Lepidoptera: Noctuidae, Cuculliinae) new to Britain. *Entomologist's Gaz.,* **44**, 183–203.

Haldane, J.B.S. (1924). A mathematical theory of natural and artificial selection. *Trans. Camb. Phil. Soc.* **23**, 19–41.

Hamilton, W.D. (1967). Extraordinary sex ratios. *Science*, **156**, 477–488.

Harris, M. (1766). *The Aurelian or Natural History of English Insects; Namely Moths and Butterflies Together with the Plants on which they Feed.* 1986 facsimile: intro by R. Mays. Country Life Books: Twickenham.

Heath, J. (1976). Habitats. In *The Moths and Butterflies of Great Britain and Ireland*. Vol. 1. (Ed. J. Heath) Blackwell Scientific Publications & Curwen Press: Oxford.

Heylaerts, F.J.M. (1870). Les macrolépidoptères des environs de Bréda. *Tijdschrift voor Entomologie* **13**, 142–157.

Hoffmann, A.A. & Turelli, M. (1997). Cytoplasmic incompatibility in insects. In *Influential Passengers* (Eds S.L. O'Neill, A.A. Hoffmann and J.H. Werren), pp. 42–80. Oxford University Press: Oxford.

Holland, W.J. (1968). *The Moth Book.* 479 pp. Dover Publications: New York.

Howlett, R.J. & Majerus, M.E.N. (1987). The understanding of industrial melanism in the peppered moth (*Biston betularia*) (Lepidoptera: Geometridae). *Biol. J. Linn. Soc.* **30**, 31–44.

Hsiao, H.S. (1972). *Attraction of Moths to Light and to Infra-red Radiation.* San Francisco Press: San Francisco.

Hudson, G.V. (1928). *The Butterflies and Moths of New Zealand.* Wellington.

James, D.G. (1986). Thermoregulation in *Danaus plexippus* L. (Lepidoptera: Nymphalidae): two cool climate adaptations. *General and Applied Entomology*, **18**, 43–7.

Jiggins, F.M., Hurst, G.D.D. & Majerus, M.E.N. (1999). Sex ratio distorting *Wolbachia* causes sex role reversal in its butterfly host. *Proc. R. Soc. Lond. B.*, **267**, 69–73.

Johnson, C.G. (1969). *Migration and Dispersal of Insects in Flight.* Methuen: London.

Jones, C.W. (1993). *Habitat Selection in Polymorphic Lepidoptera.* Ph. D. thesis: Cambridge University.

Jones, D.A. (1989). 50 years of studying the scarlet tiger moth. *Trends in Ecology and Evolution*, **4**, 298–301.

Kageyama, D., Hoshizaki, S. & Ishikawa, Y. (1998). Female-biased sex ratio in the Asian corn borer, *Ostrinia furnacalis*: evidence for the occurrence of feminizing bacteria in an insect. *Heredity*, **81**, 311–316.

Kageyama, D., Nishimura, G., Hoshizaki, S. & Ishikawa, Y. (2000). *Wolbachia* infection causes feminization in two species of moths, *Ostrinia furnacalis* and *O. scapulalis* (Lepidoptera: Crambidae). *First Int. Wolbachia Conf. Program and Abstracts*, 106–107.

Kearns, P.W.E. & Majerus, M.E.N. (1987). Differential habitat selection in the Lepidoptera: a note on deciduous versus coniferous woodland habitats. *Entomologist's Record and Journal of Variation*, **99**, 103–6.

Kettlewell, H.B.D. (1952). Use of radioactive tracer in the study of insect populations (Lepidoptera), *Nature*, **170**, 584.

Kettlewell, H.B.D. (1955a). Selection experiments on industrial melanism in the Lepidoptera. *Heredity*, **9**, 323–42.

Kettlewell, H.B.D. (1955b). Recognition of appropriate backgrounds by the pale and black phases of the Lepidoptera. *Nature*, **175**, 943–4.

Kettlewell, H.B.D. (1956). Further selection experiments on industrial melanism in the Lepidoptera *Heredity*, **10**, 287–301.

Kettlewell, H.B.D. (1958). The importance of the micro-environment to evolutionary trends in the Lepidoptera. *Entomologist*, **91**, 214–24.

Kettlewell, H.B.D. (1973). *The Evolution of Melanism*, Clarendon Press: Oxford.

Krebs, J.R. & Davies, N.B. (1981). *An Introduction to Behavioural Ecology.* 389 pp., Blackwell Scientific, Oxford.

Krieger, R.I., Feeny, P.P. & Wilkinson, C.E. (1971). De-toxification enzymes in the guts of caterpillars: an evolutionary answer to plant defence? *Science,* **172**, 579–581.

Lee, J.-K. & Strausfeld, N.J. (1990). Structure, distribution and number of surface sensilla and their receptor cells on the olfactory appendage of the male moth *Manduca sexta. J. Neurocytology,* **19**, 519–538.

Lees, D.R. (1981). Industrial melanism: Genetic adaptation of animals to air pollution. In *Genetic Consequences of Man Made Change,* (Eds J.A. Bishop and L.M. Cook), pp.129–76. Academic Press: London.

Lees, D.R. & Creed, E.R. (1977). The genetics of *insularia* forms of the peppered moth, *Biston betularia. Heredity,* **39**, 67–73.

Legrand, J.J., Legrand-Hamelin, E. & Juchault, P. (1987). Sex determination in Crustacea. *Biol. Rev.,* **62**, 439–470.

Liebert, T.G. & Brakefield, P.M. (1987). Behavioural studies on the peppered moth *Biston betularia* and a discussion of the role of pollution and epiphytes in industrial melanism. *Biol. J. Linn. Soc.* **31**, 129–50.

Luff, M.L. & Woiwod, I.P. (1995). Insects as indicators of land-use change: a European perspective. Focusing on moths and ground beetles. In *Insects in a changing environment.* (Eds Harrington, R. & Stork, N.E.). Academic Press: London.

Maier, E.J. (1992). Spectral sensitivities including the UV of the passeriform bird *Leiothrix lutea. Journal of Comparative Physiology A,* **170**, 709–14.

Majerus, M.E.N. (1981). The inheritance and maintenance of the melanic form *nigrescens* of *Pachycnemia hippocastanaria* (Lepidoptera: Geometridae). *Ecol. Entomol.,* **6**, 417–22.

Majerus, M.E.N. (1982). Genetic control of two melanic forms of *Panolis flammea* (Lepidoptera: Noctuidae). *Heredity,* **49**, 171–7.

Majerus, M.E.N. (1989). Melanic polymorphism in the peppered moth *Biston betularia* and other Lepidoptera. *J. Biol. Ed.,* **23**, 267–84.

Majerus, M.E.N. (1990). The importance of form frequency data to ecological genetics. *Bull. Amat. Ent. Soc.,* **49**, 123–132.

Majerus, M.E.N. (1993). Moths in the rain. *Bull. Amat. Ent. Soc.,* **52**, 157–159.

Majerus, M.E.N. (1994). *Ladybirds. New Naturalist Series 81.* 368 pp., HarperCollins: London.

Majerus, M.E.N. (1998). *Melanism: Evolution in Action.* Oxford University Press: Oxford.

Majerus, M.E.N. (1999). Simbiontes hereditarios causantes de efectos deletéreos en los artrópodos/ Deleterious endosymbionts of Arthropods. In *The Evolution and Ecology of Arthropods* (Eds A. Melic, J.J. De Haro, M. Méndez & I Ribera). Pp. 777–806. (In Spanish and English.) Sociedad Entomologica Aragonera: Zaragosa, Spain.

Majerus, M.E.N. (in press a). *Sex Wars.* Princeton University Press: Princeton.

Majerus, M.E.N. (in press b). *Ladybird Beetles.* Cornell University Press, Cornell.

Majerus, M.E.N. & Hurst, G.D.D.

(1997). Ladybirds as a model system for the study of male-killing symbionts. *Entomophaga*, **42**, 13–20.

Majerus, M.E.N., Brunton, C.F.A. & Stalker, J. (2000). A bird's eye view of the peppered moth. *J. Evol. Biol.*, **13**, 155–159.

Mallet, J. (1984). Sex roles in the ghost moth *Hepialus humuli* (L.) and a review of mating in the Hepialidae (Lepidoptera). *Zool. J. Linn. Soc.*, **79**, 67–82.

Mani, G.S. (1982). A theoretical analysis of the morph frequency variation in the peppered moth over England and Wales. *Biol. J. Linn. Soc.,* **17**, 259–67.

Matthews, R. (1999). Scientists pick holes in Darwin Moth Theory. *Sunday Telegraph*, **14 March,** p. 17.

Mikkola, K. (1984). On the selective force acting in the industrial melanism of *Biston* and *Oligia* moths (Lepidoptera: Geometridae and Noctuidae). *Biol. J. Linn. Soc.,* **21**, 409–421.

Morris, R.K.A. & Collins, G.A. (1991). On the hibernation of Tissue moths *Triphosia dubitata* L. & the Herald moth, *Scoliopteryx libatrix* L. in an old fort. *Ent. Rec. J. Var.,* **103**, 313–321.

Mulnix, A.B. & Dunn, P.E. (1995). Molecular biology of the immune response. In *Molecular Model Systems in the Lepidoptera*. (Eds Goldsmith, M.R. & Wilkins, A.S.). Cambridge University Press: Cambridge, U.K.

Nijhout, H.F. (1991). *The Development and Evolution of Butterfly Wing Patterns*. Smithsonian Institution Press: Washington.

Nijhout, M.M. & Riddiford, L.M. (1974). The control of egg maturation by juvenile hormone in the tobacco hornworm moth, *Manduca sexta. Biol. Bull.,* **146**, 377–392.

Nijhout, M.M. & Riddiford, L.M. (1979). Juvenile hormone and ovarian growth in *Manduca sexta. J. Invert. Reprod.,* **1**, 209–219.

Opie, I. & Tatem, M. (1989). *A Dictionary of Superstitions.* Oxford University Press: Oxford.

Owen, D.F. (1961). Industrial melanism in North American moths. *Am. Nat.,* **95**, 227–33.

Owen, D.F. (1962). The evolution of melanism in six species of North American Geometrid Moths. *Annals of the Entomological Society of America,* **55**, 695–703.

Parsons, M., Green, D. & Waring, P. (2000). The Action for Threatened Moths Project. *Br. J. Ent. Nat. Hist.,* **13**, 2000.

Pasteur, L. (1870). *Études sur la maladie des vers à soie,* **1** & **2**. Paris.

Poulton, E.B. (1892). Further experiments upon the colour relation between certain lepidopterous larvae, pupae, cocoons and imagines, and their surroundings. *Trans. Ent. Soc. Lond.,* **1892,** 293–487.

Powell, J.A. (1980). Evolution of larval food preferences in microlepidoptera. *Ann. Rev. Entomol.,* **25**, 133–159.

Renwick, J.A.A. & Chew, F.S. (1994). Oviposition behaviour in Lepidoptera. *Ann. Rev. Entomol.,* **39**, 377–400.

Rivers, C.F. (1964). Virus pesticides. *Discovery, Lond.,* **25**, 27–31.

Robinson, R., (1971). *Lepidoptera Genetics*, Pergamon Press: New York.

Rothschild, M. (1963). Is the Buff Ermine (*Spilosoma lutea* Hufn.) a mimic of the White Ermine (*Spilosoma lubricipeda* L.)? *Proc. Roy. Ent. Soc. Lond. A*, **38**, 159–64.

Rothschild, M. (1985). British aposematic Lepidoptera. In the *Moths and Butterflies of Great Britain and Ireland*, Volume 2, (Eds Heath, J. & Emmet, A.M.). Harley Books: Colchester, Essex.

Sargent, T.D. (1968). Cryptic moths:

effects on background selections of painting the circumocular scales. *Science*, **159**, 100–1.

Sasaki, T., Fujii, Y., Kageyama, D., Hoshizaki, S. & Ishikawa, H. (2000). Interspecific transfer of *Wolbachia* in Lepidoptera: the feminizer of the Adzuki bean borer *Ostrinia scapulalis* causes male-killing in the Mediterranean flour moth *Ephestia kuehniella. First Int. Wolbachia Conf. Program and Abstracts*, 109–110.

Schnitzler, H-U. (1987). Echoes of fluttering moths: information for echolocating bats. In *Recent Advances in the Study of Bats* (Eds Fenton, M.B., Racey, P.A. & Rayner, J.M.V.). Cambridge University Press: Cambridge.

Scoble, M.J. (1986). The structure and affinities of the Hedyloidea: a new concept of the butterflies. *Bulletin of the British Museum (Natural History)* (Entomology) **53**, 251–286.

Scoble, M.J. (1992). *The Lepidoptera: Form, Function and Diversity.* Oxford University Press: Oxford.

Seiler, J. (1959). Untersuchungen über die Entstehung der Parthenogenese bei *Solenobia triquetrella* F.R. I. Die Zytologie der bisexuellen *Solenobia triquetrella*, ihr Verhalten und ihr Sexualverhältnis. *Chromosoma*, **10**, 73–114.

Seiler, J. (1960). Untersuchungen über die Entstehung der Parthenogenese bei *Solenobia triquetrella* F.R. II. Analyse der diploid parthenogenetischen *Solenobia triquetrella*. Verhalten, Aufzuchtresultate und Zytologie. *Chromosoma*, **11**, 29–102.

Shaw, M.R. & Askew, R.R. (1976). In *The Moths and Butterflies of Great Britain and Ireland.* Vol. 1 (Ed. Heath, J.). Blackwells and Curwen Press: Oxford.

Sheppard, P.M. (1951). A quantita-tive study of two populations of the moth, *Panaxia dominula* (L.). *Heredity*, **5**, 349–78.

Sheppard, P.M. (1952). A note on non-random mating in the moth *Panaxia dominula* L.. *Heredity*, **6**, 239–41.

Skinner, B. (1984). *Colour Identification Guide to Moths of the British Isles.* Viking: Harmonds-worth.

Sotthibandhu, S. & Baker, R.R. (1979). Celestial orientation by the large yellow underwing moth, *Noctua pronuba. Anim. Behav.*, **27**, 786–800.

Southwood, T.R.E. (1977). Habitat the template for ecological studies? *J. Anim. Ecol.*, **46**, 337–365.

Steward, R.C. (1977a). Industrial and non-industrial melanism in the peppered moth *Biston betularia* (L.). *Ecological Entomology*, **2**, 231–43.

Steward, R.C. (1977b). Multivariate analysis of variation within the *insularia* complex of the moth *Biston betularia. Heredity*, **39**, 97–109.

Tazima, Y. (1964). *The Genetics of the Silkworm.* Logos Press: London.

Tinbergen, N. (1974). *Curious Naturalists.* Penguin Education: Harmondsworth.

Trevelyan, M. (1909) *Folk-Lore and Folk-Stories of Wales.*

Tutt, J.W. (1896). *British Moths.* George Routledge.

Tweedie, M.W.F. & Emmet, A.M. (1991). Resting postures in the Lepidoptera. In *The Moths and Butterflies of Great Britain and Ireland.* Vol. 7, part 2 (Eds Emmet, A.M. & Heath, J.). Harley Books: Colchester.

Varley, G.C. & Gradwell, G.R. (1960). The effect of partial defoliation by caterpillars on the timber production of oak trees in England. *Proc. Xith int. Congr. Ent.*, **2**, 211–214.

Varley, G.C. & Gradwell, G.R.

(1963). Predatory insects as density dependent mortality factors. *Proc. 16 Int. Congr. Zool.*, **1**, 1–24.

Varley, G.C. & Gradwell, G.R. (1968). Population models for the winter moth. In *Insect Abundance* (Ed. Southwood, T.R.E.). *Symp. R. Ent. Soc. Lond.*, **4,** 132–142.

Wehner, R. (1984). Astronavigation in insects. *Ann. Rev. Entomol.*, **29**, 277–298.

Wirtz, R.A. (1984). Allergic and toxic reactions to non-stinging arthropods. *Ann. Rev. Entomol.*, **29,** 47–69.

Wootton, R.J. (1979). Function, homology and terminology in insect wings. *Systematic Entomology*, **4**, 81–93.

Wootton, R.J. (1987). *Insects: the Ultimate Sailing Machines.* The Central Association of Bee-Keepers: Ilford, Essex.

Wright, S. (1948). On the roles of directed and random changes in gene frequency in the genetics of populations. *Evolution*, **2**, 279–94.

Wright, S. (1978). *Evolution and the Genetics of Population, Volume 4. Variability within and among Natural Populations.* Chicago University Press: Chicago.

Yagi, N. & Koyama, N. (1963). *The Compound Eye of Lepidoptera.* 319 pp. Shinkyo Press: Tokyo.

Young, M.R. (1981). Insects and oil platforms. *Ent. Rec. J. Var.*, **93**, 13.

Young, M.R. (1997). *The Natural History of Moths.* T & A D Poyser Ltd: London.

Index